New Horizons in Journalism

New Horizons in Journalism

Howard Rusk Long, *General Editor*

BRYCE W. RUCKER

THE First FREEDOM

Foreword by HOWARD RUSK LONG

Introduction by MORRIS L. ERNST

SOUTHERN ILLINOIS UNIVERSITY PRESS
Carbondale and Edwardsville

FEFFER & SIMONS, INC.
London and Amsterdam

Library of Congress Catalog Card Number 68–11651
Printed in the United States of America
Designed by Andor Braun

To Betty, Bryce Calvert, and Linda

FOREWORD

IN A WORLD ORGANIZED ALONG TOTALITARIAN LINES since the beginning of human society, the guarantee of press freedom contained in the First Amendment to the Constitution of the United States was a glorious promise that the fruits of individual reflection, of private and public discussion, would circulate freely among all the people of the United States.

Through the years our press has indeed enjoyed a remarkable freedom from governmental restraint. The courts repudiated prior censorship and upheld the right to report the news of government and to criticize governmental officials and other persons in public life. Even the summary powers of the bench were restricted by the authority of this document.

But an eighteenth-century philosophy of press freedom, as implemented on December 15, 1791 by the First Congress and the original states, is insufficient for the requirements of people ensnared in the complexities of the twentieth century. The leaders of a society composed of farmers and traders, obsessed though they were with restraining the excesses of authority, could not see beyond the despotism of central government the other real and potential threats to the rights of the people to know the truth and all the truth.

It became, therefore, the task of the spokesmen for later generations to concern themselves with such problems as access to information withheld from the public by willful officials, with the excessive influence of lobbies and pressure groups and a new tyranny of organized economic power.

At the turn of the century, writers working more or less independently but classified as "The Muckrakers," first exposed in depth the transgressions of big business. Although there was a popular outcry at the excesses of "yellow journalism," the press as a whole came out rather well in these revelations. Thus it was not until Upton Sinclair brought out his book *The Brass Check*, that wealthy publishers were placed in their proper association with the big butchers of hogs and the oil, steel, and railroad monopolists.

Much later, it was one of these American press lords, Henry Luce, who financed the first comprehensive analysis of our vast mass communications system. The resulting report of the Commission on Freedom of the Press, published in 1947 as *A Free and Responsible Press*, was received by infuriated editors, publishers, even teachers of journalism, with howls of protest, because of the rather mild criticism of existing practices, including the rapid growth of monopoly in all areas of publication and broadcasting. A year later British proprietors were shaken by a more outspoken indictment at the hands of the Royal Commission of the Press.

Meanwhile, a New York lawyer long concerned with matters of personal freedom, Morris Ernst, one of the founders of the American Civil Liberties Union, was devoting himself to specific documentation of certain evils about which the group sponsored by Luce but known as the Hutchins Commission, could only speculate. Although narrower in scope, the Ernst findings showed clearly that, as predicted by William Allen White, journalism truly had become an eight per cent business, subject to all the manipulative practices known to the corporation lawyer.

Morris Ernst published his report in 1946 under the title, *The First Freedom*. How has the public interest fared in the intervening twenty years of banker control of an industrialized system of communications? With the approval of the original author, Professor Bryce W. Rucker presents a new set of answers under an old title, in this volume also known as *The First Freedom*.

Southern Illinois University
August 4, 1967

Howard Rusk Long

ACKNOWLEDGMENTS

A complete list of those who have aided with this manuscript would occupy several pages: footnote and copy references have been made to many. However, the writer wishes to give special thanks to others, among them Morris L. Ernst, author of the original and unsurpassable *The First Freedom,* for entrusting to me the challenging task of preparing this volume and for his invaluable suggestions and kindness in providing entree to many rich sources of information. To Howard R. Long, general editor of the journalism series, New Horizons in Journalism, for his advice and encouragement. To staff members and officials at the Department of Justice, the Department of Labor, the Census Bureau, the Federal Communications Commission, the Antitrust Subcommittees of both the Senate and House Judiciary Committees, the House Interstate and Foreign Commerce Committee, the Subcommittee on Communications of the Senate Committee on Commerce, the House Select Committee on Small Business, the American Newspaper Publishers Association, the National Association of Broadcasters, the Television Bureau of Advertising, the National Association of Educational Broadcasters, Zenith Radio Corporation, the American Newspaper Guild, and many, many others for supplying information.

Special mention should be made of Southern Illinois University students who assisted in the extended research distilled in these pages, among them are Kelsey Fleming, Thomas Wu, Harry Youngren, Chien-chao Hung, Gary Coll, Barbara Brookman, and Diana Fox.

Possibly deepest gratitude is due those who without complaint received less attention from the undersigned during the past three years than they should have—my family, to whom this book is dedicated, and the journalism graduate students at Southern Illinois University.

This manuscript could not have been completed without those cited above and many others. However, they share none of the guilt for errors of fact or judgment herein contained.

Carbondale, Illinois
August 1967

Bryce W. Rucker

CONTENTS

LIST OF TABLES

INTRODUCTION *by Morris L. Ernst*

THIS IS A VOLUME OF DISTINCTION AND TIMELY SIGNIFICANCE. I take peculiar pleasure in writing these words of praise since the author used a volume I wrote in 1946 as his springboard. *The First Freedom*, published by Macmillan, remained in healthy circulation for more than a decade and Bryce Rucker's reappraisal and fresh observations should service for the next decades all men concerned with freedom of the marketplace of thought.

In 1787, when the forty-two delegates—men of elegant minds—met in Philadelphia to draft the Constitution of our Republic no mention of freedom of the press was made during the four months of great and secret debate. But before the Constitution was adopted—and it squeaked through by narrow votes in several of the key colonies—a few of the founding fathers insisted on what became our great First Amendment. In simple terms all it really did was to forbid the new United Nations of the Colonies to abridge freedom of the press. It was generally assumed that each colony would continue to wield its own blue pencil.

At that time our population was less than four million, of which about a million were illiterate black slaves or indentured white men. Of the balance less than two hundred thousand were literate in any usable sense of that term. Women were relegated to the home, the spinnet, and the needle, and not until decades later were they thought fit to be educated to literacy. Incidentally, today out of three and a third billion people on our planet about one billion over the age of fourteen are illiterate and in Africa about a third of the population has not even reached the point of reducing verbal languages into written forms. Only about one hundred nations—out of a total of more than 214—claim more than 50 per cent literacy for all those fourteen years and over.

The miracle of our own culture lay in the concept that a free marketplace of thought was in fact the matrix for man's advance in productivity. This gamble of the founding fathers has now been proven valid since except for one nation no society exists with income of over five hundred dollars per capita, without a high degree of literacy.

Maybe our greatest contribution to the history of government lies in the fact that we did believe that truth had its best chance of emerging in the competition of ideas in the marketplace of thought. At the time of the Philadelphia Convention in 1787 we had about one hundred newspapers, and the significance of such organs is indicated by an ordinance of a village which provided that no one could read—in the cooperatively purchased gazette—the advertisements, before everyone had read the news and editorials.

Little did the inventors of our government foresee the advent of photography, telegraph, telephone, movies, radio, television, or telstar. But as literacy increased and communication improved, the number of newspapers also increased. Thus, competition of thought in print increased. And then, as this volume makes clear, the tide turned and in comparison to population and literacy the economics of the "thought" marketplace went toward monopoly—whether called chains, interlocking ownership of radio and newspapers, or other techniques to deny to the people of our cities the choice of ideas or even the ability to assay for the truth.

This is the sad story of our cultural trek toward monopoly in the most precious commodity known to man. A monopoly of hairpins or sealing wax or even ships is of minor significance compared to the reduction of competition in ideas. The most frightening part of Professor Rucker's exploration may well be seen in the simple and dirty fact that the abandonment of the idea of competition of ideas can scarcely be debated in our culture today. It will be of interest to note whether the Rucker facts and thesis are even given public attention in the mass media.

The desertion of our national heritage of competition in ideas may well have reached the point where the owners of the mass media have virtually created a cartel to protect each other. Can careful readers of this volume recall many, if any, instances where newspapers have engaged in debate on issues where the press has seen fit to point to corruption of television networks, or vice versa. In fact my own studies indicate that a divorce of any reader of this volume may likely be reported in the mass media—but not if the divorce arises in the home of an owner or high official of any one of the mass media. The media and their dominant personalities live in an immune area of life—which is less than wholesome, for them or the media.

I happen to hold with our founding fathers that criticism is the single greatest corrective known to man. In this thesis lies the difference between dictatorships—of the left or right—and the few free societies of our planet. To our mass media all phases of our national life are properly subjected to criticism—all but one. The one area denied the values of cross-criticism is the mass media itself. In that field the only criticism is increasingly limited to withdrawal of advertising or sponsorship. Withdrawal of readership is no longer an available effective instrument for correction since, as this volume makes clear, choice of a daily newspaper in most areas is no longer available to the citizens of our republic. Thus inevitably even our reporting will be increasingly less responsible.

For all those who believe in freedom of the marketplace of thought, the chapters dealing with daily newspapers, radio, television, and magazines seem to me to be essential reading. I am sure that the author agrees with me that all those who favor monopolies of the marketplace might render a great service by debating with him in case he has not found the "truth" or "all of the truth" in this sensitive and vital study of our national life of communication of facts and ideas.

I fervently hope that somehow by some miracle this volume will be debated by and in the mass media—an event which in itself might be a significant turning point in our culture. Without such discourse, debate, and cross-criticism the mass media will further deteriorate, and create disaster for our culture, since the mass media of necessity vitally color and affect all of our attitudes and folkways.

In the absence of such continuing debate, the mass media will continue to report uncorrected history. And in the absence of the corrective forces of cross-criticism, the mass media will be responsible not only for such uncriticizable history but become in dangerous ways the makers of history.

Washington Square, N.Y.
August 9, 1967

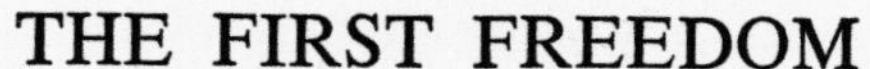

THE FIRST FREEDOM

1. The Daily Newspaper: Development and Decline

Americans, who once relied almost exclusively on newspapers for information and interpretation, are increasingly rejecting the nation's press as their primary news source. The consequences are alarming. Yet, this erosion in public confidence is understandable. The press has repeatedly borne the brunt of attacks by politicians who have blamed "biased newspapers" for their defeats, by the clergy who deplore press sensationalism, by the bar which accuses the press of thwarting justice, by social workers who fear the press turns juvenile offenders into hardened criminals, by educators who charge the press with being inane and uninformed, by scientists who claim their discoveries are misinterpreted, by governmental officials who say the press serves as a propaganda weapon for our enemies, ad infinitum.

No attempt will be made to prove or disprove these charges. They have been made repeatedly; doubtless people have been influenced by them. Hence, the Roper study results show that people regard newspapers as a less important news source and less believable than television.[1]

Declining acceptance is not the only problem faced by the press. Greedy owners have subverted opposition in legal and illegal ways to create exceedingly profitable chains and monopolies and have bought competing media—radio, television, community antenna television, weekly newspapers, and "shoppers," papers, usually weeklies, for which no subscription fee is charged. Yet every time the Department of Justice, the Federal Trade Commission, or others attempt to curb the owners' ravenous appetites they cry "freedom of the press," oblivious to the fact that the intended beneficiaries of press freedom are the news consumers, not purveyors.

Despite misleading statistics offered by the owners' lobby, the American Newspaper Publishers Association, and *Editor & Publisher*, much of the press is in dire straits. Those to blame are the selfish owners who benefit most from the alarming rate of chain growth and monopoly control. As we shall see in Chapter 13, monopoly too often includes common ownership of most, if not all, of the local news media. To argue that *Time, Newsweek,* out-of-town newspapers, out-of-town radio and television stations somehow make monopoly ownership palatable evades the question. None of those media cover local news or comment on local issues.

This blight did not descend upon us overnight. Its roots entwine the past. Indeed, the first newspaper merger in America took place in 1741, just fifty-one years from the founding of the first colonial newspaper, when the *New England Weekly Journal* bought the Boston *Gazette.* As a result Boston, then a city of less than twenty thousand population, was served by four newspaper ownerships.[2] The "honor" of building the first newspaper chain goes to the illustrious Benjamin Franklin who, prior to his retirement as a wealthy man at age forty-two, held financial interests in "at least half a dozen newspapers." Franklin, as E. W. Scripps did a century and a half later, financed talented young employees' printing and publishing ventures, for which he retained partial ownership.[3]

Early Newspapers [4]

It was in Boston, the fountainhead of early colonial journalism, where Benjamin Harris issued the first and only edition of his *Publick Occurrences Both Forreign and Domestick* on September 25, 1690. The Governor and Council suppressed the publication and forbade Harris and others to publish without authority. A more cautious John Campbell, on April 24, 1704, founded the first newspaper of continuous publication, the Boston *News-Letter.* Campbell, as both a bookstore operator and postmaster, set the pattern for other early publishers, many of whom also were one or both.

Except for Benjamin Franklin, most colonial publishers were printers rather than editors. They filled their columns largely with news from England and Europe and virtually ignored local events. But as seeds of revolution were sown, many newspaper publishers became partisans of either the rebel cause or that of England. The sheets became increasingly abusive during an era when editorial comment was the stock-in-trade of journalists. This abusive tone continued through much of the nineteenth century, especially during the political era of American journalism when each political party supported a newspaper in every sizable town. Had the early press not received political subsidies it could not have grown as rapidly as it did; equipment and newsprint were expensive and scarce. It wasn't until after the Revolutionary War that manufacture of presses began in America.

The first daily newspaper, a "sorry-looking, poverty-stricken" sheet, emerged from a triweekly begun in Philadelphia in 1775 by Benjamin Towne, a regenerated but unforgiven Tory. He switched his paper to daily publication on May 30, 1783, at which time it became the *Pennsylvania Evening Post*. The paper struggled for eighteen months without ever gaining reader or advertising support.

Only eight daily newspapers were in existence in 1790. However, with peace and stability, the total grew to twenty-four by 1800. As the number of post offices increased (from seventy-five during the Revolution to forty-five hundred in 1820) and the post road network spread, the number of daily newspapers almost doubled, increasing at a slightly faster rate than the population. Growth continued throughout the nineteenth century at such a pace that every two decades the number of dailies almost tripled.

Contributing to this rapid press development were an expanding population, increased literacy, economic growth spurred by the industrial revolution, and several important inventions. Cheaper machine-made paper plus increased advertising, a by-product of the industrial revolution, and faster presses made possible the penny press era. The first successful cheap newspaper was Benjamin H. Day's New York *Sun*, started September 3, 1833. This was a small, brash newssheet which within four months had the largest circulation in New York, five thousand. Day soon had numerous emulators, but even so, most newspapers were considerably more expensive mercantile dailies or political papers, a pattern which continued throughout most of the century.

And we shouldn't lose sight of the weekly newspapers. (Weekly newspapers here refers to newspapers issued once, twice, or three times a week.) Their rate of growth outdistanced the dailies. A mere 83 in 1790 became 210 by 1800, 650 by 1830, and exceeded 2,000 by mid-century. Men with an apron of type, a badly worn handpress, and a small stock of cheap paper followed the westward expansion, bringing printing to the frontier. This was a period when one could start a newspaper on a shoestring; practically anyone with a viewpoint and a will to express it could contribute to the marketplace of ideas.

The extension of the telegraph to St. Louis and the west in the 1840's speeded news transmission and encouraged the development of yet more newspapers. Thirty papers were started in Illinois alone in the year 1845–46, after the Morse telegraph began lacing the state. The spread of education, especially among women, introduction of incandescent lighting into the home, and postal subsidies spurred the press to additional growth. By 1860 there were 387 dailies and 3,338 weeklies; despite Civil War taxes on advertising income, the numbers increased to 1,610 dailies and approximately 13,000 weeklies by 1889. The combined daily circulations exceeded 8 million copies.

Growth continued. By 1900 there were 2,226 dailies selling more than 15 million copies. A peak was reached for both dailies and weeklies in 1909 when the numbers stood at 2,600 dailies with circulations totaling 24 million plus, and almost 17,000 weeklies. This was at a time when the total population was less than half what it is today and fewer people could read.

The Sunday newspaper was introduced by the nineteenth century's prime innovater, James Gordon Bennett. His first attempt to expand the New York *Herald* to a Sunday issue, in 1835, met with such opposition from what Frank Luther Mott called "Sabbatarians" [5] that he discontinued it shortly. It was not until his third try that Bennett, in 1841, successfully established the *Sunday Herald*. Although Sunday-only newspapers continued to flourish, the number of Sunday editions of daily newspapers did not increase markedly until the Civil War whetted readers' appetites for seven-day news coverage. Even so, as late as 1870 fewer than fifty daily newspapers issued Sunday editions; half of these were in New York, Chicago, and St. Louis. Growth then became more rapid and within a decade more than one hundred dailies published Sunday editions. But it wasn't until the 1880's that Sunday papers really began to multiply in number, size, and circulation. They quickly outdistanced and displaced the Sunday-only newspapers. It remained for Joseph Pulitzer's *Sunday World* to develop the modern Sunday edition with its wide miscellany of news and readable features copiously illustrated in a forty-eight-page package. Circulation exceeded two hundred and fifty thousand before 1890. Other Sunday newspapers followed suit.

When William Randolph Hearst bought the tottering New York *Journal* in 1895, the stage was set for what became known as the period of "yellow journalism." Hearst, and Pulitzer with his *World* vied to out-sensationalize each other in their gutter war for circulation superiority, a battle which is credited with instigating the Spanish-American War.[6] The sensational and jingoistic copy pyramided circulations of the two newspapers to beyond a million in the late 1890's. And their war-fever content spilled over into many other American newspapers, much of it supplied by the Associated Press news service. The assassination of President McKinley in 1901, after the *Journal*'s seeming advocacy of such action, shocked most newspapermen to their senses. The yellow war ceased, to be resurrected by the New York tabloids in 1920–30.

Doubtless many of the 2,600[7] daily newspapers in 1909 were poorly received and poorly supported, and many were doomed, especially when political parties began withdrawing financing. Others, operating on a thin profit margin, understandably fell victim to the depression of the 1930's. And material and labor shortages during World Wars I and II took their toll. However, not all of the 276 net newspaper loss by 1920, another 115 loss by 1930, and 221 loss by 1940 can be attributed to these causes. The extinction of a fourth of our daily newspapers between 1909 and 1940 and the further decline since to 1,749 in 1945, a level at which the total continues to stand despite marked population increases, reflects only part of the story.

This seeming stability is completely false and misleading. Actually, daily newspaper publishing resembles a bubbling cauldron wherein the strongest wages continuous warfare against its weaker competitors in an effort to gain ascendancy. Consider the number of daily newspapers which have been started and the number discontinued during the period of seeming tranquillity, 1945 to 1965. During that time an average of twenty-one new dailies, annually, established themselves by lasting for at least one year. A like number of equally "stable" newspapers ceased publication, approximately 30 per cent reverted to publishing less frequently than daily.[8] This occurred during unprecedented prosperity when the nation's population had increased by more than 56 per cent and illiteracy had almost been extinguished. During the same period circulation increased, from approximately 48.4 million to 60.36 million. Even this increase is considerably less than half of the population growth rate.

Another indicium is the trend toward monopoly newspaper cities. In 1910, 57.1 per cent of the daily newspaper towns were served by more than one newspaper ownership; within a decade the percentage declined to 42.7. By 1930 an alarming deterioration had set in; only in 21.5 per cent of the daily newspaper cities did readers have access to competing dailies. The erosion has continued and we find that by mid-1967 only in 64 of 1,547 American daily newspaper cities (4.13 per cent) did commercial dailies [9] compete. The rate of decline, contrary to popular notion, still is quite high. A ten-year peak of 45.5 per cent was set in 1920–30, the rate for the most recent decade, 1950–60, remained at 35 per cent.[10]

There are no competing dailies in 17 states (34 per cent) and in only one city in each of 20 states (40 per cent). Hence, in only 26 per cent (13) of the 50 states do daily newspapers compete in more than one city. Of the 1,547 daily newspaper cities in the 50 states, 1,400 (90.5 per cent) are single newspaper cities. In 141 of those 205 cities served by more than one newspaper, the newspapers are commonly owned. No general circulation daily newspapers compete in such large cities as Atlanta, estimated 1966 population 504,600; Indianapolis, 508,644; Memphis, 593,000; Phoenix, 607,372; San Diego, 644,855; New Orleans, 674,589; and Milwaukee, 776,810. And the newspapers which serve these monopoly newspaper cities are chain-owned except for Milwaukee. Further, 86 cities in the population range 100,000 to 499,999 are monopolies; 62 of these are served by chain-owned newspapers. Figures by population are in Table 1.

Obviously, monopolies are not restricted to small cities which lack sufficient economic base to support more than one competing newspaper. Indeed, the argument could be made that the reverse is true; that smaller cities have been more successful in recent years in supporting competing daily newspapers. Why can Maysville, Ky., population estimated at 8,739 for 1966; Murray, Ky., 14,403; and Hammond, Ind., 16,978, support competing dailies at a time when Scripps-Howard felt impelled to cease publication of its Indianapolis *Times,* the conservative Atlanta *Times* quit after fourteen months, or the *Arizona Journal,* which suspended once previously, abandon Phoenix to the chain owners of the Indianapolis *Star* and *News?* [11]

There was real carnage in New York City where at the start of the century general circulation metropolitan dailies numbered fif-

TABLE I *Daily Monopoly Cities in the United States, 1967*

Sizes of Cities	*Served by Chain-owned Newspapers*	*Served by Newspapers Not Chain-owned*	*Total*
100,000–199,999	39	18	57
200,000–299,999	15	3	18
300,000–399,999	6	3	9
400,000–499,999	2	0	2
500,000–599,999	4	0	4
600,000 and larger	3	1	4
Total	69	25	94

Sources: Statistics on daily newspaper monopoly cities from *N. W. Ayer,* 1967, and *Editor & Publisher Yearbook,* 1966, corrected to reflect changing conditions through April, 1967.

teen which have since dwindled to three. A slow decline quickened in the 1920's, during which four newspapers became hyphenated appendages of others. Another three were absorbed in the 1940's, reducing the number to eight. In 1950 the *World Telegram* devoured the *Sun,* and in 1963 the *Mirror,* a Hearst copy of the highly successful *Daily News,* ceased publication. (Bertram A. Powers, president of the New York Typographical Union, said that Roy Thomson, international newspaper-book publisher, broadcasting-chain operator, told a group of New York newspaper union leaders that he offered to buy the *Mirror* a short time before it was suspended, but was told the newspaper was not for sale.[12]) This left New York with six metropolitan dailies, only three of which were profitable. An attempt in 1966–67 to wed the heterogeneous corpses of the erudite, exceedingly well-written *Herald Tribune* to the rather bland, featurish *World Telegram & Sun* and the *Journal-American,* a newspaper still suffering from the sensational tinge of the Hearst heyday, resulted in an eight-month macabre convulsion which was predestined to fail.

Out of this nightmare at least three important points might be made. None of the hyphens succeeded; the three surviving newspapers, the *New York Times, Daily News,* and the *Post,* were never involved in Manhattan newspaper mergers. Second, the best features and columns in the world do not a newspaper make. The ill-fated *World Journal Tribune,* daily published up to one hundred inherited features, comics, columnists, including seven gossip columns! Third, a sizable city of newspaper readers was lost, upwards of 500,000. The *World Journal Tribune* retained only 56 per cent of the daily circulation and 76 per cent of the Sunday circulation of its predecessors. Growth by the three remaining newspapers left 350,000 daily circulation still unaccounted for. And when the *World Journal Tribune* died, May 5, 1967, another 150,000 circulation was lost.[13] (See Chapter 4 for discussion of problems confronting the World Journal Tribune, Incorporated.)

True, Maysville, Murray, and Hammond are the smallest cities in which dailies compete, but of the 64 competitive cities, slightly less than half (29) are cities with less than 100,000 population and a third (20) are cities of less than 50,000 population.

In only three American cities—Boston, New York, and Washington—do more than two newspaper ownerships compete. Only 16 metropolitan daily newspapers are printed in the six largest American cities, those with more than one million population.[14] As recently as 1950, there were 29 metropolitan newspapers serving the then five cities of one million population with daily circulations of 13,386,060.[15] Circulations of the 14 now serving these five cities[16] total 9,540,715, more than a 28.7 per cent decline.[17]

Before we fall victim to the argument that newspaper deaths result inevitably from the trend in American business toward fewer and larger operating units, let us look at some other possible causes. Hints as to how the strong have emasculated the weak newspapers are contained in the thirteen Department of Justice antitrust actions taken against newspapers since 1940. Obviously, the relatively few brought to book represent only a small percentage of the illegal and extralegal plots contrived to bankrupt the opposition and, thus, create highly profitable monopolies.[18] Most newspaper murders are successful; the victims have expired before legal action can be undertaken.

As a result of the first antitrust case, the Chattanooga News-Free Press Company and two individuals were found guilty of violating the Sherman Act by conspiring to restrain and attempt to monopolize interstate commerce by preventing the operation of competing afternoon newspapers in Chattanooga.[19]

Although the Chattanooga newspaper was not found guilty on a second charge, attempting to require advertisers to use that paper exclusively for afternoon advertising in the city, later decisions have centered on this question. Two important ones involve Ohio dailies and their pressure to combat radio stations. On August 29, 1950, the Lorain Journal Company was found guilty of attempting to establish a monopoly, in violation of the Sherman Act, by refusing to publish advertisements for local merchants who advertised through a local radio station, the newspaper's only local competitor. The defendants were enjoined from refusing to publish or discriminate as to price, space, and so forth against those who advertised in other media,[20] a decision affirmed by the United States Supreme Court.[21]

A consent judgment was entered January 15, 1952, against the Mansfield Journal Company and four individuals, compelling them to cease conspiring to restrain and monopolize dissemination of news and advertising by refusing to publish advertisements of those who also advertised over radio station WMAN, the *News Journal*'s sole competitor in Mansfield, Ohio. The defendants also were charged with entering into contracts with advertisers on the condition that they use the *News Journal* exclusively, thus compelling businessmen to refrain from advertising with the radio station.[22]

Attempts to monopolize news and advertising and to force subscribers to buy the morning-afternoon-Sunday newspaper package in combination were declared illegal in the Kansas City Star Company case. Not only were the defendants found guilty of refusing to accept advertising from those who used competing media, they also forced advertisers to buy space in both the morning *Times* and the afternoon *Star*, and denied advertisers access to their radio station subsidiary unless they also bought space in the newspapers. It is little wonder that more than 94 per cent of the total Kansas City newspaper advertising revenues went to the Star Company in 1951 and 1952. The Star combine—newspaper, radio, television—received around 85 per cent of the total spent on advertising in Kansas City. A consent decree forced the company to cease both forced combination sales of newspapers and of advertising space.[23]

The Wichita (Kan.) Eagle Publishing Company in 1959 was enjoined by consent decree from using forced combinations both in advertising and circulation as weapons to monopolize.[24] The *Wall Street Journal*'s advertising rate structure is under investigation as of this writing.[25]

The Justice Department had attempted to strike at the heart of unfair competition in 1950 when it brought civil action against the New Orleans Times Picayune Publishing Company. In that case, won in the Federal District court but lost in the United States Supreme Court, Justice attempted to prove that the Times Picayune Company violated the Sherman Act through forced combination advertising sales, exclusive news-vendor arrangements, and subsidizing losses in the *States* (evening paper) with income from the highly profitable *Times Picayune* (morning paper) in an effort to eliminate a competing afternoon daily, the independent *Item*.[26] The reader will note that the *Item* was absorbed into the Picayune Company in 1958 and the entire package sold for $42 million in 1962 to Samuel I. Newhouse, the modern-day haunter of wakes. The Department legal staff associated with this case still blame themselves for not having won a case they felt strongly they should have.

In the Harte-Hanks case the Department lost a second attempt to punish a newspaper for cutting advertising rates and operating at a loss to force its competitor out of business. At the conclusion of that case the Federal District Court for northern Texas granted the defendant's motion for acquittal.[27]

Justice in 1965 won its first case of this kind. However, the offending Lima (Ohio) *News* had killed off its competitor, the Lima *Citizen*, almost two years earlier. The *News*, paradoxically owned by the Freedom Newspapers, Incorporated chain, lost $6 million over a six-year period before administering the *coup de grâce* to the *Citizen*. A consent decree prohibits the *News* from ever again competing unfairly by reducing advertising and circulation rates below cost, and from offering special discounts or premiums, forcing agreements with others not to compete, and acquiring any interest in a competing newspaper.[28] Unfortunately, an attempt to establish a second Lima voice, the *Star*, failed in June 1966, after waging a fruitless $125,000, nine-months battle.[29]

Another intended victim was spared, however, when the Department entered into a consent decree in 1967 with Lindsay-Schaub Newspapers, Incorporated, an Illinois-based chain. Had the terms of that agreement been observed by all throughout the twentieth century many cities would have been saved from monopoly status. Since this is a recent case which spells out clearly many of the monopolistic pressures herein criticized, let us look at it closely. The offenses alleged in Lindsay-Schaub's "conspiracy and attempt . . . to eliminate local daily and Sunday newspaper competition in the Champaign-Urbana area, . . . Lindsay-Schaub and the coconspirators, among other things, have:

a] Intentionally operated the *Courier* at substantial annual losses which in many years totaled approximately $500,000 per year;

b] Subsidized the *Courier*'s losses out of the profits derived by Lindsay-Schaub and its subsidiaries from publishing and circulating local newspapers in communities other than Champaign-Urbana, Illinois;

c] Sold at special reduced rates national advertising in the *Courier* in combination with the Decatur newspapers (also owned by Lindsay-Schaub);

d] Sold subscriptions to the *Courier* at unreasonably low prices, particularly in the years prior to the commencement of the Government's investigation of Lindsay-Schaub;

e] Sold local advertising space in the *Courier* to selected advertisers at rates lower than the *Courier*'s published advertising rates;

f] Sold at special reduced rates pre-print advertising in the *Courier* in combination with one or more of the other newspapers owned by Lindsay-Schaub and its subsidiaries;

g] Made numerous attempts to purchase from the Champaign News-Gazette, Incorporated the *News-Gazette* and other properties owned by said corporation or to merge the *News-Gazette* with the *Courier*."

The effects of such actions are obvious. The *News-Gazette,* forced to meet this unfair competition, lost money some years and had "abnormally low" profits in others.

The final consent decree judgment forbade Lindsay-Schaub from engaging in all of the practices charged by the government. Indeed, in Provision VII, the nature of the offenses complained of is clarified. Therein, the "Defendant is enjoined and restrained among other things from directly or indirectly:

A] Selling or accepting advertisements or offering a rate of space therefore on the express or implied condition that the advertiser refrain from advertising or limit its advertising in a competing Champaign-Urbana newspaper;

B] Discriminating against any person because said person has advertised, advertises, or proposes to advertise in a competing Champaign-Urbana newspaper."

Two other of the restraints forced upon the defendant are noteworthy. 1] The defendant was barred from either gaining a financial interest in or selling an interest to another Champaign-Urbana newspaper; or 2] entering directly or indirectly into a joint production agreement, often referred to as a joint operation, with any other newspaper for six years, without prior sixty-day written notice to the plaintiff with full disclosure for reasons. The final judgment is to terminate twelve years from the date of its entry (it was entered March 27, 1967).[30]

Legal precedent to restrict joint operations comes from a little-noted but extremely important court ruling in the Justice Department's civil action against the Citizen Publishing Company, Tucson, Ariz. The Court's order stating the issues of fact and law for trial in effect declared the joint publishing agreement into which the Tucson newspapers entered violated Section 1 of the Sherman Act and, therefore, was illegal. The defense attorney, in an attempt to clarify this point, entered into the following colloquy with the judge

MR. RICHARD MACLAURY: Your Honor, this motion is made on the premise and with the understanding that the Court's order of October 26, 1965, at least as far as Section 1 is concerned, is tantamount to granting of a Summary Judgment with respect to the Section 1 charges. The Court's order of October 26 is of course the order that outlines the issues to be tried, and there is no issue outlined to be tried with respect to Section 1 as such. Issue of fact No. 6 opposes the inquiry: How can modification of the operating agreement be effective so as to eliminate price fixing, market allocation, and profit pooling and yet retain to the *Star* and *Citizen* to the fullest extent possible the joint use of staff and facilities.

Sometime ago the Government took the position this was granting of Summary Judgment. In my first appearance before the Court I questioned it. As we go along in this case and I have gotten into it further, I am inclined to come around to the Government's view without explicitly so stating there is a Summary Judgment granted with respect to the Section 1 issue. May I ask the Court if I would be correct in making that assumption?

THE COURT: Yes, the Court finds there was price fixing, there was more or less profit pooling, and other per se violations as to Section 1, there isn't any issue.[31]

Daily newspapers are published under joint operating agreements in 23 cities, as of late 1967,[32] an increase from 4 in 1940, 11 in 1945, 19 in 1954, and 18 in 1960.[33] The most serious criticism of joint operations is that they eliminate competition in important areas of newspaper production, notably in advertising and circulation where it is common practice to offer joint rates which are only slightly higher than rates for one publication. This price fixing virtually assures that no new newspaper will be established in the joint operation city, because a new paper would have to sell advertising and subscriptions at below cost to meet the unfair competition of the joint operation newspapers.[34] Further, joint operations in several instances have been preludes to merger. At least a half dozen mergers have taken place after this intermediate step, the two most recent in Tucson [35] and Salem, Ore. Another criticism of joint operations is that if Sunday papers are published by each of the entities, one invariably is suspended, as occurred with the most recent venture when Knight's Miami (Fla.) *Herald* entered into an agreement with Cox's *News* to publish the *News* and conduct its advertising and circulation operations.[36] Conversely, when the only joint operation ever dissolved by other than merger took place in 1966, residents of Chattanooga, Tenn., received a windfall, reestablishment of two newspapers providing direct afternoon and Sunday competition. These two newspapers, characteristically, had been discontinued when the joint operation was begun in 1942. No doubt the Tucson case and others encouraged dissolution of the Chattanooga joint venture.

Predictably, the American Newspaper Publishers Association in the name of "freedom of the press" has used its influence to have a bill introduced in Congress which would block the Justice Department and deprive it of its most recent gains. All but one of the bill's cosponsors understandably are Senators in whose states joint operations exist. After all, one must stand re-election every six years. It would be folly, indeed, to predict the outcome of Senate Bill 1312. Even so, Section 4 is worth quoting.

> § 4. It shall not be unlawful under any antitrust law for any person to propose, enter into, perform, or enforce the provisions of any contract, agreement, or arrangement for any newspaper combination or any joint newspaper operating arrangement if, at the time at which such contract, agreement, or arrangement is proposed or entered into, not more than one of the newspaper publications affected by such combination or operating arrangement is a publication other than a failing newspaper.

Not content to limit legislation to future actions, the bill would instruct judges to vacate "any final judgment or decree" based on antitrust actions against newspaper combination or joint operation agreements.[37] Well might those genuinely interested in preserving our basic freedoms lament, "protect us from our friends."

The "failing business" doctrine was established by the United States Supreme Court in the 1930's and extended by the Brown Shoe Company case in 1962 wherein, interpreted in terms of newspapers, no antitrust cause exists when one newspaper buys another which is in essence failing financially and acquisition by the buyer is the best among alternatives available to salvage the newspaper. Related is the concept that a particular city is a "natural monopoly," it can support no more than one newspaper.[38] As we have seen, some cities of very limited populations and resources do support competing daily newspapers. Further, it is obvious that some "failing newspapers" are failing because of the unethical and illegal business practices engaged in by the "rescuing" publisher.

Recent Justice Department actions have sought to prevent acquisitions or, if the monopoly has been accomplished, divest publishers of newspapers bought after illegal economic pressures have been exerted. Also, purchases which tend to give newspapers near-monopoly or monopoly control in an area have resulted in legal actions, pending as of this writing. The Department's suit against the Citizen Publishing Company of Tucson is of this kind as are two others, against the Times-Mirror Company and E. W. Scripps Company. Times-Mirror, publisher of the Los Angeles *Times,* has been ordered to divest itself of the San Bernardino *Sun,* a morning-afternoon-Sunday newspaper published in the fringe circulation area of the Los Angeles *Times.*[39] Scripps has been charged with monopolizing and restraining trade in Cincinnati newspapers through acquisitions of competing newspapers.[40]

Two nonnewspaper actions which have implications for publishing are the Justice Department's entry into the International Telephone and Telegraph attempt to purchase the American Broadcasting Company (see Chapter 9) and a Supreme Court decision in the merger of two small (combined sales would have totaled 7.5 per cent of sales in the Los Angeles market) grocery chains. The ruling was that the Los Angeles grocery retail market was becoming monopolistic, and this trend would be accelerated with the Von Grocery Company merger. As M. A. Wright, president of the United States Chamber of Commerce said, this decision, if it stands, might well eliminate mergers or acquisitions, including those among newspapers.[41]

Another attempt to stifle competition was cited by Loyal B. Phillips, former president and publisher of the now defunct St. Petersburg (Fla.) *Evening Independent.* "In many cases the dominant newspaper holds exclusive contracts on the best editorial columns, women's features, comics, etc.," he said. "In some instances the metropolitan dailies control publishing rights on syndicated features for smaller nearby cities, thus preventing publication in small city newspapers. Sometimes the dominant newspapers tie up syndicated features without using them." [42] The most recent action to prohibit such unfair competition was a consent decree entered into by the *World Journal Tribune,* on September 14, 1966, when that now deceased newspaper agreed to waive exclusive right to publication in the New York City area of nineteen features which formerly appeared in the three merged newspapers, the *Herald Tribune, World-Telegram & Sun,* and *Journal-American.*[43] (See Chapter 5 for a fuller discussion of how syndicated features destroy competition among newspapers.)

Businessmen, too, have used advertising as a weapon to create newspaper monopolies. They feel their best economic interests are served by the use of one medium which reaches a high proportion of their potential customers. The testimony of Mr. Phillips is again germane.

> (Ten years ago) national advertisers generally speaking began to reduce their use of secondary, underdog newspapers in cities of a half million or less. . . . Four or five years ago the large retail chain stores began to knock off the secondary newspapers. Those two sources of revenue have shown great reductions, so far as the underdog newspaper is concerned. As the top newspapers began to raise their rates and as competing media came into the field they (advertisers) began to get along without the secondary newspaper.[44]

Gene Wendorf, sales promotion manager of the Des Plaines Publishing Company, said the national food chains had discontinued advertising several years ago in the Chicago suburban weeklies published by Des Plaines, asserting they could reach Des Plaines' readers through the metropolitan Chicago dailies. However, within a year after Field Enterprises began the Arlington Heights *Day* and the Mount Prospect *Day*, two suburban dailies which compete directly with Des Plaines and other weeklies, the two Field newspapers were publishing advertising for all of the national food chains in the area.[45]

One of the most flagrant devices by newspapermen acting in concert to limit competition was overthrown in 1945 when the Associated Press was prohibited from excluding any newspaper from AP membership by reason of its competition with an AP member paper (see Chapter 5).[46] In addition to placing competitors at a disadvantage, that AP restriction led to many newspaper deaths. Throughout the later nineteenth and early twentieth centuries publishers unable otherwise to obtain an AP franchise would buy a weak newspaper which had a franchise, kill that newspaper, and utilize the franchise to strengthen the remaining newspaper.

Two recent treble damages judgments, one by a state and one a federal court, if indicative, hold promise of further restraining monopolists. Station WEOL Elyria, Ohio, obtained a $96,000 judgment against the Lorain *Journal*, a civil suit growing out of the antitrust action discussed previously. The action was first brought in 1951.[47] In 1967 the first application to newspapers of the California Fair Practices Act, making it illegal to sell a product below cost to injure a competitor, resulted in a $203,305 judgment, tripled to $609,915, in favor of one of two largely free circulation newspapers. The defendants, owners of thirteen newspapers in California, were accused of reducing advertising rates, even to the extent of running some free. As a consequence, the plaintiff claimed he lost $110,000 over a four-year period.[48]

Surely, independent publishers realize the immense value to them of these governmental successes in opposing unfair competition. It should be painfully obvious how vulnerable they otherwise are to invasion of their cities by those with large financial reserves, especially chains, who could beat them into submission and take over their properties. Why many publishers ally themselves with the misdirected efforts of the ANPA to subvert Justice Department attempts to preserve the modicum of press freedom remaining, perplexes those concerned with true press freedom.

Unless Congress or the Administration intervenes or an appellate court reverses some of these actions discussed, it may well be that newspaper publication will again become a free enterprise business, wherein the marketplace rather than illegal activities determines which newspapers will succeed and which will not. And the inexorable retrogression to monopoly may be aborted.

2. Accelerated Chain Take-over of Newspapers

Paralleling the growth of monopoly newspaper cities in the United States is the tremendous surge toward chain-domination of the daily press. A chain is defined by Raymond Nixon as "two or more daily newspapers in different cities under the same principal control" ("Groups of Daily Newspapers Under Common Ownership," *Editor & Publisher Yearbook*). This trend is nationwide and most of the large combines are adding newspapers at an alarming rate, sometimes absorbing entire chains in the process.

In 1910 when there were 2,600 dailies, 13 groups controlled 62 of them. But as the number of newspapers has declined, the number of chain ownerships has increased, slowly at first, but building to a crescendo in the 1960's. A 10-newspapers-a-year average increase from 1910 to 1960, during the first two years of 1960 skyrocketed to 33, then to 43, and finally to 46.2, for the most recent twenty-month period. Data by years are given in Table 2.

TABLE II *Rate of Daily Newspaper Chain Growth, 1910–67*

	1910	*1920*	*1930*	*1940*	*1945*	*1954*	*1960*	*1962*	*1965*	*1966*	*1967* [1]
Number of Chain Dailies	62	153	311	319	368	485	560	626	751	794	871
Increase	. . .	91	158	8	49	117	75	66	125	43	77
Percentage Rate of Annual Increase	. . .	9.1	15.8	.8	9.8	13.0	12.5	33.0	41.7	43.0	46.2

[1] As of June 1, 1967.

Sources: Data 1910 to 1960, inclusive, from Raymond B. Nixon and Jean Ward, "Trends in Newspaper Ownership and Inter-Media Competition," *Journalism Quarterly,* Winter 1961, p. 5. Data 1962 to 1967, inclusive, assembled from *Editor & Publisher Yearbooks* and *N. W. Ayer Newspaper Directories,* both corrected by information from various other news sources and updated to June 1, 1967.

As of June 1, 1967, chains own 871 of the 1,767 daily newspapers in this country, or 49.3 per cent of the total. Unless this growth trend is reversed, chains will own all of the daily newspapers in the United States within twenty years. Those who scoff might recall that press critics as recently as the 1950's took heart in the decline of the super chains, especially of Hearst and Scripps-Howard, and in the resourcefulness of large dailies in maintaining their independence.[1] Raymond Nixon, one of the closest observers of chain and monopoly trends, predicted in 1955 that the newspaper chains would continue to increase in number, but not in average size and the trend would continue away from large national chains "because of the objections to absentee control" and toward smaller regional ones.[2]

It is true that a large number of small regional chains have sprouted. Sixty-four of the 165 chains own only two newspapers. Hence, the average chain size has increased only slightly, from 5.1 in both 1954 and 1960 to 5.28 in 1967.[3] However, the 19 largest chains, those holding 10 or more newspapers, together own interests in 331 (38 per cent) of the chain dailies[4] (see Table 21, Appendix). Also, chains own 50 per cent or more of the dailies in twenty-one states, including populous and growing California (70.5 per cent), Florida (83), New York (54.1), Ohio (61.85), and Texas (62.16). The proportion of chain-owned to independent newspapers exceeds 80 per cent in Florida, Montana (87.5), and Wyoming (90).[5]

What about the comment that chains tend to own few, large circulation newspapers? Although this was true a decade or so ago, it is far from true today. Chains own the 5 largest general circulation dailies, 13 of the top 15, and 19 of the top 25. In terms of circulation, chains own 80.86 per cent of the daily and 85.4 per cent of the Sunday circulations of these 25 largest dailies (see Table 22, Appendix). Recall, also, from the section on monopoly, that of the 94 daily monopoly cities with more than 100,000 population, 69 (73.4 per cent) are owned by chains. Several chain publishers have admitted they seek monopolies when they buy, among them Gardner Cowles and Roy Thomson, the current world press lord.[6]

There is strong reason to suspect that chain operators accommodate each other to lessen competition for all. A few examples will suffice. Thirty years ago Hearst abandoned his evening *Journal* and Sunday *American* in Rochester, N.Y., giving Gannett a monopoly.

Gannett, meanwhile, combined his morning newspaper in Albany into his evening paper and discontinued his Sunday edition. Hearst moved his evening paper to the morning and continued his Sunday issue, eliminating direct Albany competition for each chain. In 1962 Scripps-Howard sold out to Hearst in San Francisco, eliminating evening competition in that city. And Hearst abandoned Pittsburgh where Scripps-Howard has an evening-Sunday publication. Also in 1962, Hearst suspended his morning paper in Los Angeles; Chandler discontinued his afternoon newspaper. As a result Chandler's morning *Times* and Hearst's afternoon *Herald-Examiner* face no direct metropolitan competition. Shortly after Hearst's San Francisco *Examiner* entered into a joint operation with the *Chronicle,* allegedly because of the *Examiner's* economic plight, that newspaper initiated a unique circulation policy. A memo was sent to circulation employees in September 1965 informing them that the afternoon *Examiner* was not to be delivered to homes in neighboring Oakland (388,000 population, 1966 estimate), only nine miles from San Francisco, nor in cities surrounding Oakland having a total population of more than 250,000. Yet home delivery was to be solicited as far away as San Luis Obispo (27,570 population), approximately 225 miles from San Francisco. Why this concession, which continued for nineteen months, was made to the politically-powerful Knowland family, publishers of the afternoon Oakland *Tribune,* is not known. Possibly the two newspapers agreed to divide the circulation area or the joint operators might have feared Knowland influence would be exerted to challenge the highly-questionable joint operation agreement.[7] In an unusual move the Cleveland *Plain Dealer* in 1960 sold its afternoon property, the *News,* to Scripps-Howard's afternoon *Press,* which promptly killed the *News.* Is there any relationship between the sale and Scripps-Howard's decision not to publish a Sunday edition in competition with the *Plain Dealer*? H. R. Horvitz, publisher of four small Cleveland-area dailies, hints there is.[8] When the Thomson chain in 1966 bought the Nicholson three-daily and one-weekly chain and spun off the Pascagoula (Miss.) *Chronicle* to Newhouse so he could effect a monopoly, several wondered if Thomson was repaying a debt or looking for future favors.

Any doubts about the rapid growth of chains should be dispelled by circulation figures. The 871 chain newspapers control 61.8

per cent of total daily newspaper circulation in 1967, after remaining at 43.4 per cent in 1930 and 46.1 per cent in 1960.[9] The 182 morning newspapers (57 per cent of the total morning papers) claim 70.1 per cent of total morning circulation. (Circulations of all-day newspapers, both chain and nonchain, were counted as morning circulation.) The 689 afternoon chains (47.6 per cent of the total) have 56.4 per cent of the afternoon circulation. Looked at more concretely, the average circulation of the morning chain is 94,795; the average morning nonchain's circulation is 52,956. Afternoon circulations generally are lower; chains average 28,936, nonchains average 19,982.

Speaking of circulations, one of the best indicators of the impact of large chains lies in their comparative weekly circulations. By this yardstick the Chicago *Tribune*'s seven-newspaper chain is largest with 26,264,990 total copies issued each week. Second is Newhouse (22 newspapers) 21,542,677, up from third within a year. Scripps-Howard (16) ranks third, 15,004,893; Hearst (8) a fading fourth, 14,604,631; and Gannett (30) fifth, 8,146,081. Other newspapers with weekly totals in excess of three million are Ridder (16), 7,458,072; Cowles (11), 7,308,068; Los Angeles *Times* (3), 6,903,210; Cox (9), 6,077,259; Thomson (36), 4,336,097; Copley (18), 3,953,574; Richmond (Va.) Newspapers (4), 3,224,584; and Block Newspapers (5), 3,211,606.[10]

The large chains have, with few exceptions, expanded in the past five years. In 1962, 15 chains held 10 or more newspapers each. As of 1967 the number increased to 19 chains. Missing from the current list are Hearst, down from 11 to 8, Ogden, 13 to 9, Brush-Moore, 13 to none, and Westchester-Rockland Center Newpapers, 10 to none. The Westchester group was absorbed intact by the expanding Gannett Newspapers, which doubled in size 15 to 30; Brush-Moore was sold for $72 million to the British-based Thomson international chain in 1967, which surged from 3 to 36 during these five years.[11] Scripps League added 11 newspapers, Southern Newspapers, 9, and Worrell Newspapers, 8, (see Table 21, Appendix).

Some of America's largest dailies became chain links during the 1962–67 period, among them the three bought by Newhouse. His most recent conquest was the one hundred and twenty-seven-year-old Cleveland *Plain Dealer*, bought March 2, 1967, for a reported $53.4 million, the highest price ever paid for a daily newspaper; Newhouse broke his own United States record of $42 million, paid for the New Orleans *Times-Picayune* and *States-Item* in June 1962. Incidentally, Newhouse's newspaper chain is estimated to be worth $200 million. This does not include his stable of four AM, five FM, and seven TV stations nor his thirteen magazines owned via Condé Nast and Street & Smith, both bought in 1959. These properties are estimated to be worth another $100 million.

Sunday Chains

As with daily newspapers, the day of competitive Sunday papers has almost ended. Only in twenty-one of the 538 American cities where Sunday newspapers are published, do Sunday editions compete. And of these, only in five do two nonchains compete.[12] There is no Sunday competition in thirty-four states. Those who argue that chains dominate because they have won in our free enterprise system circulation ballotbox might note that in only one of the eight cities where chains compete with nonchains, is the chain's circulation largest. The exception is New York City.[13]

As has been suggested, chains are increasingly monopolizing the Sunday press. And, as with the dailies, major growth has occurred in the 1960's. In 1926 chains owned 89 Sunday papers, 16.4 per cent of the total. The proportion only slightly more than doubled in the next twenty-five years; in 1952 they owned 197 of 545. The number reached 233, 42.4 per cent, by 1961. In the next six and a half years, by April 1967, another 18.6 per cent had been taken over—342 of 561.

While the percentage increases are alarming, the rate of expansion is doubly so. From 1926 to 1952, the annual rate of chain growth was 4.16 newspapers. Between 1952 and 1961, the rate skyrocketed to 13.25. It continued to increase from 1961 to April 1967, when the annual takeover rate rose to 17.2. If this rate is maintained, the chains will control all Sunday newspapers within thirteen years.

The story in terms of Sunday circulations is the same. Chains hit a circulation plateau from 1930 to 1960 when they controlled from 45.9 to 54.2 per cent of total Sunday circulation.[14] As of early 1967 they control 67.5 per cent, an annual 1960's rate increase of approximately 1 per cent.[15]

Examining the rise and fall of Sunday chain giants is akin to proclaiming "the king is dead, long live the king." As Hearst declined from 13 Sunday papers in 1952 to 10 in 1961 and 7 in 1967, other monopolists arose to replace him. Notably Newhouse, who has bought himself to the top. He parlayed 6 papers in 1952 to 9 in 1961 and 14 in 1967; their circulations have tripled, from 1,170,580 in 1952 to 3,270,879 in 1967. Other pretenders to the throne, at least in terms of numbers of Sunday chain newspapers, are Thomson and his mighty mites,[16] up from none in 1952 to 13 in 1967; Donrey, 4 to 20; Lee, 3 to 7; Cowles, 2 to 7; Ridder, 7 to 10. Virtually all of the major chains gained both in numbers and circulations during this fifteen-year period. Those with more than a million total circulation are, in descending order, Chicago Tribune, Newhouse, Hearst, Scripps-Howard, Ochs Estate, Knight, Cowles, and Ridder.

Chain expansion, both in the daily and Sunday press, obviously is spurred by high newspaper profits. If the argument that newspapers succumb to chains because they are unprofitable holds, major chain expansion would come during periods of depression and recession. As we have seen, the reverse is true. Chains, less active during "bad times," greatly intensify their buying during periods of prosperity.

Helping prime the chain pump are lush broadcasting profits, used to extend chains in all media. One need only relate profit statements of the publicly owned communications chains to acquisitions to realize the truth of this statement. A further hint comes from our Canadian-Scottish-British invader Roy Thomson. Much of Thomson's recent world-wide expansion was financed by profits from his commercial television in Scotland, where his investment of £220,000 within two years was netting, before taxes, £140,000 a month.[17] As is noted in Chapter 13, most of the large American newspaper chains also own chains of radio and television stations.

Is All Lost?

The central question now becomes, How can this almost geometric expansion [18] be reversed? Since most recent sales have been of highly successful newspapers, the logical solution is to deprive sellers of huge sales windfalls. If newspaper peddlers were charged at the regular income tax rate rather than the much more favorable capital gains rate, fewer would be attracted by fat pocketbooks. Secondly, if chain owners were discouraged rather than encouraged by the Internal Revenue Service Code and the tax courts from investing in enterprises of like kind, this whirlwind buying spree would abate. What is lamented here are tax court decisions which hold that using newspaper profits to buy additional newspapers constitutes a "reasonable need of the business." Obviously, when newspaper-broadcasting-magazine-book publishing chains make high profits, as they do, three alternatives are open: 1] buy other businesses, 2] invest in improvements on currently owned or recently bought properties, 3] pay high income taxes. Few choose the latter.[19]

Inheritance taxes should be revised so heirs are not forced to sell or form trusts to protect their ownerships. Various chain owners for years have haunted wakes, buying out bickering inheritors. Newhouse, for example, has obtained at least five newspapers in this way[20] and lost in a court fight to force sale of the Denver *Post* to himself.

The American Newspaper Guild has urged Congress to enact a law requiring that newspapers be offered for sale to the highest bidder before being permitted to merge or suspend. The Federal Communications Commission at one time attempted to offer for public auction broadcasting stations rather than approve their sale to chains and cross-media owners, but Congress and the courts intervened. Even so, this idea, as does any legal one which protects the public's informational media from monopoly or corporate control, has merit.

Various levels of government, the courts, and newspapermen should remain constantly alert for illegal and extralegal pressures exerted on the mass media. And before a newspaper, radio or television station, or magazine has been flogged to exhaustion, appropriate counter action should be taken, the offender punished, and the victim compensated. The Department of Justice has taken a limited number of actions, but it and the Federal Trade Commission must be much more aggressive. It is regrettable that in view of the shocking toll, Justice throughout history has instituted only thirteen antitrust actions against newspapers. Surely hundreds of actionable wrongs have been committed.

Those who argue that chains rescue failing newspapers have

misread the facts. Chain publishers are not operating eleemosynary institutions for weak and decrepit newspapers. Nor should they. But they shouldn't use that dodge to justify their actions. Thomson might well be criticized for his huge multiheaded complex and his niggardly salaries, but he is scrupulously honest when he says, "I am in the business of making money, and I buy more newspapers in order to make more money to buy more newspapers to make more money to buy more newspapers . . ." [21]

No agency can prevent management from implementing wasteful policies, pursuing unprofitable outside activities, failing to modernize plants and equipment, withdrawing excessive dividends to the detriment of the business, drawing up wills in such ways that ownerships are so fragmented and leadership so impotent as to doom publications. A publisher who commits these shortsighted blunders shuns his responsibility to society as surely as one whose actions or inactions endanger the democratic processes. For that is exactly the wrong he has committed.

The Nondaily American Press

3.

Few treatises on the growth, contributions, problems, and decline of American newspapers are concerned with the nondaily press. Yet the weekly (here defined as newspapers published less often than four times a week), foreign language, and Negro newspapers have contributed immensely to the development of our democracy. And they have faced many of the same problems which have plagued the daily and Sunday press. The dramatic struggle of these newspapers has taken place almost unnoticed. Yet they, especially urban and suburban operators, currently face direct, often unfair, competition from metropolitan dailies.

As we saw in Chapter 1, the weekly press predates the daily press and has expanded more rapidly, reaching a peak of 17,005 in 1915.[1] This includes 16,323 once-a-week newspapers, 616 semiweeklies, and 66 triweeklies. However, these figures and others, especially those for years prior to 1930, are open to question, largely because of the number of publications of short duration, disagreements as to what constitutes a weekly newspaper, and the practice of the major information source, N. W. *Ayer Newspaper Directory*, of not differentiating between general circulation and trade and other papers until 1927.[2] For these reasons, although various sources agree that weeklies suffered a catastrophic decline from 1915 to 1930 they do not agree on the rate. Morris Ernst reported a decline of 2,500 from 1910 to 1920 and another 1,300 plus from 1920 to 1930.[3] Malcolm M. Willey and William Weinfeld estimated a reduction of approximately 2,500 weeklies between 1915 and 1930.[4]

Obviously, many weekly newspapers, especially those in tiny villages, produced by small staffs using antiquated and inefficient equipment and yielding small profit margins were highly vulnerable to economic dips and to disruptions of supplies and manpower. It is little wonder, then, that during World War II they suffered their greatest setback, from 10,796 to 9,655 newspapers (10.6 per cent), nor that the Korean War cost them a net of 631 units (6.2 per cent). The other major reductions came during the depression, 1930–35, when weeklies declined by 467 (4.3 per cent). Short periods of growth, unless thwarted by recession or war, have tended to follow deep retrenchment, as from 1935 to 1940 and 1946 to 1950 when net increases of 291 weeklies (2.77 per cent) and 139 (1.44 per cent), respectively, occurred. But 1946 to 1950 was the last growth period of the weekly press, although the 1960's held promise until the Vietnam War intervened, reducing the number by 150 in two years. The total now stands at a new low, 8,003.

Interestingly, semiweeklies, after dropping to fewer than three hundred in 1945, have become more stable. They have enjoyed a fairly steady growth since 1933, the depth of the depression. From 1960 to 1966, after the impact of World War II, the Korean War, and the postwar recession of the late 1950's, semiweeklies increased from 324 to 363 (12 per cent). Semiweeklies, as with triweeklies, reflect newspaper growth in the cities and suburbs.

But for the growth in metropolitan areas, weeklies would show a marked decline in recent years. Wilbur Peterson [5] found that 1,055 country weeklies in the forty-eight adjacent states ceased publication from 1950 to 1959, reduced to a net loss of 708 (10.83 per cent) by new weeklies publishing in 1959 but not in 1950. Peterson shows that, contrary to common conjecture, the overwhelming majority of newspapers suspended were in existence for fifteen or more years, 813 (77.7 per cent); 384 (36.7 per cent) were established prior to 1900. Further, he punctures the pipedream that the decline has occurred almost exclusively in small communities; 567 (53.7 per cent) of the victims were published in communities of more than one thousand population. Further, Peterson found that only 46 of these newspapers changed to semiweekly and 11 to daily publication. The trend has been to revert from daily to weekly.[6] All except Arkansas and Arizona suffered losses; these states gained two country weeklies each. Major net losses were in Missouri, 64; Kansas, 49; and Illinois, 44.

Reliable circulation data on weekly newspapers are nonexistent. Even today, although weeklies are eligible for ABC audit, most publishers estimate circulations. A Department of Labor study reported in 1938 that fewer than nine hundred of the then 10,386 weeklies had circulations in excess of three thousand.[7] Ernst estimated total weekly circulation at slightly more than 15 million, based on that Labor Department study.[8] The Census Bureau placed total circulation of weeklies, including Sunday-only newspapers, at 29.8 million in 1958. However, these figures doubtlessly include

TABLE III *Weekly General Circulation Newspapers, 1956–66*

Year	*Number of Newspapers*	*Total Circulation*
1956	8,478	18,529,199
1957	8,408	19,272,826
1958	8,368	19,725,952
1959	8,287	20,186,414
1960	8,274	20,974,388
1961	8,183	21,327,782
1962	8,178	22,797,449
1963	8,158	23,433,718
1964	8,151	23,975,549
1965	8,061	25,036,031
1966	8,003	26,088,230

Source: Letter from J. Kay Aldous, administrative assistant, American Newspaper Representatives, Inc., dated Dec. 22, 1966.

publications which are not general circulation weekly newspapers. Reports on the 1963 business census included income, but not circulations, for weeklies. The 1965 *National Directory of Weekly Newspapers* estimated circulations of 8,061 weeklies (some 1,300 fewer than *Ayer*'s listed) in 1964 at 27.06 million. The directory claimed circulation increases in excess of one million for 1964 and almost 10 million since 1953. Probably as reliable as any data are these in Table 3 from American Newspaper Representatives, Inc. Obviously, the weeklies have enjoyed a heady circulation gain in recent years; 40.8 per cent from 1956 to 1966 despite the net loss of 475 papers. This growth is especially impressive when compared to the dailies' meager 7.5 per cent circulation increase for the same period.

Three major changes taking place in the weekly press are 1] a trend toward monopoly, 2] the growth of chains, and 3] expansion of the urban-suburban weeklies. Willey and Weinfeld reported that in 1900, 66.1 per cent of the country weeklies were in monopoly communities; in 1920, 82.8 per cent; and in 1930, 86.5 per cent.[9] Peterson found a further increase to 94.8 per cent in 1959.[10] Of even greater concern is the number of communities where newspapers have disappeared. Peterson reported that 488 communities lost their only newspaper, their country weekly, between 1950 and 1959. Kenneth R. Byerly cited a marked decline in the proportion of weekly newspapers to newspaper towns: in 1910, 1.62 newspapers per weekly newspaper town; in 1930, 1.18; in 1960, 1.105, when he reported 9,343 weeklies published in 8,454 towns. A slight reversal of this trend in 1940 (1.20) apparently was thwarted by World War II.[11]

Community Newspaper Chains

The stereotype of the weekly newspaper as the grass roots, democratic cornerstone published by a local owner and treating with local events persists through to today. So deeply etched is this stereotype that the trend toward chain ownership, especially among community weeklies, has never been systematically studied. Yet chains have existed throughout American journalism history. Benjamin Franklin's group, the first in the colonies, linked weekly newspapers. W. B. Harris "probably had the most extensive chain of small-town weeklies in the nation's history" during the late 1800's and early 1900's, wrote Thomas J. Scheiber.[12] Harris published 138 different newspapers at various times from his central newspaper plant in Ellettsville, Ind., for distribution in small Indiana, Kentucky, Illinois, and Ohio communities. The chain began disintegrating in 1907. Probably the major community chain of the 1930's was operated largely for political reasons by the three sons of Harry Chapman Woodyard, for five terms, between 1903 and 1927, Congressman from the West Virginia Fourth District, and state political leader. The Woodyards at their peak ran a sixteen-paper chain with headquarters at Spencer,[13] where the family still owns the *Times Record*, the Woodyards' only remaining weekly property.

Although these and other groups are known to have existed, there is reason to suspect the expansion of weekly chains has occurred fairly recently, with the tremendous development of the urban and suburban weekly press. However, before studying that phenomenon, let us consider some rather tentative information on community newspaper chains.

Despite the virtual impossibility of arriving at conclusive data, the writer as of mid-1967 identified 572 community weekly newspaper chains which held an average of 2.49 newspapers per chain. For the purposes of this discussion a chain is comprised of two or more weekly, semiweekly, and/or triweekly newspapers of general circulation published in two different locales under the same principal

TABLE IV *Number and Percentage of Community Weekly Newspaper Chains*

Number of Newspapers in Chain	*Number of Chains*	*Number of Newspapers*	*Percentage of Total Newspaper Chains*
2	409	818	71.5
3	102	306	17.8
4	34	136	5.9
5	13	65	2.3
6	6	36	1.1
7	4	28	.7
8	3	24	.5
9	1	9	.2
Total	572	1,422	100.0

ownership or control. For community newspapers, publication is in two or more towns. For urban newspapers, publication is in two or more areas of a city and/or its suburbs. Chains were most prevalent in Illinois (55 with 155 newspapers), New York (46 with 135 newspapers), California (38 with 92 newspapers), New Jersey (26 with 73 newspapers), and Texas (26 with 68 newspapers). Chains were found in 48 states; all except Delaware and Wyoming.[14] Obviously, community chains are much smaller than the daily chains, as the Table 4 figures show. Counting an additional 25 community newspapers, linked to suburban and/or urban weekly groups, as chains brings the total to 1,447; thus approximately 27 per cent of the community weeklies are chain-owned. Hardly the disaster visited upon the dailies.

However, the trend toward community chain control undoubtedly will accelerate, a by-product of central printing. Theodore Peterson said that in 1964 there were 1,100 plants printing two or more daily or weekly newspapers, totaling 2,900 newspapers.[15] Central printing usually takes one of three forms: 1] a newspaper publisher contracts to print other newspapers, 2] a printing firm which publishes no papers of its own contracts to print newspapers, 3] a group of publishers jointly finance and operate a central plant to publish their newspapers and possibly others on contract. Some of these plants print upwards of forty weekly papers, often by lithographic offset; most of them print fewer than ten.

Central printing relieves the publisher of maintaining slow, cumbersome, expensive, obsolete equipment which no longer prints newspapers as attractively, as legibly, or as rapidly as can newer processes. Too, it reduces his payroll and eliminates the need for considerable storage space. Then why the concern? When publishers wish to sell, the logical and readily available buyer is the central publisher. As with the daily press, any form of joint operation or central publishing may well be the prelude to common ownership, thus to monopoly and chain expansion.

Urban and Suburban Weeklies

The recent history of urban and suburban weeklies contrasts sharply with that of the community newspapers. Metropolitan area weeklies have expanded in numbers and circulation while increasingly falling victim to chain domination. Morris Janowitz in his excellent pioneering study linked the growth of the urban weekly press to the decentralization of retail business from the city core to suburbs and shopping areas within cities.[16] He found that most of the newspapers serving these areas, especially within city limits, were new newspapers, rather than ones which grew up there. Janowitz also reported that weeklies within the Chicago city limits, where his study was centered, increased at a more rapid pace than did those in the suburbs.

It was entirely appropriate that Janowitz's study should have been conducted in Chicago; that city's long history of a well-developed weekly press has provided a model for other metropolitan areas. As early as 1910 there were 31 urban and 51 suburban Chicago weeklies. The numbers fluctuated little until 1930 when, as a result of the highly speculative 1920's, 75 urban and 93 suburban weeklies were published there. The depression reduced the number of city weeklies by four-fifths, to 15, and cut suburban papers to 71. But by 1940, growth resumed and reached a peak of 82 urban and 99 suburban newspapers in 1950, the final year of Janowitz's study. Despite two wars, Korea and Vietnam, and an economic recession in the late 1950's, the number of urban-suburban weeklies has continued to increase. Today in excess of two hundred serve metropolitan Chicago.[17] Janowitz also reported that in the ten largest metropolitan areas, population of a million or more, 286 urban and 463 suburban weeklies were published.[18]

As the number of metropolitan area weeklies has increased so has the number and sizes of chains. In 1967, 76 paid-circulation city weekly newspaper chains linked 416 papers, an average of 5.47 per chain. After disregarding papers devoted almost exclusively to advertising, 178 free distribution, chain city weeklies remained, owned by 32 operators (5.56 newspapers per chain).[19] The free distribution, often referred to as controlled circulation, weeklies generally are concentrated in areas of intense business competition. Hence, they are found most often within the city limits.

Approximately 480 paid and free circulation chain newspapers owned by 102 groups, are located in suburbs of major cities. These suburban owners average 4.71 newspapers per chain, considerably fewer than for city weeklies.[20] But this is understandable since the proximity of individual weeklies is important to a publisher who prints several newspapers for different localities on staggered schedules from a central plant.

The largest urban-suburban chain owner is Lerner Home Newspapers with 33 paid and free circulation weeklies in northside Chicago and its adjoining suburban area. Total circulation is approximately 350,000. Close behind are the Minneapolis-St. Paul Crawford Publications, 28 weeklies, and Great Western Publishing Company of California, 21.[21] The chain with the largest circulation (575,000) is the Chicago-based Economist Newspaper Group, 16 paid and 4 free circulation weeklies. This group also became the first national weekly newspaper chain when in 1966 two San Diego papers, combined circulation 225,000, were bought.[22] All of these chains have expanded during the past year; Crawford in early 1967 absorbed a

24-publication Minneapolis-St. Paul area group with 270,000 circulation,[23] probably the largest number of American newspapers to be sold in a single transaction.

Several of the major daily newspaper chains also own weeklies, especially urban and suburban newspapers. Among them Gannett in 1966 expanded to 19 weeklies by buying two groups, one an 8-newspaper chain in Virginia and another of 10 papers in New Jersey.[24] A year later Gannett sold the Virginia papers to Globe Publications, which now owns 14 Washington-area weeklies.[25] Field Enterprises, 4 dailies, as a prelude to launching 2 suburban-Chicago dailies, bought the Tri-County Publishing Company, southwest of Chicago, in 1965; Tri-County publishes 10 suburban weeklies.[26] Ralph Ingersoll, former *Time* publisher who gained a niche in journalism history in 1940 by helping found and then managing *PM*, the adless liberal New York tabloid, heads a daily chain which bought 6 weeklies in Philadelphia suburbs at year's end, 1966, to expand Ingersoll holdings to 7 dailies and 8 weeklies.[27] Among other daily-weekly chains are Thomson, 36 dailies and 11 weeklies; Donrey, 17 dailies and at least 3 weeklies; Woodson (Southwestern Dailies), 5 dailies and 5 weeklies; and Dow Jones & Company (*Wall Street Journal*), 6 weeklies. Other daily chains with weekly holdings include Robert S. Howard, Kuser Newspapers, Lindsay-Schaub, McNaughton Newspapers, Morgan Murphy, Panax Corp., Perry, Scripps-Howard, Scripps League, and B. F. Shaw. Indeed, the owner of the giant Great Western urban-suburban chain, Lamont Copeland, also owns LDC Enterprise, a 3-daily California chain.

Among these daily-weekly chains are those comprised of metropolitan and urban-suburban newspapers bought by the large dailies to protect their vulnerable city-suburban flanks from advertising and circulation losses. That is apparently what prompted the Los Angeles *Times* recently to buy Southern California dailies and weeklies, one purchase of which triggered antitrust action against the *Times*.

In center stage of the metropolitan-suburban newspaper battle is Chicago, where both downtown owners are fighting back. Field Enterprises, publisher of the *Sun-Times* and *Daily News*, set a first year budget of $3 million with $11 million in reserve,[28] prior to launching, in 1966, two afternoon suburban dailies and companion free-circulation shoppers, the Arlington Heights *Day* and Mount Prospect-Prospect Heights *Day*. Suburban weekly publishers fear, and for good reason, they have seen the first of an evolving chain of Field Chicago-area dailies. John E. Stanton, president of the two Field dailies, put them on notice that the suburbs are not their "private hunting preserve. We will go elsewhere if successful." [29] Field recruited, largely from other papers, sizable news and advertising staffs and established a large circulation network. Within months a modern, new, newspaper plant with a ten-unit, high-speed, color-capable offset press was in operation.

The Chicago Tribune Company, publishers of the *Tribune* and *American*, took a more traditional daily newspaper approach in 1967 when the owners began a triweekly tabloid offset issued in editions for various Chicago suburbs. These publications, fittingly named the *Trib*, are inserted into the *Tribune* for distribution in the appropriate suburbs. Most metropolitan dailies have attempted to provide better news coverage of the suburbs. Boyd L. Miller found that thirty-one large dailies in 1964 published zoned editions, each containing news and advertising for different suburbs. Miller reported thirteen of the thirty-one had adopted zoning in the past five years, an increase of 72 per cent.[30] Parenthetically, at least some of these giants have been accused of resorting to questionable advertising pressures in an effort to eliminate the weeklies.[31] Another metropolitan daily solution adopted by a few publishers is a joint subscription-delivery arrangement with independent weeklies. Others, as has the nonchain Fort Worth *Star-Telegram*,[32] have bought interests in their suburban weekly competitors. But Field was the first to invade with new, directly-competitive dailies. And the outcome of Field's skirmish for Chicago's suburbs may well reshape suburban journalism.

How have those challenged by Field reacted? Most important, they have improved their news and advertising services. This has required hiring more and better-trained personnel and paying higher salaries to hold them. Several have increased the frequency of publication, from weekly to semiweekly and triweekly, and expanded the news hole by adding more pages per week. Distribution has been switched from less expensive, but slower, mail to carrier. And, also important, they have utilized research to learn more about the communities they thought they knew so well.[33]

Field, by establishing separate newspapers in the two suburbs rather than merging them, apparently learned from the aborted effort of *Time* magazine in Los Angeles. The late Henry Luce and his associate, James Parton, paid a half-million dollars for the *Down Town Shopping News,* which they attempted to expand into a metropolitan-wide, free circulation, fifteen-subedition newspaper. They increased the shopper's circulation to six hundred thousand and expanded the news staff by fifty and advertising staff by one hundred and fifty. Within the year they suffered heavy losses and quit, spurned for locally-oriented, community newspapers.[34]

Before leaving the suburban press let us consider, also, suburban dailies. The prima donna, of course, is the late Alicia Patterson's immensely successful Long Island *Newsday,* established in 1940. *Newsday*'s circulation, in excess of four hundred thousand, ranks seventh among afternoon dailies in the United States. Success, of course, invites imitation, even competition. Broadcasting-newspaper-magazine chain operator Gardner Cowles, III, launched the most recent Long Island challenge, the afternoon *Suffolk Sun,* in November 1966, with high hopes and a large bankroll. Of another stripe is the Gannett entry, *Today,* also begun in 1966. Gannett had purchased two small afternoon dailies in the rapidly-growing Cocoa area of Florida, near the Cape Kennedy space launch facilities, prior to establishing *Today.*

New York City and Los Angeles are ringed by approximately 30 suburban afternoon dailies each. Twenty encircle San Francisco. Fort Worth-Dallas, Philadelphia, and Pittsburgh metropolitan newspapers compete with 10 to 15 suburban dailies each. As of 1961, there were 145 suburban dailies serving the 15 largest cities, a post-World War II net increase of 11; downtown dailies, meanwhile, had declined from 64 to 50. And, possibly most important, circulations of these suburban dailies had increased from 1,991,100 in 1946 to 3,718,712 in 1961 (86.6 per cent); the 50 metropolitan dailies had total circulations in 1961 of 19,266,899, a decline of 2.6 per cent from the 1946 total of 19,787,196.[35] Miller found this trend continuing through 1964 in Detroit.[36]

The Foreign Language Press

Immigrant colonies dot the major American cities and have spilled over into the countryside, bringing with them virtually every language in the civilized world. And serving most of these colonies until very recent years has been a large, vernacular press. Although these newspapers are declining in numbers, circulation, and influence, they played a major role unwittingly and unintentionally in assimilating the foreign-born into American society. Their major contributions were providing information about America to those who could not read English and sprinkling American jargon through their columns. Soon their subscribers could read English-language newspaper headlines, which by their simplified writing and repetition provided language lessons to the immigrants. For an insightful and interesting exploration of these matters, see Robert E. Park's outstanding work.[37]

To understand the role of the foreign language press one must realize the enormousness of some of these foreign colonies. For example, more Italians live in New York City than in Rome, likewise, more Spanish-speaking peoples live there than in Madrid or Barcelona. In fact these 1.5 million New York residents comprise the sixth largest Spanish-speaking community in the world.[38] There are more Poles in New York and Chicago than in many Polish cities. These and other national groups have established American "capitals," most of them in New York, but the Chinese logically selected San Francisco.

American journalism's first newspaper genius, Benjamin Franklin, founded the first colonial foreign language paper, *Philadelphische Zeitung,* May 6, 1732.[39] Franklin printed only two or so issues, but the German-language press grew from this shaky beginning to become until very recent years the dominant language press in the United States. It reached a peak of more than 80 dailies and 700 other newspapers in 1893, serving all except seven states. Meanwhile, the Scandinavian press, second largest, grew to 49 dailies and 66 nondailies in 1883.[40]

However, the German press, which comprised 79 per cent of the total non-English press in 1885, began a rather rapid decline. By 1914, it fell to 53 dailies and 484 nondailies, but still German language publications comprised 46 per cent of the 1,300 foreign language newspapers and periodicals in America.[41] Foreign language newspapers were at first stimulated to growth in numbers and circulation by World War I, as immigrants thirsted for news of their homelands. Consequently, a peak was reached in 1917 of 1,323 newspapers printed in 31 languages, 523 of them in German. When the United States entered the war, large numbers of these newspapers, especially those published in German, ceased. By 1920 the German press consisted of 276 papers, 29 of them dailies, only 26.2 per cent of the total of 1,052 foreign language newspapers. Their total circulation was 7,618,497.[42]

Immigration patterns more than anything else have affected the foreign language press, and especially during the 1920's and 1930's, when our government restricted immigration rigidly, the press of many nationalities declined, while others, notably the Spanish press, increased. By 1925 there were 931 foreign language newspapers; ravaged by the depression, a mere 800 remained in 1935, at which time only 17.9 per cent were in German. Although the number of dailies has continued to decline, to 116 in 1940, 79 in 1950, 75 in 1960, 61 in 1965, and 58 in 1966, the number of non-English newspapers and periodicals, under the impetus of relaxed immigration laws, has increased; they now number 952 in 38 languages.[43]

Today, as has been true throughout the history of the immigrant press, some of it is under the control of divergent, often antagonistic, foreign political groups. A few are subsidized by foreign governments and their agents, several by deposed rulers, others by foreign political parties, including the Communist party. However, this should not surprise us since the most articulate and in many ways the best foreign language newspapers, some of those serving the Jewish community in New York, were founded and operated by socialists.[44]

The Negro Press

Deep resentment at inequitable treatment nurtures the Negro press in the United States. Born to battle against intolerable bondage, the Negro press has continued through the years the long fight for that race's birthright. Much of it is less strident, more intelligent, and more reserved today than in earlier years.[45] Indeed, as was true with foreign language journals, the newspapers which have survived have usually been those which shifted their emphasis from doctrine to news and toward commercialization.[46] However, even today many of these newspapers, as typifies special pleaders, aggressively advance the Negro's cause in highly propagandistic editorials and news.[47]

The first Negro periodical was appropriately titled *Freedom's*

Journal. It was founded in New York City in 1827 to counter another newspaper's rabidly proslavery venom,[48] and lasted three years. Others soon followed. Since 1836, when the second paper, *Spirit of the Times,* was started, also in New York, the Negro has been served by his own press. The first news publication in the South was begun in 1862 in New Orleans, *L'Union,* half in English and half in French.[49]

The pace of Negro publishing really did not accelerate until after the Civil War. As Armistead S. Pride reported, only 36 were started prior to the war and only 3 during the war, but from 1865 to 1900, 1,187 newspapers were founded; most died aborning. Pride said the average life of a Negro paper was nine years. Of the 2,700 launched since 1826, fewer than 175 were publishing in 1949.[50] This low survival rate has resulted in part from the large number of papers begun by the Republican Party during political campaigns to remind Negroes of their debt to the party of Lincoln,[51] and by various other special interest groups, especially religious bodies. Ernst agrees with Pride that poor advertising support has accounted for the suspension of many Negro papers.[52] In addition to the hardships endured by other newspapers—high costs of newsprint, labor, and equipment and their scarcity from time to time—Negro papers have faced other restrictions, especially in the South. Officials have suppressed them, mobs have sacked their plants and run editors out of town, they have been denied newsstand space and access to military camps, newsboys have been manhandled. Also, large numbers of Negro papers in the South were and are printed on contract in white shops whose operators often refused to publish "if its contents were not altogether to his liking." [53] Consequently, the truly outspoken journals and those trusted most by Negroes are located in the North, several of which have large circulations in the South.

From 1900 to 1949, the last year of Pride's study, another 1,554 publications were started; interestingly, events which ravaged other newspapers tended to stimulate the Negro press and vice versa. It isn't entirely illogical, however, that a press whose major role is to seek social and economic change, would flourish during periods of stress—depression, recession, war. During World War II, for example, when others were declining, 66 new Negro newspapers were started. And in the depression period, 1930–36, 165 Negro papers

TABLE V *Number of Negro Publications, 1910–50*[1]

Year	*Number*
1910	333
1920	216
1930	153
1940	157
1950	250

[1] These figures include all Negro publications, regardless of frequency of publication or whether general circulation or special interest.

were begun, admittedly 109 were started in election years, 1930 and 1936. Even so, the expansion rate has been above the average since 1921. Conversely, from 1947 to 1949, an era of apparent public and governmental awakening to the plight of the race, only 9 papers were started.[54] As shown in Table 5 N. W. *Ayer* figures support these conclusions. Note that during the economic boom of the 1920's Negro publications declined by 63, but experienced a net gain of 4 from 1930 to 1940, reflecting an expansion primarily in the early 1930's. The World War decade growth added almost one hundred.

The Ayer figures, of course, include other than newspapers. Pride, the foremost scholar of the Negro press, provides the informative statistics in Table 6. The two dailies are the Chicago *Daily Defender*, circulation 49,230, and the Atlanta *Daily World*, 30,100. A third daily, the Knoxville (Tenn.) *Daily Monitor*, founded in 1958, published about a year.[55] Of the 170 weeklies, six are issued semiweekly and one biweekly.[56]

TABLE VI *Circulation Growth of Negro Newspapers, 1939–66*

Year	*Number of Weeklies*	*Number of Dailies*	*Total Circulation*
1939	152	3	1,601,497
1958	170	2	1,697,560
1959	149	3	1,601,497
1961	140	2	1,470,038
1962	131	2	1,504,356
1966	170	2	1,908,520

Sources: For 1939, *Negro Newspapers in the United States,* 1939, Department of Journalism, Lincoln University. Data for years 1958–66 supplied by Armistead S. Pride, who, as chairman of the Lincoln University Department of Journalism, Jefferson, Mo., directed this continuing research.

Undoubtedly the Negro's energetic drive to eliminate discriminatory practices is reflected in press expansion, especially in recent years. However, major circulation still lies with the established chains. John H. Sengstacke, publisher and editor of the Chicago-based Defender group, in November 1966 added the large Courier press, except for the Chicago *Courier*, expanding his holdings to fourteen publications with circulations in excess of 400,000.[57] Thus his chain accounts for more than a fifth of total circulation. The second largest operator, the East Coast Afro-American five-paper chain, sells 168,000 copies weekly.[58] Circulations of the ten largest chains claim more than half of Negro newspapers' total circulation.

Axiomatically, we could take pride in the decline of the foreign language and Negro press. This would reflect an enlightenment the majority of Americans thus far have not displayed, a willingness to accept into society as equal partners those of other national origins and races. But until our society and our general circulation press serves the needs of those who have been granted less than full citizenship, they must and should rely on their own press to help solve these difficult problems.

Newspaper Problems and Outlook

4.

America's large publishers, despite inflated production costs, are riding their noncompetitive newspapers to ever higher profits during these prosperous times. Their lavish incomes stake them to more monopoly papers which further enrich them. If you doubt the formula, listen to William Randolph Hearst, Jr., editor in chief of Hearst newspapers. He said that if one were to merge independent morning and evening papers which earned $100,000 a year, the profits under monopoly ownership would be $500,000.[1] Is it any wonder chain operators try to drive competitors out of business? Or that, as we saw in Chapter 1, few competitive daily newspaper cities remain?

Because of chain-monopoly trends, newspaper economic indices show the patient to be hale and hearty, and if Newhouse buys another $40 million property we hardly notice. Only when highly publicized newspaper deaths occur, as did recently in New York City, Los Angeles, Detroit, Houston, and elsewhere, are we reminded that something is amiss. Basically what is wrong is lower general acceptance of the press, both by the public and advertisers. But publishers realize any sizable city, despite lower total circulation and advertising revenues, can support handsomely one newspaper, almost regardless of how poor the paper is. Conversely, competition is expensive, for circulation must be had, virtually at any price. If this requires costly gimmicks—life insurance, prizes, jingles, contests, gifts, promotions—then so be it.

Labor, equipment, and supply costs are high and generally rising. A few examples will illustrate. Charles L. Gould, publisher of the San Francisco *Examiner,* said the *Examiner*'s total operating expenses in 1946 were $6,322,111 compared to $29,985,531 in 1964. Similarly, the now defunct *Call-Bulletin*'s operating expense rose from $2,628,599 in 1945 to $10,336,460 in 1964.[2] Loyal B. Phillips, said it costs $2.5 million a year to publish a "consistently good" newspaper in a city of 250,000 population.[3] Ted O. Thackrey, former editor of the New York *Post,* said four owners lost $32 million on the *Post* from 1910 to 1942, before that paper first began breaking even.[4] The New York *Herald Tribune, World-Telegram & Sun,* and *Journal American* reportedly lost $15 million in 1965; their eight-month successor, the *World Journal Tribune,* lost $10 million and was losing $700,000 a month when it was scuttled.[5] Although less spectacular, losses of the Atlanta *Times* during its fourteen-month life approached $3 million.[6] Jack R. Howard, president of the Scripps-Howard Company, said the Indianapolis *Times* was profitable in only thirteen of its most recent forty-four years and failed to earn a profit from 1955 until its death in 1965.[7]

Spiraling Costs

The cost of every publishing ingredient has risen in recent years, not the least of which are newsprint and ink. Newsprint prices soared from a depression low of $40 to $134 a ton in 1958 [8] before stabilizing. Now they are again on the rise, to $139 in June 1966, and to $142 on July 1, 1967. All three figures are contract base prices in New York City. Prices in the western United States generally are $5 less and those in the South $2 to $3 less.[9] United States newsprint manufacturing in these two areas tend to lower prices of the dominant Canadian suppliers.

Accompanying and accounting for these price hikes have been huge increases in newsprint consumption, largely by the newspapers under 100,000 circulation and those in the West and South, rapid growth areas. Newspapers in cities of a million population and over increased least.[10] Although newsprint consumption failed to reach the United States Department of Commerce forecasts, the total for 1966 was 9,076,792 tons, an increase of 8 per cent over 1965 and 14.4 per cent over 1964. Both the rate and tonnage increases exceeded any since 1948.[11] Of these newsprint totals, daily newspapers consume approximately 86 per cent.

Newsprint and ink's proportion of daily newspaper costs is related to the size of the newspaper. (Small weeklies, however, which order sheet stock rather than rolls and in small quantities may pay up to four times the per-ton price of newsprint charged dailies.) According to size, the cost is as little as 16.5 per cent for those with circulations up to 25,000; and as high as 34.7 per cent for those with 250,000 to 350,000 circulation. Proportions of costs to salaries and wages and all other expenses are given in Table 7. Except for those in the 10,000 to 25,000 circulation group, expenditures for paper and ink in 1965 were higher than for the operation of any department within the newspaper. For the over 100,000 circulation newspapers

TABLE VII *Percentages of Daily Newspaper Expenses, by Circulation Groups*

Expenses	*25,000*	*50,000*	*75,000*	*100,000*	*250,000*	*350,000*	*500,000 and Over*
Salaries & Wages	52.5	50.7	45.5	52.3	37.1	44.1	43.1
Newsprint & Ink	16.5	19.9	22.2	26.7	34.7	30.8	28.3
All Other	31.0	29.4	32.3	21.0	28.2	25.1	28.6

Source: *Editor & Publisher,* March 26, 1966, p. 14.

that cost was almost three times composing room expenses, where publishers often complain of disproportionately high wages and wasteful labor practices. Percentages for the composite newspaper, representing dailies of all circulation sizes, were: paper and ink, 21.1; composing room, 14.27; editorial, 13.79; administrative and general, 13.72; circulation department, 10.57; advertising department, 9.35; building and plant, 4.64; business office, 3.73; press room, 3.54; stereotyping, 2.36; and photoengraving, 2.28.[12]

In an effort to exercise more influence on newsprint supplies and prices, several large American newspaper publishers have invested in newsprint mills, among them Newhouse, Cox, Field, Gannett, Los Angeles *Times, New York Times,* Chicago *Tribune,* and the Newark (N.J.) *News.* The *News* in 1962 opened its first mill to produce newsprint from de-inked wastepaper. Mills using this process have been built in the Los Angeles and Chicago areas, the latter by a Field subsidiary.[13] Publishers still vividly remember the world-wide newsprint-supply squeeze during World War II and the highly inflated prices in the 1940's and 1950's, when the New York delivery price advanced from $50 to $134 a ton. They and other investors, nineteen altogether, in 1967 expanded or planned to expand United States newsprint production via new mills, additional machines, or by replacing old equipment.[14]

A second major contributor to high costs is the machinery and equipment requisite to publishing. Progress has exacted its tribute. Prior to the invention of the rotary press in 1871, and linotype typesetting machines in 1887, and their rapid adoption, one could start a newspaper with relatively little capital. Even in New York City entry was easy, though few succeeded. James Gordon Bennett founded his popular New York *Herald* on $500 in 1835.[15] Horace Greeley started the premier newspaper of the day, the New York *Tribune*, in 1841, with $3,000, one-third in equipment and another third borrowed.[16] Costs greatly increased within the next decade; however, Henry J. Raymond backed by George Jones and Edward B. Wesley launched the *New York Times* in 1851 with $100,000, half of it invested in mechanical equipment.[17] As for smaller communities, crotchety E. W. "Ed" Howe in 1877 successfully challenged two other newspapers in Atchison, Kans., a town of 12,000 population, with his daily *Globe*, started on less than $200.[18] William Allen White is variously credited with saying that in the late 1800's and early 1900's one could found a weekly newspaper on $200 and a shirttail full of type, and the paper supplier would loan the $200.[19]

Prohibitive costs today preclude all but the wealthy from daily newspaper publishing, a severe blow to our democracy. When the *New York Times* was considering publishing a companion afternoon daily after the death of the *World Journal Tribune*, its staff estimated a new entrant into that market would need anywhere from $25 million to $50 million. No wonder such multimillionaire publishers as Newhouse, Cowles, and Knight, and *Newsday* and the Washington *Post* declined Mayor John V. Lindsay's invitation to start an afternoon daily there.[20] On a smaller scale, backers of the unsuccessful Atlanta *Times* in 1965 spent almost one million dollars on equipment;[21] projected equipment costs for a new afternoon daily in Bloomington, Ind., were $750,000;[22] even in tiny, population 58,000, Lima, Ohio, the International Typographical Union spent around $250,000 in 1957 for equipment to begin the *Citizen*, which died after a six-and-one-half-year struggle with R. C. Hoiles' *News.*[23] The chains pare costs of starting a new daily by shifting equipment from one plant to another, which is what Gannett did when *Today* was begun in 1966 on a meager $300,000 equipment outlay and a press moved from the Binghamton, N.Y., newspaper.[24] Others shop joint operations or suspended publications, as did two in 1966, Cowles when launching the *Suffolk Sun* on Long Island [25] and Matzner Publications when upgrading its semiweekly to daily in Wayne Township, N.J.[26] Instead of a couple hundred dollars and a shirttail of type to start a weekly, one now needs, according to Landon Wills, publisher of the *McLean County News,* Calhoun, Ky., a minimum of $75,000 to $100,000 in equipment.[27]

Modernizing established newspapers, especially to print close-register color, requires tremendous outlays. The Chicago *Tribune* in 1962 ordered $7 million worth of new presses.[28] Scripps-Howard paid $4 million for 30 Hoe Colormatic presses in 1966–67 as part of its $16 million modernization and expansion program at the Cincinnati *Post & Times-Star.*[29] Three new block-long, color-capable presses installed by the Richmond, Va., newspapers print 70,000 papers an hour, but also cost $4 million, a major item in a three-year $8.5 million expansion program.[30] The American Newspaper Publishers Association estimates new high-speed press equipment for a small daily costs $116,000; for a 50,000-circulation daily, approximately $500,000; and for a large metropolitan newspaper from $7 million to $12 million.[31] Altogether, seventy dailies installed new presses in 1966, as part of the $140.9 million spent by American daily publishers to modernize their plants in that year.[32]

Expansion of color printing and technological changes born of computers and their related hardware, may well revolutionize newspaper publishing. Unfortunately, their added expense, as have earlier innovations, further restrict publishing to those with extensive financial resources. Not only do they debar new entrants, they impel many of those now publishing to sell rather than modernize. And modernize they must or eventually fail in this highly competitive communications century. Much of the one billion dollars invested in plants and equipment by daily newspapers during the past decade has gone to install and house automated equipment and color presses. Today approximately 150 computers are used in newspaper production, 30 were added in 1965 and 71 in 1966.[33] We have seen how costly color presses are. Computers, which by themselves do not print or set type and so must be plugged into existing or new typesetting and press equipment, are expensive. The Syracuse *Herald-Journal* invested "more than a million dollars" and four years in plant-wide automating.[34] Computer equipment costs vary widely, depending on speed, capacity, and complexity of the job or jobs. Happily, competition and mass production are reducing computer costs, by one thousand times in ten years.[35] Even so, the cost of computerizing a total newspaper operation may exceed $2 million.[36] And rentals are comparably high. An automated computer-tied mailroom and dock system installed by the *Daily Oklahoman*-Oklahoma City *Times* in 1966 cost $300,000.[37] The Oklahoma City newspapers and others with the more expensive multipurpose computers use them for accounting, billing, inventory control, information storage, and circulation as well as composition.

Roy Thomson in England and John H. Perry in Florida are moving into centralized electronic editing for their newspapers. This development portends two evils if it becomes widespread among chains, as it probably will: individuality of member newspapers will suffer additionally and economies accruing to chains and improvements which independent newspapers cannot duplicate will heighten monopoly and chain trends.

Lithographic offset promises some relief for the medium to small dailies and weeklies, but the system with its accompanying platemaking machinery is presently too slow for large circulation dailies. The cutoff point apparently is around 70,000.[38] However, a $723,000, 155-foot offset press, the largest ever built, has been installed at the automated Oklahoma City papers, combined circulation more than 300,000 daily and 290,000 Sunday.[39] Other printing processes, among them electrostatic, electronic, and polography hold promise as do such gear as optical scanners, voice-actuated typewriters, laser beams, photosensitive crystals, and even our old friend facsimile transmission. But they, too, will require large financial investments, and therefore probably will accelerate rather than reduce the demise of the small investor publisher.

A third major newspaper expense factor is labor. Newspaper publishers must pay higher wages to attract and hold the kinds of personnel they so vitally need, for today skilled editorial and advertising employees, among others, are in extremely short supply. They and their bargaining agents are forcing salaries ever higher. As we have seen, wages and salaries account for around 50 per cent of the total newspaper budgets of dailies with less than 250,000 circulation, around 40 to 50 per cent of larger papers, and as high as 60 per cent of weekly newspapers.[40] Newspaper wages from 1935 to 1961 increased 203 per cent.[41] The Inland Daily Press Association, surveying newspapers with circulations ranging from 3,000 to 116,000, found salaries and wages for all classes of employees increased during the twelve months ending June 1, 1965: 6.97 per cent for back shop; 5.39, for business office; 5.23, for advertising; and 4.52, for editorial employees.[42] The American Newspaper Guild, representing editorial and other white collar newspaper employees, has set as its goal a $270-a-week minimum for key positions and $135 for all adults. This compares to the original Guild goals, announced in 1946, of $100 and $50.[43] Current contracts specify a minimum of $200 a week for experienced newsmen and photographers in several major cities.

Craft union rates, fifteen years ago the highest in the industry, are slightly lower. Their wages in major cities range from around $160 to $170 a week for less than a forty-hour week. In smaller cities their pay is often around $130 to $140 a week. But craft union pay, too, has increased in recent years. In 1962, prior to a 114-day strike, the New York day scale for printers was $141; the rate by 1970 will exceed $200.

Obviously, increased pay drives costs higher. In announcing the suspension of the *World Journal Tribune*, publisher Matt Meyer said the recent typographical union settlement (1966) with the New York *Daily News*, if applied to all unions, would increase *World Journal Tribune* payrolls by $10.5 million over the three years of the new contract. At the time the *World Journal Tribune* was losing $700,000 a month.[44] The settlement after the 114-day New York strike cost newspapers $18.5 million over the two-year period of the new contracts.[45] Newspapers in other cities, of course, also have been severely hit. For example, wage increases granted by the St. Louis *Post-Dispatch* to 250 typographers in a three-year contract ratified in 1966 exceeded $500,000.[46] Boston newspapers negotiated contracts with their 4,500 employees after a 32-day strike in 1966 which, as of

July 1, 1967, were costing them an additional $3,814,200 a year.[47] Pay raises granted by the Toledo *Blade* and *Times* after a five-month, 1966–67 shutdown raised pay by approximately one million dollars in 1968.[48]

In addition, strike-enforced shutdowns drain newspaper finances and, more important, deprive millions of Americans of their newspapers. Without attempting to fix blame, undoubtedly both management and organized labor often share the guilt, let us consider the staggering losses strikes engender. Here, too, a few examples will suffice. New York City newspapers have been especially hard hit. During a 19-day Christmas-period strike in 1958 the nine Manhattan newspapers estimated they lost $25 million in sales and advertising revenues; a 114-day strike in 1962–63, also including the bountiful Christmas advertising season, $101,250,000; [49] and a 25-day strike in 1965, $42,500,000.[50] The *New York Times* lost $1.7 million in earnings, equal to $4.14 a share, in the 1965 strike.[51] The two Detroit newspapers, the *News* and the *Free Press*, together lost $40 million in advertising and circulation revenues and in salaries paid by the *News* during a 134-day strike-enforced shutdown in 1964.[52] The Cowles-owned Minneapolis *Star* and *Tribune* lost $13 million in gross revenues during a 116-day strike in 1962.[53] Infinitely more serious than these losses has been the wholesale slaughter of New York City newspapers (see Chapters 1 and 2), attributable at least in part to repeated strikes.

Virtually every protracted newspaper strike, whether it be in New York or Terre Haute, Ind., results in circulation declines. Sometime these can be regained through expensive promotionals. Almost invariably publishers launch advertising campaigns; some resort to contests and other gimmicks, the Toledo *Blade* started two contests almost immediately upon resuming publication in early 1967. Losses in circulation may never be recouped if satisfactory alternate sources of news, comment, entertainment, and advertising are available.[54] Take New York City, for example; in late 1966 when the *World Journal Tribune* finally appeared after a 140-day strike, total newspaper circulation in that city declined by 350,000. The death of the *World Journal Tribune*, on May 5, 1967, increased total lost circulation to more than 500,000 despite sizable circulation gains, around 375,000, made by the *WJT*'s former evening competitor, the *Post*.

During prolonged strikes newspapers also lose employees, often some of their most skilled. John Hay Whitney, owner of the *Herald Tribune,* in announcing suspension of that newspaper said the loss of "more than half, of the *Herald Tribune*'s 'bright, young, talented people' during a 113-day strike was a major reason for killing the newspaper." [55] After the Minneapolis shutdown the owners complained they lost more than one hundred of their employees, "including some valued veteran news staffers." [56] The pattern has been repeated throughout the land. Obviously, such losses lower a newspaper's quality. In an effort to avoid personnel defections, many newspapers continue to pay nonstriking employees, as did the Detroit *News* during the 1964 strike.[57] But even this expensive tactic may not hold those who fear that one strike may so embitter management and labor that future strikes will follow.

For strikes tend to beget strikes. This results partly from the multiplicity of unions with which publishers must bargain. In Detroit, for example, the newspapers had reached agreements with twelve of the fourteen unions; the last two struck, closing the newspapers for the ninth time in less than a decade.[58] Metropolitan dailies must negotiate with around ten different unions, and, as has happened in New York, various union leaders seemingly bargain for dominance in pay and authority. A major issue in New York has been use of computers and wire service tape for typesetting. Thus far the affected unions, based on contracts negotiated in 1965, have barred computers from the composing rooms. As a consequence, New York newspapers are saddled with inefficient labor practices and obsolete equipment, such as thirty-five-year-old presses which they should replace and link to computers, but the unions hold a veto. Similar resistance to technological changes has been evident in other cities and through the years, invariably perpetuating wasteful practices. Costs have been increased also by various union-enforced work rules, including setting and destroying type which duplicates type originated outside the newspaper shop, control over hiring, and jurisdictional assignments of work to their own members that others could perform more efficiently and less expensively.[59]

As with lost readership, if satisfactory alternates are available, advertising volume often declines after a strike. Although the *World Journal Tribune* sold around 700,000 copies daily, advertising support was too meager to sustain the paper. Many others also suffer during newspaper shutdowns. Readers are deprived of a major source of information; certain businesses decline; freed of newspaper criticism, crooked government officials are tempted to loot the public treasury; participation in elections and other activities declines; many scheduled events are canceled or curtailed for lack of support. The United Nations Ambassador Arthur J. Goldberg, among others, has urged a "protocol of peace" be voluntarily entered into by newspaper owners and unions. He emphasizes that newspapers are as essential to a democracy as railroads, electric generating companies, waterworks, and subways and so should be regarded as public utilities. A. H. Raskin in *The Reporter* argues that as a public utility, the life or death of a newspaper should, as much as the discontinuation of a railway passenger train, be subject to independent scrutiny.[60]

Obviously, something must be done. The rate of newspaper strikes is distressingly high. After a period of intensified strike activity in the post-World War II 1940's—as many as 40 in a single year, 1947—the number declined markedly, only to increase again in 1957 when 31 strikes were called. During the next nine years there were 238 strikes,[61] 30 against forty newspapers in 1966, twenty-four of which continued to publish. Labor restiveness stems in part from inflation and high taxes, as the American Newspaper Publishers Association claims.[62] Also contributing are resistance to labor-saving technological changes, which unions fear might reduce the number of jobs, and efforts to improve the general structure of newspaper wages, especially during a period of labor shortage. Bitterness engendered in these disputes often prolongs them. The Typographical and Mailers Unions, at times joined by others, picketed the Newhouse-owned Portland *Oregonian* and *Oregon Journal* for five and a half years, until April 1965. Those two newspapers continued to publish despite repeated acts of violence.[63] The American Newspaper Guild closed the Youngstown, Ohio, *Vindicator* for 238 days in 1964–65.[64] The Wilkes-Barre, Pa., newspapers were shut down for 174 days in 1938–39, the Springfield, Mass., papers for 144 days in 1946–47,[65] and the Cleveland newspapers for 126 days in 1962–63.[66]

Income

Sources of newspaper income—circulation and advertising—have increased in recent years but not in proportion to population and economic growth, as we shall soon see. The deaths of large-circulation newspapers have contributed to the increase. Despite this, newspapers each year have failed to keep pace with their major rival, television. As more television stations enter the fray, profits for many newpapers probably will decline, for some vanish.

Since circulation holds the key to advertising, let us first consider those trends. As we saw in Chapter 1, daily newspaper circulations are increasing rapidly. But the picture is less than rosy. Daily newspapers in 1950 sold one copy per 2.87 persons. By 1960 rate of sales had declined to one for 3.11 and to one for 3.21 in 1966. The argument has been raised that these proportionate declines result from changing population patterns; ours is becoming a nation of youths. However, this appears not to be entirely true. When we relate circulation to those twenty years of age and over we find the number of newspaper copies sold increased from 1940 to 1950, from one for 2.09 to one for 1.85.[67] By 1960 a decline had set in; then there was one for 1.89, and in 1966, one for 1.95 adults. Looked at in terms of households, another "adult" yardstick, in 1950 dailies issued 1.24 newspapers per household, the rate fell to 1.12 in 1960 and to 1.05 in 1966.[68]

Unfortunately, total circulation of daily newspapers is not keeping pace with population growth. Nor is Sunday circulation. Sunday paper sales per household in 1950 were 1.07; the rate decreased to .99 in 1953, to .9 in 1960, and to .84 in 1966.[69] Doubtlessly total circulations reflect a decline in the number of newspapers per population. In 1950 there was an average of one newspaper for each 79,228 persons, falling to one for 96,684 in 1960, and one to 104,745 in 1966.[70] It is clear, then, that newspaper circulations and numbers of publications are lagging further and further behind population growth.

Although daily newspaper advertising revenues have increased in recent years, again the rate has failed to keep pace with total advertising, and especially with national advertising growth. Table 8 clearly shows that these newspaper revenues have not increased as rapidly as has the gross national product, the major and accepted economic barometer. Hence, the percentage of the gross national product devoted to newspaper advertising, which surprisingly reached a peak in 1933, has declined considerably, both in propor-

TABLE VIII *Daily Newspaper Advertising and Gross National Product, in Millions of Dollars, 1929–65*

Year	*Gross National Product*	*National Adver-tising*	*Per Cent of National Advertising to Gross National Product*	*Total Adver-tising*	*Per Cent of Total Advertis-ing to Gross National Product*
1929	$104,400	$260.	.249	$ 797.338	.764
1933	56,000	145.	.259	428.673	.765
1939	90,426	152.	.168	552.0	.610
1950	284,769	533.4	.187	2,075.6	.729
1955	397,960	788.9	.198	3,087.8	.776
1960	503,734	836.1	.166	3,702.8	.735
1965	681,207	869.4	.1276	4,456.5	.654

Source: Advertising revenue data from McCann-Erickson, Inc., as reported in *Printers' Ink*. Gross National Product from the Department of Commerce.

tions of national advertising and total advertising. Newspapers' share of mass media–newspaper, magazine, and radio–advertising fell sharply as radio prospered in the 1930's and 1940's; dailies fell from their lofty 80 per cent in 1928 to a low of 54.3 per cent in 1947.[71] Television continues each year to reduce newspapers' portion of the now four mass media advertising revenues, dropping newspapers' share to 49.1 per cent in 1966 (Table 9).

It is true that in the 1940's and early 1950's television eroded magazine and radio advertising seriously. However, television advertising increases during the past decade have been at the expense of newspapers. Note that for the years 1955, 1960, and 1966, as shown below, the proportional gains of television virtually equal the proportional losses of newspapers.

Television, primarily a national advertising medium, has criti-

TABLE IX *Proportions of Total Advertising Revenues Received by the Mass Media, 1919–66*

Medium	*1919*	*1928*	*1933*	*1935*	*1939*	*1947*	*1950*	*1955*	*1960*	*1966*
Newspapers	70.0	80.0	73.5	70.6	62.6	54.3	66.3	63.6	53.2	49.1
Magazines	30.0	18.6	16.7	17.1	17.6	20.4	16.3	13.3	13.7	13.0
Radio	. . .	1.4	9.8	12.3	19.8	25.3	14.5	9.3	9.8	10.1
Television	. . .	. . .	. . .	. . .	. . .	. . .	2.9	13.8	23.3	27.8

Sources: Data 1919–47, Harvey J. Levin, *Broadcast Regulation and Joint Ownership of Media* (New York, 1960), p. 109. Other years McCann-Erickson, Inc., reports, published in *Printers' Ink*.

TABLE X *Proportions of National Advertising Revenues Received by the Mass Media, 1950–66*

Medium	*1950*	*1955*	*1960*	*1966*
Newspapers	39.4	36.6	28.4	23.9
Magazines	37.7	30.3	32.0	32.3
Radio	18.5	8.5	8.0	8.2
Television	4.4	24.6	31.6	35.6

Source: Newspaper and magazine data, McCann-Erickson, Inc., as reported in *Printers' Ink*. Radio and TV data, FCC reports based on total billings, U.S. stations and networks after frequency and promotional discounts but before payment of commissions.

cally lowered newspapers' share of national mass media advertising, as the figures in Table 10 show. Television has replaced both newspapers and magazines as the primary national advertising medium. Further evidence of television's dominance is contained in a Television Bureau of Advertising report showing that the one hundred largest national newspaper advertisers for 1966 spent almost 370 per cent more in television than in newspapers, $1,328,122,100 in television to $361,441,115 in newspapers.[72]

Newspapers still lead in local advertising, continuing to receive approximately 80 per cent of the total placed with the mass media. However, television, which has been so luxuriously supported by national advertising, will compete energetically for local advertising as more ultrahigh-frequency stations go on the air.

The Outlook

Fortunately, all is not black. That a few beams of light pierce the cloud cover is attested by the following facts.

1] At long last the newspaper industry is seriously engaged in research which should help provide solutions to some problems and reshape the product.

2] Newspaper personnel are better educated and better trained than at any pervious time. The proportion of college graduates is steadily increasing.

3] Newer transmission equipment linked to earth satellite systems greatly speeds communication.

4] Improved presses, although very expensive, and accompanying color inks are capable of close-register, high quality color reproduction.

5] Labor leaders have joined management in expressing alarm at the number and length of strikes, giving rise to speculation that both sides may exercise greater restraint. And except in three or four major cities unions are cooperating in converting to computers.

6] The ratio of daily-newspaper revenue increases to expenditures has improved since 1958; they are approximately in balance.

7] Circulations of the weekly press, led by the mushrooming urban-suburban newspapers, are increasing rapidly, 41 per cent from 1956 to 1966.[73] (The dailies during the period increased by 6.8 per cent.)

8] Dramatic growth of the urban and suburban daily and weekly press, if it can achieve more independence, holds the potential for a grass roots resurgence.

9] In many areas where central printing houses are located, a new publisher can found a weekly newspaper and contract for its printing, thus evading heavy equipment investments. In this way those with limited financial resources again may voice their opinions in the marketplace of ideas.

In addition, some of the important recent and predicted technological developments hold promise; their impact on publishing may well be revolutionary. Offset and contract printing give some slight promise of returning competition to at least small and medium-sized cities. Competitive dailies have been started during the past three years in Athens, Ga., Oklahoma City, Tucson, and on the fringes of several large cities. An offset weekly can be started today with little cash. The minimum necessary equipment for a small weekly can be bought for around five thousand dollars, except for camera and press. And these aren't needed if a central printing establishment in the area will contract to print the newspaper. Remaining are costs of supplies, which are higher than for letterpress, and salaries and wages, which generally are lower.

Faster offset presses being developed will make it possible for large circulation newspapers to convert to offset; at present an estimated 275 dailies and 1,600 weeklies are printed by photolithography. Much good should come from this trend. Offset displaces heavy, cumbersome, expensive, antiquated composing and printing equipment and stocks of heavy metal. More important, offset printing is far superior. With offset, newspapers can print close-register color less expensively and make greater use of a wide variety of art in the form of pictures, sketches, designs and the like. Also, less skilled and therefore less highly paid employees can set copy on the newer cold-type composing machines.

Both in quality and quantity color printing has progressed. Newspapers with 88 per cent of the daily circulation are equipped to use preprinted HiFi and with 44 per cent preprinted SpectaColor rolls. Both HiFi and SpectaColor give reproduction of magazine quality. Of the 1,754 daily newspapers, 1,341 can print at least one run-of-paper color in addition to black; 909 can print two colors; and 787, three colors.[74] Color advertising linage has increased 617 per cent since 1951 and 20 per cent in 1966.[75] Color holds the greatest promise of wooing national advertising and protecting large local accounts from television.

After lying dormant for fifteen years facsimile transmission is coming of age. The *Asahi* followed by *Mainichi* and *Yomiuri*, large Tokyo dailies, in 1958 began transmitting images of newspaper pages via radio to distant regional plants for offset printing. The *Wall Street Journal* since 1961 has utilized this system to link its San Francisco newsroom with its Riverside (Los Angeles area) printing plant, more than four hundred miles away. The London *Daily Mail* in mid-1966 began printing its Belfast edition from facsimile pages transmitted via radio. RCA is conducting tests on facsimile transmission-electrostatic printing for home reception. However, facsimile, too, may work to the detriment of diversity. Chains may well use the system to improve their member newspapers and to extend their ownerships.

Automation,[76] that magical system worshipped by management, suspected by organized labor, and held in awe by the general public, could revitalize newspaper production. When computers are eventually linked to electronic gear now on the drawing boards, the publishing industry will bid adieu to techniques used since the seventeenth century. Apparently, newspapers some day will be edited by a person who, sitting at a console, retrieves information stored in computers; edits it with a "light pen"; positions copy, headlines, artwork, and advertising on the pages electronically; and activates computer-driven "presses," or funnels the product directly into the home. The latter system would permit the customer to edit his own "newspaper" to his tastes and interests. Information on any subject he selects either will be flashed on a screen almost instantaneously or "printed out," probably using some system yet to be developed.

Newspapers already are preparing for this day by acquiring community antenna television systems. They now own around 250, approximately 15 per cent of the total, and are continuing to invest heavily in this multichannel entree to the home. Already "instant pages" are printed for catalogs, magazines, and telephone directories by an electronic system which combines photographic typesetting with a cathode-ray tube and microelectronic circuitry. Input and printout are controlled by computers.[77]

Prior to that time, more and smaller newspapers will computerize type-justification and increasingly without operator-prepared "idiot" (unjustified) tapes. Scanning equipment will convert typewritten copy into electronic impulses, store these, print a "proof" on a screen for editing, then prepare justified tapes from the edited copy for either offset or letterpress composition. The computer then will proofread and correct the composing equipment's copy by comparing it with the original, edited copy.

Mechanical composition apparently will become extinct within a decade. A high-speed cathode-ray-tube typesetting device was refined in 1966 which, as soon as improved and high-speed platemaking equipment is developed, will set type almost fifty times faster than by linotype. This equipment may be adapted either to letterpress or offset or newer printing processes, as, for example, electrostatic printing. The latter process is the principle used by Xerox in its copying machines. Printing is achieved by positive and negative charges between ink and paper.

The day is fast approaching when information will be transformed into energy-bits for transmission, possibly by laser beams, over great distances, even from continent to continent via earth satellites, and converted at the receiving point into any communications form desired—visual, sound, print. Herein lies tremendous potential for evil as well as good. Obviously, we can expect enormous expansion of giant broadcasting-newspaper-magazine-book publishing communications chains. Already RCA-NBC, IBM, General Electric, Xerox, and others are expanding their cross-communications interests, well on the way to becoming "giant electronic publishers." [78] Their impact, as E. B. Weiss warns, may well require "new federal regulations to insure freedom of expression in the public interest." [79]

5. *News and Feature Services: Boon or Blight?*

It is difficult to imagine how provincial, uninformative, dull, uninteresting, and circumscribed American daily newspapers would be were they confined to staff-originated content. The large, enterprising dailies would, of course, provide limited national and international news coverage and some of the types of feature materials which comprise today's newspaper. Others, no doubt, would clip large out-of-town dailies, as they did prior to the growth of news and feature services. But no newspaper could originate as much material, even at immense cost, as is available through news services and feature syndicates.

However, the price has been high, even more in loss of individuality than in money. When one studies general circulation dailies from throughout the United States he is struck by the monotonous similarity of many of them. They contain the same news service dispatches under essentially similar headlines illustrated by the same pictures. Often many of the comics, panels, crossword puzzles, columns, feature stories, and in some, even editorials, are identical. This sameness in itself would be excusable, except that it illustrates the extent to which the mass media have placed in a few hands control over what we may read, hear, and see. The power to censor, to color news, to ignore, rests in great measure with the Associated Press and slightly less with United Press International, our two American world news services. And the serious charge has been raised that they have misused these powers, especially in relation to events which affect them or their clients directly.

Also of paramount importance, the daily newspapers for years through the Associated Press, until the courts intervened, attempted to protect themselves from competition by denying AP service to others. Would that the newspapers no longer attempted to withhold news and feature services from potential competitors. But they do, as was mentioned in Chapters 1 and 2 and will be discussed more fully.

Development of the News Services [1]

News services themselves, notably the Associated Press and its progenitors, resorted to nefarious methods to establish and maintain monopoly control over news. From the outset they entered into exclusive agreements with the major telegraph companies to bar others from the wires. Only when faced with the realities of an ongoing radio news service did they reluctantly agree to unrestricted radio broadcast of their news.

Colonial and frontier newspapers gave a greater proportion of space to nonlocal news events than do newspapers today. It may be that editors in what then were small cities and communities assumed their readers knew what was happening locally. They may have thought news grew in importance with distance, or possibly they felt readers wished their newspapers to link them with places of previous residence—England for colonists and the East for frontiersmen. At any rate, newspapers devoted much space to foreign and national news. Their sources were other newspapers, letters, and, for a few, correspondents. These, however, were slow and often unreliable, especially when weather interfered with land or river travel.

Major news events, in particular those of national importance—elections, wars, actions of Congress and the President, calamities—heightened reader interest and prodded editors to speed up news transmission. Some newspaper editors entered into news exchange agreements, others who had developed a corps of correspondents sold their news. And, finally, as costs of maintaining coverage mounted, publishers and others founded city and regional news services, among them the owners of six New York dailies who in 1846 started the Harbor News Association and the New York Associated Press. How this news service fought off competitors and achieved monopoly over foreign news and exclusive access to important telegraph lines is recounted in detail by Alfred McClung Lee in *The Daily Newspapers in America.*

As newspapers increased in western Pennsylvania, Ohio, Indiana, Kentucky, Michigan, and Missouri in the 1850's they demanded improved national and international coverage, and so the Western Associated Press, not directly tied to the New York AP, was founded in 1862. It adopted the New York AP's restrictive covenants—members were forbidden to buy news from other services, control over the association was in the hands of a few large publishers, newspapers could be admitted to membership only by unanimous vote of the members (this effectively barred competitor newspapers from obtaining the service)—and entered into news exchange agreements with the New York AP. Both Associated Presses expanded in the ensuing years and others sprang up. These, too, generally entered into news agreements with the two largest AP's.

Not unexpectedly, the Western AP soon challenged the New York AP for control. And after the New York AP effectively merged itself in 1884 with the new United Press Association (no relation to the current United Press International), the Western AP exposed these secret trust deals and forced reorganization of the Associated Press in Chicago in 1892. The offspring proceeded to extend its service throughout the country. Enforcement of its monopoly rules against the Chicago *Inter-Ocean,* however, brought a Supreme Court of Illinois ruling, on February 19, 1900, that the AP was a public utility which did not have the right to debar members from obtaining news from other sources, or to expel them. The "public utility" ruling frightened AP directors most; under it AP would be forced to sell its service to all.

Rather than live under this threat to their monopolistic rules, AP reorganized under a "Membership Corporation Law" of New York as an exclusive social club. Thus AP retained its membership restrictions until they were finally struck down by the United States District Court, southern district of New York, when on January 13, 1944, it prohibited AP from excluding any newspaper from membership by reason of its competition with a member paper.[2] The United States Supreme Court on June 18, 1945, affirmed the District Court's judgment and held that the AP members, constituting independent business enterprises, had joined together to secure a competitive advantage by barring nonmembers from using news collected either by AP or by its individual members. Further, the

Supreme Court decision pointed out that a restraint of this kind, aimed at the destruction of competition, is condemned by the Sherman Act.[3] One quotation from that decision is apropos: "Freedom to publish is guaranteed by the Constitution, but freedom to combine to keep others from publishing is not. Freedom of the press from governmental interference under the First Amendment does not sanction repression of that freedom by private interests." [4]

Although various news services attempted to challenge AP, it remained for two chain newspaper publishers to provide effective competition. E. W. Scripps, in 1907, merged his middle-western agency, Scripps-McRae Press Association, with his west coast agency, Scripps News Association, both founded in 1897, with the recently purchased Publishers' Press Association, founded in 1898, to form the United Press Association, later simplified to United Press. UPA at the outset served afternoon and Sunday morning newspapers. William Randolph Hearst combined his chain's news and features into the American News Service in 1909, reorganized the morning service into International News Service in 1910 while retaining the National News Association as an evening service for two more years before combining the entire package under International News Service in 1911. He reorganized the services again in 1918 to place the morning service under a new agency, Universal Service, and retained INS as an afternoon service. Despite other organizational changes, INS continued to operate until it was sold and merged into United Press to become United Press International in 1958. Unlike Associated Press, a member-owned cooperative, both Scripps and Hearst news agencies were private, commercial newsgathering services.

Scripps apparently was motivated by at least three considerations in founding UPA: 1] he was expanding his chain of newspapers, some of which were barred from AP membership by veto of competitor AP members, 2] he objected to the news monopoly exercised by AP, and 3] he felt that AP neglected afternoon newspapers, which it did. AP was controlled by publishers of large morning newspapers who used AP as a weapon against all others, including afternoon newspapers. It wasn't until 1915 that AP finally, ignoring objections from morning newspaper publishers, extended full service to its afternoon subscribers, from 9 A.M. to 9 P.M., and revoked its rule prohibiting members from buying news from other services.

Thus, United Press filled a news vacuum intentionally created by AP. UP also benefited from another myopic AP blunder. AP in 1870 aligned itself with the three major world news agencies in an international news cartel. Havas of France received exclusive news gathering and sales rights to France, the French colonies, Spain, Portugal, Italy, Belgium, Rumania, Serbia, and most of Latin America. Wolff of Germany was dealt Germany, the German colonies, Scandinavia, Holland, Austria, Hungary, parts of the Balkans, Switzerland, and Russia. Associated Press received North and Central America. Reuters of Britain received the rest of the world—the Middle and Far East, most of Africa, part of the Balkans, East Indies, China, and part of South America. Three major weaknesses resulted: This established an international monopoly on news. Compounding the seriousness of this ill-advised compact, Havas and Wolff were subsidized propaganda organs for their home governments. And during wartime Reuters also carried home-government propaganda as news. Hence, world news distributed by the AP included not only news as viewed through foreign eyes, but deliberate distortions largely unchallenged in AP's reverence to "objective" reporting. And the picture of the United States gained by the peoples throughout the world was altered by the national interests of these three agencies. Since our common language made London the central news distribution center, Reuters, the lesser of the three European evils, exercised more direct control over our news. The United States' entries into World Wars I and II and ill feelings generated against the United States throughout the world during these periods have been credited at least in part to AP's selling its soul for inexpensive world news reports.[5] World War I ruptured portions of the cartel. But it wasn't until 1934 that AP finally extricated itself fully from cartel agreements.

Although United Press entered into news exchange agreements with national news services, she also opened news bureaus in important world capitals. Therefore, when World War I broke out, UP had a news organizational nucleus in Europe whereas AP had none and was forced belatedly to develop a European staff under difficult conditions. As a result UP, which was already selling news to foreign clients, grew rapidly in the United States and abroad, especially in Latin America where the Havas service was recognized then as coloring war news. UP, still primarily a service for afternoon newspapers, gained also in the United States. News from each day's war activity "broke" for afternoon newspapers because of the European time differential. In addition to helping UP, this is credited with converting afternoon, largely feature papers in America into real "news" papers.

UP growth during the next twenty-five years reflects the advantages gained by challenging the news cartel. Between 1914 and 1940 UP almost tripled its number of clients, from around five hundred to more than fourteen hundred, approximately equal to the number of AP subscribers. Although AP had few clients abroad, UP sold its service to 130 newspapers in Latin America and 320 in Europe.[6] UP soon became the major news service in Latin America, virtually displacing Havas and its successor Agence France-Presse.

Meanwhile, Britain and later France, Portugal, and Japan, irritated by Hearst news treatment, around 1916 refused INS use of their postal and telegraph services. Thus shut off from its normal flow of foreign news, the Hearst agency allegedly pirated AP news, rewrote it, and supplied it to INS subscribers. The United States Supreme Court in 1918 protected AP from this unfair competition when it upheld an injunction prohibiting the wrong.[7] This blow fell at a time when INS, with fewer than four hundred clients, was in dire financial straits. INS finally established its reputation on the by-lines of several outstanding reporters and writers.

Radio posed a special problem to the three news services, which, as we have seen, were organized and supported by newspapermen to serve newspapers; all three tried to prevent radio from using their news. AP went so far as to fine a member, the Portland *Oregonian*, one hundred dollars for using AP election coverage in 1924 on that newspaper's radio station. Earlier in 1924 AP had permitted broadcasting of baseball scores. The AP convention in 1925 approved radio's use of news of "transcendent national or international importance." All three agencies provided the National Broadcasting Company with returns on the 1928 Hoover-Smith presidential election. Again, in 1932, AP reluctantly and at the last minute supplied presidential election returns to both Columbia Broadcasting System and NBC; this froze UP and INS out of the picture, both had planned to sell their election returns to the networks. Regardless, all three took strong stands against permitting radio more than brief bulletins and set stringent limits on the timing of newscasts. Nettled by these restrictions, CBS in 1933 began its own agency, Columbia News Service, Incorporated. Predictably, AP sprang into action. She hurriedly reached an agreement with CBS and NBC to provide a special service for two daily newscasts, one in the morning not earlier than 9:30 and the other in the evening not earlier than 9, both scheduled not to compete with, but to whet the listener's appetite for, newspapers. Radio could use special bulletins at any time; but none of the newscasts was to be sponsored. In return, both networks agreed to AP's demand that they cease newsgathering.

In answer to a plea from independent stations for more frequent and sponsored newscasts, alternate sources were developed, notably Transradio Press Service, begun in 1934. Transradio within a year had more than 250 customers, including some newspapers. Faced with this dilemma, UP and INS in 1935 and AP in 1936 began fuller service to radio clients; many publishers never forgave UP and INS. However, AP continued its ban on use of its reports on sponsored programs until 1939. Their precipitous action had the desired effect; it weakened their competitor. Transradio ceased operations in 1951.[8] With competition eliminated, the agencies imposed five-year contracts on broadcasters. Station owners' complaints were unheeded until late 1967 when the FCC adopted a rule prohibiting broadcasters from signing news service contracts which extended longer than three years.

Various mechanical and other improvements were made by the news services, including introduction in 1914 of the teletypewriter for sending and receiving news in typewritten form. A refinement adopted in 1929, the teletypesetter punches tapes which when run through an attachment to a linotype automatically operate the typesetting machine. (This development is a mixed blessing as it discourages newspapers from editing news agency stories and encourages filling the newspaper with news service copy rather than expending greater effort and money in gathering and setting local stories.) Another development which deserves special mention is the transmitting of photographs by wire. The three news services had previously been supplying pictures by mail, UP beginning in 1925. Various wire systems had been proposed, some of which were tested and rejected. It remained for American Telephone and Telegraph in 1933 to develop a telephoto system. AT & T negotiated an exclusive agreement with Associated Press; AP Wirephoto service began January 1, 1935. Both Scripps and Hearst, as AP members, tried to block Wirephoto. After failing, their news services developed their own photo-by-wire systems. INS introduced its "soundphoto" telephone-line system in six months and UP began NEA-Acme Telephoto a year later. AP sent the first color photos by wire in 1939.

INS, generally regarded as the least reliable of the three, had always been a marginal enterprise. Few who observed the systematic elimination of unprofitable newspapers and other Hearst ownerships after William Randolph Hearst's death in 1951 were surprised when, in 1958, INS, too, felt the ax. The service, then with some 2,000 world-wide clients including 334 American daily newspapers (20 per cent of the total), was sold to and merged into United Press to form United Press International. UP had some 5,000 clients throughout the world, including 833 (50 per cent) American dailies. AP served 7,275 total clients, including 1,196 American dailies (70 per cent). After the merger UPI had 992 United States dailies (60 per cent). Of the American dailies, 720 were exclusive AP and 516 exclusive UPI subscribers; 476 subscribed to both.[9]

AP and UPI have continued to grow. By the end of 1966 AP served a record 1,236 American dailies to UPI's 1,180; AP sold its service to 2,600 domestic radio and 324 TV stations; UPI to 3,078 broadcasters, including 320 radio-TV stations; UPI to 3,078 broadcasters, including 320 radio-TV outlets; AP reported 8,500 clients throughout the world, 2,000 more than UPI. Both news agencies speed transmission of news: to and from foreign points by radio and communications satellite; to domestic clients by high-speed equipment which they soon hope will transmit 150 words or more a minute as compared to the conventional 66; and via computer-justified tapes for both letterpress and offset composition at speeds exceeding 1,000 words a minute.[10] Both are selling a news service to CATV systems.[11] Costs continue to rise; each service spends in excess of $50 million annually, increasing by slightly less than $2 million a year since 1960.[12] Contributing heavily to high costs in

1966 was the Vietnam War coverage for which AP reportedly spent $750,000.

As a consequence of higher rates—AP in 1967 announced a 20 per cent increase [13]—more daily newspapers unfortunately are relying on one of the two major services. In 1934, during the depths of the depression, 69.3 per cent of the dailies affiliated either with AP (40 per cent), UP (24.2 per cent), or INS (5.1 per cent); reliance on one news service declined in 1948 to 66 per cent: 38.9 per cent AP, 23.3 per cent UP, 3.8 per cent INS. But by 1962, after INS had been absorbed into UPI, 70.2 per cent took only one service: 41.5 per cent AP, 28.7 per cent UPI. The deterioration continued; in 1966, 71.3 per cent were affiliated with only one service: 43.3 per cent AP, 28 per cent UPI. Of the remainder, 4.4 per cent took neither.[14]

AP's saturation of the morning field continues. In 1966 82 per cent of the dailies were AP members; 45.1 per cent also subscribed to UPI. UPI had only 15.4 per cent exclusive morning affiliations.[15] The AP services the largest newspapers. That agency has approximately four times as many exclusive affiliations as UPI among the 25,000 to 500,000 circulation newspapers; as circulations of newspapers increase, however, they tend to subscribe to both services: 3.2 per cent of 10,000 and less; 19.6 per cent, 10,001 to 25,000; 56.8 per cent, 25,001 to 50,000; 63.4 per cent, 50,001 to 100,000; 74 per cent, 100,001 to 500,000; and 100 per cent, 500,001 and over.[16]

Unfortunately, only 16.4 per cent of the dailies receive a service other than AP and UPI. And most of these are large dailies which also receive both AP and UPI. The New York Times Service has one hundred subscribers,[17] the Chicago Daily News more than seventy. None of the other approximately forty-five supplemental news agencies serve as many as sixty dailies. The only foreign world news service received by more than one or two newspapers is Reuters, with forty-one subscribers.[18]

Obviously, large segments of the population rely on AP or UPI for their picture of the world. Their newspapers and their broadcasting stations subscribe to no alternate source of nonlocal news. The seriousness of this becomes obvious when one compares the news services for disagreements, as the writer has done. A few examples should suffice. UP reported early in the Poznan, Poland, riots of 1956, a prelude to the Hungarian revolution, that people demanded withdrawal of the Russian troops; no other news service mentioned this. UP also reported incorrectly that the rioting had become a general revolt which had broken out in five Polish towns and that similar uprisings had been planned in Czechoslovakia; none of the other services so reported. Robert H. Sollen warned against a news service "tendency to place all foreign developments, regardless of their source or nature, into the context of the cold war." Every foreign event, he said, is presented as being pro- or anti-America.[19] A steel strike in the summer of 1956 was studied by the writer. Both INS and the New York Times Service blamed the steel producers for a breakdown in union-management negotiations, UP reported "the union, not the companies, is responsible." AP said each side blamed the other.[20] In a study of crowd reporting of the 1956 presidential and vice-presidential campaigns, UP favored Republican candidates more than did INS and AP; all three agencies favored Eisenhower over Stevenson.[21]

Others have complained about the inaccuracy of the news services. James A. Michener in *The Bridge at Andau* said that during the Hungarian Revolution in 1956 INS was pressing for installation of Cardinal Mindszenty as premier of Hungary and the United States government was promoting the government in exile; neither, he said, was acceptable to the Hungarians. William J. Lederer in *A Nation of Sheep* said the entire American press corps has failed to properly inform the American people. Many news service correspondents admit they seldom leave the foreign capital to which they are assigned; they rely on foreign newspapers, often as translated by foreign nationals. Blair Bolles urges fellow foreign correspondents to spend at least half of their time outside the capital, meeting and talking with the people.[22] Even today many foreign correspondents cannot read and converse in the language of the country to which they are assigned.

Edwin Lahey, chief of the Knight newspapers' Washington Bureau, chided western news services for reporting trivialities in detail while forcing American newspapers to depend on Tass, the Russian news agency, for the central feature of a 1961 Khrushchev-Kennedy conference on the then critical Berlin crisis.[23] Henry Shapiro, UPI bureau chief in Moscow, engaged in Soviet-type "self-criticism" which bares some of the hopelessness with which many correspondents approach their task of reporting on the Soviet Union.[24]

AP was berated for its coverage of the Cuban revolution, especially in the latter stages when it reported the rebels defeated the evening before they forced Fulgencio Batista, the Cuban dictator, to flee. UPI also was criticized, but less severely.[25] Criticism, which almost invariably follows the outbreak of any hostilities, again arose, concerning the aborted Cuban invasion of 1961.[26]

Wilbur Schramm pointed to one of the problems which plague all communications media in general and news services in particular. He blamed "the dangerous need to be first," whether right or wrong, for much of the inaccuracy in the press.[27] News service coverage of recent civil rights disorders illustrates Schramm's point. Ben W. Gilbert, deputy managing editor of the Washington *Post*, said early news service reports of these disturbances usually are fragmentary, inaccurate, and often contain gross over-statements.[28]

Since the news services rely heavily, in most instances exclusively, on local newspapers and those papers' employees for coverage, the charge is often made that news agency copy reflects the biases of the press in the areas of origin. With this in mind, questions have been raised concerning such reports as events involving Negroes in the South, outbreaks of diseases in tourist areas, and the political viewpoints of those favored or opposed. Evan Mecham, who started daily newspapers in competition with powerful monopoly publishers in Phoenix and Tucson, Ariz., said pointedly, "If the (Phoenix) *Republic* did not handle it (a story), then UPI and AP did not play the story, and so, therefore, the news was managed not only in the two (Phoenix) newspapers, but it was also basically blacked out of . . . other news disseminating services." [29]

A practice which vastly discredited the now-defunct French news agency, Havas, mixing news gathering with public relations business, has tinged UPI. That potential source of biased reporting surfaced in 1963 when Earl Johnson, UPI general manager, admitted in a senate committee hearing that UPI at times assigns its reporters to projects paid for by public relations firms and private industry. UPI advertised its Special Services Bureau in a brochure sent to thousands of industrial and business firms throughout the world in these terms:

UPI has 264 bureaus and over 10,000 affiliated correspondents to provide your company with a ready-made field staff capable of undertaking a wide variety of assignments on comparatively short notice.[30]

Richard L. Tobin, *Saturday Review* columnist, in writing about Earl Johnson's disclosure warned of "a natural human tendency to favor someone on whose payroll you are when you come to reporting news about him." Senator Frank Carlson (R-Kan.) illustrated the confusion which might perplex news sources: "If a reporter asked my opinion on aid in a foreign country, would he be doing this for a (public relations) client or for a news story?" [31]

Despite UPI's Special Services advertising, AP and UPI are woefully understaffed considering the enormity of their undertaking. Each employs some two thousand full-time reporters, photographers, and editors, about eight hundred of whom are stationed abroad.[32] Obviously, then, the 1,260 daily newspapers which rely on a single news service are at the mercy of that service. They have no alternate reports to alert them to possible errors and disagreements and from which they may prepare copy where those disagreements may be juxtaposed.

Finally, the news services apparently must share blame for monopoly and chain domination of the press; they stand accused of discriminating against newly founded newspapers. That is the weight of testimony by Evan Mecham and other publishers at hearings in 1967 before the Subcommittee on Antitrust and Monopoly, Senate Judiciary Committee. Seven publishers complained of difficulties encountered in attempting to obtain news agency service. Mecham said he deposited "$53,000 to get the wire (UPI) in the door" at Tucson for a paper with a daily circulation of 15,000. The $53,000 represented payment in advance of the first and fifth year assessments on a five-year contract.[33] Gene Stipe, publisher of the McAlester (Okla.) *Democrat*, cited similar difficulties. He said AP representatives failed to keep appointments to discuss serving his newspaper. UPI entered into a five-year, noncancelable contract that required payment in advance of the first year's charges, after UPI tried to impose "many arbitrary requirements." [34] Michael G. Dworkin, president of the Daily Press, Incorporated, which in 1964 published the *Daily Press* in Detroit during a four-month strike that closed the *Free Press* and *News*, blamed his inability to continue to publish after the strike in part on UPI's refusal to provide service at reasonable rates. He testified UPI insisted he sign a "five-year contract at close to $2,500 a week and pay the last year in advance—an amount in excess of $128,000." Dworkin said UPI refused his offer to pay 1] $3,000 a week, 2] two weeks in advance, and 3] installation costs. In reprisal, he has filed a civil antitrust suit against UPI and the two Detroit dailies.[35] William Loeb blamed difficulties and delays in obtaining UPI service for contributing to the failure of his Haverhill (Mass.) *Journal*. He said he eventually obtained UPI service by signing a two-year contract and paying for one year in advance. Incidentally, Loeb's brother-in-law, Charles Scripps, is head of E. W. Scripps Company, which owns controlling interest in UPI.[36] Roy McDonald, president and publisher of the Chattanooga *News-Free Press*, said that in 1939 the general manager of the *New York Times* and the publisher of the Chattanooga *Times*, Julius Ochs Adler, threatened, unless he abandoned his Sunday edition, to use the influence of those two newspapers to keep him from transferring to his *News-Free Press* an AP franchise he had obtained by purchasing the Chattanooga *News*.[37]

Two California publishers testified they were unable to obtain supplementary news services. J. Hart Clinton, San Mateo *Times & Daily News Leader*, submitted letters of refusal from the New York Times News Service, Reuters, the (Des Moines) Register & Tribune Syndicate, the Chicago Tribune-New York News Service, and the Chicago Daily News Syndicate. Yet these services are available to his competitors in neighboring San Francisco.[38] Norman Cherniss, Riverside *Daily Enterprise* and *Press*, reported he also was unable to obtain the Chicago Daily News Syndicate, primarily an afternoon service, because the morning Los Angeles *Times* subscribed.[39] More will be said about territorial exclusivity agreements relative to feature syndicates, the subject next to be discussed.

Feature Syndicates

The first newspaper syndication on a regular basis occurred in Wisconsin where weeklies during the Civil War bought sheets printed on one side from the Madison *Wisconsin State Journal*. The first purchaser, A. N. Kellogg, then publisher of the Baraboo *Re-*

public, sold his newspaper after the war and opened a syndicate in Chicago. Meanwhile, the *Wisconsin State Journal*'s readyprint service was challenged by one in Milwaukee which sold advertising for its printed sheets, thereby reducing the price. In this way the Milwaukee syndicate commandeered the business in Wisconsin and later moved to Chicago where it operated as the Chicago Newspaper Union and later as the American Newspaper Union. Both ANU and Kellogg opened branches and bought out other syndicates until in 1875 they served around eighteen hundred weeklies.[40]

To readyprint were added boiler plate and mats in the 1880's whereby features, news, and continued stories were delivered either by metal or lighter papier-mâché molds impressed with copy and pictures for casting into metal. Soon this service was extended to daily newspapers. AP and UPA contracted with the American Press Association and Kellogg syndicates, respectively, from around 1882 to 1900 to disseminate their news via metal.[41] Those arrangements were discontinued, however; AP members complained they were being scooped by syndicate subscribers. In 1884 Irving Bacheller established the New York Press Syndicate, the first one to successfully distribute features in copy form to large daily newspapers.[42] S. S. McClure, who later gained fame as a magazine publisher, established his highly successful syndicate in 1884. He and others sold works by America's brightest writers thereby contributing immeasurably to the success of many.[43]

The Western Newspaper Union purchased all of its weekly competitors in the later 1800's and early 1900's, so that by 1917 that syndicate was dominant in plate and printed syndication. It continued its readyprint service until 1952.[44] Meanwhile, new syndicates, launched primarily by daily newspapers to provide Sunday features, sprang up during the early 1900's and competed vigorously in mat and copy syndication. Many of those are still in operation: King Features, Chicago Tribune-New York Daily News Syndicate, United Features Syndicate, Newspaper Enterprise Association, Ledger Syndicate, and others.[45] Through them comics, cartoons, pictures, feature stories, poems, various columns, fiction, fillers, editorials, and other materials from large dailies, magazines, and special writers were sold to daily and weekly newspapers. Increasingly, syndicates hired known writers.

E. W. Scripps endowed a syndicate to popularize, without misinterpreting, science. The result was Science Service, founded in 1921 as a mail service; its daily wire service was begun six years later.[46] Also in the 1920's Doubleday-Doran became the first book publisher-syndicate, selling summaries of books and continued stories based on book manuscripts.[47]

Finally, in 1935, Sunday features were packaged in a weekly newspaper magazine, *This Week*.[48] Hearst two years later syndicated his *American Weekly*, established in 1896 as the first Sunday supplement.[49] The third entry was *Parade*, begun in 1941 by Field Enterprises.[50] These huge circulation magazines continued to grow until television cut deeply into their advertising in the 1950's. All but the *American Weekly* survives; Hearst in 1962 withdrew that supplement from all except the chain's own newspapers and killed it the next year.[51] *Parade*, continuing to flourish, was sold to John Hay Whitney in 1958.[52] As of the end of 1966 *Parade* was distributed in 77 newspapers with circulations of 12.85 million.[53] *This Week* was packaged into 44 newspapers with aggregate circulations of 13 million.[54] Each sells around $20 million in advertising annually.[55]

Approximately 280 syndicates in 41 classifications serve American newspapers.[56] However, half a dozen of the major ones, 2 per cent of the total, receive 40 per cent of the $100 million a year grossed by all syndicates. The largest, Hearst's King Features, accounts for 18 per cent, down from a peak of 40 per cent in the 1930's.[57] King Features in 1966 was selling 228 features to 3,154 newspapers published in 101 countries, possessions, and territories in 49 languages. Scripps-Howard is the second largest syndicator; its Newspaper Enterprise Association offers 149 and United Features 43 features. Chicago Tribune-New York News Syndicate has 133.[58] The Chandlers of Los Angeles became the fourth largest syndicator in 1967 when they bought General Features, 80 columns, comics, and special features, to add to their Los Angeles Times Syndicate, more than 30 features, and their Los Angeles Times-Washington Post News Service.[59] Other 1967 mergers include that of two large operators with some of the most popular properties in syndication; Field's Publishers Newspaper Syndicate, 52 features, absorbed the Hall Syndicate, Incorporated, 40 features, to become Publishers-Hall Syndicate. PNS was born of the merger in 1962 of Field and Publishers syndicates.[60] Also, in 1967, the Lew Little Syndicate, 12 features, was merged with the Register and Tribune Syndicate, 41. A sizable 1965 consolidation occurred when the owners of Bell-McClure, 56 features, bought the North American Newspaper Alliance, 23 features.[61] Thus a growth trend is evidenced among some of the middle-sized and large syndicates.

A major noncompetitive impact of syndicates is that those with the extremely popular features, especially comics, panels, and advice columns, can command unreasonably high prices for exclusive territorial rights. G. O. Markuson, executive vice-president of the Hearst Corporation and general manager of the Hearst newspapers, cited significant increases in the cost of feature, news, and picture services as among economic pressures besetting urban newspapers and causing some to fail.[62] At least some daily newspapers spend more for syndicated features than for their news service. Although newspaper financial data are generally unavailable, *Editor & Publisher*, in listing expenditures of an anonymous 240,000 circulation daily, reported it spent $147,715 for features and $136,528 for news services during 1966.[63]

Of even greater concern, feature services enter into conspiracies with large metropolitan dailies whereby they withhold popular features from other newspapers. One of the most flagrant violators is the Los Angeles *Times*, which by admission of Norman Chandler, chairman of the board and chief executive officer, "customarily seeks an exclusive territory for syndicated features which it purchases extending from Santa Barbara to San Diego and east to the Colorado River." [64] How the *Times* browbeats its seven morning, forty-three afternoon, and fourteen Sunday newspaper competitors in this 6,000 square mile, 8 million population fiefdom was vividly illustrated by one of its intended victims, Norman Cherniss. Cherniss said he has been unable to obtain *1*] features appearing in the *Times*, *2*] those the *Times* has bought but does not use, and *3*] those which the *Times* has rejected but the syndicate operators feel *Times* executives might later buy. He said Publishers' Syndicate, now a part of the Field-owned Publishers-Hall Syndicate, gave the latter excuse for withholding the new comic "The Wizard of Id" from sale in southern California. Cherniss added that he has repeatedly sought "Little Orphan Annie," a Chicago Tribune-New York News Syndicate comic strip, but has been refused because the *Times* has it under contract even though the *Times* ceased running it early in 1966.[65]

Other southern California newsmen have complained of *Times* tactics, including Samuel C. Stewart, executive editor of the South Bay *Daily Breeze*, a Copley newspaper. Stewart said the syndicated feature "is one place the big mets can throw their weight around—and do. The *Breeze* can't get 'Dick Tracy,' or Ann Landers, or Drew Pearson, or Walter Winchell, because the big papers have squeezed us out under a thing called 'territorial rights.' "[66]

Chandler explained that the *Times* pays higher rates to obtain territorial exclusivity because "we don't like to have all of the smaller papers scattered all through southern California acquiring the features and the comics we use. That is normal procedure in any newspaper throughout the country."[67] Apparently Chandler is correct. Loyal B. Phillips, publisher of the St. Petersburg (Fla.) *Evening Independent*, made complaints similar to those of Cherniss (See Chapter 1).[68] Mecham asserted that a major weapon used by monopoly publishers to prevent establishment of competitive papers is the exclusive rights they hold on key features, even those they do not publish.[69] H. R. Horvitz, publisher of four dailies near Cleveland, accused the Cleveland publishers of entering into contracts which prevent area newspapers from obtaining "good comics and editorial features," even those the Cleveland newspapers do not print. Horvitz raised an important point when he complained that Scripps-Howard refuses to sell its features to area publishers in an attempt to protect the Scripps-Howard newspaper in Cleveland, the *Press*, from competition. This and other previously cited restrictive practices tarnish the memory of the founder of the Scripps empire, E. W. Scripps, who, as has been mentioned, established United Press in part to thwart similar monopolistic activities then engaged in by the Associated Press.[70] J. Hart Clinton, Michael G. Dworkin, William Loeb, and other publishers testified they, too, have been unable to buy features because large dailies have control of them. Loeb said the Boston newspapers hold territorial exclusivity on features extending as far as 200 miles.[71]

What recourse is open to publishers against what both newspaper and feature service executives admit is the "standard practice of selling on an exclusive basis"?[72] The Department of Justice in 1964 began an investigation to learn whether syndicates agree "to discriminatory preferences, such as exclusive territorial rights, in connection with the distribution of certain features and in favor of certain newspaper publishers." [73] The Department reportedly is also investigating the Philadelphia *Evening Bulletin*'s $250-a-week contract for the Drew Pearson column which prevents others in Pennsylvania, Delaware, and part of New Jersey from printing it. A Justice Department statement issued to the Senate Subcommittee on Antitrust and Monopoly in 1967 said the Department is considering ways to limit exclusive syndicate feature agreements so newspapers well outside the major circulation area of a newspaper might obtain features. However, the Department placed complaining publishers on notice that it did not propose to abolish territorial exclusivity.[74]

In a 1967 Federal District Court (Buffalo, N.Y.) trial on which a verdict is pending, the Justice Department charged Newspaper Enterprise Association and Greater Buffalo Press, Incorporated, and three of its subsidiaries with antitrust practices. Six years earlier NEA and King Features Syndicate had been charged with conspiring with Greater Buffalo Press to divide and monopolize the market in color printing of Sunday comic supplements. Further, they were charged with entering into an agreement whereby Greater Buffalo would pay commissions to NEA and King Features for business received from them. Charges against King Features were withdrawn after that syndicate signed a consent order to desist from these activities. However, J. Walter Koesler, president of Greater Buffalo, said that although King Features canceled a 1958 contract with the printing firm, Greater Buffalo continues to pay that syndicate a $563-a-week "shakedown." In the 1967 suit, NEA was charged with giving a discount on comic features to those who contract with NEA to publish them. The printers, as quoted in *Editor & Publisher*, were charged with a conspiracy that:

Denied newspapers the advantages of competitive bidding for the printing of supplements.

Forced newspapers not desiring the printing services offered by the defendants to pay "arbitrary prices" for their comic features.

Eliminated price competition among the defendants and the Eastern Color Printing Co. of Waterbury, Conn.

Restrained some printers from offering their services to newspapers.[75]

The Department sought to break up the Buffalo group and eliminate tie-in sales stipulations which require newspapers to buy other features in order to obtain comic supplements.[76]

Possibly Justice Department lawyers had been heartened by their victories over the two dominant advertising mat services, Stamps-Conhaim-Whitehead, Incorporated, and Metro Associated Services, Incorporated, in 1963 and 1964, respectively. Both firms were restrained from refusing to sell or license their advertising mat and catalog services on a nondiscriminatory and nonexclusive basis to any newspaper and from entering into exclusive agreements with newspapers.[77] (Both firms supply newspapers with mats impressed with illustrations and type suitable for advertising and with suggested advertising layouts to be used by newspaper employees in preparing advertising for local customers.)

Why do newspapers invest so heavily in syndicated material? Publishers regard these features as circulation builders, and for good reason, as this example should illustrate. In the 1950's after comics and features formerly sold to the San Antonio *Express* were made available to Hearst's San Antonio *Light*, *Express* circulation almost immediately declined from its dominant position. Today the *Light* holds a circulation edge over its competitors, 35,000 over the *Express* and almost 55,000 over the *Evening News*.[78]

Newspaper publishers in their reckless search for circulation were shocked in 1959 when they learned that they had been swindled through one popular feature, puzzle contests. Two men had set up a dummy Canadian newspaper, subscribed to various newspaper contests, and fed the answers to contacts in cities where the puzzles were used. Despite these disclosures, some newspapers continue to use syndicated contests.[79]

Possibly the most serious charge that can be brought against syndicates, however, is that they limit comment and criticism in the marketplace of ideas. Regardless of how erudite, how brilliant any columnist may be, exposing his ideas to audiences of 25 to 50 million readers gives them disproportionate weight. The thoughts of few columnists, editorial writers, cartoonists, comic strip commentators, feature writers merit such wide propagation. Also, syndicated editoralists, whether by word or sketch, expound at best on national and international problems and at worst on trivia, distracting readers and taking space which often might better be devoted to local, area, and state issues of vital importance to the well-being of the newspaper's readers. Further, in an effort to please or at least not displease as large a clientele as possible, many writers, columnists, artists "water down" their material, ignore serious problems, slant so as not to offend. Therefore, despite the flood of feature syndicate and news service copy, Americans remain poorly informed on important issues of the day.

And the preponderance of space devoted to syndicated content is assigned to escape features, such as comics, panels, gossip, and pseudo advice.[80] The trend apparently favors the frivolous, newspapers' weapon against television. But the fact remains that the two daily newspapers in the United States which are gaining circulation most rapidly, the *Wall Street Journal* and the *New York Times*, do not lean on feature syndicates.

Radio's Serious Problems

6.

Standard (AM) radio faces several crucial problems, among them economic insecurity, inequitable distribution of income, overcommercialization, irritating advertising, control by broadcasting chains and by owners of the other mass media and special interest groups, the inability to serve large segments of the population, payola and plugola, rapid ownership turnover, and the failure of audience measurement firms to provide accurate information on sizes of listening audiences.

Some of the serious problems which AM shares with frequency modulation radio and television are discussed in other chapters. Those unique to AM radio will be considered here. Because some of the medium's current problems have their roots in the past let us review briefly the development of standard radio broadcasting in the United States.

Radio was at first felt to be of little commercial value, since privacy of communication was unprotected. True, it served ships at sea as a safety instrument, but telephone and telegraph companies saw no use for it. Implausible as it seems today, few visualized its potential for public communication until after three pioneering experimental stations began public broadcasting around 1920. Soon the trio was joined by others, primarily those with special interests—manufacturers who wanted to sell radio sets and retail businessmen interested in building good will. Educators soon followed and then came private citizens who enjoyed the thrill of broadcasting from tiny transmitters. Thirty stations were authorized by January 1, 1922, and 566 by March 1, 1923. They broadcast mostly recorded music and their call letters.

In a short time operators began wondering how they could finance the service. Early suggestions were that endowments be established, or that government or foundations provide support. Ever-enterprising American Telephone and Telegraph Company introduced the solution when on August 28, 1922, the utility broadcast a commercial over its WEAF New York City station. Secretary of Commerce Herbert Hoover, under whose control radio came, urged at the time that radio not be subverted to "advertising chatter."[1] AT & T, certainly not for altruistic reasons, sought to oblige Mr. Hoover. She claimed a monopoly and forbade other stations to advertise on penalty of losing AT & T services. Within two years she relented and gradually commercials began to fill the air; the first were mere announcements. Many sought to stem the tide, including the National Association of Broadcasters which, as late as 1929, urged that advertising be limited to daylight hours.

Radio at first attracted few advertisers. Broadcasters, therefore, engaged in a strong promotional campaign to woo business away from newspapers. A major inducement was a single billing by which a sponsor could buy time on all of the stations in a network; those advertising in newspapers had to bill each paper individually. The result was tremendous savings in administrative costs. Radio finally reaped its golden harvest during World War II when 1] the federal government froze station construction, thus limiting broadcast competition, and 2] a shortage of paper forced the print media to curtail advertising.

As early as 1922 the AM spectrum had become crowded. In answer to requests from broadcasters Secretary Hoover, acting under authority he assumed from the Radio Act of 1912, licensed stations and formulated regulations to minimize interference. After court decisions and an attorney general's opinion deprived him of this authority, the airways, beginning in mid-1926, became a tangled mass of indistinguishable babble. New stations went on the air without licenses, they and existing stations increased their power at will and wandered from one part of the broadcast band to the other in search of space where they might be heard. The resulting chaos induced Congress to heed broadcasters' pleas that the federal government intervene.

By the time Congress passed the Radio Act of 1927, 732 stations were on the air. Shortly thereafter 150 were forced to cease operations; no spectrum space could be found to accommodate them.[2] This Radio Act was amended by the Communications Act of 1934 that set up the present Federal Communications Commission with authority to regulate all interstate and foreign communication by wire and radio, including telegraph, telephone, and broadcast.

By these two acts Congress established that the airwaves belong to the people, whose property rights in them the federal government was required to protect. Be that as it may, spectrum space then as now limited entry into radio broadcasting. Thus, licenses granted a "temporary" monopoly to those ostensibly best fitted to serve "in the public interest, convenience or necessity." [3] However, once a license has been issued, although it must be renewed periodically (every three years at present), the FCC seldom fails to extend the license as a matter of course. Former FCC Chairman James Lawrence Fly said, ". . . there has never been a revocation of the license . . . of any responsible owner." [4]

After World War II the FCC was deluged with applications for construction permits and licenses. By January 1, 1948, there were 1,621 AM stations on the air. This increased by almost three hundred within the year and exceeded two thousand during 1949. FM, which entered World War II largely in an experimental status, bloomed. The number of commercial FM stations on the air grew from fifty-five in mid-1946 to 238 by mid-1947 and to seven hundred by January 1, 1949. Gradually, at first, the dark specter of television appeared. As recently as January 1, 1947, there were but seven commercial television stations on the air. The number increased to sixty-nine by mid-year 1949 and to 104 within the next twelve months. A freeze on new licenses from September 30, 1948, to April 14, 1952, reduced television's threat to radio.

But it was obvious that radio, especially network radio, was in serious financial trouble. After the war the income of the national networks failed to increase as rapidly as did total radio income. Then in 1949, for the first time in history, network income declined. Looked at another way, the national networks, which contributed 47.7 per cent of total radio income in 1937, became increasingly less important. By 1947 networks contributed 34 per cent. The decline continued at a rapid pace. Percentages by year were: 1950, 27.5;

1952, 21.6; 1954, 18; 1957, 9; 1959 to 1964, 6; 1965, 5. (For combined national and regional returns see Table 23, Appendix.) From 1955 to 1965 the radio networks as a group lost money except for 1963 and 1964.[5]

Although total radio income, augmented by local time sales, continued to increase each year except in 1954 and 1961, growth was such that the income per station rose only slightly while expenses were soaring.[6] The deteriorating condition of radio is reflected in other ways, too. For 1965, 1,150 of the 3,858 AM and AM-FM stations, 29.8 per cent, reported operating at losses. Radio in 1945 received 17 per cent of total advertising expenditures, a proportion that fell to 5.7 per cent in 1956,[7] the approximate proportion received since then.[8] The gross national product increased by 221 per cent from 1946 to 1965; radio total income for the period grew by only 147 per cent.[9]

Despite radio's inability to keep pace financially, both the number of stations and number of receivers have increased each year at a fairly rapid rate. Landmarks of 2,500 stations were passed in 1953; 3,000 toward the end of 1956; 3,500 in 1960; and 4,000 by the end of 1964.[10] Likewise, the number of radio sets has increased; production surpassed 10 million a year in 1939, 17 million in 1947, and 20 million in 1965.[11] Radio sets are located in almost all of the homes in the United States, although the 1960 census reported that in only 91.3 per cent of the homes were one or more sets in working condition. Even so, saturation has effectively been achieved. The problem now concerns use. The major audience measurement services report low usage, at least as compared to listening prior to the advent of television. These reports, many of questionable validity, severely limit radio advertising revenues, as will be discussed in Chapter 8.

Television has captured the mass nighttime audiences radio once nurtured. Radio has, therefore, faced the alternative of changing or dying. Even using the national radio networks as a crutch couldn't help and, as a result, radio has become much more specialized. At least a few stations are giving increasing attention to local and regional problems and events. Highly specialized formats have emerged, among them all-news, all-talk, and even all-advertising programming.[12] A number of stations program for such diverse ethnic groups as Negroes (339 stations),[13] Latin Americans, Poles, Italians, and American Indians. The number of stations offering programming in one or more of 49 languages and dialects is impressive, ranging from 235 stations broadcasting in Spanish to one in Aramaic. Thus, a minute segment of radio has found an important niche for itself, one much more vital than serving as a pipeline for network mass-entertainment shows.

Radio along with television has been given an editorial voice. Prior to 1941 except for a handful of commentators, broadcasters assumed they had no right to editorialize. In that year the FCC's Mayflower decision [14] forbade stations from editorializing in their own names. The Commission lifted this ruling in 1949 [15] with amendments in 1951 and 1959. Today a station may editorialize in its own name, but the FCC specifies that the broadcaster must air conflicting viewpoints after one side has been presented even if the station must donate time.[16] Frank Stanton, Columbia Broadcasting System president, said that CBS-owned radio and television stations broadcast 4,338 different editorials and 768 replies from January 1, 1960, to October 1, 1966.[17] However, when stations endorse political candidates, as several did in the 1966 off-year elections, politicians raised a howl.[18]

Radio Problems

Although the best of radio has made some progress, many problems remain, not the least of which are the irritatingly loud, seemingly endless stream of commercial messages some stations air. The Federal Radio Commission, predecessor to the FCC, in the late 1920's and early 1930's held radio in check, even to the extent of refusing to renew the license of Station WCRW in 1928 because of overcommercialization and "objectionable" advertising.[19] Broadcasters did not protest, because the FRC had recently rescued radio from its jumbled spectrum chaos. Even Congress saw fit to criticize overcommercialization, as shown by this resolution that was introduced in the Senate in 1932

> Whereas, there is growing dissatisfaction with the present use of radio facilities for purposes of commercial advertising: be it resolved that the Federal Radio Commission is hereby authorized and instructed to make a survey and to report to the Senate on the following questions: What in-

formation there is available on the possibility of government ownership and operation of broadcasting facilities . . . What plans might be adopted to reduce, to limit, to control and perhaps eliminate the use of radio facilities for commercial advertising purposes.[20]

The resolution was not adopted. It is mentioned here both to show the temper of the times and to contrast the strong position advocated then as against congressional wilting before broadcasting pressures today.

A peak in overcommercialization occurred in 1945 when the FCC denied renewal of a license because the station broadcast 2,215 commercials in a 135-hour broadcasting week, an average of 16.4 an hour.[21] More recently, when the Commission in 1963 refused to renew the license of WDKD Kingstree, S.C., for vulgar and suggestive programs, and misrepresentations, reference was also made to that station's broadcasting 1,448 commercials in a composite week.[22] Such harsh punishment is rare. Former FCC Chairman E. William Henry said as far as he knew no license renewal had been denied based on overcommercialization even though logs of 134 stations whose licenses were up for renewal showed that 40 per cent exceeded eighteen minutes of commercial time in one or more hours, most by only two or three minutes. Some went much further, with one devoting thirty minutes in an hour to commercials.[23]

Chairman Henry referred to eighteen minutes because the National Association of Broadcasters code specifies eighteen minutes as a maximum for Code Authority members. NAB membership is voluntary and only about half of the commercial radio and two-thirds of the commercial television stations are members. Also, code standards have deteriorated through the years. In 1929 the NAB adopted its first code, providing that there should be no commercials between 7 and 11 P.M. The code was revised in 1937. From 1937 to 1948 the NAB code limited advertising to four and one-half minutes during a thirty-minute daytime program and three minutes during a thirty-minute nighttime program. Greater proportions of commercial time were allowed for five and fifteen-minute programs during those shorter time segments. In 1948, bowing to membership pressures, the NAB raised its maximum to twelve minutes of commercial time in an hour, excluding station breaks. The present standard is eighteen minutes.

Even the NAB admits that members do not honor their code. Reports of the code authority shows that of member radio stations monitored between April 1 and September 30, 1963, 28.5 per cent violated the maximum during one or more hours. The average was a minute and a half.[24] The monitor, Phil Edwards, chairman of *Broadcast Advertisers Reports,* complained that "the air is choked with commercials in excess of industry rules" in announcing that he was discontinuing the service because his reports were ignored.[25]

FCC's more recent efforts to halt blatant overcommercialization have been strongly opposed by some congressmen. In 1963 when the Commission first proposed to adopt the NAB radio and television codes, broadcasters raised such a howl that Congress intervened by holding hearings during which the commissioners who supported the FCC proposal were rudely interrogated.[26] However, in FCC in October 1966 incorporated NAB guidelines into questionnaires sent to all licensees. Radio broadcasters were asked to justify exceeding eighteen minutes of commercial time an hour. Although NAB officers again objected, this procedure at least placed members and nonmembers on a par. Previously, FCC questionnaires had asked NAB members to justify devoting more than eighteen minutes while asking nonmembers to justify devoting twenty minutes to commercials in an hour.[27]

Commissioners apparently felt they needed more concrete guidelines as to what constituted overcommercialization. Indeed they did, if former FCC Chairman Henry's comments are accurate. He said the FCC, too, had over the years relaxed its standards. In 1949 the FCC had an "unofficial delegation" to question any daytime-only station that broadcast more than six hundred and any full-time station that broadcast more than seven hundred and fifty commercial announcements a week. The average was about seven and a half commercials an hour. This was raised to one thousand in 1955, and "I do not know what it is today. I do not think there is any specific delegation to the staff now as to when to question a station with respect to its overcommercialization." [28]

We should not be surprised to learn that the FCC, as far as Chairman Henry knew, had denied no station an extension of its license solely because of excessive commercials. Henry quoted an article from the trade press which referred to the NAB code as "window dressing designed to make broadcasting's façade look good no matter what has gone on inside the store" and added: "Neither the Government nor the NAB, moreover, has even tried to come to grips with one of the most serious problems in this field—the question of when and how often commercials should be permitted to interrupt programs." [29]

However, the FCC in the past two years has become slightly more strict. Only one station was penalized for overcommercialization with a short-term (one year) license renewal instead of the customary three year license extension during the period September 1961 to November 1963. In 1966 the Commission penalized fourteen stations (eleven AM, two FM, one TV) with one-year probationary extensions for "substantially" exceeding the amount of commercial time they had proposed in their prior license renewal applications.[30] Those who defend advertising as providing a "free" service might consider points raised by Charles A. Siepmann relative to listener investment in receivers and their depreciation and repair costs.[31] He didn't mention personal property taxes levied on radios in some areas. Others have suggested that advertising contributes heavily to the cost of products purchased.[32] As we shall see in Chapter 7, the audience has invested heavily in "free" radio and television.

Each year complaints about broadcast advertising abuses account for a large proportion of FCC mail, 43 per cent in 1964.[33] Overcommercialization was only one of the issues raised. Let us consider briefly some of the others. Many listeners have in recent years bitterly criticized loudness in broadcast advertising, both in radio and television. Pressures became so great that the FCC in December 1962 began an inquiry which culminated in a mid-1965 *Statement of Policy Concerning Loud Commercials.* In this publication the Commission attempted to set forth situations and practices which contribute to objectionable, loud commercials and urged licensees to exercise control. The FCC weapon, of course, is threat of action at license renewal time. Both the NAB and the American Association of Advertising Agencies volunteered to assist. But the major difficulty lies in setting forth criteria against which performance can be measured.[34]

Some broadcasters, aping a questionable practice of many newspapers, have engaged in double billing for advertising. This generally involves giving a local advertiser two bills, one for the actual amount charged for advertising and the other for a larger sum which the local advertiser uses to seek a higher-than-justified reimbursement under a cooperative arrangement with a manufacturer or national advertiser. The FCC in 1962 issued a warning against such practices, saying that "appropriate proceedings would be instituted" where evidence of this malpractice exists. Continued double billing led the Commission on October 20, 1965, to adopt rules against the practice.[35]

Such other advertising-related problems as payola, plugola, inequitable distribution of income by networks, questionable advertising practices, and combination advertising rates involve other media than radio and therefore are discussed elsewhere. The combination advertising-rate practice has taken on added importance recently with new Department of Justice actions.

Although the number of radio stations in the United States continues to increase, 25 million people live in "white areas," that half of the United States landmass where they can receive no primary (local or regional) night radio service. These people, many of whom also receive no television, are forced to rely on distant, 50,000 watt, clear channel stations for their evening broadcasting fare. Obviously those stations cannot program for the special needs and interests of these people—local news, weather forecasts, sports events, and advertising. How to improve service to these people has been hotly debated for years. Are the clear channel stations as now constituted providing the best service possible? Should these channels be duplicated with other stations? Should the power of the clear channel stations be increased? And, more vital to this study, who owns these powerful privileged stations?

In search of answers to these questions let us begin with 1923 when the Secretary of Commerce reserved 40 of 107 AM channels for the exclusive night-hours use of single stations. Between 1929 and 1941 the FCC authorized other stations to operate at night on 16 of these 40. The Commission in 1961, after a sixteen-year proceeding, decided to assign one additional full-time station in specified western states to all but 11 of the then 24 unduplicated channels. Congressional intervention through hearings and a 1962 House resolution urged the FCC not to duplicate assignments for a period of one year. These activities together with court appeals by stations and networks delayed assigning stations to the 13 channels until 1963. A Court of Appeals decision in October 1963, upholding the FCC position, cleared the way to duplicate on I-A clear channels.[36] Change was slow; the networks and individual stations continued to resort to court action to attempt to block duplication. As recently as May 26, 1966, the United States Court of Appeals denied NBC protection from duplicating NBC's I-A WMAQ Chicago with KBOI Boise, Idaho, a II-A applicant. The longest dispute over duplication has been ABC's continuing fight in countless FCC hearings and court actions since 1941 to move KOB Albuquerque, N.M., from 770 kc, occupied by WABC New York, a I-B station.[37] The courts have been sympathetic to ABC, citing the fact that both NBC and CBS operate unduplicated I-A clear channel stations from their headquarters in New York.

By the end of 1965, II-A full-time stations were operating on, or had construction permits to operate on, three of the thirteen channels designated for duplication. Applications were on file with the Commission as of mid-1966 to duplicate the other ten channels. It is worth noting that none of the I-A clear channel stations now to be duplicated are owned by independent broadcasters. The three major networks own seven, of which CBS owns four. Newspaper-broadcasting chains own two; industry-owned broadcasting chains own three, two by Westinghouse Electric Corporation; the other station is owned by Capital Cities, a chain.[38]

The privileged few who retain unduplicated I-A stations are: AVCO, industrial holding complex and chain broadcaster, two; Palmer, another chain broadcaster, one; church entities, two; three newspapers, one each; NBC, one; an insurance company, one; and an independent, one.[39] Thus all but one of the most powerful, widest-coverage stations in the United States are in the hands of special-interest groups, chains, and newspapers. Of the seventy-three, 50,000 watt day and night stations, only five are licensed to independent broadcasting companies with no apparent special causes to plead. Fifty-three are owned by chain broadcasters.

The problem of providing better night radio service for the more than twenty-five million who live in white areas remains. Duplicating clear channels with powerful stations in the western United States obviously will not extend service to large numbers of these people.[40] Another proposal is to increase the power of the remaining unduplicated stations so that their skyway signals will carry farther. Now their signals beyond seven hundred miles are weak and variable. Increasing their power to 750 kilowatts would extend each station's service area up to twelve hundred miles. However, the FCC reported that few people living seven hundred miles or approaching seven hundred miles from a I-A clear channel station listen to that station. Apart from economic and social arguments against licensing stations to operate on superpower, interference from adjacent channels, weather disturbances, and electrical interference make it doubtful if increased power will greatly extend the service to white areas. Too, such stations obviously could not program for the particular needs of listeners within a twelve hundred-mile radius.

Even so, pressure from the clear channel stations and from congressmen led the FCC to conduct a two-year study of the feasibility of permitting some yet to be selected clear channel stations from among those not now designated for duplication to experiment with power greater than 50,000 watts, possibly up to 750,000 watts. (WLW Cincinnati operated on 500,000 watts from 1934 to 1938.) [41] The matter has not been resolved. The duplicated stations oppose this because of the competitive advertising advantage superpower stations would gain. Others question giving these few such a dominant voice, especially since, as was noted previously, the owners of these stations have special causes to plead or already hold other major mass communications media.

7. Commercial Television and How It Grew

When picture was added to sound via television, man gained an invention that could well have revolutionized communication and education; some optimists predicted it would. All that was lacking was widespread ownership of the magic receiver sets. Now we have receivers in abundance. Latest figures place them at saturation levels, approaching 70 million distributed among an estimated 94 per cent of American households.[1] The move now is rapidly to color and by mid-1970 color sets may well replace most, if not virtually all, of the black and white receivers. Yet the genie, whether monochrome or in tint, remains in the bottle, or perhaps we should say the tube.

Why hasn't television lived up to its potential? Why has this additional communication dimension failed to provide new voices for the marketplace of ideas? Why has programming sunk into what former FCC Chairman Newton N. Minow in 1961 called "a vast wasteland"?

Before considering television's unfulfilled promise, let us first briefly sketch the background of the medium. Television advanced from the laboratory to the airwaves when public experimental telecasts were made in England in 1927 and in the United States in 1928. RCA began a second series of experimental telecasts in 1936 with improved equipment and new techniques. These first faltering attempts attracted little public notice even though seventeen experimental TV stations were operating in 1937. Not until RCA began regular experimental telecasting on April 30, 1939, timed to coincide with the opening of the New York World's Fair, did the public begin to visualize television's potential. About the only receivers in existence then were home-built instruments and those few assembled by industry for experimental purposes.

The FCC authorized commercial telecasting to begin July 1, 1941, six months before the United States entered World War II. The first license was granted, of course, to an RCA station, WNBT New York. Licenses soon were granted to other commercial stations, operated largely by networks, radio set manufacturers, and Paramount movie enterprises. Five of these stations still exist. However, of the ten stations on the air by May 1942, only six continued to provide limited service during World War II. Fewer than five thousand receiver sets were in use.

Many of television's ills can be traced directly to the selfish vested interests of the three major networks in general and RCA (NBC) in particular. RCA in 1945 convinced the FCC that television should be assigned to the extremely limited VHF spectrum. CBS favored utilizing the less-crowded higher frequencies. RCA's victory drastically limited the number of stations that could exist in any geographic area.[2] This FCC blunder earned billions for the major networks and a favored few stations at the expense of restricting the viewing public to a meager and little-varied program fare. More will be said about this in Chapter 9.

After World War II, stations that had temporarily discontinued broadcasting resumed and a few new stations were built; by the end of 1946 there were 12 commercial stations on the air. Entrepreneurs, sensing potential profits even greater than those realized in radio, began a frenzied scramble for licenses. By 1948 there were 46 stations in operation, construction had begun on another 78, and more than three hundred applications for construction permits were awaiting FCC action. Against this background the Commission on September 30, 1948, ceased licensing new stations. The station freeze continued for four years, until April 14, 1952. At that time the Commission also announced its first allocation of channel assignments, providing for 2,053 stations in 1,291 communities on both VHF and UHF bands.

Stations licensed prior to the freeze raised the total on the air to 108 by mid-1952, when the FCC began accepting applications. Fierce competition for allocations ensued: 198 commercial television stations were on the air by mid-1953. The figure rose to 402 in a year and by mid-1955 to 458. During 1956 the total exceeded five hundred, increasing less rapidly until a peak of 583 was reached on January 1, 1961. A slight decline followed, but growth resumed the next year and continues. At present the major demand is for UHF licenses, the only spectrum space available in many areas.[3]

The sale of television receivers kept pace with the station growth. Whereas one million sets were in operation in 1948, the total rose to 17 million in 1952. In a decade the figure was 55 million, and as of 1966 the total approaches 70 million, of which almost 7 million are color sets. Estimates are that 94 per cent of American homes have at least one set and 29 per cent have two or more.[4]

Despite the phenomenal growth of television, Americans, even today, are poorly served. An estimated 9 to 18 million (5 to 10 per cent) can receive no television; they live in small communities and rural areas beyond the reach of community antenna television systems, VHF and UHF translators, and satellite stations.[5] These also are white radio areas (see Chapter 6). Another 22 to 36 million (15 to 20 per cent) receive a viewable signal from a single commercial station. This is the plight of those living in 101 of the 216 markets below the top fifty markets. In another twenty communities with television service the source is a satellite station that pipes in programming from a station generally located one hundred or more miles away. Even in the top fifty markets, residents of four metropolitan areas are served by but two commercial television stations. Persons living in 47 of 215 markets (markets 51 to 266) may view only two commercial stations. Only in fifty of these smaller markets do residents have access to three or more commercial stations.[6]

The Federal Communications Commission has sought ways in which television service might be 1] extended into areas not now served and 2] expanded to provide more stations in areas where fewer than three stations now exist. Solutions thus far advanced would 1] increase the number of UHF stations, 2] use translators and satellite stations to extend the coverage areas of existing stations, 3] deintermix some markets, and 4] encourage community antenna television to expand into areas of small population. These possible solutions are discussed in Chapters 10 and 11.

Networks Control Programming

What America sees on the tube is determined largely by those who control the three major television networks—ABC, CBS,

NBC. Only about 13 per cent of all broadcast time is devoted to local-live programming.[7] Former FCC Chairman E. William Henry said that the rest of the time stations "throw the network switch, or open a syndicated film package as they would a can of beans."[8] During prime evening hours, from 7 to 11 P.M., proportions are approximately 95 per cent network to 5 per cent local.[9] For example, CBS reported that its 52 affiliates in the top fifty markets through the week of May 14, 1966, devoted an average of 12 minutes nightly during the 7 to 11 period to local-live programming and 46.4 minutes a day to all non-CBS programming, including movies, programs from other networks, and syndicated material.[10] One would expect the stations in the largest markets, with their better-trained staffs, greater availability of local talent, and larger program budgets, to feature local shows no less often than would those in smaller markets.

The FCC has attempted unsuccessfully to encourage stations to air more local-live programs in keeping with each licensee's pledge to operate "in the public interest." The "weapon" has been gentle persuasion applied at license renewal time. This failing, under pressure from the Antitrust Division of the Department of Justice which threatened to take action if the FCC did not, the Commission, in September 1963, prohibited contractural arrangements between stations and networks whereby stations are required to option to the network specified amounts of time.[11] Networks, after imposing the option-time system upon affiliated stations in 1945, have fought all efforts to alter option arrangements. A Senate committee in 1954 urged, among other things, abolition of option time.[12] The *Barrow Report* in 1957 recommended outlawing option time.[13] At this point the FCC began to take notice. It first (September 14, 1960) reduced the option time permissible from three to two and one-half hours in each time segment.[14] However, this decision was appealed by KTTV Los Angeles, a nonaffiliated station, which opposed option-time agreements and favored reducing by 75 per cent the amount of prime-time programs a station might receive from any single source.[15] The Commission, on April 19, 1961, vacated the 1960 action pending reconsideration. Then on May 28, 1963, the FCC concluded that "option time is not essential to successful TV network operations, . . . it restrains the freedom of choice of licensees as to what programs to present and at what times to present them, and restricts access by non-network groups to desirable evening time." [16] The rule prohibiting option time and "any other practice having a like restraining effect on TV" became effective as of September 10, 1963.[17]

In addition, the FCC on May 28, 1963, after taking a similar position a year earlier, declared illegal a CBS affiliate compensation plan which had been adopted to become effective in the spring of 1961.[18] The plan provided for a graduated pay scale that "varied sharply according to the number of hours cleared for CBS programs." [19] As would be expected, CBS fought the Commission's "incursion."

Despite prophecies of doom, such as ruination of the networks and degrading of programs,[20] the end of option time had no appreciable effect on the amount of network programming cleared by affiliates. In fact, *Television* reported in March 1965, that the networks were clearing programs with less difficulty than before option time was banned. Figures and percentages cited earlier in this chapter prove that eliminating option time has had no impact.

Why did outlawing option time fail? First, it must be recognized that station licensees have amassed great wealth merely by riding the networks. Telecasting nonnetwork programming may be more profitable, especially in large markets where commercials may be sold readily and at higher profits than would be realized from network advertising. However, providing nonnetwork programming, especially local live shows, requires outlays of time, larger staffs, and, possibly more critical, ideas. In addition, the FCC did not reduce network pressure on affiliates merely by eliminating option-time agreements. Prior to the chain-broadcasting regulations, adopted in 1941, networks imposed on affiliates five-year noncancelable contracts which the networks could abrogate with a one-year notice. Current Commission rules, however, now limit network affiliation contracts to two years.[21] As if holding the implied threat of disaffiliation after two years over the heads of station licensees were not sufficient, CBS specifies that

> Where a station is affiliated with the CBS Television Network, the CBS Television Network in normal course reviews the station's record of delayed and non-cleared Network programs and the result of such review is an important factor in determining whether it is in the interest of the CBS

Television Network to affiliate with another available station. If an affiliate's pattern of clearance of CBS Television Network programs evidences a disinterest in those programs or unreasonably impairs the ability of the Network effectively to serve national advertisers and the public, the Network's need to effect substantial clearance may outweigh the disadvantages of disrupting an existing relationship.[22]

The myth that the networks merely serve as pipelines for programs produced by others dies hard. Actually, the networks have appropriated control of programming to further enrich themselves.

TABLE XI *Number of Mass-Appeal, U.S. Produced Series Released Annually by Major Suppliers to the First-Run Syndication Market, 1956–64*

Year	*Number of Series*
1956	29
1957	20
1958	16
1959	15
1960	10
1961	7
1962	3
1963	3
1964	1

Source: "Notice of Proposed Rule-Making," docket 12782, FCC mimeo. 64453, March 22, 1965, p. 15.

Despite denials by network officials, the FCC reported that only 6.9 per cent of prime evening programming (6 to 11 P.M.) was not "under direct network ownership or proprietary control." [23] Put another way, the networks have squeezed independent producers (herein defined as those who do not assign financial interest and/or program control in their productions to others, especially network corporations) out of business, so that most broadcast time not preempted by networks is given to movies or to reruns of old network shows. As proof, in 1956 the independent major suppliers to the television first-run, mass-appeal syndication market released twenty-nine program series. An FCC study committee reported that it could find only one such series released in 1965 (see Table 11).[24] As former FCC Chairman Minow pointed out, "television networks made use of the economic leverage derived from their control of scarce broadcast time and facilities of affiliate-licensees to acquire financial or proprietary interests in programs exhibited on networks in favorable time periods."[25] The interests to which Minow referred are merchandising rights (such as dolls, records, and clothes, based on a program), foreign and domestic syndication rights, and sharing in revenue from the sale of the program by the network to advertisers at an amount in excess of the program cost to the network.

Network control over program production has evolved because the three national television networks comprise the sole major market for independently produced television programs.[26] Hence, competition cannot flourish either for national television or for domestic or foreign syndication. Indeed, as figures cited earlier clearly show, virtually no programs are available in syndication that were not originally exhibited on one of the three major networks. The FCC Notice of Proposed Rule-Making, March 22, 1965, summarized the plight of independent program producers succinctly.

> 23] Under present conditions independent producers who wish to exhibit their product first on a network and then to offer it in the domestic syndication or foreign markets are subject to an extreme handicap. They must bargain for the network exposure necessary to establish the subsequent value of their program properties with the network corporations who are among their principal competitors in domestic and foreign distribution. In this bargaining process independent producers often grant to their competitors—the network corporations—large shares in the subsidiary rights in the programs which are their stock-in-trade in domestic and foreign markets. Also, independent producers who attempt to sell their programs for original exhibition through the domestic syndication market must compete with "off-network" programs which are owned or controlled by network corporations. Similarly, an entrepreneur who attempts to compete in foreign markets finds his source of supply of the programs which constitute his stock-in-trade controlled and limited in large measure by his principal competitors—the network corportions.[27]

Although network officials deny heatedly that residual financial interests influence their decisions to exhibit a program series, evidence clearly refutes their argument.[28] The Report of the House Committee on Interstate and Foreign Commerce (a committee then not unfriendly to broadcasting) concludes,

> The net result appears to be that the networks, through these activities, place themselves in a situation where very compelling economic motives arise to choose for network exhibition and thus to popularize those film

series in which they have been able to acquire a right to share in continuing values from syndication and other values which may be created or enhanced through network exhibition.[29]

The syndication facts of life are that programs do not sell unless they have been popularized, either by network exposure or, in the case of movies, exhibition in movie theaters.

Network officials argue that since they must provide "risk" capital to produce pilot programs, the networks should share in the residual profits. However, at least some of the major motion picture companies testified before Congress that they did not need network financing, but "preferred" to accept it for business reasons. It is obvious that accepting network "risk" capital in return for licensing a program to a network and permitting that network to participate in the profits results from coercion.[30] *Television* magazine put it rather bluntly, ". . . it (is) almost impossible for a producer to sell a show without cutting the network in on the profits in some way." [31]

The question then arises: Are the really independent program producers barred from television? Let us turn to the small number of persons who have testified on the subject, despite probable reprisals from their only customers, the networks. Most outspoken has been Robert Montgomery, whose "Robert Montgomery, Presents" weekly dramatic series appeared on NBC from 1950 to 1957. He told a House subcommittee that his series was canceled even though advertisers wished to continue it; he quoted unidentified NBC personnel as hinting that the network should be given "a very large portion of the profits" if the program were to continue.[32] He said he had been contacted recently by a large insurance company which wished to back a program but was unable to without assigning ownership of the program and control of its content to a network. Montgomery said that when an independent producer takes a story idea to a network, "they (network personnel) will be glad to experiment with (the) idea and take the control completely away . . . and take at least 50 per cent of (the) profits . . . But they will not let (the producer) do it as an independent." [33]

Montgomery urged the government to open program production to young people by forcing the networks to relinquish at least part of their control over programming. And in reply to the networks' contention that without network "risk" capital television screens might go dark, he offered to program any hour at any time on any network and broker it to advertisers.[34]

Don McGuire, a writer, director, and producer of motion picture and television shows, in 1965 filed a civil antitrust suit against CBS and General Foods, alleging that CBS refused to exhibit two McGuire-produced shows because CBS did not have a financial interest in them. He charged that CBS took this action even though General Foods, Procter & Gamble, and Phillip Morris Company said they wished to sponsor one or both of them and contacted network officials, seeking permission to place the shows on CBS. Each potential sponsor, so McGuire charged, was told by CBS personnel that they should sponsor other programs, ones in which CBS held financial interests.[35]

The March 22, 1965, Notice of Proposed Rule-Making was issued by the FCC to rectify some of these wrongs. The proposed rule was an attempt to stimulate competitive conditions in television program production by

> 1] eliminating network corporations from the syndication business within the United States and from the sale, licensing and distribution of independently produced television programs in foreign markets; 2] prohibiting network corporations from acquiring distribution or profit-sharing rights in syndication and foreign sales of independently produced television programs; and 3] limiting economic and proprietary control by network corporations of the programs included in their schedules in desirable evening network time. The proposed rule, however, would preserve the right of network corporations to sell or otherwise dispose of syndication, overseas and other subsidiary rights in programs produced by them or by persons controlling, controlled by, or under common control with them and to distribute programs of which they are the sole producers in foreign markets.[36]

The major feature of the proposal is the so-called 50–50 rule whereby, if adopted, networks could hold financial interest in no more than 50 per cent, or fourteen hours, whichever is greater, of weekly evening programs (6 to 11) in their schedules. Excluded are news, special events, and sustaining programs.[37]

In essence, the Commission and many critics of television programming are reversing themselves. During the quiz show scandals (see Chapter 8) of the late 1950's a solution which was proposed to prevent future scandals has become known as the "magazine format" of programming—advertisers would buy time but exercise no control over program content.[38] Reserving to the networks a total control over their programming, so they might resist such wrongs as plugola and quiz show rigging, appeared then to offer promise. Today few advertisers buy programs for network placement; almost all merely buy commercial minutes on network-owned or network-licensed programs with virtually no voice as to program content. The "solution" did not work. Network officials' tastes are no higher and, in some cases at least, are not as high as those of advertisers and advertising agency personnel. One would have to disregard the fine dramatic and musical programs of the 1950's were he to argue that television programs today are superior. Some of those excellent programs were produced by networks. The matter at issue relates to program quality and variety more than ownership, at least as far as viewers are concerned. It is the long-suffering viewer who has been ignored through all of the discussions about "wastelands" and programming. For networks, advertisers, and others to argue that Nielsen, *et al*, provide a guide to viewer tastes is pure rot. Viewers may select only from among those programs networks choose to exhibit. Drama has all but disappeared; in 1965 the only drama in prime evening hours was "Chrysler Theatre." Reacting, at least momentarily, to the glare of unfavorable publicity, FCC pressure, and congressional inquiries, the networks increased amid much fanfare the budget of drama programs for the 1966–67 season. Too, they scheduled a few programs by independent producers, both predictable moves calculated to forestall adoption of the 50–50 rule.

Would the FCC 50–50 rule open program schedules to "competitive and competent elements" so Americans could enjoy a greater diversity of programming? The majority of commissioners say it would.[39] But shifting half of network programming from the greedy control of one group (networks) to a second (advertisers) would merely redistribute the wealth slightly. Neither group can be trusted to provide program diversity and quality viewers deserve. The Commission should consider barring both networks and advertisers from imposing their program concepts on, and extracting financial concessions from, independent program producers. In this way a freer marketplace for writers, directors, composers, performers, and producers—those with the talent and skills to develop worthwhile shows—could emerge.

The Cost of "Free" Television

Repeatedly, network officials and other industry spokesmen have pleaded with Congress, the FCC, and the public to protect our beloved "free" television. But how free is television? The answer isn't as simple as it might appear. One must consider the initial outlays for equipment, television advertising costs included in the prices of products and services, and the cost of operating television sets and keeping them in repair. Few realize that the public has invested far greater sums in tangible broadcast property than have the television networks and stations. The Television Bureau of Advertising estimated in 1962, that the capital investments by the television industry in the physical facilities which then composed the broadcast structure was 4 per cent; viewers invested 96 per cent.[40] At that time the ARB said the public had invested $19.5 billion in sets then in use. The industry investment in tangible broadcast property was $641,030,000.[41]

However, most estimates of public investment in receiving sets and maintenance run higher. CBS President Frank Stanton in 1956 placed the figure at $17 billion;[42] Robert W. Sarnoff in 1959 estimated $40 billion. Sarnoff said, further, that the public was spending $4 billion a year for sets and maintenance.[43] F. G. Osbarh, editor, *Electronic Industries*, estimated that 121.68 million television sets had been sold from 1946 to mid-1966 for $26.5 billion.[44] If one were to include the cost of antennas, repairs, and parts, the total would run to at least $30 billion. The investment by broadcasters in tangible television property was $1,013,451,000 as of the end of 1966, depreciated to $549,725,000.[45] Few viewers qualify for tax depreciations on their television sets. Disregarding depreciation, the cost to broadcasters is less than 3 per cent of the total equipment outlay.

The average family's bill for television advertising runs slightly more than $34 a year,[46] more than three times the annual combined British television and radio set tax ($11.20). As Harry J. Skornia points out in his penetrating book, *Television and Society*,[47] persons with high incomes may well pay considerably more. He estimates that those families with an income of only $5,000 would pay approximately $65 a year.[48] In reply to arguments that advertising benefits society by reducing production costs, he says that any such economies are not reflected in lower prices and cites evidence where the opposite has occurred. Skornia estimates that the average family pays $150 a year for its "free" television service.[49]

A License to Print Money

Roy Thomson, British press lord, reportedly confided that obtaining a franchise to operate commercial television in Scotland was like receiving "a license to print money." He has used the huge profits realized from his commercial television holdings to build his international newspaper chain into the world's largest. His American broadcasting cousins have also constructed industrial empires and publishing-broadcasting chains out of profits earned in television. But that subject will be treated in Chapter 13. More germane to our discussion is the television profit structure.

Annual television revenues continue to soar, reaching $2,203 million for 1966, an increase of 2 per cent over 1965 and almost double the 1960 rate. Profits before federal income taxes for 1966 also set a record, $492.2 million, a rather healthy profit-to-tangible property rate of almost 100 per cent (see Table 24, Appendix). One might assume that dividing this amount among the 608 stations reporting to the FCC gives each a sizable gain. The arithmetic is accurate; the logic is not. The three network corporations earned $78.7 million and their 15 owned-and-operated stations another $108 million, leaving the other 593 stations $307.1 million to divide.[50]

Why networks should retain such a large amount and their stations should earn profits averaging more than $7.2 million while the stations not owned by the three major networks average earnings slightly more than $500,000 each is a question worth pursuing. Quite obviously the networks through their control over television programming also hold television's purse strings. Of the $614.1 million the networks received from sales in 1966, they magnanimously assigned $201 million, an average of $414,433, to 485[51] affiliates while retaining $372.6 million plus $40.6 million under the guise of paying it to their 15 owned stations, an average of $2.84 million per station.[52] It is little wonder owners of affiliated stations have long complained that network stations receive a disproportionately large share of network advertising revenues.

Unfortunately, the FCC does not as a matter of policy release financial data in such a way as to divulge information about individual stations. Occasionally, as when the *Barrow Report* was issued in 1957, the previously hidden is briefly exposed. This report revealed a fact that network officials have since openly admitted, that the average station affiliate receives less than 30 per cent of the proceeds from the sale of its time by a network. A station with an advertising rate of $3,250 an hour normally receives approximately $975 for a sponsored hour of network programming, approximately $162.50 for a commercial. If that station sold the spots through its own station representative, it would receive approximately $650 to $700 each, 30 per cent of which it would have to pay the network were the spots carried on a program provided by the network. It should be noted that affiliates may sell such spots only when the networks cannot sell them.[53]

Close study of the FCC television financial report for 1966 is revealing. The 15 network owned-and-operated stations earned profits before taxes of $28,818 per full-time employee as compared to $11,512 for the other VHF stations, $10,053 for the nonnetwork-owned VHF and UHF stations, and $8,449 for the network corporations. The figures are slightly lower but comparable when part-time employees are included.[54] Obviously, the network stations employ highly efficient personnel!

An examination of the 1966 profits in relation to tangible property may help clarify the situation. The FCC report did not give a breakdown of property owned by the networks and their stations, hence that information is not available. However, the three networks and their 15 stations earned profits before taxes equal to 91 per cent of their original investment and 148 per cent of the depreciated cost of their properties. The 479 VHF stations not owned by networks earned a 31 per cent profit on original investment and 83.5 per cent on the depreciated value of their properties.[55] Indeed, excellent earnings rates, but not nearly as favorable as rates enjoyed by those who control television finances. The 114 black sheep UHF's as a group lost $7.4 million.

We can present further evidence in two slightly different ways. The 15 network stations earned 70 per cent profits on expenses; the 479 VHF stations' rate was 47 per cent.[56] And, finally, network-owned stations earned at the rate of 35.3 cents and the 593 other VHF and UHF stations at 26.6 cents on the sales dollar. Combined network and network-owned station data yield rates comparable to those of the nonnetwork stations—27.5 cents.[57] A major contributor to the network stations' high earnings is the success networks have achieved in selling national spot advertising for their own stations. The proportion of national nonnetwork spots to total sales was 75.4 per cent, 20 percentage points greater than for the 593 other stations.[58]

The counterargument that the network stations obviously would be more profitable since they are located in the largest twelve markets is persuasive.[59] Meager contravening evidence exists, primarily because of the FCC's policy of withholding financial data. One nugget of evidence worth considering, however, is contained in the FCC 1966 television financial report. The income structure of stations in the only two comparable markets of the top twelve suggests favoritism to an ABC-owned station. Network-time sales shares allocated to the three affiliated stations in Boston, fifth market, were $4,944,000, $561,000 less than were allocated to the Detroit, sixth market, where ABC owns a station. It should be pointed out that in both of these cities three VHF stations were carrying network programs; a fourth commercial station, a UHF, was not affiliated. Further, the four stations in Boston, despite lower network sales shares, earned $18,937,000 in profits before taxes compared to $12,806,000 for the four Detroit stations.[60] The differences cannot be ascribed to higher advertising rates in either city; *Broadcasting Yearbook*, 1967, listed combined hourly rates for the three VHF stations in Boston of $10,250 and in Detroit of $9,600. Rates quoted by the networks reverse these slightly, listing Boston at $9,300 and Detroit at $9,500.[61] But let's not extend these figures further. Arguing from the single case is dangerous; this instance, however, offers supportive evidence to the charge that the networks pay their own stations at higher rates, generally, than they pay nonowned affiliates. The financial information ABC filed with the FCC in an effort to gain FCC approval of International Telephone and Telegraph's purchase of ABC supports this argument. ABC reported that for the period 1962–65 it earned its greatest share of market profits on its owned-and-operated Detroit and San Francisco stations, 29.9 and 26.4 per cent, the only markets where ABC does not compete with another network-owned station. ABC's share of markets in other cities were New York, 14.9 per cent, Los Angeles, 14.9 per cent, and Chicago, 19.3 per cent.[62]

Harlan M. Blake and Jack A. Blum point out that the affiliated stations have repeatedly battled with the networks to get a larger share of total revenues.[63] Since network affiliation is highly profitable,[64] these licensees can do little more than grumble, while those with whom networks have chosen not to affiliate have no recourse. In fact, the nonaffiliated could not carry network programs rejected by affiliates in the same market until the FCC started applying pressure by means of a Proposed Rule-Making (docket 16041) adopted June 2, 1965. Now the networks generally offer programs not cleared by an affiliate to nonaffiliated stations in the same market, to VHF stations first, if available.[65]

Television has its losers as well as winners. While 33 stations earned $3 million or more in profits in 1966 and 116 earned one million dollars or more, 13.2 per cent (62) VHF stations and 41.5 per cent (39) UHF stations operated at losses. Thirteen (5 VHF, 8 UHF) lost $400,000 or more, one of them despite total revenues of between $1.5 and $2 million.[66]

Advertisers, Too Large and Too Few

Television relies too heavily on a few large advertisers for its sustenance, an invitation to censorship of news and entertainment content. Evidence suggests that some programs and reports of events have, indeed, been affected. For example: *1*] Procter & Gamble, by far television's largest advertiser, has a policy of eliminating from programs any material which might reflect adversely on business and especially on grocers and druggists,[67] *2*] Chrysler, a major munitions manufacturer, in 1966 killed a proposed war-story program, *Barbed Wire,* because the plot was too antimilitary,[68] *3*] a gas company edited a "Playhouse 90" series on the Nuremberg trials to eliminate references to "gas" as cause of death in Nazi concentration camps,[69] *4*] Alcoa moved the locale in a dramatic program *Tragedy In A Temporary Town* from a trailer lot to a shanty mining town because Alcoa is a major supplier to trailer companies,[70] *5*]

Networks generally have underplayed or ignored events and statements unfavorable to food processors and soap manufacturers. Recent examples are the short shrift given Senate subcommittee hearings on, and comments favorable to, the 1966 "truth in packaging" bill and the high cost of food processing. Could it be that such behavior reflects concern for the best interests of, say, the top-fifty grocery products advertisers who spent $1,314,983,000 in television in 1965, 52.3 per cent of television's total advertising income? [71]

Let us look at some of these major advertisers and groups of advertisers in relation to proportions they contribute to television's income, remembering that television gets 83 per cent of its total income from advertising. Procter & Gamble clearly dominates television advertising; that conglomerate spent $179,156,960 in 1966, $1 of every $15.43 (6.5 per cent) spent on national, regional, and local television advertising.[72] Procter & Gamble's expenditure on network television alone ($101,251,200) exceeded the amount Bristol-Meyers, the second largest TV advertiser, spent on network and national and regional spot advertising ($93,602,370).[73] The five largest advertisers in 1966 contributed 17.8 per cent ($491,224,830); the 35 top advertisers supplied 50.7 per cent of television's total advertising income.[74] These figures assume greater significance when one realizes that the other thirteen hundred TV advertisers [75] furnished less than 50 per cent.

Further, many large corporations concentrate their advertising on one network to earn maximum discounts.[76] CBS-TV network President John T. Reynolds reported that in 1964 the CBS network had 138 prime-time advertisers.[77] A study of prime-time (7:30–11 P.M.) commercial announcements on the three network owned-and-operated stations in New York City during March 1966, showed that 1,697 commercials were presented, almost equally divided among the three major networks. Five companies placed 337 commercials, approximately 20 per cent of the total. Table 12 shows how these five companies distributed their messages.[78] Thus, Bristol-Meyers bought 14.5 per cent of ABC's commercial spots during the period; General Foods bought slightly more than 9 per cent of CBS's spots. General Foods, American Home Products, and Procter & Gamble together bought approximately 22 per cent of CBS commercials.

The impact of the largest advertisers permeates the entire network financial structure. The largest five network advertisers in 1966 accounted for approximately 22 per cent of network advertising revenues. The top ten contributed one-third and the top twenty, just under 50 per cent. The other 345 advertisers accounted for the remainder.[79] The major national advertisers also contribute heavily to the direct income of local stations. *Broadcasting Advertisers Reports* for March 1966, revealed that national advertisers bought 68.53 per cent of the sixty-second nonnetwork commercials during a full week in 75 leading television markets. The figures were 8,121 national advertisers to 3,730 local advertisers.[80] Approximately 90 per

TABLE XII *Number and Distribution of TV Commercials Among Networks*

Company	*Networks*			
	ABC	*CBS*	*NBC*	*Total*
American Home Products Corporation	10	36	0	46
Bristol-Meyers Company	82	6	9	97
Colgate-Palmolive Company	10	7	29	46
General Foods Corporation	8	51	7	66
Procter & Gamble Company	29	36	17	82
Total	139	136	62	337

cent of the total television advertising expenditures are in the top 75 markets.[81] A *BAR* report for February 1966, showed that of 67,491 commercials in the 75 major markets they had studied, 39,280 (58.2 per cent) were network commercials, 17,590 (26.1 per cent) were national nonnetwork spots, and 10,621 (15.7 per cent) were local.[82] Since the networks sell one-minute spots and restrict affiliated stations to very few nonnetwork commercials as long as a minute, the amount of advertising time commandeered by the networks is even greater than these figures suggest.[83]

Organized Labor

Probably fewer than half of the local television stations have union contracts covering employees.[84] Obviously, the industry does not lend itself to unionization, since each station employs a relatively small number of technicians and, except for the major markets, few cities have more than one station. Conversely, the national television networks are highly unionized; here is where the major labor-management disputes have arisen. Television is at somewhat of a disadvantage in its negotiations with the unions; its product, time, cannot be "stockpiled" should work stoppages occur. Indeed, television networks fear interruptions which undoubtedly would alter at least some viewers' entertainment patterns, possibly to the detriment of television. Consequently, unions usually have little difficulty gaining their demands from the networks, even unions representing small numbers of employees.

As with other mass media, the networks and large stations must bargain with a great number of unions. In 1958, CBS and NBC each negotiated one hundred separate union contracts on behalf of their networks and owned stations.[85] A strike by any one group generally forces curtailment of network operations even if other union members cross picket lines, as they did during the 13-day strike of the American Federation of Television and Radio Artists against ABC, CBS, NBC and their owned and operated stations, and Mutual Broadcasting System in March–April 1967. That was the first AFTRA national strike, but an AFTRA and Screen Actors Guild strike, also against the four networks, was narrowly averted in November 1966. Network officials fear these disputes may spark other broadcasting labor unrest.

As a consequence of the labor unions' strong bargaining position, pay rates generally are high, a pattern which grew out of concessions granted during the high profit license-freeze years, 1948–52. The AFTRA, in 1967, sought for its newsmen a minimum weekly base of $225 plus $225 fee guarantee for camera appearances, a total of $450. (Star newscasters, such as Walter Cronkite, Chet Huntley, and David Brinkley, reportedly earn in excess of $100,000 a year.) Both the Guild and AFTRA sought a $25-a-day pay increase for performers on television commercials, giving them $130 a day.[86] Details of the contracts were not made public. Unions have struck individual stations. However, the stations have continued to operate, using supervisory personnel to replace those on strike and relying heavily on networks and syndicates for the bulk of their nonnews programming.[87]

Even a cursory discussion of television union-management problems should include mention of agreements with representatives of authors and composers. Networks, both radio and television, and individual stations pay for the right to broadcast music composed by the 8,468 writers and 2,836 publishers who are members of the American Society of Composers, Authors and Publishers and the approximately 9,000 writers and 5,000 publishers represented by Broadcast Music, Incorporated. Together, ASCAP and BMI license an estimated 98 per cent of all music broadcast,[88] for which stations and networks pay ASCAP approximately $38 million and BMI $14 million annually.[89] Rates are based on income.[90]

Broadcast Music, Incorporated was formed in 1939–40 by CBS, NBC, and a group of other broadcasters to provide an alternate source of music. When broadcasters and ASCAP failed to reach agreement on rates in 1940, radio was denied the right to use ASCAP-licensed music. The reader may recall with something less than pleasure the inundation of radio by Stephen Foster melodies during the period of disagreement, January 1 to November 1, 1941, a deluge that possibly has forever damaged "I Dream of Jeanie," "Kentucky Babe," and other public domain music.

One final discordant musical note, the Department of Justice issued a consent judgment against BMI, November 29, 1966, the culmination of a civil antitrust suit filed December 10, 1964. The major concern was with BMI's growing domination of popular music which was brought about by its broadcaster-owners who hold the power to popularize music via radio and television.[91] That suit also charged that broadcasters use BMI as a bargaining weapon to depress and control license rates of other music licensing organizations.[92] Major provisions of the consent decree prohibited BMI from publishing or recording music and distributing sheet music and recordings, from entering into a contract with a writer or publisher for a period longer than five years, from negotiating contracts which would prohibit a publisher from conducting business with any other performing-rights organization, from prohibiting member writers and publishers from issuing nonexclusive licenses for performances of their works, and from forcing others to record or perform any stipulated percentage of music to which BMI has licensing rights. Broadcasters feared they might be forced to divest themselves of financial interests in BMI, but they were not.[93]

Although quite obviously broadcasters founded BMI as a

weapon to force ASCAP to reduce its rates, as ASCAP did in 1940, rather than as a direct profit-making venture, BMI has yet to pay a dividend. And it is obvious that broadcasters have used their entree to the public to popularize BMI music to the detriment of ASCAP music. To BMI's credit, it has encouraged numerous authors, composers, and publishers who were not admitted to ASCAP, by helping them publish, record, and popularize their works. One might well question the quality of music BMI has promoted, yet musical taste involves subjective evaluations not properly at issue here; one man's treasure is another man's trash.

Recent TV Developments

COLOR TELEVISION

Essentially a phenomenon of the mid-1960's, color television has its roots in the 1920's when an early color system was demonstrated by John Baird in Scotland, July 3, 1928. Bell Telephone Laboratories in New York sent color pictures over wire on June 27, 1929. Network activity came later. RCA began an experimental color television demonstration in February 1940; CBS tested its color television system in August 1940, and the next month successfully demonstrated its "field sequential system" to the then FCC Chairman, James L. Fly. The CBS system used large color filters which revolved mechanically to convert the three color images transmitted into one, but in three tints.

Thus, RCA and CBS competed for Commission approval of their color systems. CBS won the first round when on October 11, 1950, the FCC licensed its 405-line color wheel-synchronized switch system, despite protests by General Sarnoff that the CBS system would make the 8 million black and white receivers then in use obsolete because of its incompatibility. CBS argued that black and white sets could be converted with an adapter (cost estimated at $30 to $50) and a converter (cost estimated at $75 to $100) to receive the CBS color.[94]

After being delayed by an RCA preliminary injunction, CBS began limited commercial color broadcasts on June 25, 1951, over a five-city hookup. Few tint shows (25:35 hours—25 hours, 35 minutes—in 1951) were broadcast. However, before CBS could exploit its system, the National Production Authority, activated to allocate strategic materials during the Korean War, on November 20, 1951, "approved CBS colored TV production provided no strategic materials or skilled manpower be lost to war production." [95] This delay effectively killed the cumbersome CBS system and gave RCA, whose skilled research men obviously utilized the lull to improve RCA's system, an opportunity to forge ahead. In the spring of 1953 RCA telecast a twenty-minute variety show in color before the House Interstate Commerce Committee, for which it won "rave notices." [96] In October, RCA, CBS, and Dumont all demonstrated compatible color broadcasts for the FCC. The Commission reacted rapidly and favorably, approving on December 17, 1953, the RCA compatible color system and the standards that had been adopted earlier by the National Television System Committee.[97] Thus, the present color system evolved, setting the stage for commercial colorcasts.

The approved color system utilized the RCA three-gun tube or variations on it and broadcast at 525 lines definition, the same as is used in the United States for black and white broadcasting. RCA's system uses a "dot sequential system" with a screen in the receiver which permits only electrons for the appropriate color to reach and "turn on" the phosphor dots of its respective tint.[98] It will be recalled that CBS from the outset favored utilizing UHF spectrum exclusively for television. RCA prevailed and the FCC established television in the more restricted VHF (channels 2–13) space. CBS then argued 1] television should from the start broadcast in color and 2] picture quality either black and white or color would be enhanced by utilizing a finer line screen than the 525 imposed by the narrowness of the VHF spectrum. CBS arguments appear convincing today. Picture quality of European television is superior to ours; Europe uses a 625-line definition. France adopted a 819-line system at the outset.

Commercial color telecasting resumed in this country in 1954 when NBC telecast 75:30 and CBS 38:30 hours. However, CBS failed to keep pace as NBC steadily increased its broadcasts in color to 643:15 hours in 1957; CBS telecast 56:45 hours that year. CBS reduced its colorcasts to 24 hours in 1958, 10 hours in 1959, and 4:30 hours in 1960 while NBC ran 668, 725, and 1,035:30 hours, respectively. ABC began telecasting a half-hour a week in color in September 1962, and increased to a three-hours-a-week schedule shortly thereafter. CBS resumed colorcasting (5:30 hours) in 1963, after two years of inactivity.[99]

The major surge in colorcasting came with the 1965–66 season after NBC had released research results that claimed programs in color drew slightly larger audiences than the same programs in black and white. NBC led the way by broadcasting 96 per cent of its 1965–66 prime evening programs in color, at the rate of approximately four thousand hours for the broadcast year. CBS and ABC also tremendously increased their colorcasts; CBS scheduled half and ABC 40 per cent of their prime evening programs in color. All three increased their color schedules during the broadcast season[100] with NBC telecasting its total schedule in color beginning November 7, 1966.[101] CBS and ABC are scheduled to achieve total colorcasting in 1968.

Station capabilities to broadcast in color also have risen rapidly, especially during the past two years. A *Broadcasting* survey conducted in mid-November 1965, reported that 506 stations (84 per cent) could carry network color. This compares with 77 per cent with network color capability at the end of 1964. Although 48 per cent at year's end 1965 could telecast color film and 23 per cent could transmit color tapes, only 76 (12 per cent) could produce local live color shows, an increase from 11 per cent in 1964.[102] A large backlog of orders were on file with color equipment manufacturers in 1966 and 1967, indicating that virtually all television stations will shortly have color capability although the cost of converting from black and white to color is approximately $250,000, according to Norman E. Cash, president, TV Bureau of Advertising.

Early color receivers were of uneven quality; sales were low. *Television Age Yearbook*, 1958, reported that by January 1, 1955, only 9,690 color sets were in operation. The total reached 428,000 by January 1, 1958, and did not pass a million until 1963. The number has risen sharply since, to approximately 11 million in mid-1967.[103] Jack Gould, New York Times News Service, has pointed out that producing films in color costs an additional $7,500 per half hour, further inflating already high television program costs. This, Gould said, "is one more economic pressure that can only put added emphasis on winning the largest audiences to justify the mounting expenditures . . . curbing any temptation to take a gamble or to get away from well-tried merchandise (program formats)."[104]

SATELLITE COMMUNICATION

Communications via earth satellite was born when Echo I, a ten-story high balloon, coated with a thin film of aluminum, was launched by the National Aeronautics and Space Administration on August 12, 1960. Two-way transcontinental telephone conversations and other transmissions, including facsimile pictures, were bounced off this ten thousand miles high, visible-from-earth satellite.[105] The Courier, the first "active" satellite, one equipped both to receive and to send, was launched by the United States Army on October 4, 1960. The Courier received and recorded messages from earth which it retransmitted upon command.

American Telephone and Telegraph created an international sensation with its 170-pound Telstar I, which it built and paid NASA to launch. The three-foot spherical satellite relayed live television programs between the United States and Europe beginning fifteen hours after its launching, on July 10, 1962. Telstar I established a number of firsts: first repeater satellite to transmit internationally, first to transmit still pictures in color, first to telecast test television live and in color, and first to be financed by nonpublic funds.

Congress was so impressed by AT & T's dramatic Telstar I demonstration that in August 1962 it rushed passage of a slightly modified Kennedy Administration proposal, the "Communications Satellite Act of 1962." This act authorized creation of a profit-motive corporation, under federal government (FCC) regulation, charged with building and operating a commercial communications satellite system.[106] The act was adopted despite charges by a few congressmen and others that Congress was being stampeded into giving away valuable resources on which the government had lavished hundreds of millions of dollars.[107]

Relay I, built on contract by RCA for NASA and launched at NASA expense[108] on December 13, 1962, like Telstar, was a medium-altitude repeater satellite. Overdrain of its power supply during the first three weeks after its launching, however, made the satellite inoperative. An alternate system activated January 3, 1963, made it possible to conduct television, telephone, teletype, and facsimile tests with stations in England, France, Italy, and, for the first time, Brazil. Improved versions of these three satellites were launched: Telstar II, in 1963, and Echo II and Relay II, 1964.

But only sporadic transmissions were possible through the use of these low level (Echo) and medium altitude (Telstar and Relay) satellites. To establish continuous world-communication service would require some thirty medium-altitude relays. Also, tracking the diverse orbiting patterns of each would require that expensive equipment be installed at each land relay station. Therefore, the Communications Satellite Corporation (Comsat),[109] incorporated January 31, 1963, has begun to establish a high-altitude synchronous satellite system of three satellites in orbits of approximately 22,300 miles and positioned over the equator. At that height each of the three space satellites would travel at the same rate of speed as does the earth and provide twenty-four-hour service to 90 per cent of the world.

The three Syncom communications satellites, designed and constructed by Huges Aircraft Company on contract by NASA and launched by NASA at public expense, were the first 22,300-mile altitude synchronous satellites. A malfunction occurred while injecting Syncom I into orbit during its February 14, 1963, launching. Consequently, its communications equipment never functioned. Syncom II was launched in orbit over the Atlantic Ocean, July 26, 1963, and Syncom III was put into orbit over the Pacific Ocean on August 19, 1964. Both Syncom II and III performed numerous communications experiments, the most spectacular being Syncom III's relay of live television coverage of the 1964 Olympics from Tokyo to the United States. Thus, the research had been done and innumerable problems had been solved to make possible placing in high orbit properly positioned satellites that could provide the long-sought continuous satellite communications.

The stage was set for the first commercial synchronous satellite, Early Bird I. This eighty-five-pound hatbox-shaped relay satellite, owned and financed by Comsat, was launched April 6, 1965. From its position over the Atlantic, between the east coast of Brazil and Gabon on the west coast of Africa, Early Bird I, with a capacity to relay two hundred and forty two-way telephone or one two-way simultaneous television service, has provided continuous commercial service between North America and Europe since June 27, 1965. Four larger satellites capable of relaying twelve hundred telephone or four two-way television transmissions were launched in 1966 and 1967, only two of which achieved proper synchronous orbits. Both of these, one launched January 11 and one September 27, 1967, plus another launched October 26, 1966, which went off course, are in orbit over the Pacific where they provide commercial telephone, telegraph, and television service between continental United States and Asia. An attempt on March 22, 1967, to place a larger satellite into synchronous orbit over the Atlantic was unsuccessful. Despite failures, satellites are rapidly linking vast areas of Asia, Africa, Europe, and the Americas into a giant satellite communications network which is invaluable to world communications.

Comsat has ordered a design for satellites capable of relaying twelve to twenty television channels, six thousand to eight thousand two-way voice transmissions, a dozen circuits for communications between aircraft and ground stations, or a combination of each.[110] These satellites, expected to be launched in 1970, would be designed to relay television signals directly from sending transmitters to television stations for retransmission. Opponents have challenged 1] Comsat's apparent monopoly of commercial satellite communications and 2] the rates the corporation charges. Black and white one-way television rates as of July 7, 1966, were $3,000 for ten minutes of prime use between Andover, Maine, and a European terminal and $48 a minute thereafter. Costs for two-way or color transmission were 150 per cent of the quoted rate.[111] Charges previously had been higher and the minimum rate based on thirty rather than ten minutes. The corporation has proposed lowering the ten-minute rate to $1,100 plus $30 for each additional minute.[112] During 1965, Early Bird I was used by United States television to relay thirty-three and one-half hours of programming.

What is the future of satellite communications? Long-time dreamer and, incidentally, one whose predictions have often come true, aging General David Sarnoff, chairman of the board of RCA, visualizes simultaneous communication with the entire population of the earth by 1970 via satellites that broadcast directly to FM radio and television receivers. A variety of sound channels would permit each viewer to select the one in his own language. Ultimately, General Sarnoff predicts, "total mass communications on a global scale" at which time all communications will be converted into identical bits of energy for transmission over vast distances. Electronic signals at the receiving end will be translated into printed, oral, and/or visual matter, that will be projected on a wall-mounted, all-purpose television screen. The individual then may obtain news and entertainment from throughout the world and factual information on an almost limitless number of subjects from computer facilities linked internationally by satellites.[113]

Another visionary, John Richardson, executive officer with Huges Aircraft, builder of several satellites, predicted that by 1970 the world would wear "a necklace" of satellites at the equator that could provide in addition to world-wide television and telephone service, world-wide weather and navigational information. He sees as a major benefit to mankind this service's transmission of educational television to peoples of newly emerging nations.[114]

Although Sarnoff, Dr. Harold A. Rosen of Huges Aircraft Company, some FCC members, spokesmen for NASA, the director of the United States Information Agency, advertising agency officials, and others have predicted satellite-to-home broadcasts, powerful forces are allied against such a development. The hardware and knowledge to accomplish direct satellite-to-home service exist, except for a small nuclear power plant. The first person in a position to know, who has hinted that such direct broadcasts are not in the future, is Lieutenant General James D. O'Connell, retired United States Army Chief Signal Officer, and telecommunications adviser to President Johnson and director of telecommunications management of the Office of Emergency Planning. He pointed out that increasing demands on the radio spectrum make it necessary to limit space satellite utilization, including direct-to-home broadcasting.[115] However, another factor is the tremendous political power wielded by broadcasting station owners. Congress virtually never rebuffs this pressure group and always has given them an attentive hearing. Obviously, these broadcasters, who lean so heavily on network programming, will oppose any such threats.

More realistic is the proposal by radio, and especially television networks, to relay programs to their affiliated stations via satellites.

The networks reportedly pay approximately $55 million a year to AT & T for wire lines and microwave relays to their affiliates. ABC asked the FCC in September 1965, for permission to build its own satellite, but the Commission returned the application without taking action. ABC estimated that it would save approximately $6 million a year by feeding programs to affiliates by its own satellite. Comsat, which claims exclusive right to own and operate satellite communications systems, announced in April 1966, its intention of establishing within three to three and one-half years a domestic satellite-communications system that would serve the networks at an annual charge of $35 million, affording them a combined saving of $20 million. The FCC in December 1966, adopted an interim policy to remain in effect until 1969 granting 50 per cent ownership of ground stations to common carriers; Comsat retains 50 per cent interest and will continue to manage the stations. The action was taken in an effort to speed development of the global system.[116] In 1967, the FCC was considering the possibility of licensing a domestic, privately owned satellite system. The Ford Foundation in a dramatic proposal petitioned the Commission for approval to establish a nonprofit domestic satellite system with income to be used to finance educational television (see Chapter 12). Others also seek FCC permission to develop domestic satellite systems. Who will own and operate the system which is destined to replace cable and microwave as network television and radio carriers is a question still to be answered.

Broadcasting's Embarrassments

8.

Broadcasting has attracted more than its share of "get-rich-quick" investors, shyster promoters, and unethical performers. Unfortunately, many of them have reaped sizable financial gains, thus encouraging others to emulation. As their questionable practices have become increasingly flagrant, exposure generally has resulted. Then segments of the industry are called to task by one or more federal regulatory agencies, congressmen, or, less often, by the public. The pattern which evolves has become so repetitive that one can predict, with almost certainty, that spokesmen for broadcasting will prevail on the regulatory agency or congressional subcommittee to permit them to "clean their own house." The "scandal" will soon cease to be reported by the mass media, if it ever was; public attention will be focused on other matters; and the practices will soon resume. Despite pious pleas, broadcasters have an abysmal record of self-regulation, consequently broadcasting has been plagued periodically by such problems as trafficking in licenses, the quiz-show payola-plugola scandals, and the highly questionable audience-measurement services.

Trafficking in Licenses

The public is best served by broadcasters who make a determined effort over a period of years to operate in the public interest. FCC leadership has repeatedly emphasized the need for long-time ownership of broadcasting facilities by reputable persons who thereby can best learn the needs of their audiences and can program accordingly.[1] But this is not what has happened in much of AM,

FM, and TV broadcasting. From the time radio first started earning profits to the present, transfers of stations have taken place at an alarming pace. During the thirteen-year period 1954 to 1966, for example, 4,369 broadcasting stations, as well as 538 television stations, changed hands at a total cost of $1,536,041,367 (see Table 25, Appendix). Activity built to a peak in standard broadcasting in 1959 when the FCC received 917 applications for transfers, more than 26 per cent of the number of AM stations on the air. The FCC granted approval of 712 AM transfers, equal to more than 23 per cent of the number of stations in existence. The turnover was particularly high among stations held for less than three years. More than 50 per cent of the applications for transfers in 1960 were from such short-term ownerships. Obviously the FCC is correct in its concern for resulting "disruptions" of service that may lead to "deterioration in programming."[2]

In an effort to reduce wholesale trading in stations, the FCC on March 15, 1962, amended its rules (docket No. 13864) to require that applications for transfers of stations held less than three years be designated for hearing unless the potential seller can establish that unanticipated changes in circumstances beyond his control make the sale necessary.[3] The results have been discouraging. Applications from both television and FM station owners for transfers of licenses in 1965 reached new peaks, 151 in TV and 358 in FM. Previous highs had been 132 for TV in 1957 and 159 for FM in 1960. AM station trading slowed slightly. From a peak of 917 applications in 1959 and 821 in 1960 it declined to 758 in 1963 but increased to 793 in 1964, the third highest in history.

The FCC in taking action which it hoped would curb station sales referred repeatedly to trafficking in licenses. It is clear that many broadcasting station owners behave like other owners of scarce merchandise: wherever demand greatly exceeds supply competitive bidding results. Scalpers, in this case called license traffickers, arise to exploit the advantages open to them. Basically, this is how it happens. A radio or television allocation is available in an urban center. Let us say that five groups file applications with the FCC for this construction permit and license.[4] Each probably will hire a highly skilled communications attorney, a person who has previously been successful in winning cases before the FCC. Each attorney then prepares a dossier which will meet all of the criteria. The FCC holds hearings, enough in and of itself to discourage the less well-financed applicants.[5] Each group presents its best arguments and attacks the other four. After a "potential" winner has been selected, the other applicants "gang up" on him in an effort to defeat the then leading contender. Amid all of this "noise" and while laboring under an avalanche of detailed trivia contained in the five applications, the FCC selects a winner.

The drama often doesn't end here. If the successful applicant wishes to make a quick killing, as so often he does, he sells the construction permit or builds the station and operates it for a brief interval. Then he sells it to the highest bidder. Unless the FCC can find good cause, it is virtually powerless to deny the transfer. FCC Commissioner Robert E. Lee severely criticized this procedure as "a helleva way to run a railroad." His primary concern was that a chain broadcaster, or someone else who could not have prevailed over the other four applicants in our example, could shortly gain control of the station.[6]

Traffickers also buy inexpensive stations, possibly stations losing money, and shortly after apply to the FCC for authorization to move them to more profitable cities or to increase their power or otherwise improve the property. Then they are "open to offers." This was the mode of operation of the Tedesco brothers, Nicholas and Victor, who were accused by the FCC of trafficking in transactions involving at least three radio stations (WISK St. Paul, Minn.; KFNF Shenandoah, Iowa; and KBLO Hot Springs, Ark.). How successful the Tedesco brothers were is reflected in FCC's denial of their application for a construction permit for a Bloomington, Minn., radio station.

> 32] Nicholas and Victor Tedesco have profited substantially from their buying, selling and trading in broadcast authorizations. . . . On September 1, 1948, and May 10, 1949, Nicholas and Victor showed a net worth of $14,577 and $8,870, respectively. In the fall of 1960 (after they had sold their interest in Station WISK, St. Paul; their interest in WCOW, Sparta, Wisconsin; their interest in KWEB, Rochester, Minnesota; and their remaining 40 per cent interest in KCUE, Red Wing, Minnesota,) their joint net worth exceeded one million dollars . . .[7]

It is interesting to note that the FCC did not confront Nicholas and Victor Tedesco until six years after this event and then only after a rival for a radio station construction permit called attention to their trafficking activities. Incidentally, this case illustrates one reason why many broadcasters will agree not to sell a station after being threatened with an FCC hearing. But let us leave the Tedescos, whose brother, Albert S., holds ownership interests in four radio stations,[8] and move on to larger operations. Metromedia, broadcast chain owner, with other interests that include direct mail and outdoor advertising, documentary production, and an ice review, has been accused by the FCC from time to time with "speculating in the public domain," as the FCC prefers to label trafficking. Unquestionably, Metromedia has profited from trading in stations. In 1959–60, for example, Metromedia bought two UHF stations—WTVH (TV), changed to WIRL-TV Peoria, Ill., for $610,000, and WTVP (TV) Decatur, Ill., for $570,000. The two stations were sold in 1965 for approximately two million dollars each, a 239 per cent profit.[9] It should be explained that station trading of this sort is widespread. Here Metromedia was selling so that she might "trade up," buy two television stations in more populous and more profitable markets. FCC rules, adopted in 1954, limit ownership by any one individual or group to seven AM, seven FM, and seven TV stations of which no more than five may be VHF.

Probably the most flagrant case of trafficking in licenses was by Transcontinental TV Corporation which over a period of less than six years had acquired thirteen stations, usually by intricate stock exchange agreements. Transcontinental sold eleven of these in 1964 for $38,539,310,[10] the biggest station transaction in history. Examination of purchase and sales data on file at the FCC indicates Transcontinental realized a profit of approximately 85 per cent. Former FCC Chairman E. William Henry commented, "I can vote to approve such a transaction only on the assumption that none of Transcontinental's major stockholders plan to re-enter television within the foreseeable future. If any of them should file applications for television facilities in the future, his intention to operate in the public interest, rather than traffic in licenses, should be subjected to the most searching and critical scrutiny." [11] After the sale Transcontinental dissolved itself and split the profits among its several stockholders. The FCC would not authorize transfer of WDOK-AM-FM Cleveland because Transcontinental had not held the property for three years. This property, therefore, was retained by Northeastern

Pennsylvania Broadcasting, Incorporated, a long-time Transcontinental subsidiary. It is not surprising, then, to learn that shortly after this station had been held the requisite three years it was quietly sold for a profit of approximately $780,000.[12]

As the number of purchasable choice stations in the major markets diminishes, pressures mount on owners to sell. Concrete evidence is reflected in the record prices recently paid. Cox Broadcasting Corporation, a publishing-broadcasting chain, paid $20.5 million for WIIC (TV) Pittsburgh (FCC approved November 20, 1964). WIIC (TV) at the time had tangible assets of only $3.8 million. A major AM-FM-TV chain, Storer Broadcasting, in 1962 paid $10.95 million in cash for radio station WHN (then WMGM) New York City. Westinghouse broadcasting stations, chain operator and manufacturer, paid $9.1 million in 1966 for KFWB Los Angeles in another high bid. Even prices for UHF stations have increased. The Sonderling radio chain bought WLKY-TV Louisville for $6.85 million in 1967.[13] An FM station, WRFM New York City, was sold (FCC approved May 11, 1966) to Worldwide, Incorporated, a subsidiary of the Mormon Church's Bonneville International Corporation broadcasting chain, for $850,000.

Capital gains tax laws stimulate station trading by permitting sellers to pay taxes on their sales at lower rates than they otherwise would. Court decisions which permit corporations to reduce taxes by expanding into allied enterprises also contribute to the turnover in broadcasting stations and to monopoly trends in all branches of our economy. There are also other laws which allow a licensee to deduct operating losses for tax purposes, even losses accumulated under previous ownerships, that motivate many to buy. Little has been written on the subject, but the practice of acquiring money-losing stations to gain tax write-off benefits on profits from other sources is widespread in radio broadcasting. The procedure works very simply. A businessman or industrialist whose income is quite high will buy a radio station that is losing money and will deduct these losses and depreciate the value of the station. He then sells it, usually for more than he paid, acquires another station to avoid paying taxes on the sale, and "the pattern begins all over again," in the words of Chairman Henry.[14] Even if the seller chooses not to buy another station his taxes on the sale are at the highly favorable capital gains rate.

At least two serious evils result from these tax evasion schemes.

Many stations with little public acceptance continue to occupy frequencies which might well be assigned to other broadcasters or other nonbroadcast users.[15] Secondly, these money-losing stations usually reduce advertising rates or give more commercial time for the same price in an effort to increase their income. Other stations, including those which have been offering better service in terms of more local news coverage, more live programs, and more editorial comment on local events, often attempt to meet the competition. As a result some of them reduce their services in an effort to pare costs. Soon the radio service of the entire city becomes diluted.[16]

The following FCC statistics are pertinent to the discussion. In 1965, 29.8 per cent of the radio stations in the United States reported operating at a loss. Taken as a group the AM and FM radio stations in 40 of 195 standard metropolitian statistical areas for which information was available operated at a loss during that year. In 87 nonmetropolitan areas with three or more stations the radio stations in 22 as a group lost money. And, finally, in none of the 19 standard metropolitian statistical areas with three or more FM stations did those stations as a group report earning a profit. Total losses ran as high as $405,324 for twenty-one AM and FM stations in Seattle-Everett, Wash., and $324,302 for six FM stations in New York City.[17]

Fear that television may increasingly fall victim to the "depreciable assets" racket which is damaging radio was expressed by Chairman Henry.[18] Unfortunately, the FCC has encouraged broadcasters and virtually anyone else willing to invest to enter UHF, as it had done and continues to do with unassigned FM channels. Financial data released by the FCC for 1966 show that despite total revenues for stations not owned by the networks of approximately $1,208,900,000 and income before taxes of $307,100,000, 101 of the 593 TV stations reporting operated at a loss. Further, 12.9 per cent of the 479 VHF and 34.2 per cent of the 114 UHF stations reported deficits for 1966.[19] Obviously conditions are ripe for the kind of increased transfers Chairman Henry fears.

Scandals: Quiz Shows, Payola, Plugola

Because the stakes are so high in television, networks, in pursuit of maximum audiences, are loath to experiment with program formats. Therefore, when a different idea attracts large audiences, dozens of slight variations on that theme soon saturate the tube. The public shortly loses interest and the search is on for a new crowd-pleaser. The magic formula in 1955 was the quiz program. In typical show business fashion, some producers were not content to gamble on honest contests. They determined in advance the winners and losers based, of course, on the contestants' audience appeal. Viewers who vicariously struggled through weeks of torturous questions with their favorite contestant were unaware that often the tenseness, brow mopping, and faltering responses had been rehearsed to elicit maximum audience involvement.

By the spring of 1957, some of the less well-planned shows were discontinued. This was true especially of those whose jackpots paled in competition with the inflated prizes offered on "The $64,000 Question," "Twenty-One," and other leading shows. Even at that early date faint rumors of rigging were heard but almost universally rejected amid a chorus of assurances from network officials that the shows were honestly conducted. On August 28, 1958, however, the New York *World-Telegram & Sun* shattered viewers' hypnotic trance when it quoted a former "Twenty-One" top money winner as saying that the program producers had given him the answers. Finally, after almost two years of charges and denials, none of which attracted wide public attention, the quiz-show fixing scandal was in full public view.

Lesser shows, such as "Dotto" and "Big Surprise," had been more suspect than "Twenty-One." Both the sponsor and CBS announced on August 16 that they were canceling "Dotto" immediately. But "Twenty-One" bore the stamp of highest ethical standards, affixed by Charles Van Doren, an instructor at Columbia University, author of three books, the offspring of a family of historians, biographers, and novelists. He had been heralded as TV's Socrates for fourteen weeks. Even academicians voiced pride in respect gained for "egghead" professors by Van Doren's seeming brilliance.

Testimony given at the subcommittee hearings, under the chairmanship of Representative Oren Harris, made clear that rigging was widespread and had been since the earliest network quiz programs went on the air.[20] Finally, the big money quiz shows with their highly publicized but not always paid jackpots [21] were forsaken by a public which became incensed at being duped and by sponsors who wanted to extricate themselves from unfavorable publicity, especially after audience interest had waned.

Were those who perpetrated this fraud punished—the network executives, the program producers,[22] the sponsors, the cooperative contestants? No, only the guilty contestants really suffered. In addition to irreparable damage to their reputations and careers, several of them received suspended sentences for lying to a New York grand jury.[23] Unfortunately, the many contestants who were not involved in the rigging and were unaware of it were deemed guilty by association.[24]

Congressmen while investigating quiz-show rigging unearthed another malpractice that was even more extensive and of much longer duration—payola. Record manufacturers and distributors paid radio and television disk jockeys to play selected records and falsify their popularity. Compensation was made in such forms as under-the-counter cash payments, gifts of stock in record companies, assignments of copyrights of songs, and percentage shares in profits. In a sense payola to disk jockeys was an extension of the 1920's practice of paying vaudeville performers to plug songs; in the 1930's and early 1940's orchestra leaders often received stock in music publishing houses in exchange for popularizing the publishers' songs.

The Harris subcommittee in May 1960, revealed that $263,245 in payola had been given to 207 disk jockeys working for stations in 42 different cities.[25] This probably was merely a fraction of the payola involved.[26] It certainly did not include the amounts Dick Clark earned from his record company and other interests. The New York *Times* in April 1960, reported that Clark had received over a twenty-seven-month period $576,770 in salary and increased value of his stock from his holdings in thirty-three companies. Clark owned interests in three record companies, a record distributing company, a record pressing company, an artists' management company, copyrights to 162 songs, and many other music-related enterprises. Eleven records by Duane Eddy, a rock 'n roll singer under the management of Clark's firm, were played by Clark on his "American Bandstand" 240 times in twenty-seven months, topping the 173 times nineteen records of rock 'n roll originator Elvis Presley were played. Records by such other popular singers as Bing Crosby were played once, Perry

Como, 4 times, and Frank Sinatra, none, during the period. Incidentally, Clark also owned a 25 per cent interest in the company that pressed the Eddy records.

Congressman John E. Moss (D-Calif.) estimated that Clark probably would owe ABC $25 million were he required to pay for plugs he gave records in which he had a financial interest.[27] Clark shows were at the time estimated to gross $12 million for ABC. Is it any wonder that ABC came to his defense and continued his program on ABC television daily for another seven years?

Congress in 1960 passed legislation making quiz-rigging and payola illegal, with maximum punishment of a year in prison and a $10,000 fine. Incidentally, payola and plugola were in violation of FCC rules adopted almost twenty-five years earlier.[28] Since the big-money quiz programs have gone off the air, concern about rigging quiz shows has abated. However, rumors persist that payola is still widely practiced. The FCC in almost unprecedented actions held closed-door hearings in Los Angeles during June–July 1966 and New York in January 1967, to investigate "alleged widespread payola activities among certain record companies and rock 'n roll stations." [29] These hearings were an outgrowth of an eighteen-month FCC investigation into payola.[30] As a result, the FCC threatened licensee Crowell-Collier Broadcasting corporation with sanctions against its KFWB Los Angeles station. However, the commission relented and granted approval of Crowell-Collier's sale of the station to Westinghouse Broadcasting Company, December 9, 1966.[31]

A kissing cousin of payola and plugola, also surfaced while congressmen were looking into the muck of the quiz-scandal cesspool. Plugs for a client's products and services made on programs not sponsored by him, for which the client paid persons appearing on or involved in producing various radio and television programs, has been a long-standing promotional technique. Automobile manufacturers pay to have entertainers and other prominent persons seen in their cars; [32] airlines pay for the statement "travel arrangements on . . . show are arranged by . . . airlines"; clothing manufacturers pay for wardrobe credits, and so on. The practice of receiving pay for plugs was widespread in vaudeville where, for example, touring entertainers would mention the hotel where they were staying. Car manufacturers have for years bid to have their automobiles selected as gangster get-away cars in movies. Gossip columnists continue to drop names of promising starlets for fee or favor. And those who are skilled at placing a client's name or picture of his product in a national magazine or a large newspaper are highly paid.

Companies have been formed that specialize in bribing radio and television personnel to mention products and services. "Some of the country's largest and most reputable companies" engage in plugola, wrote Jack Gould, *New York Times* columnist.[33] The FCC can take action against broadcasting personnel engaged in plugola under the 1960 act. But the harried, underbudgeted, pressure-sensitive FCC hasn't the manpower even if it had the inclination to police the industry.

The concern here with quiz-show rigging, payola, and plugola is that these manifestations of corporate behavior in pursuit of profits cheat the viewing and listening public in many ways. All three malpractices have deprived us of access to the creative talents of those who refuse to stoop to deceit, trickery, and unethical practices. In addition, the trio of vices has quickened the monopolistic[34] trend that favors the less skilled but less scrupulous and, thereby, have further debased mass communications. Perhaps most serious of all, modes of conduct rampant in business and industry are first abhorred and then adopted by a society that has been taught to revere unrestrained free enterprise. The effect on our moral standards is incalculable.

The Rating Game

Radio and television need some method by which they can determine the size of their audiences. Obviously, no system as precise as that used by the Audit Bureau of Circulation to provide certified, audited circulation data on member newspapers and magazines is available to broadcasting. Yet advertisers want information on the audience size for programs on both the network and individual stations. Several measurement services have been established to provide for this need. Reports of a few of them have gained high credibility among advertising agency personnel, advertisers, broadcasters, and the general public. The most successful has been the A. C. Nielsen Company of Chicago.

Techniques used in drawing samples and collecting, analyzing, and interpreting data had remained carefully guarded secrets until Representative Oren Harris of the House subcommittee of the Committee on Interstate and Foreign Commerce held hearings in 1963–64. Many weaknesses were found in virtually all of the rating services, so many, in fact, that a careful reading of the four-part report, *Broadcast Ratings*, leads one to surmise that the research on which various listening-viewing reports are based is open to serious question.

Before summarizing some of the pertinent evidence from these hearings, however, let us first consider why the work of broadcast rating services merits serious examination by those concerned with preserving our basic freedoms. First, rating services' reports determine which network programs Americans may view. If a program scores much lower than 20 on a national Nielsen survey, it is in dire danger of being canceled. Such important programs as "Playhouse 90," "The Firestone Hour," "See It Now," "You Are There," "Omnibus," to name but a few, have succumbed to what is flippantly called "the numbers game." A few of these programs have been killed even though advertisers were willing and, indeed, anxious to continue them.

Secondly, television rating reports which lead to predictions of mammoth audiences have lured advertisers away from other of the mass media. Several important magazines have ceased publication and newspapers, especially in large cities, have lost or failed to gain advertising needed for success. But the most serious loser has been radio, both individual stations and the networks. The most successful television rating surveys that also conduct surveys for radio have, possibly not by design, grossly underestimated radio listening. As a consequence many advertisers assume that radio is no longer a good advertising buy. Underestimates of radio audiences result primarily from the inherent difficulty in measuring automobile and transistor radio listening. A few broadcast rating companies have attempted to overcome these weaknesses, with varying degrees of unsuccess.

Finally, a concerted effort had been made by the largest of the rating services, Nielsen, to eliminate the others, as evidenced by letters and testimony introduced in the Harris subcommittee hearings.[35] Robert E. L. Richardson, associate counsel, summarized part of this evidence in a question

MR. RICHARDSON. Mr. Seiler, according to the testimony yesterday and according to your knowledge of this business, knowing, for example, that Nielsen bought out the only competitor it had in 1950, Hooper; that it forced Sindlinger to quit operating with its metering device; and that through its patent infringement suit with ARB which caused, at least partially, ARB to stop its syndicated service, would you state that Nielsen has been successful in keeping a virtual monopoly in the television network rating business?

MR. SEILER (James W., American Research Bureau, C-E-I-R Inc.). Up until now, yes, sir.[36]

Concern here is not necessarily with relying on audience sizes to determine which programs succeed, although strong arguments exist to oppose always giving the public what it says it wants. Rather the point is that although the research methodologies of virtually all rating services were shown to be highly unscientific, their ratings continue to determine 1] who and what will grace the TV screen, 2] program formats for the bulk of network entertainment shows, 3] whether a fifth rerun of "I Love Lucy" or a Senate subcommittee hearing on vital issues concerned with national survival will flow through the CBS TV network, and, on a local level, 4] whether loud music and yelling announcers will dominate the radio spectrum. It doesn't matter how popular a network program is, if it does not score high on the major rating surveys, it almost invariably dies for lack of sponsorship.

Advertising agency personnel, entertainers, network officials, station owners, program syndicators all agree that a point or two difference on an accepted rating survey could mean thousands of dollars, gained or lost, for the network or station. Advertising agency officials say they buy radio and television time periods, stations, and programs on the basis of rating points, even taking into consideration fractions of points. This obviously is rank misuse of rating report information. Were the reports not so badly misinterpreted at least some of the criticism aimed at those preparing the reports would be blunted.

HEARINGS SHOW RATINGS TO BE FAULTY

Evidence presented before the Harris subcommittee [37] disclosed numerous serious deficiencies in all but one of the audience measurement services. A number of these weaknesses will be mentioned here,[38] but the point should be made that these hearings were conducted largely before mid-year, 1963. Some of these deficiencies may have been corrected, although little has appeared in the trade press to assure us of this.

Robert S. Conlan Associates, Incorporated, claimed to have hired telephone interviewers for surveys that those interviewers denied having conducted. This and other evidence led the subcommittee to conclude that reports on radio audiences were issued when in fact no interviews were conducted.[39]

Videodex, Incorporated, claimed to be operating as an Illinois corporation when in fact the company had been involuntarily dissolved in the state of Illinois, January 4, 1954, and voluntarily dissolved in the state of New York, June 16, 1954. Subcommittee investigators complained that Videodex gave them the "run-around" to such an extent that they were unable to locate any recent program diaries, although the rating service allegedly was based on diaries.[40]

Reports by American Research Bureau, division of C-E-I-R, Incorporated, were described by a Federal Trade Commissioner as being a guess at best. And the ARB director admitted the ratings given in metro (local) markets meant little in terms of station audience sizes. Yet advertisers and television station managers and owners testified that a minute metro rating difference would greatly affect advertising revenue. The Federal Trade Commission issued a cease-and-desist order to ARB (FTC docket C-289) requiring ARB to refrain from saying in its published reports that respondent data presented were based on other than estimates and that data were based on probability samples without properly qualifying the term "probability sample."[41]

C. E. Hooper, Incorporated, was criticized for prorating listening percentages based on listening patterns received from telephone calls completed to all calls made—those not answering and refusals. Hooper also was criticized for inflating sample sizes printed in its reports.[42] The only one of the rating services generally exonerated in the hearings was Sindlinger and Company, Incorporated. That firm reportedly used the telephone recall technique based on a minimum sample of seven thousand.[43]

Trendex was criticized for, among other things, issuing audience data based on samples smaller than the number of stations in the market; in Charlotte, N.C., ratings of eight radio stations were based on as few as six listeners. Trendex also was accused of encouraging "hypoing" by informing subscribers when surveys were to be conducted. Thus their clients could, and many did, conduct contests and other special promotionals during the rating period in an effort to increase audience sizes.[44]

Among weaknesses in The Pulse, Incorporated, work were these: "not at homes" were included in the sample; several questionable adjustments were made in the survey results, including weightings which the subcommittee staff said followed no discernible pattern; interviews were not always done in the areas prescribed by the home office; and interviews, at least in one market, were done outside the B contour of the television stations surveyed. A Federal Trade Commission cease-and-desist order (docket C-291, December 28, 1962) ordered Pulse to reflect these and other weaknesses in its reports. The subcommittee staff conducted a field investigation of the work of various of the rating services in Louisville. Pulse interviewers, following faulty central office instructions, conducted interviews over a four-year period in Winchester, Ky., eighty miles from Louisville, and Prestonburg, Ky., 160 miles from Louisville, for data for at least eight "metropolitan Louisville" television surveys. Herbert Arkin, statistical consultant to the subcommittee, criticized some of the Pulse ratings as being "not better than nothing." In reference to Pulse, subcommittee Chairman Harris said "This appears to me to be a con game." [45]

Committee investigators trained their biggest guns on the giant of the audience measurement service, A. C. Nielsen Company.[46] As with the other audience measurement firms, weaknesses revealed in the subcommittee hearings on Nielsen operations are too numerous to detail here—subcommittee counsel and members quizzed Nielsen executives, other employees, and former Nielsen employees during ten days of hearings. More than seven hundred pages of testimony and evidence, virtually all of Part 3 of *Broadcasting Ratings*, concerned the Nielsen company.[47] Many of its weaknesses are cited in the following list.

1] Nielsen samples were small. Two national audimeter [48] samples were used to compile data for the national Nielsen Television Index, approximately twelve hundred homes, and the Nielsen Radio Index, approximately one thousand homes. On the average 10 per

cent of the audimeters were said to be inoperative at any given time. Local radio and television samples, from which the data for Nielsen Station Index reports were compiled, averaged 175 to two hundred homes.[49]

2] The national sample was out of date. The one used in 1963 was based largely on 1940 census data with modifications. Nielsen's chief statistical officer admitted that Nielsen would not revise its national audimeter sample to base it on 1960 census information until around 1970, at the rate preparations for this changeover were being made.

3] Randomness, so carefully built into selecting each home in which the audimeter was to be placed, was badly violated; few randomly selected homes appeared in the sample. Three former fieldmen, whose jobs required that they place audimeters, said they called on an average of six to ten homes to place an audimeter. One former employee said he called on four hundred homes before placing one audimeter.

4] Because randomness in selecting the sample was violated and other errors committed, the Federal Trade Commission ordered Nielsen to cease-and-desist from implying that "its measurements, data, or reports are based upon a probability sample." The order specified that certain other claims to preciseness in ratings not be made.[50]

5] The subcommittee staff found evidences of oversampling certain demographic characteristics.

6] The Nielsen company used a sample which was fairly static, that is, many homes were continued in the sample over long periods of time. Some had been in the sample since 1945 and quite a number for ten years or longer. Nielsen officials said they went to great lengths to prevent others from learning which homes were in the national audimeter sample, to avert "tampering" by those who might wish to influence ratings. Subcommittee staff members learned the names and addresses of fifty-three Nielsen audimeter homes, enough if "influenced" to alter national network program ratings by five points.

Further, three former Nielsen fieldworkers testified that virtually all, if not all, of the forty Nielsen fieldmen would sell anyone a list of their audimeter homes for, say, $25,000. One, Eugene Davis, said he could locate all twelve hundred audimeter homes in the national sample for $100,000, and "would make a real good stab at getting 1,200" for $50,000.

Nielsen filed a $1.5 million damage suit in March 1966, against Rex Sparger, former special assistant to the subcommittee, charging him with stealing trade secrets for his own financial gain. Nielsen alleged that Sparger had learned the location of fifty-eight audimeter homes. Sparger told the Oklahoma City *Times,* March 25, 1966, that he had learned the location of "considerably more" than fifty-eight homes and had rigged Nielsen ratings on four network shows, including the "Bob Hope Vietnam Special," a program which won the highest rating ever for a show of its type.[51] Nielsen dropped the charges against Sparger on September 2, 1966, after Sparger signed a consent order in which, among other things, he promised not to further influence Nielsen samples, use information gained, or make damaging statements about the Nielsen system.[52]

7] Fieldmen more often than randomness would justify placed meters (audimeters and recordimeters [53]) in apartment building superintendents' apartments.

8] UHF television stations were undersampled. A former fieldman said it took longer to attach a meter to a UHF than to a VHF receiver.

9] Sample sizes in reports were misrepresented (inflated) prior to a Federal Trade Commission cease-and-desist order, issued December 28, 1962.[54] Incidentally, the FTC ordered the Nielsen Company, among other things, to quit saying or implying that "its measurements, data or reports are . . . other than estimates . . ."

10] One of Nielsen's major national television survey selling points was and is that survey results are based on the precise measuring characteristics of the audimeter. Thus recall, failure to report, not at homes, reporting errors, and the like are eliminated. However, there were problems connected with the use of this instrument. The company attempted to check the accuracy of audimeters by requiring that fieldmen run test film strips on each audimeter periodically. Three former fieldmen testified that they sometimes instead ran the required test strip checks on audimeters in their own homes and represented them to the company as having been run on audimeters in the radio-television sample. They said this faking of audimeter checks was "widespread."

Although Nielsen discontinued measuring national radio audiences after these hearings, information from the hearings relative to that firm's radio audience measuring practices is included here to illustrate the methods of the operation. The same former fieldmen testified also that it was general practice among fieldmen to adjust audimeters so radio listening on a wide band of stations (up to ten stations over a range of up to 450 kilocycles) would be recorded as listening to a single station.

They said the audimeter cams were sometimes adjusted so the meter would not record all of the radio stations in a metropolitan area. A former New York City fieldman said he calibrated audimeters in that city for fifteen stations when in fact thirty-nine stations were broadcasting in the market. He added that he did not calibrate the same stations in every home. These and other steps were taken, the fieldmen said, in an effort to improve "usable returns" from their territories. Promotions and pay increases were based on the "quality" of their work. Hence, the poorly paid fieldmen often resorted to various makeshifts to reduce unidentified radio listening and rejected diaries.

11] Fieldmen testified that they and others "quite frequently" instructed those in the diary sample to write in the front and back of the diary that the radio was broken or not in use, thus reducing the possibility of errors in completing the diary. Such diaries were counted as "good" and fieldmen given credit toward the par of 77 per cent usable diaries. (The subcommittee associate counsel, Richardson, said that about a third of the Nielsen diaries he had examined were blank on radio.)

12] In a local radio study (Louisville, June and July 1961) thirty-nine diaries were not counted because the diary keepers skipped a day or erred in some other way. Yet when the completed data from these diaries were included in the results, the station Nielsen had rated first (a Nielsen subscriber) became third, and the station rated third (not a subscriber) became first.

13] The subcommittee counsel learned that diaries often were edited and sometimes in what he regarded as questionable ways.

14] The radio report for Louisville was based on 87 homes, although language in the report gave the figure of at least 150 different homes and an average "base-case" of 2,590 for Monday-Friday. Further, of the 87 homes, 10.7 per cent on the average were listening to radio across the day—an average of nine homes; ten commercial AM radio stations are located in the metropolitan Louisville area. Nielsen officials admitted that all stations in the Louisville report fell within statistical variance at two sigmas[55] and "at this level I don't believe you could call it (station audience measurements reported) anything else (but a calculated guess) . . . it is of very little value."

15] Sometimes the number of homes reported in breakouts were fewer than the number of stations in a market. Reports on New York City listening, for example, were based on 365 audimeters with only 10 per cent on the average reporting listening (36 homes in 17 counties) to measure listening to 39 AM stations.

16] For some local radio markets Nielsen received only 60 per cent usable returns (diaries).

17] Nielsen policy excluded radio stations outside a metropolitan area regardless of the level of their audience if those stations did not provide a "unique service"—Los Angeles stations received in San Diego, for example.

18] Nielsen began a special car-radio and transistor listening service in mid-1962, built on the company's national radio sample. However, in these surveys only the amount of listening was tabulated, not stations or networks. This listening time was then prorated among the networks in proportion to the regular in-home listening of the respondent's family. Auto-listening data collected in national studies were broken down into time zones and equated to the number of automobiles registered in each metropolitan area. These results were then included in radio ratings for individual metropolitan markets.

19] The three fieldmen who testified at the hearings estimated that only 30 to 50 per cent of the plug-in radio sets in recordimeter homes were metered. They added that owners often refused to permit them to place recordimeters on the newer and more expensive sets, apparently fearing the meter might damage the sets. They surmised that considerable listening was thus not measured.

20] The fieldmen testified that many recordimeters were placed on sets of friends and relatives of other recordimeter and audimeter families. In St. Louis a fieldman asked for volunteers at a Parent-Teacher Association meeting. Nielsen company learned of

this approximately a year after the recordimeters were placed in service.

21] The subcommittee staff concluded that "The recordimeter, as far as its being used as a check on the accuracy of data in radio is concerned, does more harm than it does good." The three fieldmen agreed that the audilogs-recordimeters do not measure correctly or adequately.

22] Possibly the most telling blow was the introduction by the subcommittee counsel of a confidential letter addressed to the chairman of the Nielsen board by a Nielsen vice-president and chief statistical officer which, among other things, said, "These governmental investigations were trying because we preferred not to let these people learn and publish some of our vital weaknesses."

Despite the highly damaging evidence the Harris subcommittee developed, the subcommittee's final report, issued January 23, 1966, just prior to Representative Harris' retirement from the House, opposed government supervision of broadcast rating companies as a possible corrective measure and advised against legislative action against that industry. Instead, the report suggested that the Broadcast Rating Council, the audience measurement services, and the Office of Statistical Standards of the United States Budget Bureau work closely to improve sampling methodology.

Subcommittee members apparently were impressed by the work of the Broadcast Rating Council, established by the National Association of Broadcasters to certify rating firms. The council, however, determines merely if an audience-measurement service "does what it says it does." It does not certify that ratings are accurate. Other committees have been formed to study the rating services since the subcommittee hearings, one of which was the Committee on Nationwide Television Audience Measurements. That committee, formed by the three television networks, essentially cleared the rating services of wrongdoing. They did, however, point to some minor problems, such as significantly inflated ratings caused by cooperator bias. But they said this rarely would change the rank order of the programs rated. Obviously, inflated television ratings would work to the disadvantage of the other media by overestimating television audience sizes, a weakness which does not displease television network officials.

Competition among television rating services has become more spirited, with each company guaranteed a freer access to use of meters and less pressure from Nielsen, due to the restraints imposed by the FTC cease-and-desist order, issued October 23, 1963, docket C-613. In addition to Nielsen, Pulse, Sindlinger, and American Research Bureau conduct television surveys. And the directors of the Audit Bureau of Circulations has set up a new affiliated corporation, the Audit Bureau of Marketing Services, "which will explore the expansion of the ABC's traditional print auditing role to other media, possibly including broadcasting." [56] Also, various attempts are being made to measure both AM and FM radio more effectively, even including the use of electronic devices.

Recent public disclosures, however, suggest that broadcasting ratings are still unreliable. Nielsen and ARB results in 1967 differed as much as 20 percentage points.[57] Hypoing of ratings, the seemingly insolvable broadcasting problem, continues now as for several decades to haunt radio and television. WNEW-TV New York, a Metromedia station, in 1966 hired a Metromedia subsidiary, O. E. McIntyre direct-mail firm, to send a number to two million New York area residents, informing them that if they saw their number on WNEW-TV they could win a prize. The contest was scheduled for a period when Nielsen and ARB were surveying. And worse, both Nielsen and ARB drew their samples from lists supplied by O. E. McIntyre Company.[58] In what was probably the first such court case, WPOP Hartford filed a $500,000 damages suit against WDRC Hartford, charging that that station from September 1965 to March 23, 1966, urged people through radio and newspaper advertising not to say "hello" when answering the telephone but to say "I am listening to WDRC radio . . . big D in Hartford." Prizes were awarded to those responding in this manner to periodic calls placed by WDRC personnel. The objective, the plaintive charged, was to inflate rating figures on WDRC listening. In years past this and other hypoing techniques have been used in an estimated 90 per cent of the markets during rating surveys.[59]

One might wonder why clients of the audience measurement services use information so fraught with weaknesses. An obvious answer is that nothing better is available. If this be true, why don't those who spend millions annually with these services demand a better product? They have, of course, obtained some improvements. Nielsen no longer attempts to measure national radio, Conlan quit the business, committees have been formed to study the operations of the rating services. Granted then some improvements have been made since the Harris subcommittee hearings of 1963–64. It becomes obvious, however, that those who utilize the television rating reports benefit financially from them, regardless of their accuracy. Network officials really don't care which of their programs have high ratings as long as reports indicate that television attracts huge viewing audiences. They can replace low-rated programs with new ones based on formats the services report are attracting large followings. And despite temporary inconveniences, the networks continue to amass large fortunes. To put it bluntly, the rating reports sell advertising.

The large advertising agencies funnel as much as 80 per cent of their domestic billings into television.[60] Why? Agency executives would rationalize by arguing that TV sells more efficiently. This may be true, but another reason agencies concentrate on television is that agencies earn higher profits on their TV billing. In some agencies the net profit is six times greater for television than for the print media. Gerald T. Arthur, former senior vice-president in charge of media for Donahue & Coe, Incorporated (now known as West, Weir and Bartel, Incorporated), New York advertising agency, told the Senate Antitrust subcommittee June 2, 1966, ". . . it takes up to $6 of print media to equal $1 of television billing." Thus he explained why "agencies that are heavy percentage-wise in broadcast billings, particularly network billings, have a greater profit ratio than those that have the majority of billings in print." [61] It becomes rather obvious that advertising agencies find TV rating reports highly useful in justifying 1] spending clients' budgets in television and 2] placing advertising on particular shows.

Obviously, rating results are highly useful to those most vitally interested. It is, then, small wonder that the network committee that investigated rating services exonerated them. Nor is it surprising that executives of the six major advertising agencies (that reportedly bill $750 million a year in television) when interviewed by a Los Angeles *Times* staff member shortly after Sparger announced he had tampered with Nielsen ratings said they would continue to use the Nielsen ratings. Some comments quoted in the *Times* article are interesting.

How would we get information without Nielsen? We have to have audience information and Nielsen dominates the field.—J. Walter Thompson official.

Nielsen is the only source of information on network television on a weekly basis. We have to continue using it.—Ted Bates & Co. officer.

If Nielsen were thrown out we would all be in the jungle for a couple of years until we figured something else. It would be chaos.—John Allen, a vice president of McCann-Erickson, Inc.[62]

But what about the advertising departments of advertising agency clients? They, too, need to justify advertising allocations. Ratings serve their purpose. The net result, however, has been disasterous to the professional careers of countless performers, writers, and independent program producers. More important, the great bulk of TV programming has reached a low qualitative level, a pall of sameness which former FCC Chairman Newton N. Minow characterized as a "vast wasteland."[63] The real sufferers, then, are those who have invested most heavily in money and time, the American people who have been deprived of the benefits television could provide were it not solely the instrument of business and industry.

Broadcasting Networks Dominate Programming

9.

What broadcasting is today it owes to the national networks. Both credit for thousands of hours of news and entertainment and blame for the low quality of much of it, interspersed with millions of raucous commercials, is theirs. But perhaps the greatest network sin is coercing affiliates to settle for trivia. In television, as was true in radio prior to the networks' decline, local programming is virtually nonexistent, local voices are stilled. The point must be made, however, that the few locally produced programs on most television stations contain no local talent, present no local flavor, and often are copies of cheap network fare, not so well presented. Networks have, of course, contributed to this sorry state of affairs by killing local initiative.

What America sees is determined by three men in New York, according to a charge repeatedly made and most recently by President Lyndon B. Johnson.[1] In a sense this is true, but in reality it is the few men deputized by broadcasting's oligarchy who make these decisions, with, of course, their bosses exercising veto power whenever they wish. The networks have stifled competition, used their tools to propagandize for and against causes, formed large holding corporations which supply their own needs, built industrial empires whose tentacles penetrate every sphere of commerce; they wield tremendous political influence, wheedle from government rights and concessions private citizens could not hope to win, pressure public opinion to do their bidding—the charges are endless. In a word, networks are far too powerful for the good of the United States.

A brief look at the founding of Radio Corporation of America helps identify the roots of the problem. RCA was formed in 1919 by

General Electric, Westinghouse, and American Telephone and Telegraph through its Western Electric subsidiary.[2] They banded together to form a radio-communications cartel whereby they 1] would "patriotically" displace British Marconi from domination of American communications,[3] 2] form a repository for radio and other patents, 3] enter into cross-licensing on these patents, and 4] divide the communications spoils. GE and Westinghouse were granted a monopoly to manufacture sets which RCA would sell. AT & T was given the exclusive right to manufacture, lease, and sell radio transmitters.

However, they had not anticipated the formation of networks. AT & T and RCA fought over this plum. To her WEAF New York station AT & T, on January 4, 1923, tied WNAC Boston for the first network link. Shortly, the AT & T Washington, D.C., station was added. Growth was rapid; by 1924 AT & T had a 23-station national network. When RCA began forming a network, AT & T fought back, denying RCA the right to broadcast commercials and to use AT & T lines. This resulted in AT & T owning the dominant network.

However, AT & T and RCA, in true corporate spirit, reached an agreement in 1926 whereby AT & T would be given a monopoly over wire transmission facilities in exchange for abandoning network operations to RCA. AT & T sold its headquarters station, WEAF, to RCA for one million dollars, transferred its other radio holdings to its coconspirators (RCA, Westinghouse, and GE), and settled back to earn huge profits by leasing its telephone lines to RCA and other networks as they were formed. RCA, on September 9, 1926, formed NBC as its broadcasting subsidiary, which on November 15 launched amid much publicity its twenty-one-station network. Four nonaffiliated stations carried parts of the four-hour program, one as far west as Kansas City, Mo.

NBC had not one, but two networks, designated by its engineers as Red and Blue. By January 1, 1927, the fifteen-city Red network had stretched coast-to-coast to carry the Rose Bowl football game (Stanford and Alabama tied, 7–7). Two years later regular coast-to-coast programming came, December 23, 1928, when there were fifty-eight stations in the network. NBC exploited her advantage, buying stations in the largest cities and affiliating with the most powerful and best-located stations elsewhere. Thus for years she dominated chain broadcasting. Finally, in 1943, the federal government forced NBC to sell one of its chains; she chose to sell the weaker Blue network.

Radio stations not affiliated with NBC were hard pressed to compete. So when United Independent Broadcasters, Incorporated, was formed on January 27, 1927, it had little difficulty lining up sixteen affiliates. After weathering early financial crises, the firm adopted the name Columbia Broadcasting System and began its competitive fight for survival. In 1928 controlling interest was bought by William S. Paley and his family, owners of the Congress Cigar Company. The Paley family still controls CBS.[4]

A third radio network, the Mutual Broadcasting System, evolved from an agreement, in 1934, among stations WGN Chicago, WLW Cincinnati, WXYZ Detroit, and WOR New York to offer an advertising sales package. The station-owned chain became a coast-to-coast network in 1936, but has been hampered by financial problems throughout its history despite the large number of affiliates (more than five hundred, mostly low-powered stations) utilizing what now is largely a news feed. In 1960 the Minnesota Mining and Manufacturing Company bought the scandal-ridden[5] system for $1.3 million and operated MBS until July 1, 1966, when 3M Company, shortly after being fined $190,000 on charges of unfair trade practices, sold it for $3.1 million. The new owners were the seventh in nine years.[6] The principal interest is held by L. M. Berry & Company, Dayton, Ohio, a firm which operates several small telephone exchanges and a nationwide telephone directory advertising company.[7] In contrast to the other networks, MBS has never owned radio or television stations nor has it developed a television network. However, the new owners have said they wish to expand by acquiring radio and television stations and community antenna television systems.

American Broadcasting System bought the NBC Blue Network in 1943 for $8 million after the federal government in December 1941, had ordered NBC to sell. On October 12, 1943, the FCC approved transfer of three Blue-owned stations. The name was changed shortly to American Broadcasting Company. On May 23, 1951, United Paramount Theaters, Incorporated, announced purchase of ABC for $25 million. Thus, Leonard Goldenson, UPT president, assumed control of what became American Broadcasting-Paramount Theaters, Incorporated. The argument that persuaded the FCC to approve the sale was repeated in 1966 and 1967: The transaction will provide ABC with vitally needed capital so it can compete more successfully with NBC and CBS.[8] In 1965 AB-PT reverted to ABC shortly before another merger was announced. Again, the FCC, flouting the advice of the Department of Justice, several congressmen, and some of its own staff members,[9] approved ABC's merger into another corporation. This time it was International Telephone and Telegraph, a giant international holding company, of which 6.85 per cent is owned by foreign interests.[10]

Enter Television

NBC on October 27, 1945, linked WNBT New York with WRGB Schenectady and WPTZ (TV) Philadelphia for its first network telecast, the appearance of President Harry S. Truman at a Navy Day celebration in New York. Several NBC programs, including major boxing matches and football games, were carried over a four-station network in 1946. The network added stations as new ones went on the air and, by 1948, was offering such programming as "The Milton Berle Show," "Howdy Doody," "Kraft Television Theater," "Voice of Firestone," "Philco Television Playhouse," the NBC Symphony, the World Series, and the national political conventions.[11] NBC's two present competitors began trying to catch up. In 1948, ABC signed the first of its television affiliates, WFIL-TV Philadelphia, March 22, and linked it to its WRGB Schenectady;[12] CBS, on March 25, signed WCAB-TV Philadelphia and on March 29, WMAR-TV Baltimore to add to its New York headquarters station. Early CBS programming featured horse racing at Pimlico, the Preakness, and the Dixie Handicap.[13]

Both NBC and CBS supplied programs by tape to stations not directly linked, and as early as 1948, NBC serviced WLWT Cincinnati and WTVR Richmond and CBS WMAL-TV Washington with tapes.[14] By July 1, 1949, coaxial cable tied the four networks to stations as far west as Chicago and St. Louis; they then also had West Coast affiliates they served by tapes.[15] Cable and microwave links were completed in time for NBC to inaugurate coast-to-coast television service on September 4, 1951, when 52 affiliates, almost half of the 107 stations then on the air, carried activities of the Japanese Peace Treaty convention in San Francisco.[16] As of January 1, 1951, ABC had 67, CBS 61, Dumont 62, and NBC 63 stations. However, few of these were exclusive affiliates; most selected programs from two or more networks.[17]

Some Problems Arose

It is beyond the scope of this book to trace the history of these four radio and three television networks. Rather, let us consider some of the problems these vociferous chains have generated. Of major concern to Morris Ernst in his edition of *The First Freedom* was the tremendous power the networks exerted,[18] especially NBC and CBS. CBS has ceased its unprofitable electronic manufacturing, but RCA, owner of NBC, has expanded and is now, as it was then, a major defense contractor. Organized to sell receiver sets, the firm first entered manufacturing in 1930 through the old RCA Victor Company, Incorporated. After years of absorbing other companies, launching new ones, spinning off some, mostly under government pressure, RCA and its subsidiaries now manufacture

> AM and FM receivers, black and white and color television sets; computers, data processing systems; records, phonographs, magnetic tape, tape recorders; radio and television tubes and other components, television picture tubes for black and white and color sets; consumer, industrial, and computer semiconductors; microwave equipment; direct energy conversion devices; integrated circuits; aviation, communication, radar, and guided missile equipment; electronic printing equipment; radio and television broadcasting equipment; closed circuit television equipment; audio-visual equipment; marine and mobile communications, control, and automation equipment; electron microscopes; motion picture sound recording equipment; books, educational study aids, teaching machines; and much more.

Moody's Industrial Manual (Vol. 37, Nos. 3 to 79) listed government prime and subcontracts amounting to more than $120 million. RCA's major work was with ballistic missile early warning networks, other electronics equipment, and computers. The United States Air Force was the major purchaser.

One might ask, as many have, can we trust an industrial giant which enriches itself with military contracts to provide us with news? Surely the temptation to prolong the cold war, if not to encourage hot war, must be great. For this and other reasons, Harry J. Skornia, former president of the National Association of Educational Broadcasters, advocates divesting the television networks of their non-broadcasting activities.[19]

As if having one huge electronics-defense-communications combine determining what we may hear is not sufficient disregard for peoples' rights, the FCC on December 21, 1966 approved, 4–3,[20] a second such conglomerate corporation—the absorption of ABC into International Telephone and Telegraph[21] in a $350 million stock transaction.[22] Not only is ITT a major international defense contractor, it derives 40 per cent of its domestic income from defense and space contracts and receives 60 per cent of its total income ($1.8 billion in 1965 from sales in 118 countries) from foreign sources. Prior to the purchase, ITT ranked forty-first among world and thirtieth among United States corporations. Its assets included plants and facilities in two hundred United States cities and towns in all fifty states.[23]

(Although the ITT on January 1, 1968 canceled its proposed merger with ABC in the face of Department of Justice court actions,[24] the fact that the FCC twice approved such a merger raises serious questions about the entire regulatory machinery of government. Hence, the merger is discussed at considerable length here.)

The FCC was involved in the decision only to the extent of approving transfer of licenses for seventeen radio and television stations, the largest such transfer ever approved by the Commission. Press reports suggest that no concern was shown at the FCC with such potential conflicts of interests as ABC's president holding a directorship in Western Union and Western Union's chairman holding a directorship in ABC; cross directorships with other corporations holding broadcasting properties; ABC's being bought by one of its important suppliers which thereby would create an RCA-NBC type of protected market.

The FCC, by the same 4–3 vote, affirmed its December decision on June 22, 1967, despite testimony during a hearing instituted by the Justice Department in April when incontrovertible evidence was presented showing that ABC did not need the financial support of ITT.[25] Justice's case was so persuasive that Thomas B. Fitzpatrick, chief of the Broadcast Bureau, the bureau assigned by the FCC to hear the testimony, concluded that ABC in fact did not need ITT's financial underpinning, its ability to compete with CBS and NBC would "not materially" be enhanced by the proposed merger, and the public interest would not be served by the FCC's approving the merger.[26]

It might be asked, Did the yea-sayers hear Fitzpatrick's recommendations or read the transcript of the hearing? And if they did, with open minds? One of the central questions raised by Justice and of major concern here, the possibility of ITT exerting influence over ABC news operations, was dramatically exposed. Three reporters who were covering the hearings—Miss Eileen Shanahan, *New York Times*, Jed Stout, United Press International, and Stephen M. Aug, Associated Press—testified that ITT press officials had attempted to influence their stories, both by applying pressure on them and through their superiors.[27] What more evidence did Commissioners committed to the merger need to counter pious promises by ITT officials that they would not interfere in ABC news decisions? (We shall explore in Chapter 15 the matter of ownership influence on news.)

Interesting speculation as to the reason for such hasty approval has arisen. Application had been made less than nine months previously. It takes longer to get Commission approval to increase power on a small radio station.[28] Strong hints that the approval was politically motivated appeared in the press.[29] The initial vote, which freshman Commissioner Nicholas Johnson called "a foregone conclusion . . . from the outset," was taken only sixteen hours after the FCC received Assistant Attorney General Donald F. Turner's letter warning that anticompetitive consequences could result from the merger, but that the Department of Justice would bring no antitrust action. Turner, head of the department's Antitrust Division, cited ITT's $7 million investments in community antenna television systems and development of satellite communications and the likelihood that buying ABC would deter ITT from developing technology for competitive broadcasting systems: an interconnected CATV grid and direct satellite-to-home broadcasting. Turner also emphasized that ITT had the wherewithal to develop a fourth television network were it blocked from obtaining ABC. However, with the merger, ITT-ABC could exert pressure that might kill a fourth network. He urged the FCC to seriously consider "these anticompetitive possibilities." Obviously, little weight was given Turner's request. His letter was received after closing hours on Tuesday; the FCC voted at 10 A.M. on Wednesday. Apparently *Broadcasting* was correct when it said the majority "had been ready to act for months." [30]

What was FCC's reason for approving after only a cursory two-day public hearing at which only ABC, ITT, and FCC witnesses appeared and affirming despite evidence presented at the later hearing? To strengthen ABC competitively by giving it greater financial resources.[31] Apparently, however, the two corporate leaders had never discussed such assistance; prolonged Commission questioning was required before Goldenson could calculate, while testifying, ABC's need for $50 million over three years and ITT's agreement to provide the funds. Commissioner Johnson, quite correctly, emphasized that ABC was in a healthy financial condition and was perfectly capable of improving its facilities without outside financing.[32]

Possibly, the FCC was swayed by ABC's tear-jerking performance in July 1966, while "baring its financial bosom," to quote *Broadcasting*. Goldenson pleaded that ABC-TV, which earned $20.2 million on its network and owned-and-operated stations, received 18 per cent of total television network income for 1962. But in 1964 the network had lost $8.4 million while its stations earned only $21.9 million, leaving ABC a mere 9 per cent of the network income. Further, the ABC network lost $5.6 million and its stations earned only $25.5 million in 1965. How ABC reports its profits is of little concern; what is important is that ABC profits had dipped from a high of $20.2 million in 1962 to $11.6 million in 1963 (8.5 per cent of network earnings). However, the network rebounded in 1964 and 1965 with earnings of $13.5 million (8.6 per cent) and $19.9 million (12.3 per cent), respectively. Actually, while ABC's earnings and share of network earnings increased, both income and share of network income of NBC and CBS combined fell off in 1965.[33] ABC's profits from 1960 to 1966 were $125 million and in 1966 ABC's share of TV network revenues rose to 27 per cent.[34]

A major argument for selling to ITT was to gain funds needed to convert to color. Yet ABC already was transmitting its prime-evening entertainment schedule in color and had entered into a $25 million loan agreement with four banks to expand color facilities.[35] As for converting its five stations to color, Norman E. Cash, president of the TV Bureau of Advertising, estimates such costs at up to $250,000 per station, an insignificant expenditure for a company with profits of $19.9 million. If funds were so badly needed, ABC could have accepted some of the $5 million in advertising the radio network turned down in 1965[36] or plowed more of its 1965 profits into capital improvements. ABC in 1965 earned at the rate of $3.35 a share and paid $1.50 dividends, higher than ITT paid ($1.23 ¾).[37]

As Harold S. Geneen, chairman of the board and president of ITT told his stockholders, except for color retooling, growth in broadcasting is based on "very little capital."[38] Justice Department quizzing of ITT personnel, assistant attorney general Turner said, revealed ITT expected ABC's income to reach $100 million by 1970 or earlier, almost all of which would be available for reinvestment in nontelevision businesses.[39] ABC earned $15,565,000 after taxes in 1965; depreciated properties were valued at $17.5 million; thus earnings were 89 per cent, a rather healthy sick corporation.[40]

To argue that ABC could not effectively compete is reminiscent of the alibis and arguments so long offered the FCC, Congress, and the public by NBC and CBS, relative both to radio and television. When broadcasting's many sins were exposed the rejoinder was "we're so young," "ours is a young, struggling industry," and "don't upset the delicate financial balance of broadcasting, to do so threatens our democracy." It is a matter of record that ABC's share of audience, as proclaimed by the demigod the networks so gleefully quote, A. C. Nielsen Company, has increased to the point that it is not significantly different from that of NBC and CBS. For instance, for the period September 1966 to August 1967, Nielsen reported these prime viewing average audience ratings: CBS 18.0, NBC 17.8, and ABC 15.7.[41] Hertz, the largest car rental firm, sold to RCA in 1966; its number two competitor, Avis, an ITT subsidiary, was joining ABC. The networks could *give* these and other subsidiaries advertising without the matter ever being made public; their books are not open for inspection. Also, they may attempt to coerce suppliers into advertising with their networks, as the Justice Department has charged General Tire and Rubber Company with doing relative to its chain of radio and television stations.[42] And if ABC could not compete against CBS and NBC, how can a fourth national television network hope to succeed against these three well-entrenched, ruthless financial giants?

The most plausible reasons for the ABC sale, Geneen said, are ITT 1] needed to improve its image in the United States and 2] wished to expand its business here into more consumer areas so as to strike a 50–50 balance, United States to foreign income. As for ABC, the major value apparently accrues to its president, Leonard H. Goldenson, to whom ITT has offered an attractive five-year contract with lucrative stock option rights and incentive compensation.[43] In addition, the merger would bar plans of a rival, industrialist-magazine publisher Norton Simon, to assume control of ABC. Simon, the largest single shareholder (9 per cent of ABC stock), was blocked by Goldenson forces from a seat on the board of directors unless he obtained 50 per cent ownership. When an FCC commissioner asked Goldenson why he didn't sell stock to raise money, he replied that it would be "highly undesirable." No doubt. In addition to pay, Goldenson gained a $3,142,349.89 windfall on his ABC stock even prior to consummating the sale.[44]

For these selfish interests, Goldenson contracted to turn ABC's five television and six AM and six FM stations[45] over to an international holding corporation that already controlled 187 foreign companies and held minority interests in another eleven.[46] Accompanying the stations are 138 primary television and 348 basic radio affiliates, television and radio networks, 400 movie theaters, record manufacturers, International Telemeter Corporation (a pay-TV system), numerous feature length films, a television film distributing company, three farm publications, amusement centers, and other enterprises—a $400 million company.[47] ITT, which claims to be the world's largest manufacturer and supplier of electronics and telecommunications equipment, engages in international communications, defense and space work, automobile rentals, insurance, publishing, copper exploration, and other activities, including Press Wireless, Incorporated, a news service operating in sixty-five countries. (See Table 35, Appendix, for list of holdings.)

Investments of the proposed ABC-ITT conglomerate would exceed those of RCA.[48] ITT itself owns from 5 per cent to 49 per cent interests in forty broadcasting stations in twenty-six countries, concentrated mostly in Central and South America.[49] ABC controls Central American Television Network, Limited, and holds minority ownerships of television stations in twelve countries, seven of which are in Central and South America. ABC also owns News, Limited, an Australian newspaper-magazine publishing corporation, and has business relationships with television stations in ten other countries, of which five are in the Americas.[50]

Although all concerned denied that the merger would affect ABC's news and documentaries, even about foreign countries where ITT has major holdings, Commissioner Robert T. Bartley raised the specter of ABC as 13 per cent of the new entity, wishing not to damage the other 87 per cent.[51] Commissioner Johnson suggested pointedly that the reason NBC gave much greater coverage to the visit of Philippine President Ferdinand E. Marcos to the United States in 1966 than did CBS or ABC was because of RCA's "important interests" in the Philippines.[52] Little evidence exists to support the "self-righting" theory suggested by Geneen, whereby the news services and other networks would reveal any coloration of facts that ABC might be guilty of.[53]

Finally, what does approval of the transfer of five television stations, all VHF's and in the top seven markets, do to the FCC interim policy announced June 21, 1965, of designating for hearing any transfers that would result in anyone owning more than two VHF stations in the largest fifty markets? This policy had been ignored four times before in sales of single stations. But now the dam has broken; a rush by chain broadcasters to expand can be expected.

Regardless of finances, ABC has faced much the same problem that CBS overcame. NBC, the first to develop both radio and television networks, obtained the most desirable affiliates. CBS was often forced to take those unclaimed by NBC and with television to wait until second stations were built in many markets. Latecomer ABC has generally affiliated with what was left. Hence, NBC has 204 primary television affiliates; CBS, 192; ABC 138. NBC claims it can reach 99 per cent of all television homes in the United States; CBS, 99.2 per cent; and ABC, 93.4 per cent.[54] In the top fifty markets, NBC relies on one UHF for its primary affiliation, CBS on two, and

ABC on three. The key to ABC's problem is a shortage of affiliates in one and two-station markets, not money. The merger can't solve this problem. It isn't that ABC programs do not draw so well; fewer persons have an opportunity to see its programs. And, although improving, the condition is really worse than here presented: several of ABC's 138 affiliates and most of its supplementary stations also are affiliated with NBC and/or CBS; they may, and often do, select programs from those other networks rather than from ABC.[55]

The DuMont Television Network succumbed to similar frailities. Inventor-manufacturer Allen B. DuMont, without benefit of radio experience, launched a television network in 1949, using his three owned stations as the nucleus, WABD (TV), now WNEW-TV, New York, WTTG (TV) Washington, and WDTV, now KDKA-TV, Pittsburgh. Although DuMont carried the first commercial network program and developed a nationwide network of some one hundred stations, most of those stations carried few DuMont programs. The network ceased operations in September 1955.

The *Report on Chain Broadcasting,* issued in 1941, revealed the strong-arm tactics used by the networks to stifle other efforts to establish competing networks.[56] Morris Ernst cited the exterminations of the American Network, in 1933, and the Transcontinental and Atlantic Coast networks, in 1939–40.[57] Of three regional radio networks bought by General Tire & Rubber Company—Yankee and Colonial in 1943 and Don Lee in 1950 [58]—only Yankee remains. And many more have been absorbed or muscled out.

Great odds must be overcome for a new television network to have a chance of succeeding. First, AT & T rates discriminate against those using less than its eight-hour-a-day interconnection service. A newcomer obviously must start with less than a full program schedule. The instigator of an FCC study of AT & T's discriminatory practices, Sports Network, Incorporated, which feeds special sports programs to about 150 stations coast-to-coast, reported paying higher rates for thirty-five occasional-use hours from Washington to Chicago (six hundred miles) than the networks did for a full month of eight-hour-a-day service between these two cities. Consequently, SNI in 1964 paid $7 million for occasional service; the three major television networks together paid $50 million for full service.[59]

Secondly, when competition develops, the three established

networks rise to suppress it. Several examples might be cited, but let us consider a recent battle. During the period March 2, 1961, to May 1, 1966, when Newton N. Minow and E. William Henry were chairmen, the FCC encouraged development of alternate television program sources. The Commission, under the leadership of these chairmen, made concessions to financier Daniel H. Overmyer by granting him licenses to six UHF stations in the top fifty markets, more than FCC guidelines permit (see Chapter 7). The reason for this was that Overmyer said he wished to establish a network. The Overmyer Network, reorganized as United Network, broadcast a two-hour late-evening variety show, filmed in Las Vegas, for thirty-one days before ceasing operations on May 31, 1967, $1.7 million in debt.[60] Its only network competitor when the venture was announced was NBC's "Tonight Show." Shortly thereafter, ABC announced it had signed a top TV star, Joey Bishop, to head a late-night show beginning in April 1967, over 110 stations. CBS said it will begin a late-night program in 1968. These are merely the publicly announced efforts to destroy UN. We may never know what was done by way of pressure on individual stations and on advertisers, attempts to withhold talent, and other nefarious behind-the-scenes infighting. UN had planned to expand to fifty-six hours of night entertainment a week in the Fall 1967.

The dominant networks previously had strangled the proposed Prime Network, the brainchild of Sylvester (Pat) Weaver and Oliver Treyz, a Sunday-night chain that was to begin in mid-1966. Apparently also dead or floundering are Trans-World Broadcasting and Unisphere Broadcasting System, two recent attempts at network operations.

How Networks Operate

National radio networks were forced by the medium they spawned, television, to retrench. Today, except for weekends, they no longer attempt to provide large blocks of programming. Instead, they feed affiliates periodic newscasts and commentary, occasional features, and coverage of special events and sports. Almost forgotten is the battle radio fought in the 1930's to obtain full Associated Press, United Press, and International News Service coverage. Only after CBS launched its own world news service was freer access to news service news obtained (see Chapter 5).

Today, the radio networks provide programs, sell advertising for those programs, and, except for MBS, reimburse affiliates for their time. Fifty-five regional networks, some appendages of the national networks, and Keystone Broadcasting System, Incorporated, a transcription service, also supply limited programming. However, most of the regional networks are little more than group advertising sales organizations.

Television networks developed along the lines of radio networks. They first offered a few hours of evening programs, expanded into a full evening schedule, and then developed daytime fare. In this way they provide affiliates such a full budget of shows that most affiliates broadcast virtually no local programs other than news and weather. ABC, CBS, and NBC supply programs, sell advertising, pay line transmission fees, pay advertising discounts and agency fees, and reimburse affiliates at the rate of approximately 30 per cent of the affiliates' advertising rates. Affiliates supplement their income by selling advertising for station breaks, nonnetwork programs, and spots in programs the networks are unable to sell; they pay the networks approximately 30 per cent of the income from sales of spots on network shows. Large city affiliates generally prefer to sell or have their station representatives sell advertising, thereby earning at a much higher rate. However, networks can and do sell time on these stations with relative ease. The reverse is true with affiliates in small cities.

Licensees, although charged by the FCC to operate "in the public interest," [61] stand mute on network programming. If they were to exercise their rights under network contracts to reject commercial programs, they soon would lose their highly profitable affiliations; the result for most would be bankruptcy. On this dilemma hangs the inability of the FCC to improve programming, for the network corporations are licensed by no one. Minow and other critics of the networks advocate licensing as a way to curb excesses and improve programming.

Although networks easily clear mass appeal shows, clearances of public service programs are low. A recent study showed that an average of approximately 30 per cent of network affiliates reject network public affairs programs, the rate ran as high as 70 per cent for a February 13, 1966, NBC special documentary on Vietnam.[62] At the time the United States had committed 170,000 United States military forces in a war that threatened to expand into a confrontation with China. Many stations close the television switch on documentaries; instead, they broadcast syndicated material easily sold to national, regional, and local advertisers, no doubt "in the public interest." [63] One cannot blame the networks for reducing their expensive and unremunerative public service broadcasting,[64] especially when audience measuring systems say they attract small numbers.[65] Were it not for FCC pressure, these all too infrequent probes into serious problems doubtless would disappear. Now they serve as credits to be stored against the periodic FCC and congressional investigations. When a network seeks Commission favors, that network characteristically behaves as a child does the week before Christmas—ABC announced its 1966–67 season cultural concession, "ABC Stage 67," shortly after reaching agreement to merge into ITT.

Virtually all advertisers still demand mass appeal, low level programming. Few concessions are made to those with minority tastes. However, at present no more than a dozen advertisers "package" shows, as they did in the 1950's. Networks, under FCC and congressional goading after the quiz-show scandals, assumed almost total direction of their programs. Also, advertising now is sold on a spot basis: 90-second, minute, 40-second, 30-second, rather than on program sponsorship. Most advertisers seem pleased with the so-called magazine format; they can spread their advertising over several shows and diverse audiences rather than gamble huge sums on a single program which may prove unpopular. If the FCC adopts rules limiting network ownership interest to 50 per cent of prime evening-hour entertainment programs, the advertiser-packager probably will reappear. CBS, followed by ABC, and, finally, NBC, bowing to pressure from the Senate Antitrust and Monopoly subcommittee, revised television rate cards in 1966, ostensibly to reduce discounts to volume advertisers. At least one witness at the subcommittee hearings was skeptical; he said that Procter & Gamble with its four thousand minutes of CBS spots could save $4 million, "no other advertiser probably could get (that great a savings)." [66] ABC and NBC rates, announced later, followed the pattern of CBS, each providing "modest price advantages" for early buyers of large numbers of minutes. All three eliminated discounts only on time charges for sponsored programs. As noted, very few network programs are sponsored; advertisers buy participation spots. In addition, the new rates are designed to discourage adherence to the FCC's proposed 50-50 rule, should it be adopted.[67]

Two marked network programming trends were evident in 1966 and 1967, the rush was to sports and movies. Networks bid against each other for rights to recent movies. ABC and CBS during 1966 paid approximately $118 million for rights to exhibit twice each, some 180 movies on their networks. (CBS paid a record $5 million for rights to show *Cleopatra* twice.) [68] These transactions do not include a "multi-million dollar" outright sale of twenty-six features to ABC-TV by David O. Selznick, consummated in March 1966. These and other movies are to be shown over several seasons, some as late as 1970. NBC in 1967 contracted to pay $115 million for 94 United Artists feature films, to be shown over a nine-year period.[69] The bidding is keen for rights to baseball, football (the three networks paid $41.1 million for TV and radio rights to college and play-for-pay football for the 1966–1967 season),[70] hockey, boxing, the Olympics, and even soccer from a league that had not begun play. Both NBC and CBS telecast professional football during prime evening hours in the fall of 1966 and 1967. Movies dominated each network's programming two nights a week, leaving Monday the only movieless network night. Thus, twelve hours a week, approximately 20 per cent, of prime television network entertainment schedules were devoted to movies, up from a movie-a-week in 1961. Jack Gould, *New York Times* television columnist, sees TV's reliance on movies as "buying its way out of trouble again" after for years neglecting to develop "its own reservoir of entertainment resources," which he says the networks ultimately must do "even if it does involve a temporary drop in income." [71] Television's soothsayer, General Sarnoff, warned in 1961 that TV in ten days uses more material than the three largest movie makers produce in a year.[72]

All three networks began searching for original dramas following the acclaim of CBS-TV's presentation of the Arthur Miller Broadway hit *Death of a Salesman* in May 1966. "ABC Stage 67" has already been mentioned. NBC announced plans for an experimental theater,[73] and CBS-TV reached agreement with the Royal Shakespeare Company of Stratford-on-Avon to produce two Shakespearean dramas for the 1967–68 and one for the 1968–69 seasons.[74] Also, TV has financed several "movies" produced for television and NBC and CBS have backed Broadway shows, notably CBS's incredibly successful *My Fair Lady.*

Networks adroitly maneuver to thwart government attempts to hold them in check, including immediate resort to the courts should the FCC rule against them. Other successful devices used on congressional subcommittees as well as on regulatory agencies are (1) the filibuster and (2) inundation. Whenever investigative proceedings are begun, those under the magnifying glass submit impressive, lengthy pleadings, reports of studies, and other documents. Two examples will illustrate this. When the FCC expressed concern for networks' control of programming (see Chapter 7), broadcasting hired Arthur D. Little, Incorporated, to prepare a rebuttal, *Television Program Production, Procurement and Syndication.* Data from this report were cited *ad nauseam* by industry witnesses at FCC and congressional subcommittee hearings, and highlights were released to the press. The *Little Report,* presented to House Subcommittee No. 6 of the Select Committee on Small Business during its 1966 hearings, occupies one hundred and fifty pages of six-point type in the report of that subcommittee.[75] When ABC-ITT filed for permission to transfer ABC-owned stations, seventeen applications, each of which was more than six inches thick, were filed—eight cartons of legalistic trivia to overwhelm the Commission.[76] A single FCC staff member was assigned part time to the task of unraveling that riddle.

When the FCC schedules a hearing on broadcast matters the Commission receives pleadings and requests to testify from large numbers of industry spokesmen; seldom any from those not financially involved. They, friendly congressmen, affiliates, and paid "experts" jam congressional subcommittee hearing rooms to protect broadcasting's vested interests. Scan the transcript of any pertinent hearing: Clear Channel Broadcast Stations, Regulation of Community Antenna Television, All Channel Television Receivers and Deintermixture, Television Network Program Procurement, Broadcast Advertising, to name a few. And through it all, broadcasters ally themselves with congressmen to "prevent the FCC from usurping congressional power," a highly successful recurring industry dodge.

Occasionally monopolistic practices surface. It is then, if the FCC or, more likely, the Department of Justice is up to the long legal ordeal which inevitably ensues, that the network is called to task. A recent representative case can illustrate this more clearly. NBC owned WKYC-AM-FM-TV Cleveland, eighth market, and wanted to trade up. Westinghouse owned KYW-AM-TV Philadelphia, fourth market. Under the threat of losing its network affiliation, Westinghouse agreed in 1955 to trade stations. NBC helped salve hard feelings and made the trade appear legitimate by adding $3 million to the deal. The FCC rubber-stamped the trade "despite informal allegations" that NBC had threatened disaffiliation. The Justice Department entered the fray and began antitrust proceedings; finally, ten years later, NBC signed a consent decree, agreeing to dispose of the Philadelphia station. A stronger FCC on July 29, 1964, ordered return of the two stations to their former owners by June 19, 1965; an original deadline of December 31, 1962, had been extended several times.[77]

NBC and its parent RCA have been at loggerheads with the FCC, Justice Department, and the courts from the 1920's to the present as that network has sought to perpetuate and extend its broadcasting monopoly. Against FCC's overworked and undermanned legal staff RCA repeatedly has aligned the most skilled battery of attorneys available, placing a heavy financial burden on taxpayers that an industry whose subsidiary is supposedly operating in the public interest should not impose. Only on those rare occasions when the FCC undertakes comprehensive investigations, as with the Chain Broadcasting study of the 1940's, do these strong-arm network tactics gain public attention. Even then, broadcasters ignore the findings and most of the press and the news services give them scant notice. For ownership of the press, including magazines, and broadcasting is so intertwined (see Chapters 13 and 14) that an attack on one is an attack on both. Few are the newspapers that reported in full the opposition to the ABC-ITT merger. Can the day be far off when criticism of the mass media will be published only by the university presses? Would Random House, bought by RCA for $37.7 million in 1966, publish a book critical of NBC? Would Holt, Rinehart and Winston, merged into CBS in 1967, accept a manuscript in which CBS was attacked? Mergers beget mergers to the point where little is open to objective scrutiny. Here, more than in governmental censorship or news management, lies the critical threat to press freedom.

UHF and FM: Broadcasting's Stepchildren

10.

While broadcasting in general has been merrily amassing large fortunes for its owners, two communications outcasts, ultra high frequency television and frequency modulation radio, have been struggling to gain their place in the sun. Thus far they have been largely spurned by the masses and therefore are unable to attract the advertising revenue so necessary for their existence. At this point there are grave doubts if UHF and FM will ever live up to their potential of providing greater program variety, especially programs that appeal to minority tastes, but unless they do, public access to a greater variety of ideas will be blocked. At least the entry into national television advertising will remain essentially a monopoly of a few major industries and businesses.

Ultra High Frequency Television

Let us examine UHF and FM to determine why they are in such distress. The plight of UHF was methodically charted by the giants of the television industry to reduce competition and thus enhance profits. The FCC was the instrument used to achieve these ends. Two major FCC blunders, the first early in public telecasting and the second in 1952, placed UHF in a strait jacket from which it has never been able to extricate itself.

In 1945 the FCC, unmindful of the tremendous growth potential of television, bowed to industry pressure and allocated thirteen channels (later reduced to twelve) [1] to television in the VHF spectrum. Frequencies in this spectrum already were limited by heavy demands from noncommercial broadcasters, primarily the military. The FCC at that time told licensees that all telecasting would be moved to the more spacious higher frequencies if the medium proved successful. This was easier said than done. Therefore, by permitting stations to begin broadcasting on VHF the FCC doomed TV to this narrow spectrum for years to come.

As financial success came to these early telecasters others demanded licenses. It became obvious that the twelve VHF channels capable of accommodating a maximum of 650 stations for the entire nation could not provide enough spectrum space, so on September 30, 1948, the FCC ceased licensing new stations. The freeze was lifted on April 14, 1952, at which time the FCC announced its first allocation of channel assignments. The plan utilized both VHF and UHF bands to provide for 2,053 stations in 1,291 communities.[2]

By this action the FCC committed mistake number two, actually two mistakes in one. First, freezing construction on new stations gave those occupying these select VHF channels an opportunity to build viewer loyalty; enrich themselves under monopoly or near-monopoly conditions during a time when virtually all receiving sets had only VHF tuners; and improve their equipment, programming techniques, and relations with advertisers. Thus the UHF newcomers were placed at a distinct disadvantage. Most of the highly lucrative VHF licenses, especially in large urban areas had been awarded.[3] It was therefore obvious to all that growth in the major cities could be achieved only through utilizing UHF channels. But in assigning these channels the FCC committed a second major mistake, one that cost UHF broadcasters millions of dollars and stymied use of the UHF spectrum for commercial broadcasting for almost fifteen years: the FCC intermixed channel assignments so that VHF and UHF stations competed. At that time all 108 television stations were VHF and few sets could receive UHF. As might have been expected, virtually every UHF station, more than one hundred, failed.[4] In 83 areas where one or more UHF stations once operated, none were on the air in 1967. Among the failures were at least 36 areas that now have no local TV service, including such cities as Allentown, Pa., Atlantic City, N.J., and Battle Creek, Mich.

Congressman Emanuel Celler of New York summarized the plight of UHF succinctly and well when he said

> although from the beginning the Commission (FCC) laid down clear perspectives for a nationwide and competitive system and declared the wide use of the ultrahigh frequencies to be essential, for many years it not

only failed to encourage the development of UHF broadcasting but, on the contrary, its every action and inaction—the 4-year freeze, the deadly intermixture provisions of the 1952 report and order, the failure to stimulate all-channel set manufacture, and the vacillation with respect to deintermixture—further strengthened and entrenched VHF. The result is that in so-called intermixed areas, where UHF stations must compete with established VHF, they face an almost insuperable disadvantage.[5]

Three major obstacles have blocked the growth of UHF:

1] as previously mentioned, except in areas where UHF-only stations existed, few television receivers prior to 1965 had UHF tuners. Production of all-channel television sets declined consistently from 1953 to 1961. For example, 20.2 per cent of the 7,126,000 TV sets manufactured in 1953 contained UHF tuners. By 1957 only 12.2 per cent were so equipped, and by 1961 production of UHF-capable receivers was down to 6 per cent.[6]

2] UHF stations were limited largely to telecasting reruns of old network shows, shows that networks rejected, old movies, documentaries prepared by special interest groups, and extremely expensive station-originated programs. Networks have long followed a practice of not affiliating with UHF if a competing VHF station is available. At the beginning of 1966 NBC had exclusive affiliations with two and combination (with CBS and ABC) affiliation with one UHF station in the top fifty markets. CBS had exclusive affiliation with three, all in the same UHF-dominated market, and joint affiliations with one or both of the other networks in three other markets. ABC had three exclusive affiliations and three joint affiliations with one or both of the other networks. None of the UHF exclusive affiliations were in cities closer than sixty miles to a VHF exclusive affiliation with the same network. We find, then, that out of 149 VHF-UHF network-affiliated stations in the top fifty markets, only 11 were UHF stations. Governor William W. Scranton, then a United States representative and former part-owner of a UHF station in Scranton, Pa., said, ". . . it is absolutely essential for a UHF station to have a network (affiliation)."[7] Statistics bear out Scranton's viewpoint; only four nonnetwork UHF stations that went on the air in the 1950's were still in operation in 1966.[8]

Clear indication of the higher operating costs UHF stations must bear is given in the information released by the FCC which shows that among television stations reporting losses for 1966, 41.7 per cent of the VHF stations with gross revenues of less than $200,000 reported earning a profit; only 25 per cent of the UHF stations grossing less than $200,000 earned a profit. Further, of the UHF stations reporting gross revenues in excess of $600,000, 20 per cent operated at a loss; only 6 per cent of the VHF stations in this revenue classification reported losing money.

3] Scarcity of UHF receivers and inaccessibility to network affiliation convinced most advertisers that UHF, even at much lower rates, was a poor advertising buy. UHF network-affiliated stations generally charge approximately one-third or less for time than do VHF network stations in the same markets. Rate differences are greater for nonaffiliated UHF stations; in one instance the rate quoted was one twenty-fifth.[9] Even more revealing, a report of revenues of eight television (seven UHF, one VHF) stations in central Illinois for 1960 shows that the single VHF station in that area received 35 per cent of the total $5,697,000 earned by this group of eight stations. None of the UHF stations receive as much as 15 per cent. Further, of the pooled profits of the eight stations, before federal income taxes, the VHF accounted for 78 per cent; the most profitable UHF retained 11 per cent. Three of the seven UHF stations in this predominantly UHF market reported deficits. Also, the VHF station had a return of 308 per cent on its investment in 1958 and 212 per cent in 1960. The most profitable UHF station had a return of 35 per cent on its investment in 1960.[10] A staff member of the FCC, who has worked for the Commission for twenty-five years, told the writer that advertisers and networks still, as of July 1, 1966, "avoid UHF stations with channel assignments above 40." [11]

It must be admitted that rejection of UHF by potential station owners, networks, and advertisers was somewhat justified, at least prior to 1965, largely because of technical and developmental problems. UHF signals do not travel as far or bend to avoid obstructions as well as do VHF signals. A VHF station generally will provide a high-quality signal within a radius of sixty-five to seventy miles of the transmitter. A comparable UHF station will provide similar service to within a radius of about forty-five miles. Increasing the power of a UHF station and utilizing an extremely tall antenna will extend that station's coverage area, but its signals still cannot be received as far as can those of a much lower-powered VHF.[12] Also, UHF receiving set tuners are not as efficient as are VHF tuners. They are less sensitive and need repairs more frequently. Both problems may well be solved shortly.[13]

Although the UHF fiasco inflicted huge financial losses upon thousands of station investors, the major concern here lies with the effects on society. It is clear that an unsuspecting and largely unaware populace has by these unwise actions and inactions been unnecessarily deprived of access to a greater diversity of viewpoints.

The FCC Seeks Solution

Certain members of the FCC were horrified at the carnage inflicted upon UHF stations by their muscular and ruthless VHF cousins. As a result the FCC recently, under more liberal chairmen, have attempted to find a solution to the over-extended VHF, virtually abandoned UHF spectrums. One highly unpopular "solution" that VHF broadcasters killed through pressure on congressmen was deintermixture. The FCC as early as 1954 proposed switching channel assignments so that all stations in a market would be either UHF or VHF, thus making possible more equitable competition among all stations. Only two markets were deintermixed; one was Fresno, Calif., 133,939 population (1960 census), where residents may view two independent local as well as three full-time network channels, a privilege available in only seven other American cities. The other was Bakersfield, also in California, where a city of 56,848 population (1960 census) has three full-time network affiliates, a rarity among cities of this size.[14]

The FCC-instituted rulemaking (dockets Nos. 14239 to 14246) on July 27, 1961, whereby eight cities would be deintermixed: Montgomery, Ala.; Hartford, Conn.; Champaign and Rockford, Ill.; Binghamton, N.Y.; Erie, Pa.; Columbia, S.C.; and Madison, Wis. These areas, to be the first of several deintermixes, were selected because 1] they at that time were served by at least one UHF station, and 2] a high proportion of receivers in each city could receive UHF. But, as with many other attempts by the FCC to solve serious problems, Congress, responding to heavy broadcasting pressure, intervened. The impotent FCC, attempting a two-pronged solution, then agreed to relent on deintermixture under threat of congressional action. Congress itself acceded to a second, less politically volatile FCC proposal; it passed a law enabling FCC to require that after an FCC-specified date all television sets shipped in interstate commerce be capable of receiving VHF and UHF channels (Public Law 87–529, July 10, 1962). In exchange FCC promised to delay any deintermixture plans for five years.[15] The FCC all-channel public notice set the effective date as April 30, 1964; hence, the number of homes to which a UHF station could gain entry had increased almost fourfold by 1966.[16] By 1970 "conservative FCC estimates" are that 70 per cent of American television homes will have all-channel capable receivers.[17]

Interest in establishing UHF stations, especially in the larger markets, has grown tremendously. FCC figures show that in July 1961, when 62 applications for new television stations were pending, only 23 were for UHF, 9 of which were for educational assignments. In early 1965, of the 134 applications pending, 105 were for UHF, of which 82 were for commercial allocations.[18] What thus far has been one of the most unfortunate debaucheries in the history of mass communications currently offers the brightest hope of introducing new voices into public discussion. But, as we shall soon see, a cloud hovers over this rainbow, too.

During a recent seven-month period the number of UHF commercial stations on the air increased from 108 to 122, the number of construction permits issued to stations not on the air increased from 78 to 98, and the number of applications for new stations, both VHF and UHF increased by 25.[19] Obviously, more UHF stations will be built, and a major objective of the FCC will be gained. However, in encouraging this growth the FCC has committed other errors of judgment that might well reduce the benefits of these gains to television viewers. Although the FCC seeks to limit chain ownership to three stations in the top fifty markets, of which no more than two may be VHF,[20] it has ignored these guidelines in relation to UHF. For example, the FCC in September 1967 approved transfer of a sixth UHF station in the top ten markets to Kaiser Broadcasting

Corporation, a subsidiary of the giant industrial complex.[21] Channel 61, Cleveland, thereby joined Kaiser stations in Los Angeles, Philadelphia, Boston, Detroit, and San Francisco. Apparently commissioners were persuaded by Kaiser's plan to begin a fourth TV network by 1970. In the meantime, the Kaiser chain sought a seventh UHF, either in New York or Chicago.[22] What sort of Frankenstein might this bending of rules to foster growth in a favored new area release upon the American public? Here concern is not specifically with the Kaiser grants but with a policy of expediency that through the years has caused the FCC to yield on basic philosophical points in an effort to encourage change.

As has been pointed out, the three major networks and the advertisers often for sufficient, albeit selfish, reasons shun UHF in general and channels higher than forty in particular. UHF is faced, therefore, with the twin problems of providing programming that will attract audiences of sufficient size and complexion to interest advertisers and to overcome advertiser predisposition to ignore UHF. Certainly, NBC, CBS, and ABC cannot be expected to cancel affiliations with VHF stations to affiliate with new UHFs. The question then arises, from whence cometh the programs? The ill-fated United Network had promised affiliation to several UHF stations.[23]

Earlier, the new owners of the Mutual Broadcasting System announced they were planning eventually to develop a television network. No target dates have been set.[24] A Canada-based color network, Transworld Broadcasting, has announced plans to serve "principal television stations across the United States."[25] Also, encouraging the formation of a fourth national television network is a stated objective of the FCC, which sees such a development as providing additional variety in programming and serving the needs of UHF stations. But the early financial difficulties of ABC and the failure of United Network, which were discussed in a previous chapter, are such as to forewarn any group interested in launching a network that there are considerable risks involved.

In only one respect, then, are UHF's prospects rosier now than they were in 1954 when disaster plagued efforts to develop stations in that spectrum: the number of all-channel receivers has vastly increased. Incidentally, this FCC-Congressional solution has cost the public an estimated $200 million during the first eighteen months after the all-channel law went into effect.[26] UHF still faces network and advertiser resistance;[27] the dominant audience-measurement service, A. C. Nielsen Company, still largely ignores UHF pleas to measure their market penetration; and, possibly most important of all, the general public has been so long addicted to NBC-CBS-ABC offerings and conditioned to watching their affiliates that weaning them away and into UHF channels may prove disheartening.[28] UHF momentum suffered a serious setback when Harcourt, Brace and World, a major book publisher, returned construction permits for five UHF stations in large intermixed cities to the FCC and asked the Commission to withdraw another pending UHF application. The company president said "UHF is . . . too big a cash risk." Indeed it is; as previously mentioned, the 114 UHF stations in 1966 as a group lost $7.4 million. Bad "omens" cited by Harcourt for abandoning UHF included competition with VHF stations, possible impact of satellite communications, competition with a projected noncommercial TV network, failure of United Network, and dominance of networks over programming.[29]

Frequency Modulation Radio

The developer of frequency modulation, Major Edwin A. Armstrong of Columbia University, blames RCA for stifling FM. There is much to support his charge, but it should be noted that the other radio networks and many broadcasters pressured the FCC into launching commercial FM under conditions that virtually assured its failure. Again, RCA led the fight.

Major Armstrong developed FM in the 1930's and submitted it to RCA for study in 1934. Despite favorable recommendations by RCA engineers, RCA officials did not mention FM as a possible use for frequencies above 30,000 kilocycles when the FCC called a hearing in 1936 to obtain information as to how best to use this then unassigned spectrum space. Instead, RCA, even at that early date, tried to sell television as the proper occupant and opposed assigning FM to these frequencies.[30] The FCC finally authorized commercial FM operations to start on January 1, 1941, setting aside 35 channels for its use. WSM-FM Nashville, owned by the licensee of WSM, the National Life and Accident Insurance Company, was the first on the air, May 29, 1941.[31] However, World War II intervened.

As the United States emerged from war, many predicted that FM would shortly replace AM, in two to three years according to the FCC chairman in 1946.[32] FM's static- and interference-free reception, much higher fidelity, and, most important of all, space for an additional five thousand stations were cited as its advantages. Small stations could be built at a fraction of the cost of building or buying an AM station, and they could be operated for much less. FM, of course, had some drawbacks, the major ones of which were 1] no AM sets could receive FM without a converter and 2] FM signals travel in a straight line and are not reflected back to earth by the ionosphere. Consequently, the coverage area of an FM station is less than that of an AM station of equal strength and antenna height, especially at night. Conversely, more stations per spectrum space can be accommodated on FM than on AM since stations may occupy the same or adjacent channels within from sixty-five to one hundred and eighty miles of each other, depending on the power of each station.

Those in control of the industry, fearing competition which undoubtedly would reduce profits, convinced the FCC to permit FM development under conditions which foredoomed it. The FCC, in 1945, proposed to require AM broadcasters who built FM stations to offer a minimum of two hours a day of programming different from that offered on their AM stations. As has happened with disgusting frequency, the FCC deleted this requirement in the face of overwhelming opposition from the networks and broadcasters. This action, probably more than any other, forced FM into second-class status, where it remains. As might have been expected, all of the existing stations which operated FM appendages merely duplicated 100 per cent their AM programming; they gave advertisers AM and FM coverage, such as it was, at no extra cost. How could an independent FM-only station compete? It could not, and most went out of existence.[33] Channel assignments that in 1945 and 1946 were so energetically sought were by 1950 unclaimed.[34] For example, in June 1946, there were 55 FM stations on the air; the number had skyrocketed to 733 by January 1, 1950. In 1951 a decline set in and by January 1, 1957, the number had dropped to 530.[35]

The fears expressed by Commissioner C. J. Durr, in dissenting to the FCC's decision to permit 100 per cent duplication by AM broadcasters of their AM and FM programming, were borne out. He said, in part:

It seems to me that the use of two radio channels for only one program service is not only a waste of frequencies but will retard the development of FM broadcasting. FM will develop at the speed of the increase of listening sets in the hands of the public and, in my opinion, listeners will not be encouraged to buy FM receivers if their investment means only that they can have a little more clearly the same programs which they now receive.[36]

By 1958 manufacture of FM sets had only reached 764,000 a year;[37] by contrast, approximately 12.55 million AM and 5.3 million TV sets were produced that year.[38] And virtually every household contained at least one AM set.

The FCC, then with FM as with UHF today, sought to stimulate growth in the new, promising, broadcast service, hence, AM licenses and newspaper publishers were encouraged to pour money into FM. (Incidentally, the FCC still invites virtually anyone willing to take the gamble to invest in FM and to use it in highly unusual ways.)[39] Newspaper publishers, most of whom had missed out on the AM bonanza of the 1930's and 1940's saw FM as opening new and potentially profitable opportunities to them. Too, facsimile publication, wherein a newspaper could be "delivered" to the home via the airwaves, captured their imaginations. Newspaper executives felt they would 1] be ready to utilize facsimile as soon as it became better developed and 2] prevent potential competitors from launching facsimile newspapers by preempting this service, while in the meantime 3] reaping financial rewards to be gained in FM broadcasting. It is little wonder, then, that newspapers owned more than 30 per cent of the FM stations on the air during the decade beginning in 1945. Their peak penetration was in 1948 with 72.3 per cent.[40] Virtually all of the other FM stations were owned by AM broadcasters. The National Association of Broadcasters reported in 1949 that 91.9 per cent of all FM stations were owned by AM broadcasters, some of whom also owned newspapers. Based on financial reports published by the FCC, this grew to 92.3 per cent in 1955 (see Table 26, Appendix).

Development of FM outside the domination of AM broadcasters and newspapers still has not been achieved, although some slight gains have been made. Ownership of FM by AM broadcasters in the same city had declined to 72.4 per cent in 1960. But this trend toward independent operations was reversed in 1961 and has essentially moved in the direction of AM-FM affiliation since, rising to 1,043 of 1,381 stations (75.5 per cent) reporting financial data to the FCC for 1965.[41] Newspapers as a group have tended to hold their FM stations and to add slightly to them in recent years. Despite this, the percentage of FM stations thus owned declined markedly until in 1966 it stood at 13.5 per cent (see Table 27, Appendix). In 1967, however, the percentage increased to 14.5.

Although the number of independent FM stations reporting profits has generally increased during the past dozen years at a slightly higher rate than the number reporting losses, FM is still largely a bankrupt enterprise. In 1965, for example, of the 338 FM stations reporting, not operated as AM affiliates, 236 (69.8 per cent) reported deficits. Total income for the 338 stations set a new record, minus $3.3 million. FM stations as a group have never earned a profit. In fact, losses have continued to increase each year since 1955, with one exception. The rate of loss declined from previous peaks of $3.2 million in both 1962 and 1963 to $3 million in 1964 (see Table 28, Appendix). However, revenues have increased steadily since 1954 to $15.7 million in 1965, of which $14.5 million was from advertising. This is a healthy indication that more advertisers are being attracted to the medium, but not nearly rapidly enough. In fact rising costs are more than offsetting income increases. FM stations on the average had revenues of $26,315.79 and expenses of $36,315.79 in 1955 for an average loss of $10,000. In 1965 each FM-only station had average revenues of $42,899.41 and expenses of $56,213.02 for an average loss of $13,313.61.[42] Further, FM stations not affiliated with AM stations in 1965 received advertising support at 21.8 per cent the rate of AM stations.[43] As was true of UHF, FM has been largely ignored by virtually all the major audience-rating firms. This accounts, at least in part, for the lack of advertising support.

A few bright spots appear in this dismal picture. Most important, the number of FM sets is increasing. Sales in 1965 set a new record, 7,852,000.[44] The number of homes with FM sets have increased to more than 50 per cent in New York City and more than 30 per cent in nine other cities.[45] Even so, FM in most areas is still broadcasting in a vacuum, and its supporters have failed to convince Congress that all radio sets should be capable of receiving both AM and FM. Nor does there appear to be any discernible move afoot to push for an all-channel radio set law. However, another plus is that the number of FM stations has continued to increase since 1957 after attrition had reduced the number to 530. A slow recovery became accelerated and by 1963 there were 1,081 and by June 22, 1967, 1,642 FM stations on the air.[46] But as has been noted, the great bulk of these do not enlarge the circle of public debate; they are adjuncts of AM and TV stations.

Finally, local radio service has been extended in many localities by FM. Some daytime-only AM broadcasters are utilizing FM at night. And greater use of FM's unique full fidelity is being made, especially with newer concepts of broadcasting, such as stereophonic sound. An increasing number of FM broadcasters, however, are devoting their finely tuned instruments to programming on the same commercial level as the successful AM's. See, for example the large number of FM stations that have adopted "country and western music" and "rock 'n roll" formats. The major battle, therefore, still concerns the duplication of AM programming on FM. The FCC has ordered FM stations in the largest one hundred markets not to duplicate AM programming more than 50 per cent of the time. Exceptions have been made in several instances, but those FM stations not granted a reprieve were required to comply with the rule starting no later than December 31, 1966.[47] This isn't quite as stiff a penalty as it at first appears. Quite obviously AM's can comply by broadcasting at night over FM and duplicating during peak and more profitable daytime hours, to the detriment of the independent FM broadcasters. Expense to the AM-FM broadcaster will be nil since he can automate his station to virtually run itself. And the omnipresent networks have again come to the rescue; they have developed program material for FM, but obviously this programming service is available only to AM network affiliates which operate FM stations. Of the four major radio networks only Mutual Broadcasting System has admitted independent FM stations to affiliation and only two stations were so blessed as of October 1, 1965.[48]

Despite FM economic doldrums some of the problems associated with AM and television are beginning to appear: trafficking in licenses, repeated sales of stations, inflated station prices, chain ownership, and industry ownership.[49] FM always has offered attractive tax-loss write-off benefits, as is pointed out in Chapter 8. But these and other special industry problems transcend any one spectrum and so are discussed elsewhere.

STV and CATV: Supplementary TV Services

11.

The free-enterprise television industry, as always, attempting to protect its monopolistic position, has leveled its most vicious attacks, with varying degrees of success, against two supplementary television services: subscription television and community antenna television. For years pay television has been prevented from serving more than very restricted areas. However, largely because the networks are only mildly concerned,[1] the broadcasters' battle against CATV has accomplished less and, in increasing numbers, they have bought into CATV so as to have "a piece of what knocks them out,"[2] if CATV replaces television, as some predict.

Against both the industry has argued variously that these services have siphoned off investment money which logically should go to television and will *1*] kill "free" television, *2*] bankrupt the networks, *3*] destroy small-city television stations, *4*] stunt the growth of UHF, *5*] place communications in the hands of undesirable (hinting at underworld) elements, *6*] ruin program producers, *7*] wreck "professional" sports, and *8*] otherwise cripple the American free enterprise system. These are only slight exaggerations of ills broadcasters predict will befall the nation unless pay TV and CATV are scuttled. Fortunately, they apparently delayed their attack too long to kill CATV, and it may well be that pay TV will develop largely through CATV.

Subscription Television

A service which would go far toward tempering objections to the present inanity of television fare as well as providing program variety at least in urban areas, subscription television has been denied an opportunity to prove itself. Television networks, station owners, movie producers, movie theater owners, and other special interest groups have used every ruse and delaying tactic available to destroy pay television.[3] Networks in 1966 and 1967 paid huge sums to obtain recent first-run movies and professional sports rights, fare toll TV prizes.[4] It appears, despite a House committee delay, that the FCC will authorize nationwide subscription television, a matter the Commission has had under consideration since shortly after the end of World War II.

As early as 1950 the FCC authorized preliminary over-the-air toll-TV experimentation. In that year the Skiatron system was tested over WOR-TV New York. The next year the Telemeter system was tested over KTLA (TV) Los Angeles, and Zenith tested Phonevision over its experimental station in Chicago, a system it had begun developing nineteen years previously.[5] A limited number of special receivers were used in those tests. The first pay-TV experiment in which programs were made available to the public was conducted by International Telemeter Corporation, a division of Paramount Pictures Corporation, in Palm Springs, Calif., 1953–54. A second wired subscription television system operated in Bartlesville, Okla., 1957–59. In the Bartlesville experiment, about five hundred subscribers received two movies daily for a monthly fee of $9.50. International Television Corporation launched the largest wired pay-TV system to date in Etobicoke, Canada, a suburb of Toronto, on February 26, 1960. This system was moved to Montreal, April 30, 1965.

On March 4, 1966, the FCC for the first time assumed control over wired broadcasting systems; the Commission ruling related to community antenna television. However, subscription television which also did not use the airwaves had previously been assumed to be beyond the control of the FCC. Indeed, the best-financed ($25 million) of all pay television ventures, conducted by Subscription Television, Incorporated,[6] was not authorized or controlled by the Commission. Thus, the first nonexperimental pay-TV operation in the United States, was begun in Los Angeles, July 17, and in San Francisco, August 14, 1964.

But as with other attempts to establish experimental or nonexperimental subscription television, broadcast and movie interests fought it savagely, forcing STV to cease operations by the most ingenious method yet devised to block pay television. Opponents, led by the Southern California Theater Owners Association, succeeded in placing initiative referendum Proposition 15, outlawing subscription TV in the home, on the November 3, 1964, California ballot. They spent in excess of a million dollars to wage a "pay television will kill free television" campaign. As a result, Proposition 15 passed by a 2–1 margin.

The movie interests, however, thus tangled with one of broadcasting's most astute entrepreneurs, Sylvester L. (Pat) Weaver, Jr., former NBC president, who was president of Subscription TV until April 30, 1966. Weaver had built the three-channel system into one which had attracted wide attention and support and, more important, six thousand subscribers during its brief existence. His court appeal resulted in the proposition's being declared unconstitutional by Judge Irving H. Perluss, Sacramento County Superior Court, on May 19, 1965. This decision was upheld by the California Supreme Court, 6–1, on March 2, 1966, and by the United States Supreme Court on October 10, 1966. Meanwhile, two Subscription TV suits are pending, a $117 million suit against the movie theater owners and a $14 million suit against the state of California. In two other pay-TV court victories, Twentieth Century Fox paid RKO an undisclosed amount for refusing to release motion pictures to the Hartford station and the Antitrust Division of the Department of Justice forced film producers to release first-run movies to subscription television operators.

The FCC, in 1957, considered granting permission for experimental over-the-air pay TV. However, pressures applied on Congress by the "free" television industry and movie producers and exhibitors forced a two-year delay. As an example of pressures used, CBS gave a lavish party in Washington for congressmen to which local CBS affiliates were urged to send representatives. These local broadcasters were conveniently seated at tables with their home-state senators and representatives so they might discuss "the threat to the American way of life posed by pay television."[7] It was also during this period (1958) that Robert W. Sarnoff, then president of NBC, sounded the oft-repeated but entirely unconvincing argument, in testimony before the FCC, that subscription television would kill free television.[8] Here the son was merely parroting what his father, David, had put so well in testimony before the FCC three years earlier when he pled "Keep American radio and television broadcasting free to the public." [9]

Congress, as usual, was impressed and prevailed on the FCC to delay authorizing further toll broadcasting tests until Congress had an opportunity to consider legislation.[10] Finally, on March 24, 1959, the Commission issued a third report announcing that it was prepared to consider any pay-TV application by a commercial television station. Thus, the groundwork was at last laid for the first public test of pay-TV over the air. On February 23, 1961, the Commission granted Hartford Phonevision Company, now RKO General Phonevision Company, authorization to conduct a three-year trial subscription-TV test over that company's Channel 18, WHCT Hartford, Conn. The station began its pay broadcasting experiment on June 29, 1962, delayed by theater owners' court attempts to block final approval.[11] Participants in the experiment, in addition to RKO General, were Zenith Radio Corporation, supplier of the equipment used, and Teco, Incorporated, licensed by Zenith since 1949 to commercially develop Phonevision systems.

The Hartford test, still under way, received approval on May 21, 1965, to continue for a second three-year period or until the FCC terminates its outstanding subscription-television rulemaking. Zenith and Teco asked the Commission on March 10, 1965, to authorize subscription TV on an "extended nation-wide basis" and to make toll TV available to all operating or proposed TV stations as a supplemental broadcast service.[12] This petition, plus earlier ones, primarily from Zenith and Teco, were supported by the results of the Hartford test which showed that the subscription television operation there 1] did not unduly siphon off advertising-supported television viewers, 2] won moderate viewer-acceptance, 3] although operated on a limited (five thousand subscribers adopted as a maximum) [13] basis and at a financial loss ($3,538,000 in three years), demonstrated that subscription television should break-even financially with twenty thousand subscribers, 4] provided viewers with kinds of "box office" programming unavailable by way of regular television, and 5] attracted subscribers largely from the middle-income group rather than from high-income families, as had been forecast.[14]

Comments favorable to extending subscription television punctuate the proposed rulemaking and inquiry notice adopted by the FCC, March 21, 1966.[15] This and more recent Commission actions suggest that unless Congress interferes the FCC will permit expansion of subscription television in some form.

What is the future of pay TV? Proponents, of course, foresee unlimited success. Some other economically disinterested sources agree. For example, as a result of interviews the Stanford Research Institute predicts that some 15 million American households, wherein reside 50 million people, will receive subscription programs by mid-1970 and that they will pay $2 billion a year for the service.[16] The late Gary A. Steiner found in his scientifically conducted poll that 22 per cent said subscription television should be tried out on existing stations, replacing current programming, at $1 a program, and that 13 per cent would be willing to pay $31 to $100 a year for current programs without advertising.[17] The matter is not settled. But should subscription television survive the "pocket veto" applied by Congress, and flourish, as it well may, vitally needed new voices will be added to the pitifully few now heard in the marketplace of ideas, entertainment, culture, and the arts.[18]

Community Antenna Television

A second avenue to diversity of programming, at least for viewers in some areas, is community antenna television. This service, by picking up signals of stations which cannot be received by viewers, amplifying the signals and distributing them by wire to subscribers' homes, provides programs not otherwise available.[19] Most CATV systems are located in small towns and cities which either are too far from television stations to receive the three networks or are shielded from stations' signals by obstructions, most often hills and mountains and, in urban areas, tall buildings (500,000 on Manhattan Island do not get adequate off-the-air television service).[20]

The first noncommercial CATV was built in Astoria, Ore., in 1949. In early 1950, the first commercial CATV delivered programs to Lansford, Pa., a community walled-in by mountains. Gradually the number of systems increased until in 1953 an estimated 240 were serving some 150,000 subscribers, largely in mountainous areas of the East and sparsely populated areas of the West and Southwest. The number had more than doubled by mid-1956 and subscribers had multiplied fourfold. By 1966, the number of systems had increased to an estimated 1,675 serving approximately two million subscribers. At that time an additional 1,503 franchises had been granted and 1,420 cities were considering applications; the figures had increased to 2,138 systems in operation or under construction, 1,082 additional franchises granted, and 1,630 applications pending in 1967.[21] Such growth leads the more optimistic to predict that the number of systems and subscribers will double in two years.

Increasingly, CATV has invaded large urban areas,[22] where systems improve signals within the cities. In less populous areas, they import programs from distant stations, except where restricted by FCC rules. Most of the largest American cities have granted or are considering granting franchises to one or more CATV operators to "wire" portions of the cities, sometimes at fantastic compensation to the cities. A Hughes Aircraft Company-Teleprompter Corporation-owned company was highest bidder among six for a ten-year franchise for three areas of Los Angeles not then serviced by CATV (five other companies are licensed for other areas of Los Angeles). The high bid was $845,100, plus an agreement to pay the city 3 per cent of gross receipts.[23] Those two companies also jointly own the CATV franchise for the northern half of Manhattan Island, New York City. The Asheville, N.C., franchise was granted to an operator who agreed to give the city 16 per cent on the first $600,000 gross and 50 per cent on the income over that figure, annually, plus clear title to the cable system after twenty years.[24]

The television industry and, therefore, the FCC and Congress largely ignored CATV until the mid-1950's. The first broadcaster objections concerned CATV interference with AM and TV reception. Also, the FCC received a complaint as early as 1954 from a UHF station owner who charged that many CATV systems were carrying commercials and competing directly with television stations, without regulation, control, or restraint by any governmental body. The Commission was urged to classify CATV either as a broadcasting service or as a common carrier and subject it to FCC jurisdiction.

In 1956, thirteen broadcast licensees filed a formal complaint against 288 CATV system operators located in thirty-six states. The FCC, in what has become known as the *Frontier* case, in April 1958 dismissed the complaint, saying that CATV was not a common carrier. But the Senate Commerce Committee, under the chairmanship of Senator Warren G. Magnuson, began a series of hearings, "The Television Inquiry," which included a study of CATV. The committee's report, known as the *Cox Report* because it was written by Kenneth A. Cox, now FCC Commissioner, who then was counsel for the Senate committee, criticized the Commission for not assuming control over CATV and urged commissioners to request legislation if they found that the Communications Act did not vest the regulatory body with this authority. The tenor of the *Cox Report* was that CATV must be regulated "in order to prevent damage to the orderly development of the country's television system," [25] a view Cox still espouses.

During the Senate hearings broadcasters testified that many CATV's refused to carry local stations, that local stations' signals when carried often were degraded to a poor quality, and that CATV connected clients' sets in such a way that subscribers could get no signals except those fed over the wire. The FCC essentially ignored the *Cox Report* and, in addition, denied that it had the power to force CATV systems to obtain consent from originating stations prior to distributing their signals. However, the FCC report recommended legislation which would require CATV system operators to obtain consent of TV stations whose signals they transmitted and to carry signals of any local TV station requesting it, without degrading that station's signals.[26] TV broadcasters testifying at the FCC and Senate hearings pleaded that CATV be prevented from simultaneously duplicating programs carried by local stations.

Pressure from broadcasters and congressmen, following the FCC report and order, coerced the Commission into amending its rules to begin limited regulation of CATV's utilizing microwave systems to import television signals.[27] Senator Magnuson introduced a bill to bring CATV under FCC control and impose other restrictions on the industry; a substitute bill lost in the Senate by one vote.[28] An FCC-proposed bill in 1961 died for lack of action. Against this gathering storm the Carter Mountain Transmission Corporation applied for additional microwave relay facilities to serve its

CATV systems in Wyoming. The FCC, on February 14, 1962, denied the application unless the carrier agreed not to duplicate programming of KWRB-TV Riverton, Wyo., the only local television station in one of the communities served by Carter. Further, the FCC specified that Carter must carry programs requested by KWRB-TV.[29] A federal court of appeals upheld the decision on May 23, 1963, and the United States Supreme Court declined to review the decision.[30]

Based largely on the Carter decision the FCC, as early as December 1962, required microwave applicants not to duplicate local stations' programming and to carry their programming, unless those stations waived this right. Finally, on April 22, 1965, the Commission formally adopted rules to regulate microwave-served CATV systems, ordering local station carriage and nonduplication for fifteen days before and after local airing.[31] Some four hundred CATV systems serving 6.6 million TV viewers were utilizing microwave transmission.[32] At the same time, the FCC reported it had reached an initial conclusion that it had jurisdiction over all CATV systems.

On March 8, 1966, the Commission assumed jurisdiction over all CATV systems (except those which serve fewer than fifty customers, or which serve only as apartment house master-antennas) and set forth certain requirements, among them carriage of local television station programs and same-day nonduplication of programming on local stations.[33] Also, the FCC established guidelines as to which commercial and noncommercial stations the systems must carry and which ones they must protect by nonduplication, and required that CATVs seeking, henceforth, to import signals from distant stations into the grade A (primary service) area of a station in the top one hundred markets must obtain FCC permission.[34] This latter requirement was to control the CATV invasion of the major markets, especially to protect UHF stations and encourage development of a fourth national television network.[35] Again, the Commission requested legislative guidelines to clarify FCC authority in this area, but to date Congress has not acted. This is understandable since congressmen have been caught in the crossfire of two vocal pressure groups—from broadcasters demanding restraints on CATV and from the CATV industry which incites its subscribers through a

"Don't Let the Government Turn Off Your TV Set" campaign to flood congressmen and the FCC with mail opposing restrictions.[36]

CATV suffered another major blow on May 23, 1966, when a federal judge in New York ruled that the owner of television rights to movies could collect royalties when the movies were shown on a CATV system.[37] The United States Court of Appeals, second circuit, affirmed the decision May 23, 1967. In the meantime, House and Senate committees held hearings on copyright liabilities of CATV. It appears quite obvious, therefore, that some systems, especially those which import signals beyond a station's normal service area, possibly its B contour, will be liable to copyright provisions on at least some programming.[38] However, the copyright question involves much more than CATV. Congress in 1966 and 1967 was studying other changes needed to modernize copyright laws; laws which have received no major revisions in over fifty years.

TV broadcasters' opposition, FCC regulations, and copyright law problems are harrassing CATV operators into developing their own programming, an eventuality which really could challenge television. Consequently, broadcasters have urged Congress to prohibit CATV program origination and have been attempting to tie nonorigination to other issues, even including copyright legislation. Despite the Commission's request that Congress bar CATV systems from originating programs "in the public interest," such prohibition seems highly questionable, unless one assumes the public interest to coincide only with the rights of broadcasters. Surely CATV subscribers would be better served were they to receive alternate program choices.

Indeed, a Key West, Fla., CATV system has been originating programs since 1954. Today more than three hundred systems provide a twenty-four-hour weather service; both AP and UPI deliver news for on-camera transmission,[39] an estimated seventy-five systems produce live local programs. One system, in Chillicothe, Ohio, after investing $140,000 in local origination equipment, has employed a six-man staff to develop three or four hours of local programming daily, none of which is sponsored.[40] Conversely, some systems do sell commercials[41] and more probably will unless prohibited from doing so. Frederick W. Ford, National Community Television Association president and former FCC member, along with other industry leaders have urged CATV operators to originate programs. Dal-Worth Microwave, Incorporated, Dallas, has applied to the FCC for permission to build two microwave stations to transmit three channels of programming exclusively to CATV systems in Texas.[42] That company and others have been buying programs suitable for CATV use. Local origination of programs has been made possible by improved equipment. Early CATV systems had capacities generally of from one to five channels. Even today the majority are five-channel systems; the second largest number are twelve-channel systems.[43] Twenty-channel systems were placed in service in 1967 and others with up to eighty channels are being planned. A rather typical modern twelve-channel, small-town CATV operation is the one in Parsons, Kan. Viewers who previously could receive off-the-air signals from two stations now may select from eleven stations in Kansas, Missouri, and Oklahoma, plus a news and weather channel.

A major limitation on CATV in some areas is the need to feed signals from the antenna to the home via wire. This is impractical in 1] large urban areas where utilities, including CATV, are required by law to be placed underground, New York City, for example, and 2] rural areas where population densities are so low that wire costs are prohibitive. Both problems may be solved by a short-range microwave unit developed by Hughes Aircraft and Teleprompter, the two involved jointly in CATV operations in New York and Los Angeles. The equipment transmits twelve channels of color with clarity up to six miles. In New York the system has been used to feed signals received off the air by an antenna atop the Empire State Building to receivers in each block served; signals then are distributed by wire to individual subscribers. Hughes predicts that receiving equipment eventually will be so inexpensive that receivers can be attached to television sets in rural areas.[44] CATV's rapid growth is attributable to its immense profitability. Martin Seiden, an economist who conducted a special study for the FCC, reported that the twenty-eight systems he studied averaged a 57 per cent profits-to-revenues ratio. He found profits as high as 68 per cent.[45] Waterbury (Conn.) Community TV, Incorporated, estimated that in 1965 it had received a 400 per cent profit on its investment.[46]

Broadcasters individually and through their organizations have fought CATV,[47] yet many have embraced it. A survey released in 1966 showed that 548 broadcasting licensees own 833 CATV franchises which serve approximately 501,000 subscribers and have a potential of 1.4 million.[48] Further, although the National Association of Broadcasters has opposed CATV, 364 NAB members, 225 radio and 139 TV, have financial interests in 538 systems.[49] Virtually every issue of the trade press reports additional penetration. Martin Seiden advised the FCC that broadcaster ownership of CATV posed no problems unless they owned systems in their station's service areas, as many do. Then, he warned, they might be tempted not to improve poor signals in an effort to enlist CATV subscribers. More important, cross-ownership would seem to discourage program diversity. The FCC had considered placing limits on broadcaster ownership of CATV until Congress intervened.[50]

CATV, as with other communications systems, is increasingly falling into chain hands. The 25 largest CATV chain owners reportedly hold interests in more than 670 franchises (31 per cent of the 2,178 franchises granted) and have applications pending for almost 400 others. According to the *Seiden Report* the nine largest CATV chains owned 179 systems, 15 per cent of the industry, at the end of 1964. The largest chain owner, General Tire & Rubber Company, through interests in Vumore of Oklahoma City and H & B Communications of Beverly Hills, Calif., has interests in 72 systems.[51] Approximately 225 newspapers have interests in CATV and 300 more are seeking franchises "because they don't want to be left at the post in this development like they were when television came in . . ."[52] The Major Robert McLean family, owner of the *Philadelphia Bulletin, Santa Barbara* (Calif.) *News-Press,* and WPBS-FM Philadelphia, in 1966 paid approximately $2.2 million and assumed obligations of $1.8 million for 66 per cent of a Santa Barbara CATV, so anxious were they not to be left at the post.[53]

CATV owners' lists read like a *Who's Who* of broadcasting and publishing. NBC and CBS, virtually all of the major broadcasting chains, most of the newspaper-magazine chains, many independent newspapers, theater interests, various manufacturers, bankers, and radio station owners are scrambling wildly in heated competition to obtain lucrative franchises from local governments. Some of them plan to spend immense sums to develop their systems; a CATV operator in Philadelphia, for example, plans to invest $40 million and, if the FCC permits, import signals of independent New York stations. Other systems seek permission to relay TV signals as far as 1,350 air miles, from Los Angeles to Texas.[54] The FCC estimates that the cost of a CATV system serving 1,000 customers is about $150,000; 5,000 customers, $400,000; 10,000 customers, $800,000.[55]

Despite monopoly trends and many other problems, CATV still is, as a former director of research for Philco Corporation said, the most efficient of all systems for distributing television signals without further crowding the already over-taxed spectrum space. He and others see CATV as providing additional services and supplanting TV broadcasting in twenty to twenty-five years.[56] The two major telephone utilities, AT & T and General Telephone, fear that CATV with its tremendous signal-carrying capacity (thousands of times the capacity of a telephone line) might well compete with them by providing such services as shopping via color TV, home banking, access to computers to retrieve information and solve such problems as income tax calculations, direct burglar and fire alarm contact with the nearest police and fire stations, classroom instruction in the home, stock exchange quotations, classified advertising, and possibly even direct satellite-to-home communication. Since AT & T was prohibited by a 1956 federal consent decree from operating CATV systems,[57] that utility has sought other protection, primarily through (1) leasing Bell-owned and installed systems to CATV operators at attractive rates[58] while (2) prohibiting those operators from offering other than traditional TV transmission plus such incidentals as weather, music, and time channels. Other uses of the CATV systems are reserved to the telephone company.

CATV is still in a developmental stage. Its future rests largely in the hands of the federal government—Congress, the FCC, the Justice Department, and the Courts. They will determine whether it will 1] continue in its present pattern, 2] retrench, 3] cease to exist, 4] expand to serve half or more of the United States, 5] provide services which are now only figments of the imagination, or 6] supplant television and movies, or, conversely, fall victim to direct space satellite-to-home communications. Pressures are fast building to a climax. But for once broadcaster influence on Congress and the FCC is counterbalanced by a CATV industry whose millions of loyal subscribers reject violently any attempts to interfere with their beloved, multichannel entertainment link.

A Bright Future for ETV?

12.

But for the combined energetic efforts of a dozen or so educators who enlisted support among a few highly placed people in government, educational television would have fallen victim to the same ruthless treatment that killed educational radio. In 1934 Congress was considering the Wagner-Hatfield amendment to the Communications Act which would have reserved 25 per cent of AM radio frequencies for educational purposes. However, commercial broadcasters, especially network officials, prevailed. Their argument was that the networks were already devoting up to 70 per cent of their time to noncommercial programs, including education.[1] After the Senate defeated the amendment, and as radio became increasingly profitable, CBS's tacit promise to serve the needs of education was forgotten. Radio channels were not reserved, and as a consequence, all but thirty noncommercial educational stations are confined to the twenty channels, 88 to 92 megacycles, on the FM band reserved in 1945 by the FCC for educational use. Actually, few of the noncommercial radio stations should be called "educational"; their only truly educational role lies in providing practical experience to students preparing for careers in broadcasting. Most of them, of course, broadcast "cultural" programs, primarily recorded music.

Two groups of educators, realizing that unless they acted wisely and speedily the commercial broadcasters would again defeat them, in the 1950's joined forces to plead educational television's case. The Joint Council for Educational Television and the National Citizens Council for Educational Television, provided with a desperately needed respite by a "freeze" on television channel allocations from 1948 to 1952, marshaled funds, recruited congressional support, enlisted the evangelistic backing of FCC Commissioner Frieda B. Hennock, and obtained the invaluable aid of such allies as the late Franklin Dunham, chief of Radio-Television, United States Office of Education. In contrast to a poorly conceived and presented case in 1934, these proponents outlined their ambitious needs clearly before the FCC in 1950. Although they failed to achieve their goal of VHF channels in the 168 metropolitan areas, they prevailed upon the Commission to reserve 242 channels, of which 80 were VHF, thanks largely to Mrs. Hennock's one-woman crusade within the FCC. However, since only 10 to 15 per cent of the receiving sets were equipped for UHF, those 162 UHF channels were of little value.

The fact that fewer than a half-dozen commercial broadcasters had testified against the educators should not be misconstrued as assent; they were merely biding their time until conditions improved. Especially during the middle and late 1950's they exerted tremendous pressure on the Commission and on Congress to redesignate idle educational channels for commercial use. But the FCC, faced with congressional counterpressure to preserve the noncommercial channels, resisted.[2] Commercial broadcasters exerted influence on the state level, as Senator Ralph Yarborough of Texas pointed out "the people who wanted to get those channels for commercial purposes got riders put in our State appropriation laws and for years it prohibited the legislature (Texas) from appropriating any money for educational TV."[3]

In the most recent (1966) FCC allocation, 116 VHF and 516 UHF channels were reserved for education.[4] Had the channels not been reserved through the years, they would have been lost, commandeered by those eager to exploit these valuable national resources. Most states, universities, school districts, and community groups have been slow in building educational television stations. Only in the past three years have the number of stations increased appreciably. As recently as 1960 only 51 educational stations were on the air; the number did not pass 80 until 1963. As of late 1967, there were 67 VHF and 51 UHF educational stations on the air.[5] Yet large areas of the country still were poorly served, if at all, by ETV. No stations were on the air in 11 states; only one station in each of 15 states. Conversely, large numbers of stations were concentrated in a few states; 72 of 130 were located in 11 states.[6] For the number of ETV stations on the air at the end of each calendar year see Table 13.

Despite the increase, educational television allocations are so badly drawn that, nationwide, comparatively few people have access to ETV programs. Only three VHF ETV channels have been reserved for the eight populous Northeastern states, two in Pennsylvania and one in Massachusetts. None are located in New York,[7] New Jersey, Maryland, Delaware, Connecticut, and Virginia. The more sparsely populated areas fare better. Texas has seven VHF allocations; New Mexico, six; Montana, North Dakota, Nebraska, and South Dakota, four each.[8] However, considering the limited number of unassigned channels and the demand for them at the time educators began their fight, they were fortunate to salvage these. Partially because educational stations are located for reasons other than financial gain, many serve television "white areas." ETV stations provide the only local television in forty-one communities, including Wilmington, Del. (1960 census, 95,827), and Ogden, Utah (1960 cen-

TABLE XIII *Number of ETV Stations at End of Calendar Years, 1953–66*

Year	*Number*
1953	1[1]
1954	10
1955	17
1956	21
1957	27
1958	35
1959	44
1960	51
1961	62
1962	75
1963	83
1964	99
1965	113
1966	116[2]

[1] KUHT Houston, licensed to the University of Houston and the Houston Independent School District, was the first noncommercial educational television station to go on the air, the date, May 23, 1953.

[2] *Broadcasting,* Jan. 2, 1967, p. 143; Jan. 10, 1967, p. 85.

sus, 70,197). They supplement the single commercial station in each of another nine cities.[9]

Educational television scored a major breakthrough in 1962 when Congress passed the Educational Television Facilities Act. That act provided matching federal grants up to one million dollars per state for construction and expansion of educational television stations. Although Congress failed to fund the program in 1962, it subsequently provided $32 million. President Johnson asked Congress to appropriate an additional $20 million to continue the program another year beyond the June 30, 1967, expiration date. As a consequence of the ETV act, an increasing number of states have interconnected their stations into state-wide networks. A second major contributor to ETV growth has been the all-channel receiver law, passed in 1962 and instituted in 1964. As a result the number of sets capable of receiving UHF has vastly increased, a boon to all UHF stations, including educational ones.

Unless unforeseen problems arise, educational TV is on the threshold of fuller development. At long last, serious proposals to solve ETV's ever-present financial problems have been presented. And various of these have received support from those in positions to guarantee success—high government officials ranging from the President to Congress to federal agencies, rich foundations, educators, leaders of business and industry, and even influential segments of the mass media. In 1966, both the Ford Foundation and a special Carnegie Commission on Educational Television offered proposals to finance television programming. The Ford Foundation urged the FCC to sanction formation of a nonprofit corporation to build, launch, and operate a domestic satellite communications system, the profits to be used for ETV programming. AT & T and COMSAT both opposed; the latter countered with a proposal to levy a surcharge on users of the forthcoming commercial, domestic satellite system, the income to be earmarked for ETV.

The Carnegie commission suggested three sources of funds for ETV: 1] an excise tax on new television sets,[10] 2] grants from federal, state, and local governments, and 3] contributions from foundations and others. The commission considered, but rejected, a proposal to tax commercial television stations. Yet even some broadcasters agree that they should pay for the privilege of enriching themselves on the priceless public airwave franchises.[11] And why not? Clearly, those who flood these scarce public resources with mass audience-appeal trivia have the responsibility of underwriting programming which would appeal to the growing number whose interests and tastes they have slighted. As of this writing Congress was pondering another Carnegie commission proposal, formation of a nongovernmental nonprofit corporation to receive and expend monies to develop programming, interconnect educational television stations for live coverage of major news events and cultural programs, and conduct research, primarily on programming. Finally, the commission advocated a new name, "public television," since educational television has become synonymous with uninteresting, poorly executed fare. (The Public Broadcasting Act of 1967: 1] established a government-funded Corporation for Public Broadcasting, 2] authorized CPB to make grants for programs for noncommercial stations, 3] appropriated $9 million to CPB, 4] extended five years the program of federal grants in aid to states building educational television and radio stations, and 5] appropriated $10.5 million for these grants.)

Regardless of which proposals are adopted, a fourth network of broader cultural, public affairs, and educational scope than the presently constituted National Education Television network[12] probably will be in operation by the time you read this. Whether it will be an improved version of NET, which has since 1957 maintained a virtual monopoly over everything other than in-school ETV programming, or some other entity, the network will attempt to make a wider appeal with improved programming made possible by a broader financial base than NET has enjoyed; NET, since its inception, has been almost 100 per cent dependent on the Ford Foundation.[13] Also, the ETV stations will shortly be forged into an evening hours, live national network; stations will no longer be forced to rely on taped programs shipped by mail.[14]

The best bet as of this writing is for an Americanized BBC-type network providing an alternate evening program source, hopefully on a higher cultural yet entertaining plane, available to millions of Americans.[15] As public television programs gain in popularity, however, commercial broadcasters undoubtedly will attempt to prohibit noncommercial TV from engaging in "entertainment."

Broadcasting Control by Chains and Newspapers

13.

The United States Supreme Court in 1945 declared that the First Amendment guarantees of a free press "rest on the assumption that the widest possible dissemination of information from diverse and antagonistic sources is essential to the welfare of the public." [1] If doubt had existed previously as to the intended beneficiaries of the First Amendment, none could remain. Yet on local issues the First Amendment is dead, as far as millions of Americans are concerned. They have access to no local media voice, or receive only what a single owner of their radio station and newspaper and, in a few instances, television station deems desirable. Thus, those who have most often invoked the First Amendment to protect their pocketbooks have effectively killed it. We saw in Chapters 2 and 3 how chains have expanded their control over daily and weekly newspapers. Let us complete our study of monopoly trends in the local media by next examining both chain and newspaper ownership of radio and television. In this way the evidence can be weighed and a decision be made on just how dead the First Amendment is.

Radio

We have followed radio's development from a toy into a highly effective seller of products and services (see Chapter 6). As radio prospered, broadcasters sought to control more than one station. Both the number of chains and the number of chain-owned commercial AM stations have increased at rapid pace,[2] especially in recent years, so that today approximately a third are held by persons owning three or more stations (Table 14).[3] And the trend continues.

Of seventy radio station transfers approved by the FCC during October–November–December 1966, more than half (thirty-nine) were to licensees who already owned broadcasting properties; twenty had two or more radio stations prior to the sale.[4] Despite disclaimers, AM radio chains have tended to become larger. The number of six-station chains increased from eighteen to twenty-five, five-station chains from twenty-seven to thirty-six, and four-station chains from forty-six to fifty-two during the period 1960 to 1964.[5] Many chains doubtlessly would be larger were it not for FCC maximums of seven

TABLE XIV *Chain Ownership of Commercial AM Radio Stations, 1939–67*

Year	*Number of Chains*	*Chain-Owned Stations*	*Total Number of Stations*	*Per Cent Chain Owned*
1939 [1]	39	109	764	14.3
1951 [2]	63	253	2,232	11.3
1960 [2]	185	765	3,398	22.5
1964 [2]	215	900	3,937	22.9
1967 [3]	373	1,297	4,130	31.4

[1] Warren K. Agee, "Cross-Channel Ownership of Communications Media," *Journalism Quarterly*, Dec. 1949, p. 414.

[2] Data for years 1951, 1960, 1964 from *Activities of Regulatory And Enforcement Agencies Relating to Small Business,* Part I, p. 88.

[3] Data for 1967 is from FCC records, *Broadcasting Yearbook*, 1967, and information released when broadcasting property sales were approved by the FCC.

AM, seven FM, and seven television stations of which no more than five may be VHF.

As has been noted previously, chain broadcasters control virtually all of the most powerful (50,000 watt) stations in the United States. Seven of the eleven clear channel AM radio stations not now designated for duplication are owned by chains: AVCO industrial complex, two; NBC, one; Palmer, one; religious organizations, two; and the Minneapolis *Star* and *Tribune* newspaper-broadcasting chain, one. Two of the four not chain-owned are owned by newspapers and another is licensed to an insurance company. Only KFI Los Angeles is owned by persons with no other mass media holdings or obvious special interest causes to plead.

The situation is almost as bad with the other 50,000 watt day and night stations. Forty-seven of these sixty-two stations are in chain hands, of which the networks control twelve; newspaper-broadcasting chains, eight; industrial-broadcasting chains, seven; insurance-broadcasting chains, three; movie theater-broadcasting chains, one; and a church-broadcasting chain, one. Of the fifteen maximum-power stations not owned by chains, newspapers control four; a labor union, one; industry, one; and a movie operator, one. Only six of the seventy-three full-time, 50,000 watt stations are independently owned.

Obviously, licensees of these powerful stations hold valuable franchises obtained at little cost and for which they pay the public nothing. Although evidence is not needed as to the worth of these channel assignments, it is readily available in the form of network affiliations. Only one of the eleven unduplicated and not to be duplicated clear channel radio stations is not affiliated with a major network, and this obviously is by choice. (NBC is affiliated with seven, one in combination with ABC; CBS, three; and ABC, one in combination with NBC.) At the lower end of the broadcasting hierarchy, none of the FM stations, not operated in conjunction with an AM station, holds affiliation with the three major radio networks; only three are affiliated with Mutual.[6]

Incidentally, chains also have invaded FM, where they own 31 per cent of the stations (496 of 1,602). The great majority of them, however, are in AM-FM combinations (402 or 81.5 per cent) which largely duplicated programming on their AM counterparts until the FCC, beginning in 1964, started pressuring AM-FM licensees in cities of one hundred thousand population and greater to provide alternate programming on their FM facilities during at least 50 per cent of the time.

As has been suggested, newspaper penetration of radio is of serious proportions. Members of Congress objected to newspaper-broadcasting combines as early as 1927, when Senator Clarence C. Dill of Washington raised the question during a debate on the Radio Act of 1927. However, newspaper control expanded unabated; by 1941, of one hundred and eleven communities where one radio station and one newspaper existed, eighty-seven stations and newspapers were commonly owned. At that time the FCC issued two orders wherein the Commission 1] questioned the wisdom of newspaper domination of broadcasting,[7] 2] in effect barred further penetration,[8] and 3] launched a three-year study of the problem.[9] After this flurry of activity, the FCC reversed itself in 1944. Congress considered the problem in the 1950's and in 1960, but passed no restrictive legislation.[10] Daniel W. Toohey, in a *Federal Communications Bar Journal* article, summarized the current practices of the Commission that are based on precedent.

As a comparative factor, newspaper ownership: 1] is a discrediting, not a disqualifying factor; 2] will be decisive only where all other comparative criteria have been equally met by the applicants; 3] will depend for its importance upon the nature and extent of newspaper interests of the applicant; and 4] where a non-comparative proceeding is involved, there will be no hearing save where collateral public interest matters, such as suppression of competition, are material.[11]

The same precedents hold for television. Newspaper domination of radio, however, has clearly subsided since 1940 when the press held ownership interests in 30.8 per cent of all AM stations. Gradually, newspaper ownership declined until it reached 9.5 per cent in 1966.

A similar pattern, but on a grander scale, developed with FM. Many newspaper publishers, obviously aware that they had erred in not entering AM radio, seized upon FM. As of January 1, 1948, newspapers owned interests in 72.3 per cent of all FM stations on the air. Again, when more stations began broadcasting, the newspaper domination abated slightly. However, as recently as 1950, newspapers still owned 36.8 per cent of the stations. Publishers along with others lost interest after it became obvious that FM could not compete with AM, much less with television. Many let their stations go silent. In 1957 only 530 FM stations were in operation, of which 142 were held by newspaper interests. As of 1967, newspapers had interests in 223 of the 1,533 commercial FM stations, 14.5 per cent, slightly reversing the downward trend. (For statistics on newspaper ownership of AM and FM radio and television for selected years see Table 27, Appendix.) As is often true, these general statistics conceal several important facts. First, newspaper penetration of AM-FM combinations is much greater than of either AM- (8.4 per cent) or FM-only (4.7 per cent) stations. Of the 1,147 AM-FM combinations on the air as of November 30, 1966, newspapers held financial interests in 205 (18 per cent).

Stronger evidence of serious newspaper domination appears when ownership patterns are examined regionally and by states and communities. In the five midwestern states of Illinois, Indiana, Michigan, Ohio, and Wisconsin plus Pennsylvania, newspapers have invested heavily in radio. More than 42 per cent of the newspaper-owned AM-FM stations are located in this contiguous area (87 of 205). Indeed, of the total AM, AM-FM, FM newspaper licensees, 34 per cent are located in these six states. And domination within a state, for example Illinois, runs as high as 41 per cent of all AM-FM stations (20 of 49). A slightly lower proportion, 30 per cent, of all AM-only stations in Illinois (35 of 117) are owned at least in part by newspapers. Conditions in neighboring Indiana are not much better. There, newspapers hold ownership interests in 14 of 41 AM-FM stations (34.1 per cent) and of 18 of 79 AM stations, including AM-FM combinations (22.8 per cent).

Equally as alarming, newspaper-radio monopolies exist in 85 cities where the only daily newspaper owns an interest in the only AM station. In 78 cities newspapers own majority interests. Only 14 of these 85 cities are in metropolitan areas where listeners receive some measure of local radio service as an alternate (see Table 29, Appendix). Residents of another 51 American cities fare only slightly better. In each city, the only daily newspaper holds ownership interest in one of two AM stations. And only 8 of these cities are in metropolitan areas. In 48 of these cities, the daily newspaper owns a majority interest (see Table 30, Appendix).

Again, domination is largely regional. Ten monopoly cities are in Illinois, ten in Pennsylvania, nine in Ohio, seven in Oklahoma, and five each in Indiana and Wisconsin. In another five Illinois cities the only daily owns one of two AM stations (see Tables 29 and 30, Appendix). And these newspaper-owned AM stations in two-station cities clearly are choice properties. All but nine of these stations (82 per cent) are licensed to operate day and night, whereas just over half of all AM stations are licensed to broadcast at night.

Further evidence that newspapers own the choice AM radio stations is contained in data submitted by then FCC Chairman Newton N. Minow to the Antitrust Subcommittee of the House Judiciary Committee in 1963,[12] information which, incidentally, has never been published. Citing financial reports available only to authorized FCC personnel, he said that after discounting network-owned and operated stations, the newspaper-owned stations, which comprised 9 per cent of the total number of AM stations, earned 15 per cent of the total AM radio station revenues for the year 1961. This testimony reveals that of 222 newspaper-owned stations in 82 markets of two stations or more, 92 earned the highest profits, 66 earned second highest, and 25 earned third highest. Only 10 ranked lower than tenth in earnings, a rather remarkable profit-showing since his figures included 13 markets with from 16 to 31 stations and 18 markets with 10 to 15 stations. (For more complete information see Table 31, Appendix.)

Why are the newspaper-owned radio stations more profitable? Obviously newspapers own a disproportionate share of the older, better established, more powerful day and night stations which are affiliated at a much higher rate with the major networks. Networks have for years preferred newspaper-run radio stations, as was pointed out by Morris Ernst in 1946[13] and by others since. A sample of AM radio stations analyzed for this study shows that slightly more than 20 per cent of NBC affiliates and slightly fewer than 20 per cent of CBS affiliates are newspaper-owned AM stations.

We will return to this question of higher earnings among newspaper-owned stations later in this chapter, since the matter is common to all of broadcasting. However, first let us consider chain ownership of television.

Television

No other local medium of mass communications in American history has become so chain-dominated as television. Financed by high television profits based on low investments and protected by valuable monopoly FCC grants, enterprising chain broadcasters have virtually taken over television. They now control 73.6 per cent of all commercial stations. Although penetration had reached alarming proportions by 1956, the number of chain-owned stations has since more than doubled and the percentages almost doubled, as the figures in Table 15 show. At the beginning of 1967 there were 183 broadcasting chains which held interests in one or more television stations (147 owned two or more stations); they outnumbered single ownership station licensees by 49. Further, the number of separate television entities as of mid-year 1966 was 317, 12 fewer than in

1956.[14] This decline coincides with an increase of TV stations on the air from 443 in 1956 to 611 on June 2, 1966.[15] Obviously, chain domination has grown at an alarming rate.

Not only have the number of chains increased, they have become larger. Doubtless they, as with radio chains, would be much bigger if there were not FCC restraints. Even so, two chains, Capital Cities and Taft Broadcasting, own full complements of seven stations, all on the air. Several other chains hold construction permits for new stations which, when operative, will give them full complements of seven TV stations. Eight chains own six stations each,[16] an

TABLE XV *Number and Per Cent of Chain-Owned TV Stations 1956–67*

Year	*Number of Chains*	*Number of Stations Chain-Owned*	*Total Number Stations On the Air*	*Per Cent of Stations Chain-Owned*
1956 [1]	81	203	443	45.8
1964	134	372	582	63.9
1967	147	459	623 [2]	73.6

[1] FCC Public Notice B, docket 60894, Dec. 18, 1964.

[2] The number of television stations on the air, or projected as scheduled to be on the air by Jan. 1967, in *Broadcasting Yearbook*, 1967, was 623. The number actually on the air Jan. 1, 1967, was 618. Data for 1967 herein cited are based on the 623 figure.

increase from three in 1956 and five in 1964. As Table 16 shows, similar increases for other sizes of chains have occurred in recent years. Even a cursory glance at these figures shows that the average size of multitelevision ownership chains has increased from 2.7 in 1956 to 2.94 in 1964 and to 3.87 in 1967.[17]

Several radio and television chains are linked to other chains by commonly owned stations, suggesting that some chains may own more than the FCC-imposed limit by the subterfuge of financing other stations through nonstockholding officers. A complete audit of broadcasting ownerships of mutual funds, banks, and other financial institutions no doubt would reveal that many investors exceed the FCC ownership maximums, as did Merrill, Lynch, Pierce, Fenner and Smith, Incorporated. That brokerage house on March 10, 1965, owned 1 per cent or more of 14 broadcasting chains with holdings of 51 AM, 39 FM, and 56 TV stations. A mutual fund, Keystone S-4, at that time held interests in 18 AM, 14 FM, and 23 TV stations. Nine mutual funds owned 1 per cent or more of two or more publicly held chain broadcasting companies.[18]

The bitter pill of chain domination has been made even more unpalatable by extensive newspaper ownership of television. As of the beginning of 1967, publishers held interests in a third of the VHF stations (156) and in 22 per cent of the UHF stations (28). They owned interests in half or more of the VHF stations in eight states and the District of Columbia.[19]

TABLE XVI *Growth in Sizes of Television Chains, 1956–67*[1]

Sizes of Chains	*Number of Chain Owners* 1956	1964	1967
Seven Stations	0	0	2
Six Stations	3	5	8
Five Stations	4	11	19
Four Stations	5	20	21
Three Stations	22	32	34
Two Stations	46	65	63
Totals	80	133	147

[1] The column totals for any one year exceeds the number of television stations held by chains. Ownership interests in some stations are held by more than one chain.

Source: Data for 1956 and 1964 is from FCC Public Notice B, Dec. 18, 1964. The total number of chains given here for 1956 and 1964 is one less than figures given in Table 15. The FCC notice did not explain this obvious discrepancy. Data for 1967 is from *Broadcasting Yearbook*, 1967, corrected by cross-checking with an FCC computer print-out of station ownerships and revised to reflect station sales through mid-1967.

Further, newspaper-television monopolies existed in 27 American cities; the owners of the only local daily newspaper also held financial interests in the single TV station, majority interests in 23 stations (see Table 32, Appendix). And in 17 of these 27 cities, viewers, unless they installed tall outside antennas or subscribed to community antenna television, received no other television service. The only daily newspaper in another 17 cities owned a share of one of the only two local television stations and majority interests in 14 (see Table 33, Appendix).

Absolute local monopolies existed in three American cities in

1967: Rock Island, Ill.; Zanesville, Ohio; and Temple, Tex. There the only daily newspaper owned majority interests in both the only television station and the only AM radio station. Hastings, Neb., was a monopoly communications city until a new AM-FM station went on the air in 1964.[20]

An interesting newspaper-chain ownership pattern evolves when we reassemble the data; 81.3 per cent of American VHF television stations as of the beginning of 1967 were owned either by chains or newspapers or both. Ownership of the less profitable UHF stations was at a lower rate, 62.8 per cent. And either newspapers or chains or both owned interests in all VHF stations in eleven states and the District of Columbia;[21] they owned interests in all but one station in another thirteen states.[22] Thus, in only twenty-three states were there two or more VHF stations owned by others than chains and/or newspapers. At the time, no VHF stations were located in Delaware and New Jersey, and the only VHF station in Vermont was independently owned and, therefore, is not considered in this data.

The task of providing complete, accurate data on radio and television, nationally, defies solution, partly because of subterfuges used to conceal ownerships.[23] When one analyzes the major markets, however, monopoly ownership trends emerge more clearly. Wealthy chains and newspapers have outbid the competition to buy these scarce, prized stations and thereby monopolize these largest markets, markets which are doubly important because of the vast populations the stations serve.

In the top ten television markets, which, incidentally, include almost 40 per cent of all television households, 37 of the 40 VHF stations are owned by chain broadcasters. The remaining 3 are licensed to companies owning daily newspapers in the same cities. And 7 of those 37 chain stations are licensed to companies which also own newspapers. Since neither chains nor newspapers are expected to voluntarily sell these immensely profitable stations, only the development of UHF can alter this grim picture.

Of the 156 VHF stations in the top fifty markets, wherein are located 75 per cent of all TV homes, 127 (81.5 per cent) are licensed to chain broadcasters. Networks hold 15 and newspaper chains, 42. Seventeen of the 29 stations not forged into chains are owned by newspaper interests, 3 others by insurance companies, and one by a Roman Catholic university. Therefore, only 8, 5.13 per cent, of the 156 VHF stations in the top fifty markets are owned singly by broadcasters who have no other obvious special interests. And the move is toward greater chain-newspaper domination. During the period December 18, 1964, to January 1, 1967, 16 stations in these largest fifty markets were sold to chains.[24]

Further, lucrative and highly influential network television affiliations in the top fifty markets are held almost exclusively by chain, newspaper, and other special interest owners. The bulk of affiliations are held by chain owners, 102, including 41 that are licensed to publishers who own chains. Newspapers owning only one station each, hold another 16 network affiliations. The networks themselves own and operate 15 VHF stations, 5 each, all but one in the top ten markets. Only 12 of the 149 VHF and UHF affiliations are held by others, and none of these are in the top twenty-three markets. Newspaper-owned stations dominate the NBC and CBS affiliations, holding 47[25] of 103. Affiliation, especially in television, holds the key to financial success, both for stations and networks. A logical question is, then, Why do networks prefer to affiliate with newspaper-owned stations? Because of ownership stability? Newspapers do tend to retain their broadcasting properties.[26] Because newspapers operate better stations? This is only conjecture. Or because of the assurance that network programs will receive generous newspaper publicity? The latter obviously is true, and since profits rise and fall with audience ratings, this is sufficient justification for networks to prefer newspaper-owned stations.

The networks, of course, own and operate five each of their own affiliates. It should be noted that all of the networks also own publishing, movie, record, and other communications and industrial corporations. Many of the other TV chains also own diverse industrial-communications facilities. And in this mad scramble for ever-greater profits, the public, as usual, suffers. In only eight of the largest fifty markets may one watch a local, independently owned VHF station. Broadcasting chains operate VHF stations in 48 of the markets and newspapers in 38. Newspapers also own UHF stations in another four markets.

The FCC has long publicly deplored the sale of television

stations in the largest urban areas to chains and those with other communications interests. In a woefully tardy [27] attempt to curb this trend, the FCC, on June 21, 1965, adopted proposed rule making and an interim policy to limit common ownership of TV stations in the top fifty markets to three, no more than two of which may be VHF. At the time the proposed rule was adopted nineteen chains owned more than the prescribed number of TV stations in the largest fifty markets. No attempt was made to divest these ownerships of any of their stations.[28] Applications for station transfers which would contravene this proposed rule were to be designated for hearing,[29] in the absence of "a compelling affirmative showing." [30] But, as we have seen, the FCC has violated this guideline by approving at least four sales to chains holding more than the maximum, and without full-scale hearings.

Much evidence exists to support the Commission in its historic opposition to newspaper ownerships of broadcasting. Major concern, of course, is with maintaining a diversity of communication voices in the marketplace of ideas; another lies with advertising rates. Newspaper-owned stations obviously charge higher rates. Of the thirty-nine markets in which publishers own network affiliated stations, these stations charge the highest advertising rates in seventeen markets and tie for the highest rates in seven others. Stations owned by chains (nine) and networks (three) charge the highest rates in twelve markets. Only in three (6 per cent) do independently owned stations charge highest rates.[31]

For indisputable evidence that newspaper-owned television stations are more profitable, let us return to the testimony of former FCC Chairman Minow. He said that excluding the fifteen network owned-and-operated stations, newspaper-owned TV stations, which comprised 24 per cent of the total, earned 36 per cent of total television station revenues in 1961.[32] Newspaper-owned stations were relatively most profitable in the seven four-station markets; six earned 25 per cent or more of pooled profits and only one earned less, 20 to 25 per cent. These comparisons are in all-VHF or all-UHF markets, hence, the lower profitability of UHF stations did not affect these data. (See Table 34, Appendix.)

Mere profitability, however, isn't to be condemned. The problem is that at least some newspaper-TV station owners are suspected of amassing disproportionate profits through questionable advertising practices. Newspapers have for years granted advertising discounts based on volume and on insertions in more than one commonly owned publication. Indeed, several groups of newspapers not commonly owned sell group advertising at reduced rates. Does the practice of granting discounts to multiple-publications advertisers extend to radio-television-newspaper units? The Kansas City *Star* at one time enforced a combination radio-newspaper advertising rate,[33] and, until the courts intervened, discriminated against advertisers using competitive media.[34] Chairman Minow cited two cases the FCC was investigating in 1963 in which newspaper-owned television stations and their newspapers were accused of offering joint advertising rates. And he placed in the House Antitrust Subcommittee record a letter sent to another broadcaster, WKRG-TV Mobile, Ala., wherein the FCC said its evidence was insufficient to justify hearing proceedings on complaints that WKRG-TV and the Mobile Press Register, Incorporated, 50 per cent owner of the station, offered newspaper and television advertising rates in combination. The letter said the complaints were "neither frivolous nor completely unfounded" and urged "a degree of vigilence by licensee which may have been lacking in the past" to protect the public from monopolistic practices. The FCC noted that the *Press Register* was the only daily newspaper in Mobile at the time.[35]

The FCC on January 30, 1963, took a strong position against combined broadcasting-newspaper advertising rates, saying they involve price fixing "by independent parties who should be competing." Authority to act against such parties derives from the *Radio Fort Wayne, Incorporated,* case.[36] The Commission emphasized that its concern was not merely with providing advertisers entry to an open and competitive broadcasting industry, but was with protecting all broadcasters so that they might compete fairly, rather than against combinations. The statement pointed out that a station, not a party to such combination-rate arrangements, might well lose substantially because of this unfair competition, and its service to the public might then deteriorate as a result.[37]

From the evidence here presented, it seems clear that millions of Americans have lost their First Freedom birthright on local issues. It is small wonder, then, that the wholesome criticism and competition which once pitted broadcasters against newspapermen has waned.

14. *Magazines: Will Suicidal Tendencies Abate?*

Any generalizations about magazines are by necessity oversimplifications. Unlike newspapers and broadcasting, magazines fit into no convenient classifications. Circulations are decreasing, yet they are at an all-time high; advertisers have forsaken them for television, yet advertising set new records in 1966; as some die others flourish. Many magazines have lost touch, but new ones are in the mainstream of thought. It's a strange industry wherein self-destruction on the part of individual publications seems inevitable. Throughout history immensely successful magazines have almost without fail run full circle, ending in suspension or merger, the victims of impertinent upstarts. Success seemingly lies more in an idea than in publication skill, and a fickle public which enthrones its kings just as quickly forsakes them. The magazine publishing business is strewn with carcasses of once vastly popular journals which lost touch with an on-rushing world and wouldn't or couldn't change their formulas to keep pace.

At a time when many of the monstrous, mass-appeal, general-circulation magazines have succumbed or are apparently en route to oblivion, highly specialized publications thrive. Some of these, started on little capital by new entrepreneurs, built audiences in this other-directed society, gained advertising support, and flourished. Their publishers launched other magazines of equally limited appeal and soon became new magazine-chain owners. Flushed by success, they, as have others, invested in business and industry. Herein lies the formula, expansion-diversification. The system often produces wealth but propels the move toward cross-media ownership and publisher-industrial links. Also contributing are the sales of established magazines to these interests. Consequently, today few magazines are owned by those with no other investments.

Disregarding the many nonprofit publications, and there are a surprisingly large number of these, magazines have been victimized to a much greater extent than have newspapers and broadcasting by unfair competition, chain domination, monopoly within specializations, subscription wars, and advertising rate cutting. Add to this the greater penetration by special interest groups and one has a picture of some of the problems. The results have at times been disastrous.

Development of Magazines

Benjamin Franklin set out to introduce magazine journalism to the colonies. Learning of his plans, Alexander Bradford, a competitor, rushed into print with his *American Magazine* three days before Franklin's *General Magazine,* in January 1741. Both founded as monthlies, Franklin's lasted six issues; Bradford's three.[1]

The foundation for today's magazines was laid in the nineteenth century. *Knickerbocker,* founded in New York, 1833–65, was the first of the general-circulation popular monthlies;[2] *Godey's Lady's Book,* 1830–98, was the first successful national woman's magazine, achieving a circulation of 150,000 in the 1850's;[3] *Harper's Monthly,* the first of the successful, finely illustrated, quality magazines, began its long career in 1850 and soon had the largest monthly circulation in the world, 200,000;[4] *The North American Review,* 1815–1940, appealed to scholars. By 1870 precursors of today's highly specialized publications were rolling off the presses[5]—magazines for sportsmen, artists, stamp collectors, spiritualists, brewers, for various professions, and for a wide range of political ideologies, including communism.[6]

Newspapers, the communications mainstay during the colonial and revolutionary periods and early years of nationhood, gave way to magazines prior to the Civil War. In 1860 approximately six hundred nonnewspaper periodicals were in existence, the largest with circulations exceeding 200,000.[7] Spurred by war, the number was increased by around one hundred in five years; in the early 1870's they approached 1,400, reached 3,300 in 1885, and 3,500 in 1900.[8] These, of course, are estimates. The guessing game becomes even more clouded in the present century. Best estimates available for various years in the twentieth century are shown in Table 17. Obviously magazines have continued to increase in number, although at a slower pace in recent years. Not considered, of course, are the "10,000 institutions or firms issuing 50,000 publications reaching 160 million people." [9] Many of those free-circulation publications are in magazine format.

TABLE XVII *Estimated Number of Commercial Magazines, 1900–1965*

Year	*Number*
1900	3,500
1925	3,635
1929	4,500
1936	5,483
1940	6,261
1948	6,657
1954	7,429
1965	8,000

Sources: Years 1900–1954, Theodore Peterson, *Magazines in the Twentieth Century* (Urbana, Ill., 1956), p. 53. For 1965, Paul S. Swennson, director of The Newspaper Fund, in Sigma Delta Chi speech, St. Louis, Mo., May 20, 1965.

Probably a better measure of growth lies in circulations. Reliable figures for certain classes of magazines are available, but totals for all commercial periodicals can only be estimated, which is what Theodore Peterson did (see Table 18). The Magazine Advertising

TABLE XVIII *Estimated Circulations of Commercial Magazines, in Millions, 1900–1947*

Year	*Circulation*
1900	65.0
1925	128.6
1929	202.0
1933	174.8
1939	239.7
1947	384.6

Source: Theodore Peterson, *Magazines in the Twentieth Century* (Urbana, Ill., 1956), p. 54.

Bureau has reported circulations of Audit Bureau of Circulation general circulation and farm magazines since 1914. Their figures (Table 19) for representative years support the contention that

ABLE XIX *Circulations of Audit Bureau of Circulation Member Magazines, eneral and Farm (Excluding Comics), 1914–64*

ear	*Number of Magazines or Groups*	*Combined Circulation per Issue*			*U.S. Adult*[1] *Population (in thousands)*	*Circu-lation Per 100 Adults*
		Single Copy	*Subscription*	*Total*		
914	54	. . .	. . .	17,912,922	67,556	26.5
916	96	. . .	. . .	32,638,114	69,514	47.0
920	146	. . .	. . .	44,094,717	72,675	60.7
925	200	19,770,855	41,505,812	61,276,667	79,905	76.7
930	232	27,366,763	51,477,685	78,844,448	87,074	90.5
933	187	23,564,124	45,783,305	69,347,429	90,436	76.7
936	206	31,690,147	51,544,973	83,235,120	94,067	88.5
940	224	39,005,215	55,812,023	94,817,238	99,012	95.8
945	219	65,707,419	55,533,066	121,240,485	97,903	123.8
950	250	61,988,611	85,270,929	147,259,540	110,471	133.3
955	272	71,073,877	108,891,354	179,965,231 [2]	115,505	155.8
956	282	73,874,770	111,856,119	185,730,889	116,743	159.1
959	274	62,609,711	122,979,455	185,589,166	121,438	152.8
960	273	62,295,487	128,136,349	190,431,836	123,890	153.7
963	274	62,578,172	140,645,067	203,223,239	129,797	156.6
964	282	64,953,619	142,917,837	207,871,456	132,005	157.5

[1] Population 15 years of age and older.
[2] Includes *Reader's Digest* for the first time as an A.B.C. publication—circulation 10,361,531.
Sources: Magazine Advertising Bureau of Magazine Publishers Assn., Inc. That association's ublication, "Circulation 1A," credits as its sources: Circulation—ABC records covering the *second* x months of each year. Population—Bureau of Census, population aged 15 years and older, mid-ear estimates excluding members of the armed forces.

magazine circulations are continuing to increase. These figures obviously exclude large numbers of magazines, but two points should be made: The data is based on ABC-audited circulations; publishers have no opportunity to inflate through estimates. Second, large magazines are included. Thus these figures represent a sizable portion of total circulation; more than a third each year of Peterson's estimates.

These Magazine Publishers Association data reflect a major problem confronting large circulation magazines, a heritage of the 1890's. At that time *McClure's, Cosmopolitan,* and *Munsey's Magazine* slashed newsstand prices to attract huge circulations. The formula evolved of earning immense profits from high advertising rates which more than offset losses on circulation. Ballooning circulations continued to reap ever higher advertising profits until television's needle deflated the system. Magazine publishers, however, loath to abandon the success formula, reacted by reducing subscription rates even more, many of them to half. The huge subscription increases since 1950 reflect this unhealthy ritual. *Coronet* is a recent example of how the system has bankrupt even growing magazines. *Coronet* had built a circulation of 3.2 million and went out of business in 1961. Comments made by Lewis Gillenson, *Coronet*'s last editor, are illuminating.

> Contemplate the cost of a subscription. A giant weekly publisher begs you to sign up for a year with enticing "9 cents per copy" offer. The magazine sells weekly on the newsstand for 25 cents. The following are, roughly, average costs to the publisher: production, 40 cents; mailing, 4 cents; fulfillment, billing, delinquency, 3 cents. Total, 47 cents. In all, the magazine is behind 38 cents an issue on subscriptions, or about $20 for the year. Multiply this figure by three million, a reasonable estimate of the number of cut-rate subscribers a big magazine might carry, and you begin to get an idea of the deficit that must be made up by advertising.[10]

Many of the large magazines have been ensnared by the "numbers game." In 1959, *Life* was estimated to be selling approximately 78 per cent of its subscriptions at cut-rate prices; *Look*, 51 per cent; *Newsweek*, 63 per cent. So rampant has become the practice that by 1961, 99 per cent of *Reader's Digest*'s and 59 per cent of *McCall's* new subscriptions and renewals were sold at reduced rates.[11] Publications other than *Coronet* have been destroyed by the lag between rapidly expanding subscription lists and the advertising rates quoted on lower totals. This squeeze almost bankrupted S. S. McClure in the 1890's during the early years of his magazine publishing career. Later, *Saturday Evening Post*, *Life*, and many others suffered similar deficit-inducing results.[12]

Heavy reliance on advertising has given business and industry dominant influence over the content of many magazines, as Theodore Peterson has illustrated.[13] An advertising agency head who pleaded for editor control over content to maintain the quality needed, said he felt in many instances that the business office and promotion departments had taken over, consigning the editor "to an office down the hall with no carpets, one window, and a pension fund."[14] Certainly conclusions based on a *Life* research study support his charge: "The delivery of an audience for the advertiser is the fundamental function of any medium. . . . on the one hand, it (the medium) should give maximum pleasure; on the other hand it should give minimum offense." [15] Mass circulation magazines are prima facie evidence that this attitude prevails among publishers. No longer will magazines risk publishing attacks on Standard Oil, the meat packing industry, or the railways, as did *McClure's*, *Collier's*, *Cosmopolitan*, *Everybody's*, and the *Arena* in the first decade of this century. It is worth noting in passing that of these magazines only an anemic version of *Cosmopolitan* remains while several of their lesser, untainted competitors now flourish.

Magazines, other than the muckrakers, which were gaining in circulation have suspended because advertisers had a bad impression of them. A magazine may be *hot* or *cold*. And *Collier's*, despite a growing 3.75 million circulation,[16] was scuttled in 1957. *Saturday Evening Post* has for years been at death's doorstep although its circulation exceeds 6.7 million and is increasing, the victim of a 53.2 per cent decline in advertising from 1950 to 1961.[17] (Curtis Publishing Company reportedly lost $18.9 million in 1962 [18] and $14 million in 1964,[19] and on January 16, 1965, reduced *Saturday Evening Post* to biweekly publication.)

Mortality rates have been staggering. Thirteen of the twenty-one general magazines with a million or more circulation in 1930 have died. A hundred magazines were suspended between 1950 and 1957, two of which had circulations in excess of 4 million.[20] J. K. Lasser and Company reported thirty-two of the two hundred and fifty largest magazines between 1950 and 1960 either ceased publication or were merged into other magazines.[21] Mass circulation periodicals which have expired during the past thirty years include such giants as *American, Collier's, Coronet, Country Gentleman, Delineator, Household, Liberty, Literary Digest, Pathfinder, Pictorial Review, Scribner's, St. Nicholas, Woman's Home Companion*. Also gone, but less lamented, are a bundle of cheap pulps.

The profits of those remaining have declined.[22] Magazine profits hit bottom in 1960 when the thirty-five largest publishing houses reported profits after taxes of 1.7 per cent of total sales. This compares to 19 per cent for television and 7.6 per cent for radio stations. The Magazine Publishers Association reported that 39 per cent of its members in 1960 operated at losses and another 25 per cent had profits of less than 5 per cent of revenue before taxes.[23]

In an effort to lure advertising, one magazine cuts rates; almost immediately others join the price war as they attempt to regain linage lost to television; magazines' share of total mass media advertising declined from 20.4 per cent in 1947 to 13.3 in 1955, a proportion which has fluctuated little and remains at 13.0 per cent. Although magazine advertising revenues have increased, they continue to lag behind the other media except for newspapers. From 1960 to 1966, magazine advertising increased from $940 million to $1,295 million, 37.8 per cent; newspapers from $3,700 million to $4,876 million, 31.8 per cent; but radio, the supposedly sick media, rose from $690 million to $1,001 million, 45.1 per cent; and television, after gaining 835 per cent in the previous decade, grew another 73.9 per cent, from $1,590 million to $2,765 million.[24]

Meantime, production costs have soared. J. K. Lasser and Company, using 1947–49 as their base, reported these index increases during the decade of the 1950's: paper, 131; printing, 144; second-class postage, 189; and salaries, 141. During the same period the Consumer Price Index rose to 127 and Wholesale Commodities Index to 119. Paper, printing, postage, and salary costs consume 80 per cent of magazine revenues.[25]

As the MPA circulation figures show, publishers during World War II, forced by paper shortages and reduced advertising revenues, shifted their emphasis from subscriptions to more profitable single copy sales. The trend actually began around 1935 and reached a peak in 1945 when 54.2 per cent of total ABC-member general and farm magazine sales were by single copy. As the figures show, subscription totals remained stagnant until after the end of the war. Then the rush resumed for mass cut-rate circulation, peddled again by traveling subscription teams, by club and organization fund-raising schemes, in combination with newspapers, and, of course, by enticing mail offers and gifts.

Single sales dipped in the late 1950's and through the mid-1960's, resulting from a monopoly which squeezed publishers for years and cost them untold millions. Distribution of copies to newsstands and other dealers, shifting copies from places where they are not selling well to others where they are, returning unsold copies, and otherwise servicing single sales of magazines soon became too complex for individual publishers to untangle. They relied on distributors. As a result, American News Company through its Union News subsidiary monopolized newsstand distribution of magazines. Union News refused to sell to those not supplied through American, thus enabling the parent company to pressure publishers into granting exclusive distribution rights. Justice Department antitrust action brought in 1952 terminated in a cease and desist order entered in 1955. In the meantime, Union News was quietly sold to other interests, against whom monopoly practices charges continued to be levied until Union News went out of business in 1957.[26] The resulting disruption lowered single copy sales by more than 13 million between 1956 and 1961; publishers have not yet regained lost newsstand sales.

S-M News Company, formed in 1919 by two companies, publishers of *Popular Science Monthly* and *McCall's*, early began to challenge Union News, especially after *Reader's Digest* in 1947 and Meredith Publishing Company in 1948 became part owners of S-M. With the shift of *Reader's Digest* and Meredith's magazines and, the following year, of Street & Smith Publications to S-M News, that agency became a major competitor. Its impact reduced American News' net income from $4,495,000 in 1948 to $817,000 in 1953 and $434,000 in 1954.[27]

Vying for dominant display on, and exclusive agreements with, newsstands continues to be a struggle among publishers. They and their distributors often are accused of coercing store owners into giving their magazines preferential display under threat of withdrawing franchises, and of pressuring outlets to accept quotas of less popular magazines to get those with large circulations.[28]

Magazine Ownership

Squeezed between inadequate advertising income and soaring production and subscription-maintenance costs, magazine publishers have fought among themselves for survival. As a result magazines increasingly have been taken over by industrialists, businessmen, and cross-media chains. One of the largest is Norton Simon of Hunt Foods and Industries, Incorporated.[29] In 1953 he began buying into the McCall Company and gained control in 1956. Pouring his millions into *McCall's*,[30] a fourth-place, woman's magazine, he, through subscription price cutting and the most extensive promotional campaign ever waged in the mass media, pushed *McCall's* into first place by 1961 and continued to widen the gap over the former queen, *Ladies Home Journal*, 6,839,882 circulation. That magazine has now fallen to fourth position, behind *McCall's*, 8,531,091, and two grocery-chain distributed magazines, *Family Circle*, owned by Cowles, 7,938,170, and *Woman's Day*, Fawcett Publications, 6,984,510. In addition to *McCall's*, the Simon interests publish two other large magazines, *Redbook*, 4,350,987, and the literary weekly, *Saturday Review*, approximately 463,138.[31]

Altogether, only one of the nineteen general consumer, shelter, and woman's magazines with circulations in excess of a million is not chain-owned, *Reader's Digest*. And it, of course, along with every other million-plus magazine has outside financial interests. Chain ownership among these million-plus circulation journals may be measured in another way, total circulation by chains; Curtis owns four giants with 18 million circulation; Cowles, two, 15.7 million; McCall, two, 13 million; Time-Life, three, 12 million; Triangle Publications, two, 10.8 million; Fawcett, three, 10.7 million; Hearst, five, 10.5 million; Meredith, two, 8.2 million.[32]

Newspaper chain owners apparently have an affinity for magazines. As we have seen, early magazines were started by newspapermen. One of the major investors was and is Hearst, who founded his first journal in 1901, *Hearst's Magazine*. In 1905 he bought *Cosmopolitan*, and twenty years later merged the two into *Hearst's International Cosmopolitan*.[33] He started new magazines and bought various others while building his newspaper-magazine-radio chain; by 1935, at his peak, he owned 13 magazines, 26 daily newspapers, 8 radio stations, 2 motion picture companies as well as King Features Syndicate, International News Service, International News Photos, Universal Service, and *American Weekly* Sunday newspaper supplement.[34] Through the years he and his successors have started, bought, and killed various magazines. Today most of the chain's newspapers and magazines lag behind competitors. Those remaining are *Good Housekeeping, Cosmopolitan, Harper's Bazaar, Town and Country, House Beautiful, Bride and Home, Motor, Motor Boating,*

Sports Afield, Popular Mechanics, Science Digest, American Druggist, and eight British magazines.

A second major newspaper-broadcasting chain invasion of magazines was by Newhouse. He bought controlling interest in Condé Nast publications (*Vogue, House & Garden, Glamour, Bride's Magazine* of Great Britain, and *Jeune Mariée* of France) for his wife in 1959 as a $5 million, thirty-fifth wedding-anniversary gift.[35] And for another $4 million he gained control of Street & Smith (*Mademoiselle, Charm, Living for Young Homemakers, Astounding Science Fiction, Air Progress, Hobbies for Young Men, Baseball Annual,* and *Football Annual*). He combined *Charm* and *Glamour,* but kept the others intact.[36] Newhouse turned these two money losers, Condé Nast had lost $534,528 and Street & Smith in excess of $200,000 the previous year,[37] into profitable properties; Condé Nast, which operates Street & Smith, in 1966 earned $2,447,000, or $1.66 a share, on $57.5 million sales. Profits rose 25.8 per cent in a year.[38]

Other newspaper-broadcasting chains which own major magazines include Triangle Publications, *Seventeen, TV Guide, Official Detective*; Cowles Communications, Incorporated, *Look, Family Circle, Venture, Accent on Leisure*; Washington *Post, Newsweek, Art News*; Oklahoma City *Daily Oklahoman, Farmer Stockman*; Minneapolis *Star* and *Tribune,* half interest in *Harper's*; Stauffer, *Capper* farm publications; Cox, 80 per cent interest in United Technical Publications, electronics, medical-electronics, and office-equipment fields; Ridder Publications, *Electronic Design,* and trade magazines in hotel and restaurant fields; Whitney Communications, *Parade, Interiors*; Corn Belt Publishers, *Drovers Journal*; Fred A. and Richard M. Seaton, *Western Farm Life.*

Magazine-broadcasting chains own these journals: Time-Life, *Time, Life, Fortune, Sports Illustrated*; Meredith, *Better Homes and Gardens, Successful Farming*; Bartell Media Corporation, *True Story, True Romance, True Detective, True Love, Climax, True Experience, Photoplay, Sport, Saga, TV-Radio Mirror, Master Detective, True Confessions, Motion Picture, Official Detective, Silver Screen, Screenland, Pageant.*

The line separating magazine and book publishing, as the late Frank Luthor Mott predicted in 1954,[39] grows dimmer each year. Thirty-five of forty-nine magazine publishing houses responding to a questionnaire by Sherilyn Cox Bennion in 1962–63, reported they were engaged in nonmagazine activities. Of these, twenty-one, the largest number, said they published books.[40] Movement between these two fields is in both directions. Publishers of some of the largest special interest as well as mass circulation magazines filter the flow of ideas through progressively fewer minds, for these owners throw communications switches to let ideas germinate or die. Book publishers expanded into magazines in the nineteenth century; among them Harper & Brothers (now Harper & Row), *Harper's Monthly Magazine, Harper's Young People, Harper's Bazaar*; D. Appleton & Company, *The Popular Science Monthly, Appletons' Journal*; P. F. Collier, *Once A Week*; Dodd, Mead & Company, *The Bookman*; Doubleday, Page & Company, *The World's Work*; J. B. Ford & Company, *The Outlook*; Lippincott's, *Lippincott's Magazine*; Phillips, Sampson & Company, *The Atlantic Monthly*; Putnam's, *Putnam's Monthly Magazine*; Scribner & Company, *Scribner's Magazine*.[41]

Magazines which began diversifying into other than book publishing around the 1930's, have continued to do so at a quickening rate, heeding the advice of such trade publications as *Ad Age, The Gallagher Report*, and *Magazine Industry Newsletter*.[42] Sherilyn Cox Bennion found that twenty-seven companies had divisions and subsidiaries in 1950, another seven were founded or acquired through 1954 and an additional thirteen through 1959. The number of subsidiaries increased to forty-six from 1960 to 1963.[43] Miss Bennion's study listed the following magazine publisher ownerships.

1] American Heritage Publishing Company, Incorporated, six book publishing houses, some of which also issue special interest magazines. And this company entered into agreements with others to publish, to make movies from, and to distribute their works to newspapers.

2] Bartell Media Corporation, annuals, book publishing, broadcasting, community antenna television, pay television, distribution, periodicals, printing.

3] Curtis Publishing Company, book publishing, magazine and book subscription sales and distribution, Jack and Jill food and clothing merchandising, catalog subscription sales, job printing, paper manufacturing, data processing.

4] The Chilton Company, books, contract printing, films, market research, microfilm information retrieval, iron mines, paper manufacturing.

5] Crowell-Collier (returned to magazine publishing with *Grade Teacher*), books, broadcasting, education by mail company, encyclopedia publishing and marketing, professional and technical programs.

6] Davis Publications, Incorporated, books, handbooks, manufactures kits and craft plans.

7] Esquire, Incorporated, Scott Stamp Publications, instructional films, manufactures outdoor lighting equipment, owns real estate including an office building, broadcasting, magazine subscription firm.

8] Farm Journal, books, book club.

9] Flower Grower Publishing, Incorporated, books, sells flower products by mail, plans and sponsors tours.

10] Hearst, books, newspapers, Sunday supplements, features syndicate, broadcasting, publishing service, real estate, ranching, mining, foundations, art collections.

11] HMH Publishing Company, Incorporated, books, Playboy clubs, tours, gifts, hotels, motion pictures, calendars.

12] Hunt Foods and Industries, books, dress patterns, two large printing divisions, photoengraving, investment corporation, broadcasting.

13] McGraw-Hill Publishing Company, Incorporated, books, bookstores, book distribution warehouses, catalogs, business newspapers, broadcasting, educational films, educational research services, programmed instruction, paper mills, iron mines.

14] Meredith Publishing Company, books, broadcasting, geographical globes, printing.

15] National Geographic Society, books, atlases, globes, maps, school bulletins, information services, sponsors expeditions and scientific projects.

16] Parents' Magazine Enterprises, Incorporated, book publishing and wholesaling, national subscription sales companies, printing.

17] Premier Industries, Incorporated, battery additives, venetian blinds.

18] Popular Science Publishing Company, book publishing, filmstrips.

19] Reader's Digest Association, Incorporated, books, book club, record clubs, advertising agency, educational materials.

20] Time-Life, book division, book club, textbook publishing, foreign book and magazine publishing, broadcasting in the United States and three foreign countries, weekly news service for elementary and junior high schools, newsstand circulation service, printing facilities, paper-making facilities.

21] Universal Publishing and Distribution Corporation, paperback books, career guidance manuals.

Universal exemplifies the immense success open to one who attunes magazines to the special interests of a large body of readers. *Ski* magazine was the first and continues to be the most popular of Universal's three ski industry journals; the others are *Ski Business* and *Ski Management*. The company has branched into other sports-hobbies with *Golf, Gold Business*, and *The Family Handyman*. Universal prints a wide variety of fiction and nonfiction, includng vocational guidance manuals and books on sports topics. Revenues of the publicly owned business have grown from $2.8 million in 1961 to $7.2 million in 1966.[44]

Another of the fabulously successful new publishing empires is the sole property of Robert Petersen. This, the largest magazine publishing company west of the Rockies, is an outgrowth of Petersen's keen interest in cars. His first magazine, *Hot Rod*, founded in 1948, remains his most profitable property, with 770,000 circulation. He, like Universal, offers a complete array of magazines to appeal to buffs: *Motor Trend, Car Craft, Rod & Custom, Sports Car Graphic, Hot Rod Cartoons*, and *Cartoons*. He also issues *Guns & Ammo, Skin Diver*, and a boy-watching magazine for teenage girls, *'Teen*. Petersen publishes hard and soft cover books, owns a film production company, holds large interests in a stock car race track and a 470,000-acre cattle ranch, and has valuable real estate.[45] Gene Booth, associate editor of a Petersen competitor, *Car Life*, said, in 1964, that there were twenty-five magazines devoted to cars published in the Los Angeles area.[46] These are only a tiny part of the 2,486 specialized publications which were in existence in 1963, an increase of more than seven hundred since 1950.[47]

A comparison of 1938 and 1963 circulations by Robert and Christine Root shows these special interest magazines lead all others (Table 20). Although the Roots excluded from their study the special interest magazines alluded to here, they included what might well be classified as special interest publications in their categories "Outdoor," "Leisure," "Business," and "Science-mechanic." And these four were among the five enjoying the largest circulation growth. However, as has been noted and as the authors point out, circulation is not always a barometer of prosperity.

TABLE XX *Magazine Groups Ranked by Percentage of Increase 1938–63*

Type of Magazine	*Percentage of Growth*
Outdoor	393.6
Leisure	336.5
Idea	244.2
Business	210.2
Science-mechanics	164.2
Shelter	150.1
Quality	148.2
Women's	135.8
News	131.3
General	61.0

Source: Robert Root and Christine V. Root, "Magazines in the United States: Dying or Thriving?" *Journalism Quarterly,* Winter 1964, p. 22.

One other spectacular recent success, *Playboy,* merits mention. Founded in 1953 on a $10,000 investment, the magazine, which *Time* says peddles "spectator sex," circulates 4 million, 85 per cent sold at newsstands. Its trademark, the bunny, has bred Playboy Clubs throughout the world, resorts, gifts, and sex symbols.[48] Many earlier magazine success stories might be mentioned—*Reader's Digest,* begun in 1922 on a $5,000 loan; *Time,* started a year later on $86,000 capital; *Life,* started in 1935; *The New Yorker,* 1925; *Look,* 1937; *U.S. News & World Report,* 1948; *TV Guide,* 1953; and many more.

The gold these and others have reaped has enticed many to enter magazine publishing. Since most magazines, including many of the largest, are printed on contract, a new entrant into the field need not invest in expensive equipment. But this open invitation to fabulous fortune is more illusion than fact, as Harlan Logan pointed out. He calculates the odds against success for a new publisher as ranging from 2 to 1 in the Specialty Service (*Harper's Bazaar, Mademoiselle*), Miscellaneous Monthly (scientific, travel, youth, the arts), and Pocket Size (*Reader's Digest, Pageant*), to 10 to 1 in the General Monthly (*American, Cosmopolitan*) groups. And these figures presuppose financing to support the publication for four years.[49] It is doubtful if the odds have improved, judging by the large number of journals which regularly die in infancy.

A Few Encouraging Signs

Fortunately, a few bright spots appear in the magazine industry. Quite obviously the special interest publications will continue to thrive, fed by a population whose leisure time continues to expand. Who knows what journals may join *Antique Airplanes, Amateur Rocketeer,* and *Gambling Illustrated* to plow these fertile fields. Only if publishers fall victim to the numbers-phobia of the general circulation books should special interest magazines falter.

General circulation magazines, forced by television to subdivide into regional editions, are striving to improve their advertising acceptance. The *New Yorker* in 1929 introduced this concept, but large magazines generally resisted until 1959 when *Life, Look,* and *Saturday Evening Post* offered advertisers placement in less than the full run. As a result, regional editions attracted $48 million in advertising that year; the total reached $162 million in 1965.[50] Regional editions helped increase advertising pages from seventy thousand in 1961 to eighty thousand in 1965. Some advertising men predict split-run advertising will account for one of every four dollars spent on magazine advertising in 1970.[51]

Look offers advertising in seventy-five "Magazones"; *Saturday Evening Post,* in a wide variety of "Select-A-Market" combinations. *Life* permits one to choose any of the largest twenty television markets as long as his total circulation is 750,000 or more. Thus an advertiser may make such selections as Philadelphia, 325,000, Milwaukee, 65,000, much as if he were buying spots on television stations in these cities. *Reader's Digest,* under a similar plan, has built a circulation of more than a million for its metropolitan New York edition. Conversely, *Farm Journal* will sell space for any one of the 3,070 counties in the United States; in March 1966, it ran 126 different editions.[52] *Time* offers ten regional and three demographic editions, one each for physicians, educators, and college students.[53] Geographic and demographic splits make possible keying advertising to subscribers' weather, local customs and styles, consumer patterns, and professional interests. Although the procedure is complex and probably too expensive for small-circulation magazines, split-run publishing doubtless will expand. Computer-programmed press runs make it possible to tailor magazines to the individual advertising and editorial interests of each subscriber. Characteristically, few editorial changes are being made from one edition to another.

In addition to general improvements in the print media, as discussed in Chapter 4, a few others of particular value to magazines are three-dimensional photography, combination of sound with copy, electronic distribution, and, of course, improved equipment, paper, and ink. Harris-Intertype, Eastman Kodak, and *Look* cooperated to develop 3-D color photography reproduction, which when perfected will inject new realism into illustrations. *National Geographic*, in its August 1965 issue, distributed a record on which television newsman David Brinkley's narration of the funeral of Sir Winston Churchill is recorded together with excerpts from Churchill speeches. A couple of years earlier, the publishers of *Practical Builder* bound into their magazine a recorded demonstration of sound transmitted through "quiet home" partitions, to accompany an article on "The Quiet Home."

More important to the theme of this book is the significant increase in "little magazines." From around sixty in the 1920's, when they first attracted attention, the number went to 180 in 1955, 250 in 1960,[54] and 323 in July 1965.[55] The only reason for the existence of these "individual intellectual rebels," as *Publishers' Weekly* labeled them, is that they publish the ideas of those whose views and writing styles are unwelcome in the commercial press.[56] And although few circulate more than one thousand copies, free or by sales, and the total audience for all of them is less than fifty thousand—mostly other writers, literature students, and editors[57]—they enable the author to air his views, regardless of how unpopular, unconventional, ill-advised they may be. E. Oatman, quoted in the *New York Times*, expresses the point well: "The importance of the little magazines cannot be measured solely by any greatness they may nurture. Their true worth is in their independent spirit which defies the thick skin of bigness and favors the individual who has something to say but cannot say it on larger platforms." [58] Topics range the broad political, economic, social, and religious spectrum. Contents are varied—essays, fiction, plays, poetry, reviews, art reproductions, and proclamations. Most are mimeographed; a few are printed. Virtually none are handsome or lavish. Actually, the only things they have in common are their unprofitability, tiny circulations, and often evangelistic advocacy of causes. At present they represent press freedom in its purest, most elemental form.

A Blueprint for Action

15.

As we have seen, our mass media are increasingly falling into the hands of monopolists. Multimedia webs span the nation and at times control all of the local news communications outlets. Most media owners have other financial and, hence, special interests for which their newspapers, broadcasting stations, magazines plead, either at the insistance of the owners or by indirection. Let us consider for a moment this latter charge; it is indeed a damning one.

That the owners have used the mass media as weapons for their selfish interests has been well-documented, and a few examples will further illustrate this. Probably the greatest abuser of press freedom was the Anaconda Copper Mining Company, the world's largest nonferrous mining industry, which from the early 1900's to 1959 owned the major daily newspapers in Montana. Anaconda used its seven-newspaper chain to help maintain its state political domination and at times to influence actions in Washington. Thor Severson began the first of a six-article investigative series for the Denver *Post*, on "The Copperdust Shadow Over Montana," with this biting description:

> BUTTE, Mont. — Montana lives under the captive shadow of one of the world's most fabulous corporation giants — a giant so powerful it virtually ghost-writes this state's legislative program and wields enough dictatorial power to all but still the voice of the state's free press.[1]

One of the most severe indictments of the owners' use of an American newspaper's news and editorial columns and political influence to further their economic interests was lodged against the Los Angeles *Times*. William G. Bonelli, who observed from his vantage point as a member of the California State Board of Equalization, accused the Chandler family of using their newspaper in many and diverse ways to enrich themselves. One criticism concerned their campaigning for an expensive, tax-supported system to pipe water two hundred and thirty miles to the San Fernando Valley from where it would then flow to Los Angeles. Harry Chandler and two others, Bonelli said, had previously bought land in the valley for from $5 to $20 an acre which they sold shortly thereafter for a profit of around $100 million.[2] In a 1964 study, the *Times*, whose owners are among the largest landholders in California and New Mexico, opposed ending the Mexican farm labor ("bracero") program, both in editorials and news stories.[3]

S. I. Newhouse has been pictured as one who does not interfere in the editorial operation of his newspapers. The convenience of a noninterference policy to one who operates large newspapers in the North and South is obvious, especially when success demands that divergent views on civil rights be expressed. As his critical biographer, John A. Lent, pointed out, Newhouse's brothers and sons hold managerial positions on half of his newspapers, long-time associates on the others.[4] Under these circumstances he obviously can exercise all the anonymous control he wishes. Further, his interference to prevent his St. Louis *Globe-Democrat* from endorsing Senator Barry Goldwater for the presidency in 1964, after that nominally conservative Republican newspaper had urged the party to nominate him, is well known among *Globe-Democrat* staff members. It is little wonder that President Johnson found time to speak at the dedication of the Newhouse Communication Center at Syracuse University in August 1964.

In an earlier period, William Randolph Hearst was accused of using his newspapers to foment the Spanish-American War;[5] undoubtedly he used them to plead many of his special causes, including his own candidacy for the presidency. News and editorial columns of the Denver *Post*, under Fred G. Bonfils and Harry H. Tammen, often were used for personal gain, even to the extent of blackmailing through threats of disclosure, oil lessees involved in manipulations which were later exposed in the Teapot Dome scandal.[6]

Some newspaper, radio, and television owners also browbeat local city councils into granting special favors. A current activity is to apply pressure to gain approval of community antenna television systems in which they hold financial interest. Their weapon is to support candidates who do their bidding and to destroy those who oppose them; so charged Representative Thomas L. Blanton (D-Tex.).[7] A recent victim was Senator Thomas J. Dodd (D-Conn.), whom, regardless of the merits of his case, broadcasters had fought ever since he began investigating the impact of television on juvenile crime. They gleefully reported all the actions leading up to and including his censure, June 23, 1967, by the United States Senate. And the commonly owned media jointly defend and promote each other and attack their enemies. CBS complained that RCA-owned Random House published the book by the former head of CBS news, Fred W. Friendly, *Due to Circumstances Beyond Our Control,* to harass CBS.

These few examples illustrate how owners' economic interests affect mass media content. And we have seen in previous chapters the extensiveness of media operators' ownerships of cross-media, business, and industrial interests. Few of those who read, listen to, and watch the mass media know of these ties. Therefore, in all fairness, should they not be informed, so that they may better evaluate news and comment related to outside ownerships? If a newspaper owner also holds oil interests, shouldn't the readers know so that they might understand that newspaper's stand on such matters as the oil depletion allowance? If a radio-television station combination is owned by a large airline, shouldn't listeners and viewers be told this during a bond-issue campaign to expand or build a new air terminal? When a large defense contractor owns a radio-television network, shouldn't those who view and hear that network's news and public affairs programs be so informed when hot war, cold war, and armaments are under discussion? And shouldn't magazine readers know that their publication is being underwritten by men of great wealth who use it as a propaganda weapon against the public schools in a short-sighted attempt to lower their taxes? These and thousands of other conflict-of-interest communication-ownerships exist. The very least that should be done is to inform communications consumers so that they may be less deceived. Every medium should be required regularly not only to publicize the names of those who own even small interests in that medium, but also the communications and noncommunications businesses and industries in which they hold interests. There are precedents for such action. Names of those owning 1 per cent or more of the stock in a broadcasting station are on file at the Federal Communications Commission. The Post Office Department requires semiannual ownership disclosure by newspapers mailed second class; publishers negate the regulation by setting names in the smallest type available and burying the information where it will be least noticeable. In view of this experience, ownership disclosure regulations would have to be explicit in what, where, how often, and how the information would be released.

Doubtlessly, media spokesmen will reply, "We do not dictate news policy." Few such proclamations of piety are true, as Per Holting, Walter Gieber, and David R. Bowers learned. Holting found that more than half of the hundred television news directors surveyed said that they had friction with their management. Friction with those charged with carrying out policy was considerably greater with managers who had never worked with news.[8] Not unexpectedly, Fred W. Friendly's comments about difficulties he and Edward R. Murrow had with CBS board chairman William S. Paley and president Frank Stanton corroborate Holting's findings.[9] Gieber stated that if a reporter accepts the existence of policy, he is likely to act according to a set or accepted "line" or to his interpretations of that policy; reporters on none of the papers he studied felt free to pursue a civil rights story at will. They said that under certain circumstances they would not attempt to write a story.[10] Bowers in his study of managing editors, those charged with carrying out newspaper policies, found that publishers were most active in areas affecting the revenues of the newspaper directly or indirectly, and less active regarding social issues, unless they related to economic considerations. More than three-fourths of the managing editors said their publishers were active in affecting news and editorial treatment of subjects included in Bowers' questionnaire.[11]

Actually, whether the owners ever speak to newsmen about policy, other interests of the company, special likes and dislikes, is not at issue. Warren Breed and Lewis Donohew learned that publishers' desires get translated into newspaper content, regardless. Breed, in an important early study, found that staff members assimilate policy through "osmosis": rewards and punishments, observing the work of others, corrections and hints, discussions in news conferences and staff meetings, talking with other employees, fear of being given less desirable assignments, obligation to and esteem for superiors, desire for promotion either within or without the news medium, also a desire to maintain an "in-group" posture. He pointed out that much news is objectively presented, but news relating to policy is altered by slanting, burying it, or presenting only those aspects of it which support policy.[12]

A vital link in this chain of evidence was supplied by Donohew. He found publishers' attitudes overshadowed all other considerations in determining the treatment newspapers gave to news about Medicare. The newspaper performance was correlated with thirteen variables: publisher's attitude, publisher's estimate of community opinion, circulation, an attitude-opinion index, and community demographic criteria such as the proportion of white collar workers, proportion receiving old age assistance, proportion with incomes of $3,000 or less, proportion of age sixty-five and over, proportion voting for President Kennedy, proportion unemployed, educational level, number of physicians per one thousand population, and whether urban or rural.[13]

Obviously, newsmen learn their medium's policy and reflect that policy in news treatment, even subconsciously. A study conducted by Jean S. Kerrick, Thomas E. Anderson, and Luita B. Swales further illuminates this problem. They found in a University of California laboratory experiment that students selected certain facts and ignored others so as to reflect policy in both editorials and news stories. Surprisingly, those whose own opinions disagreed with policy wrote the most partisan editorials and the most one-sided news stories favoring the policy. The attitudes of the students tended to change after writing editorials and stories in the direction of policy.[14] A considerable body of literature supports this attitude-change phenomenon.

Clearly, who owns the mass media is of vital concern to all of us. Those persons can and do determine what information and interpretations the American people receive. It is an unusual person who disseminates information deterimental to his economic interests. We have seen ample evidence, and we have only scratched the surface, that the interests of the media owners and those of the general public at times conflict.

The problem is compounded when individuals or groups amass large chains, thereby dangerously extending their power to persuade. The nearer we approach communications monopoly in any given area, the more restricted our freedom. Few would dispute that our press freedom is predicated on the concept of a marketplace of ideas from which the public may select. The United States Supreme Court in *Associated Press* v. *United States* held that the First Amendment to the Constitution of the United States "rests on the assumption that the widest possible dissemination of information from diverse and antagonistic sources is essential to the welfare of the public." Thomas Jefferson said we can tolerate error of opinion if truth may freely combat it. Walter Lippmann told members of the International Press Institute:

> A press monopoly is incompatible with a free press; and one can proceed with this principle; if there is a monopoly of the means of communication—of radio, television, magazines, books, public meetings—it follows that this society is by definition and in fact deprived of freedom.[15]

Clearly, then, press freedom is a civil right accruing to news and information consumers, not a license granted media owners to enrich themselves at society's peril.

Who says we are powerless against the tide of monopoly and cross-media expansion? If our laws can prevent railroads from owning steamship lines and aircraft manufacturers from owning more than small percentages of airlines, why can't we prevent newspaper-broadcasting-magazine-book publishing combines? Are ocean and air travel more sacred than ideas? Are we irrevocably condemned to an Orwellian one-think world? Surely ways to reverse the trend toward chain-monopoly control of our information sources can be found; they must be found if we are to preserve our basic freedoms.

Complex problems often defeat us because we see a single, difficult, all-embracing solution. A beginning, advocated in previous chapters, would be to revise our tax laws. They make selling to a chain so attractive that few can resist, and, thereby, encourage chain and multimedia expansion. Further, tax laws complicate the disposal of property by will to a survivor.

The postal subsidy should be increased for small, single ownerships and lowered or eliminated for large, multiple ownerships. India bases postal rates on circulation and, along with Great Britain, Germany, some of the Scandinavian countries, Japan, and others, has established a press council to, among other things, try to slow the trend toward chain and monopoly ownership. Formation of a press council in the United States has been advocated, and for good reason. Realistic proportions of space that a publication may devote to advertising and still be classified as a newspaper for mailing purposes should be explored. Spreading life-sustaining advertising among more media would reverse monopoly trends. If the heavily over-staffed and fantastically featherbedded British press profitably operates on around 35 per cent advertising, why can't ours? Sir Cecil H. King, head of the largest publishing combine in the world, told the American Society of Newspaper Editors that his largest newspaper, the *Daily Mirror*, earned $15 million before taxes in 1966, a poor year. Yet the *Mirror* received only 32 per cent of its revenues from advertising and sold for less per copy than half the standard American rate. He, of course, limits his tabloid newspaper to thirty-two pages; it averaged twenty-six in 1966.[16] Admittedly, the *Daily Mirror* is the world's largest circulating newspaper and panders to some of the baser reader-interests; it also offers considerable serious material and treats more intelligently with society's problems than do many American newspapers.

Permitting large publishers and broadcasters to monopolize features, news, programs, is senseless. Such practices are alien to a free exchange of ideas; they smack of censorship, cartels, profits at any price to society. Since the airwaves belong to the people who also own more than 96 per cent of the real broadcasting property, we should demand a stronger voice over what comes through the speaker and picture tube. But first, regulatory control must be vested in a body which can regulate; one armed with sufficient autonomy, authority, administrative procedures which simplify rather than complicate decision-making, and one protected from politics. The Federal Communications Commission undoubtedly is the most frustrated agency in Washington. Some of the commissioners, as accused, have been influenced by the broadcasting industry. The great majority, however, have been honest, if poorly qualified, men. A few of the more competent FCC members have striven courageously to right some of the obvious wrongs. Their rewards have been Congressional reprimands. After realizing the hoplessness of their task, most have resigned. Former Chairman Newton N. Minow proposed to President John F. Kennedy that the administrative and judicial functions of the FCC be split, with the former vested in a single individual and the latter in an administrative court. Similar suggestions had been made by the Hoover Commission in 1949, Louis Hector in 1959, and the Federal Communications Bar Association Committee in 1963. Minow's points are well taken; his suggestions would go far toward streamlining FCC operations. But the one major hurdle facing the Commission, as Minow argues, is antiquated, cumbersome procedural rules which sap the members' time and energies.[17] Congress resists changing these rules because they serve the vested interests of congressmen. Approximately twenty-five congressmen or members of their families own interests in radio and television properties, clearly these men are open to conflict of interest charges. Less well known, but even more serious, probably half of the senators and representatives through their law firms represent broadcasters. Is "influence" the polite term? Some might call it bribery. What should we call the free radio and television time given to two-thirds of the members of Congress by their local stations?[18] No wonder incumbents almost always win re-election. Finally, it is no secret that some committee chairmen, primarily concerned with broadcast problems and with review authority over the FCC, have received generous campaign contributions from the broadcasting industry.

Contrast this mess with the autonomy enjoyed by the Independent Television Authority, the body which regulates commercial television in Great Britain. Members perform tasks in a day which embroil the FCC in red tape for months if not years, as for example, awarding station licenses. Further, their decisions stick. The ITA in mid-1967 deplored the lack of imagination and originality in broadcasting. So have some FCC members; but they are capable of doing little about it. ITA proved it is no mere FCC rubber stamp. When awarding new six-year monopolies, to begin in July 1968, it refused to renew the license of one large company, ordered others to merge, granted monopolies to three new companies, and demanded that

Roy Thomson, the international newspaper-magazine-book-broadcasting chain owner, reduce his stock in Scottish Television from 55 to 25 per cent. The odds are high that British commercial television will become more imaginative and original in its programming. ITA earlier prevented British commercial television from becoming an appendage of United States television when it limited the importation of programs to 14 per cent of program time.[19] Meantime, our rudderless television drifts more deeply into mediocrity.

Educational television, now being referred to as public television, offers some hope. At least evening programming improvements now projected will provide greater program choices for millions. As ETV improves its offerings and woos away commercial television audiences, however, we can expect pressures on Congress to reduce ETV funds, enact restrictive legislation, curtail hours and program formats, for commercial television cannot tolerate an equally convenient, high quality, truly entertaining competitor. Let it be clearly stated, no argument is raised here against entertainment; no plea is made to replace situation comedy with opera, or variety shows with ballet. But entertainment should be more varied, more imaginative, more entertaining. Commercial television already is gradually losing its vast audiences, even without ETV competition. They can anticipate greater defections, especially with the ever rising educational level in this country.

There is Hope

Have we, through neglect, forfeited the right to have society's problems ventilated in the mass media? Has press freedom been completely lost? An unmitigated pessimist would answer "yes" to both questions. And unless changes occur to reverse monopoly trends, both in ownership and ideas, we can expect little from most of the daily press, radio, television, and mass circulation magazines. And even book publishing, as we have seen, is engulfed in this tangled morass.

However, the media are operated by individuals, some of whom place service above riches; their products reflect it. Daily newspapers have exposed government graft, television networks have initiated reforms through their documentary investigations, magazines have explored some of man's previously ignored problems. But by and large they have limited themselves to matters which neither related to owners' investments nor disturbed advertiser sensibilities. There are exceptions—the Little Rock *Gazette* and its burdensome advertising and circulation losses which are attributed to its stand on integration, ABC radio's advertising cancellations because of a program in which Alger Hiss was interviewed, the bankruptcy of Ralph Blumberg by an advertising boycott imposed to punish him for his opposition to the Ku Klux Klan over his WBOX Bogalusa, La., radio station.

Our greatest hope lies not with the behemoths of the mass media; they have been taken over by the businessman-communicators whose forte is balancing ledgers rather than pursuing ideas. They long ago learned the cardinal principal of success: profits do not accrue from challenging the *status quo*. Nor do the little magazines, the other extreme, hold real promise despite their almost limitless freedom. They fail to attract large enough audiences; more important, most of those they wish to influence unfortunately equate them with irresponsibility, the lunatic fringe, eggheads, idealistic do-gooders. The real hope lies with the weekly press, for here an advocate of causes may enter the public debate at relatively low cost, in a medium which has the aura of respectability long associated with farm life, the grass roots, and "the American way of life." Only here can we hope to produce a twentieth century Horace Greeley, Joseph Pulitzer, Benjamin Franklin. Indeed, some of the most refreshingly persuasive, responsible, articulate, outspoken voices in the land speak from this rostrum. Let us consider a few.

Hazel Brannon Smith in her Lexington (Miss.) *Advertiser* could not remain silent while a Negro family suffered brutal persecution meted out by the local sheriff and his deputies. She soon found herself the defender of her county's racial majority. Because of her protection, Negroes in Lexington suffer fewer physical attacks, sleep more soundly at night, walk the streets with impunity, less often are targets of police brutality. They have learned that the dignity of man also refers to them and, thereby, have gained renewed confidence in the future. The cost to Mrs. Smith was disastrous. She has lost hundreds of thousands of dollars, and her once prosperous three newspapers are near bankruptcy, the victims of protracted, fear-enforced advertising and circulation boycotts. The Ku Klux Klan and White Citizens Council members and other racists have threatened her life. Society has attempted to remove some of the hurt by recognitions money cannot buy: the Elijah Parish Lovejoy Award for Courage in Journalism, 1960, the Golden Quill Award for Editorial Writing, 1963, and the Pulitzer Prize for Editorial Writing, 1964. Most cherished is the $2,852 Negroes in her town raised to help their friend. At the presentation ceremony their spokesman paid tribute to Mrs. Smith and her paper, saying that without them "your eyes would be put out," [20] figuratively, at least, if not physically.

Another fighter who lost all is Gene Wirges whose exposures of a corrupt political machine in his Morrilton (Ark.) *Democrat* broke the machine's back. Conway County's sheriff, kingpin of the machine, now faces trial. The impact on Arkansas politics of Wirges' attack was unexpected. It helped focus public attention on other long-entrenched and corrupt political machines and on state problems; consequently, the electorate cleaned house in the next general election, 1966, and returned Arkansas to a two-party status. The expense of defending himself against an avalanche of law suits cost Wirges his newspaper; he is mired in debt. And only on June 5, 1967, was his name finally cleared when the Arkansas Supreme Court dismissed a three-year prison sentence on a perjury conviction, the last major case against him.

J. R. Freeman is living proof that some weekly editors fear no man; he has challenged the oil industry, congressmen, and the United States Department of Interior in his tiny, Frederick (Colo.) *Farmer & Miner*. Here the prize is public shale oil lands, some of which the Interior Department proposes to give away and others to lease for oil exploration at the ridiculously low rate of $2.50 an acre. Freeman claims that the untapped oil's value is worth $8 to $10 trillion. He has convinced some people that this give-away of public resources is infinitely worse than the infamous Teapot Dome debacle. At long last, some congressmen and editors of national magazines and major newspapers have heard this 809-circulation voice; challenges have been raised in public hearings and the mass media. As a result, the program has been revised; still unsatisfied, Freeman continues his almost solo search for more evidence. He has accumulated insurmountable debts, his newspaper continues to receive such minuscule advertising and subscription support that he doesn't know from one week to the next if he will publish; he can afford only a small trailer for his family's home; and attempts have been made on his life.

Least likely of all weeklies to challenge the wrong-doing of the wealthy and powerful is a financial newspaper. But Gene Cervi in his *Cervi's Rocky Mountain Journal,* Denver, repeatedly does just that. He often prints disclosures his richer, daily neighbors ignore. One was the 1966 housewives' protest against inflated chain-grocery store prices in a city where, after eliminating 80 per cent of the independent grocers, the chains raised prices to the highest levels in the nation. Through Cervi's pages others were alerted, grocery-chain boycotts erupted across the land, Congress initiated hearings, the relationships of trading stamps-prizes-contests-frills-advertising and food processing to prices were aired. Several large chains lowered prices, at least temporarily, and housewives received a lesson in the economics of the food industry. *Cervi's,* predictably, lost advertising. And that is why the two Denver dailies ignored the protest until after it was front-page news in New York City; then they buried the story for they dared not risk disturbing huge newspaper profits regardless of the importance of the event.

It is unfortunate that so few of the large dailies, with their infinitely greater financial and manpower resources and louder voices, choose not to attack society's serious problems. Need they be so shy, those who have, to paraphrase Sir Cecil King, driven the weak to the wall to become the most cosily protected businessmen, whose newspapers are the most sheltered from the bracing effects of competition of any in the world? [21] They less than anyone should fear advertiser pressures; the advertisers have helped them eliminate alternate, locally printed advertising outlets. Where else can advertisers turn? Anyway, can they lose more than did Wirges and Mrs. Smith? Those two lost everything, and that leaves one broke whether the loss is ten thousand, a million, or a hundred million dollars. As Carl Lindstrom so accurately put it, the problem with monopoly publications lies not in remaining in business, but staying in journalism.[22] But we forget; to a countinghouse publisher profits, not ideals, are the goal.

That is why we had to rely on the weekly Pecos *Independent* and its young editor, Oscar Griffin, Jr., to unearth in 1962 the Billy Sol Estes government swindle. Even after the exposé, other Texas newspapers ignored the affair. Estes retaliated by pressuring advertisers to boycott the *Independent* and by reducing advertising rates on a competing weekly Pecos newspaper Estes had founded the previous year when the *Independent* refused to endorse his candidacy for the school board. The national scandal unleashed by Griffin is well-documented. His payment came in protecting the public treasury from further plundering, recognition, and a well-earned Pulitzer Prize. The nation again was served by what Howard R. Long calls the "mighty mice,"

(who) as they scurry about the skirts of the Establishment, seem to come to grips with matters in the public interest which escape the eyes of the giants of their profession. . . . It is the mice of the press, therefore, who are the legitimate heirs to the American Journalistic tradition.[23]

The view that in the weeklies lies journalism's final chance is comfortingly shared by others, including the author of the first edition of *The First Freedom*, Morris L. Ernst. His conviction of this view has been stated both in recent talks and in his column in the Greenwich Village (New York City) paper, *The Villager*.[24] Admittedly, comparatively few editors have risen to the heights of Mrs. Smith, Wirges, and Freeman. They sacrificed dearly to serve society. Society should repay part of the debt by giving financial assistance to those who have fought and bled for worthy causes. Our large foundations could scarcely find a more effective way to revive America's democratic keystone, freedom of the press.

APPENDIX/NOTES/INDEX

Appendix

TABLE XXI *Chains Holding Interest in Ten or More Dailies in 1967*

Chains	Number of Chain Dailies 1962	1967	Total Circulation, 1967 Daily	Sunday
Copley	14	18	619,218	485,876
Cowles Publications	8	11	1,017,860	1,319,852
Donrey Media Group	14	21	166,528	173,170
Federated Publications	5	13	355,959	264,797
Freedom (Hoiles)	12	14	346,242	179,374
Gannett Newspapers	15	30	1,253,540	617,749
Harte-Hanks	11	12	478,969	341,727
Lee Newspapers	16	16	398,719	323,166
Newhouse Newspapers	19	22	3,199,516	3,011,707
Palmer Newspapers	10	10	83,943	63,093
John H. Perry Newspapers	15	17	317,981	203,735
Ridder Publications	14	16	1,128,825	1,101,738
Scripps-Howard Newspapers	19	16	2,307,743	876,135
Scripps League	16	27	231,068	95,104
Southern Newspapers [1]	9	18	206,235	148,910
Speidel Newspapers	8	10	215,345	133,011
Stauffer Publications	13	14	226,454	133,146
Thomson Newspapers [2]	3	36	697,366	344,993
Worrell Newspapers [1]	8	16	182,383	164,287

[1] Southern Newspapers and Worrell Newspapers jointly own six dailies.

[2] Thomson Newspapers bought the Brush-Moore chain of thirteen daily and four weekly newspapers, the sale consummated in Dec. 1967.

Source: *Editor & Publisher Yearbook,* 1962, 1967, ownerships corrected to late 1967.

TABLE XXII *Twenty-five Largest Daily Newspapers, with Chain Ownerships Designated*

Newspaper	*Daily Circulation*	*Sunday Circulation*	*Chain Ownership*
Daily News (New York)	2,122,982	3,135,155	Chicago Tribune
Times (Los Angeles)	847,869	1,170,360	Times-Mirror
Tribune (Chicago)	832,146	1,158,975	Chicago Tribune
Times (New York)	767,239	1,473,981	Ochs Estate
Herald-Examiner (Los Angeles)	726,424	706,971	Hearst
News (Detroit) [1]	684,705	936,410	. . .
Bulletin (Philadelphia)	670,123	728,906	McLean
Sun-Times (Chicago)	547,381	701,460	Field Enterprises
Free Press (Detroit)	537,203	580,412	Knight
Inquirer (Philadelphia)	517,229	943,731	Triangle Publications
Chronicle (San Francisco) [1]	490,027	. . .	. . .
News (Chicago)	466,424	. . .	Field Enterprises
Post (Washington)	455,825	574,751	Post Publications
American (Chicago)	439,360	494,530	Chicago Tribune
Newsday (Garden City, N.Y.) [1]	413,391	. . .	. . .
Press (Cleveland)	381,708	. . .	Scripps-Howard
Post (New York) [1]	380,764	279,928	. . .
Plain Dealer (Cleveland)	377,089	526,401	Newhouse
Journal (Milwaukee) [2]	366,398	556,693	. . .
Post-Dispatch (St. Louis) [1]	356,722	572,583	. . .
Press (Pittsburgh)	345,762	739,431	Scripps-Howard
Times (Kansas City)	341,634	. . .	Star Group
Long Island Press (Jamaica, N.Y.)	339,064	402,307	Newhouse
Star (Kansas City)	337,733	399,319	Star Group
Globe-Democrat (St. Louis)	318,459	. . .	Newhouse

[1] Not owned by a chain.
[2] Not owned by a chain, but owns both dailies in that city.
Source: *N. W. Ayer Newspaper Directory*, 1967.

TABLE XXIII *AM and AM-FM Radio Financial Data, in Millions of Dollars, 1935–66*[1]

	National & Regional[2] *Networks*		*National Spot*		*Local Time*		*Total*	
Year	*Sales*	*Per Cent of Total*	*Sales*	*Per Cent of Total*	*Sales*	*Per Cent of Total*	*Sales*	*Per Cent of Change from Previous Year*
1935	$ 39.7	50	$ 13.8	17	$ 26.1	33	$ 79.6	. . .
1937[3]	59.0	50	23.1	20	35.7	30	117.9	+48.1
1938	56.6[4]	48	28.1	24	32.7	28	117.4	− 0.6
1939	62.6[4]	48	30.0	23	37.3	29	130.0	+10.7
1940	73.8	47	37.1	24	44.8	29	155.7	+20.5
1941	82.4	46	45.7	25	51.7	29	179.8	+15.4
1942	85.2	45	51.1	27	53.9	28	190.1	+ 5.8
1943	105.6	46	59.4	26	64.1	28	229.1	+20.0
1944	129.4	45	73.3	25	85.0	30	287.6	+26.1
1945	134.0	43	76.7	25	99.8	32	310.5	+ 7.9
1946	134.8	40	82.9	25	116.4	35	334.1	+ 7.6
1947	134.7	36	91.6	24	147.8	40	374.1	+12.0
1948	141.1	34	104.8	25	170.9	41	416.7	+11.4
1949	134.9	32	108.3	25	182.1	43	425.4	+ 2.1
1950	131.5	29	118.8	26	203.2	45	453.6	+ 6.6
1951	122.5	27	119.6	26	214.5	47	456.5	+ 0.6
1952	109.9	23	123.7	26	239.6	51	473.2	+ 3.6
1953	98.1	21	129.6	27	249.5	52	477.2	+ 0.9
1954	83.7	18	120.2	27	247.5	55	451.3	− 5.4
1955	64.1	14	120.4	26	272.0	60	456.5	+ 0.7
1956	48.4	10	145.5	30	297.8	60	491.7	+ 7.7
1957	50.6	9	169.5	32	316.8	59	536.9	+ 9.3
1958	46.5	8	171.9	32	323.2	60	541.6	+ 0.9
1959	35.6	6	188.2	32	359.1	62	582.9	+ 7.6
1960	35.0	6	202.1	32	385.3	62	622.5	+ 6.8
1961	35.8	6	200.0	32	381.4	62	617.2	− 0.8
1962	37.3	6	212.1	32	415.8	62	665.2	+ 7.8
1963	41.8	6	224.7	31	445.2	63	711.7	+ 7.0
1964	43.8	6	237.3	31	482.6	63	763.7	+ 7.3
1965	44.6	5	254.1	31	529.0	64	827.7	+ 8.4
1966	47.2	5	284.6	31	580.2	64	912.2	+10.2

[1] Excludes independently owned FM stations.

[2] Regional networks contributed from $1,869,583 in 1940 to $8,481,000 in 1951. Most often regional networks had incomes of from $3.5 million to $7 million. Breakouts for both national and regional networks are given for the years 1937 and 1940–58 in recent editions of *Broadcasting Yearbook*. See, for example, p. 19 of the 1967 edition.

[3] Information not available for 1936.

[4] Data not available on regional networks income for 1938 and 1939.

Sources: Data for years 1954 to 1965, *AM-FM Broadcast Financial Data*, 1964 and 1965, FCC mimeo., October 1965 and 1966. Data prior to 1954, *Broadcasting Yearbook*, 1966, p. 10.

TABLE XXIV Broadcast Income Before Taxes, 1948–66, in Millions of Dollars

Year	*AM*[1]	*FM Only*[2]	*TV*
1948	64.1	(3.1)[3]	(14.9)[3]
1950	70.7	(2.6)	(9.2)
1952	61.1	(1.0)	55.5
1954	42.5	(0.6)	90.3
1955	46.3	(0.4)	150.2
1956	49.6	(0.4)	189.6
1957	54.3	(0.5)	160.0
1958	38.0	(0.7)	171.9
1959	44.0	(1.6)	222.3
1960	48.3	(2.4)	244.1
1961	32.0	(2.6)	237.0
1962	46.7	(3.2)	311.6
1963	58.1	(3.2)	343.2
1964	73.8	(3.0)	415.6
1965	81.1	(3.3)	447.9
1966	100.6	(3.3)	492.2

[1] Includes combination AM-FM operations.

[2] Independent FM stations not operated with AM license.

[3] Parentheses denote losses.

Source: Annual financial reports, FCC.

TABLE XXV A Thirteen-Year Record of Station Trading, 1954–66

Year	*Total Dollar Value*	*Radio Only Dollar Value*	*Combined Radio-TV Dollar Value*	*TV-Only Dollar Value*	*Number of Stations Changing Hands*		
					Radio	*Radio-TV*	*TV*
1954	$ 60,344,130	$ 10,224,047	$ 26,213,323	$ 23,906,760	187	18	27
1955	73,079,366	27,333,104	22,351,602	23,394,660	242	11	29
1956	115,605,828	32,563,378	65,212,055	17,830,395	316	24	21
1957	124,187,560	48,207,470	47,490,884	28,489,206	357	28	38
1958	127,537,026	49,868,123	60,872,618	16,796,285	407	17	23
1959	123,496,581	65,544,653	42,724,727	15,227,201	436	15	21
1960	99,341,919	51,763,285	24,648,400	22,930,225	345	10	21
1961	128,804,167	55,532,516	42,103,708	31,167,943	282	13	24
1962	101,742,903	59,912,520	18,822,745	23,007,638	306	8	16
1963	105,303,078	43,457,584	25,045,726	36,799,768	305	13	16
1964	205,756,736	52,296,480	67,185,762	86,274,494	430	20	36
1965	135,123,766	55,933,300	49,756,993	29,433,473	389	15	32
1966	135,718,316	76,633,762	28,510,500	30,574,054	367	11	31
Total	$1,536,041,367	$629,270,222	$520,939,043	$385,832,102	4,369	203	335

Note: Dollar value figures represent total considerations reported for all transactions, whether majority or minority interests were involved. In many transactions involving joint radio-television properties, individual values were not assigned to the radio and television stations. Such sales are reported in the column headed "Combined Radio-TV."

Source: *Broadcasting*, Feb. 27, 1967, pp. 77–79.

TABLE XXVI Number of Frequency Modulation Stations Owned by Standard Broadcast Stations, 1954–65

Year	Total FM Stations Reporting	FM Stations Not Owned by AM Licensees Reporting	Percentage FM Stations Owned by AM Licensees
1954	528	43	91.9
1955	493	38	92.3
1956	472	51	89.2
1957	499	67	86.6
1958	533	93	82.6
1959	662	148	77.6
1960	789	218	72.4
1961	938	249	73.5
1962	993	279	71.9
1963	1071	294	72.5
1964	1175	306	74.0
1965	1381	338	75.5

Source: *AM-FM Broadcast Financial Data—1965*, mimeo., Oct. 18, 1966.

TABLE XXVII AM, FM Radio, and TV Stations: Number and Percentage with Newspaper Affiliations, 1931–66

	AM			FM			TV		
Year	On Air	Affiliated	Per Cent	On Air	Affiliated	Per Cent	On Air	Affiliated	Per Cent
1931	612	68	11.1	...	...	...	...	...	...
1936	632	159	25.2	...	...	...	...	...	...
1940	814	250	30.8	...	...	...	...	...	...
1945	943	260	27.6	...	...	...	...	...	...
1948	1,621	444	27.4	53	17	32.0	9	1	11.1
1949	1,912	463	24.2	458	331	72.3	17	...	...
1950	2,086	472	22.6	700	280	40.0	50	13	26.0
1952	2,331	485	20.8	733	270	36.8	97	41	42.3
1956	2,824	463	16.4	637	212	33.3	108	49	45.4
1960	3,398	415	12.2	540	156	28.9	482	160	33.2
1962	3,693	399	10.8	688	141	20.5	573	178	31.0
1966	4,033	385	9.5	960	140	14.6	563	172	30.5
				1,390	188	13.5	595	175	29.4

Source: *Broadcasting Yearbook* (titled *Broadcasting-Telecasting Yearbook* for some of years).

TABLE XXVIII *Financial Data, by Millions of Dollars, for FM Stations Operated by Non-AM Licensees, 1954–65*

Year	*Total FM Stations Reporting*	*Revenues*	*Expenses*	*Income*	*Number Reporting Profit*	*Number Reporting Loss*	*Per Cent of Reported Loss*
1954	43	$ 0.8	$ 1.4	$(0.6)	. . .	. . .	. . .
1955	38	1.0	1.4	(0.4)	. . .	. . .	. . .
1956	51	1.4	1.8	(0.4)	. . .	. . .	. . .
1957	67	2.0	2.5	(0.5)	. . .	. . .	. . .
1958	93	2.5	3.2	(0.7)	. . .	. . .	. . .
1959	148	4.3	5.9	(1.6)	. . .	. . .	. . .
1960	218	5.8	8.2	(2.4)	50	168	77.06
1961	249	7.1	9.7	(2.6)	59	190	76.3
1962	279	9.3	12.5	(3.2)	71	208	74.55
1963	294	11.4	14.6	(3.2)	86	208	70.7
1964	306	12.8	15.8	(3.0)	93	213	69.6
1965	338	15.7	19.0	(3.3)	102	236	69.8

Source: "FM Financial Data—1954–1965," *AM-FM Broadcast Financial Data—1965*, mimeo., Oct. 18, 1966. Parentheses denote losses.

TABLE XXIX *Eighty-five Communities with One AM Radio Station and One Daily Newspaper, with Newspaper Having Ownership Interest in Station*

City	Call Letters	Year Station Began Operations	Station Under Original Licensee	Population Code [1]	Station Class [2]	Power: Day	Power: Night	Extent [3] of Newspaper Ownership
SEVENTY-ONE COMMUNITIES OUTSIDE OF METROPOLITAN AREAS								
Hope, Ark.	KXAR	1947	Yes	15	IV	250w	S.H. [4]	Majority
Magnolia, Ark.	KVMA	1948	Yes	15	III	1kw	. . .	Minority
Paso Robles, Calif.	KPRL	1946	No	15	IV	1kw	250w	Majority
Santa Cruz, Calif.	KSCO	1947	Yes	13	II	10kw	500w	Minority
Cour d'Alene, Idaho	KVNI	1946	No	14	IV	1kw	250w	Majority
Bloomington, Ill.	WJBC	1925	No	13	IV	1kw	250w	Majority
Canton, Ill.	WBYS	1947	Yes	14	II	250w	. . .	Majority
Effingham, Ill.	WCRA	1947	Yes	15	II	1kw	. . .	Majority
Kankakee, Ill.	WAKN	1947	Yes	13	III	1kw	500w	Majority
La Salle, Ill.	WLPO	1947	No	14	II	1kw	. . .	Majority
McComb, Ill.	WKAI	1947	No	14	II	250w	. . .	Majority
Mount Carmel, Ill.	WVMC	1948	No	15	III	500w	. . .	Majority
Connorsville, Ind.	WCNB	1948	Yes	14	II	250w	. . .	Majority
New Castle, Ind.	WCTW	1960	Yes	14	II	250w	250w	Majority
Vincennes, Ind.	WAOV	1940	No	14	IV	1kw	250w	Minority
Warsaw, Ind.	WRSW	1951	Yes	15	III	1kw	500w	Majority
Washington, Ind.	WAMW	1955	No	15	II	250w	. . .	Majority
Boone, Iowa	KWBG	1950	Yes	14	III	1kw	500w	Majority
Marshalltown, Iowa	KFJB	1923	No	14	IV	1kw	250w	Majority
Arkansas City, Kan.	KSOK	1947	Yes	14	III	1kw	100w	Majority
Coffeyville, Kan.	KGGF	1930	No	14	II	10kw	5kw	Majority
Great Bend, Kan.	KVGB	1937	No	14	III	5kw	5kw	Minority
Manhattan, Kan.	KMAN	1950	Yes	14	III	500w	. . .	Majority
McPherson, Kan.	KNEX	1949	No	15	II	250w	. . .	Majority
Middlesboro, Ky.	WMIK	1948	Yes	14	III	500w	. . .	Majority
Paris, Ky.	WPDE	1955	No	15	III	1kw	. . .	Majority
West Yarmouth, Mass.	WOCB	1940	No	16	IV	1kw	250w	Majority
Albion, Mich.	WALM	1952	No	14	III	1kw	500w	Minority

TABLE XXIX (cont.)

City	Call Letters	Year Station Began Operations	Station Under Original Licensee	Pop.[1] Code	Station[2] Class	Power Day	Power Night	Extent[3] of Newspaper Ownership
Benton Harbor, Mich.	WHFB	1947	Yes	14	II	5kw	1kw	Majority
Niles, Mich.	WNIL	1956	No	14	III	500w	. . .	Majority
Owosso, Mich.	WOAP	1948	Yes	14	II	1kw	. . .	Majority
Saulte Ste. Marie, Mich.	WSOO	1940	No	14	IV	1kw	250w	Majority
New Ulm, Minn.	KNUJ	1949	Yes	14	II	1kw	. . .	Majority
Brookfield, Mo.	KGHM	1955	No	15	III	500w	. . .	Majority
Warrensburg, Mo.	KOKO	1953	No	15	IV	1kw	250w	Majority
Miles City, Mont.	KATL	1941	Yes	15	IV	1kw	250w	Majority
Norfolk, Neb.	WJAG	1922	Yes	14	II	1kw	. . .	Majority
Elko, Nev.	KELK	1948	No	15	IV	1kw	250w	Minority
Asbury Park, N.J.	WJLK	1926	No	14	IV	1kw	250w	Majority
Grants, N.M.	KMIN	1956	No	14	III	1kw	. . .	Majority
Fredonia, N.Y.	WBUZ	1958	No	15	II	250w	. . .	Majority
Oneonta, N.Y.	WDOS	1947	Yes	14	II	1kw	. . .	Majority
Coshocton, Ohio	WTNS	1947	Yes	14	II	1kw	. . .	Majority
Findlay, Ohio	WFIN	1941	No	13	III	1kw	. . .	Majority
Newark, Ohio	WCLT	1949	No	13	III	500w	. . .	Majority
Wooster, Ohio	WWST	1947	Yes	14	III	1kw	. . .	Majority
Zanesville, Ohio	WHIZ	1924	No	13	IV	1kw	250w	Majority
Altus, Okla.	KWHW	1959	Yes	14	IV	1kw	250w	Majority
Ardmore, Okla.	KVSO	1935	Yes	14	IV	1kw	250w	Majority
Durant, Okla.	KSEO	1947	No	14	II	250w	. . .	Majority
Henryetta, Okla.	KHEN	1956	Yes	15	III	500w	. . .	Majority
Ponca City, Okla.	WBBZ	1927	No	14	IV	250w	250w	Majority
Shawnee, Okla.	KGFF	1930	Yes	14	IV	1kw	250w	Majority
Stillwater, Okla.	KSPI	1947	Yes	14	II	250w	. . .	Majority
Bedford, Pa.	WBFD	1955	Yes	16	III	5kw	. . .	Majority
Bradford, Pa.	WESB	1947	Yes	14	IV	1kw	. . .	Majority
Clearfield, Pa.	WCPA	1947	Yes	15	II	1kw	. . .	Majority
Du Bois, Pa.	WCED	1941	Yes	14	III	5kw	500w	Majority
Gettysburg, Pa.	WGET	1950	Yes	15	III	1kw	500w	Majority
Huntingdon, Pa.	WHUN	1947	Yes	14	III	5kw	. . .	Majority
Stroudsburg, Pa.	WVPO	1947	No	14	II	250w	. . .	Majority
Sundbury, Pa.	WKOK	1933	Yes	14	IV	10kw	1kw	Majority
Gainesville, Tex.	KGAF	1947	Yes	14	II	250w	. . .	Majority
Waynesboro, Va.	WANV	1964	Yes	14	III	5kw	1kw	Majority
Logan, W.Va.	WLOG	1940	No	16	IV	1kw	250w	Majority

Fond du Lac, Wis.	KFIZ	1922	No	13	IV	250w	250w	Majority
Janesville, Wis.	WCLO	1930	Yes	13	IV	1kw	250w	Majority
Shawano, Wis.	WTCH	1948	Yes	15	III	1kw	1kw	Majority
Wisconsin Rapids, Wis.	WFHR	1940	Yes	14	III	5kw	500w	Majority
Rock Springs, Wyo.	KVRS	1938	No	14	III	1kw	500w	Majority
FOURTEEN COMMUNITIES WITHIN METROPOLITAN AREAS								
San Rafael, Calif.	KTIM	1947	Yes	01	II	1kw	. . .	Majority
Stamford, Conn.	WSTC	1941	No	07	IV	1kw	250w	Majority
Pekin, Ill.	WSIV	1946	No	09	II	5kw	1kw	Majority
Rock Island, Ill.	WHBF	1925	No	08	III-A	5kw	5kw	Majority
Waukegan, Ill.	WKRS	1949	Yes	01	II	1kw	. . .	Majority
Attleboro, Mass.	WARA	1950	Yes	03	III	1kw	. . .	Majority
Lockport, N.Y.	WUSJ	1949	Yes	02	IV	250w	250w	Majority
Alliance, Ohio	WFAH	1953	Yes	04	III	1kw	. . .	Majority
Elyria, Ohio	WEOL	1948	Yes	06	III	1kw	1kw	Majority
Kent-Ravena, Ohio	WKNT	1946	Yes	04	II	1kw	. . .	Minority
Warren, Ohio	WHHH	1941	No	03	III	5kw	5kw	Majority
Bethlehem, Pa.	WGPA	1946	Yes	04	II	250w	. . .	Majority
Lansdale, Pa.	WNPV	1960	Yes	01	III	500w	. . .	Majority
Temple, Tex.	KTEM	1936	Yes	08	IV	1kw	250w	Majority

[1] Population Code: 01 = 2 million or more; 02 = 1–2 million; 03 = 500,000–1 million; 04 = 250,000–500,000; 05 = 225,000–250,000; 06 = 200,000–225,000; 07 = 175,000–200,000; 08 = 150,000–175,000; 09 = 125,000–150,000; 10 = 100,000–125,000; 11 = 75,000–100,000; 12 = 50,000–75,000; 13 = 25,000–50,000; 14 = 10,000–25,000; 15 = 5,000–10,000; 16 = 2,500–5,000.

[2] A Class I station operates on a "clear" channel and employs 10,000, 25,000 or 50,000 watts power to serve remote rural areas as well as a large center of population. (1 kilowatt = 1,000 watts.)

A Class II station is a secondary station which operates on a clear channel with a power of 250, 500, 1,000, 5,000, 10,000, 25,000, or 50,000 watts. It serves a population center and an adjacent rural area, and is operated so as to not interfere with the extensive services rendered by major clear-channel stations.

A Class III station, which shares a "regional" channel with several similar stations, uses power of 500, 1,000, or 5,000 watts and serves a center of population and adjacent rural area.

A Class IV station operates on a "local" channel (shared by many similar stations elsewhere) and employs up to 250 watts nighttime and not more than 1 kilowatt daytime.

[3] Majority ownership comprises 50 per cent or more.

[4] S.H. designates "Special Hours of Operation."

Note: Stamford is the only community of the fourteen with *no* other radio station in the metropolitan area.

Sources: Testimony of Former FCC Chairman E. William Henry before the Antitrust Subcommittee of the Judiciary Committee, House of Representatives, 88th Congress, 1st session, 1963. The transcript of these hearings, held March 13, 1963, was never published. See transcript in files of Representative Emanuel Celler's office, House Office Building.

TABLE XXX *Fifty-one Communities with Two AM Radio Stations and One Daily Newspaper, with Newspaper Having Ownership Interest in One of Two Stations*

City	Call Letters	Year First Station Began Operations	Station Under Original Licensee	Population Code [1]	Station Class [2]	Power: Day	Power: Night	Extent of Newspaper Ownership [3]
FORTY-THREE COMMUNITIES OUTSIDE OF METROPOLITAN AREAS								
Camden, Ark.	KAMD	1946	Yes	14	III	5kw	500w	Majority
Waycross, Ga.	WAYX	1936	No	14	IV	1kw	250w	Majority
Danville, Ill.	WDAN	1938	No	13	IV	1kw	250w	Majority
Decatur, Ill.	WSOY	1925	No	12	IV	1kw	250w	Majority
Galesburg, Ill.	WGIL	1938	Yes	13	IV	1kw	250w	Majority
Jacksonville, Ill.	WLDS	1941	No	14	II	1kw	. . .	Majority
Quincy, Ill.	WGEM	1948	Yes	13	III	5kw	1kw	Majority
Elkhart, Ind.	WTRC	1931	Yes	13	IV	1kw	250w	Majority
Burlington, Iowa	KBUR	1941	No	13	IV	1kw	250w	Majority
Dodge City, Kan.	KGNO	1930	Yes	14	III	5kw	1kw	Majority
Garden City, Kan.	KIUL	1935	No	14	IV	1kw	250w	Majority
Pittsburg, Kan.	KSEK	1947	Yes	14	IV	1kw	250w	Majority
Corbin, Ky.	WCTT	1947	Yes	15	II	1kw	1kw	Majority
Owensboro, Ky.	WOMI	1938	Yes	13	IV	1kw	250w	Majority
Holland, Mich.	WHTC	1948	Yes	14	IV	1kw	250w	Majority
Port Huron, Mich.	WTTH	1947	Yes	13	III	5kw	5kw	Majority
St. Cloud, Minn.	KFAM	1938	Yes	13	IV	1kw	250w	Majority
Columbus, Miss.	WSBI	1940	No	14	III	1kw	500w	Majority
Vicksburg, Miss.	WQBC	1931	Yes	13	III	1kw	500w	Majority
Hastings, Neb.	KHAS	1940	Yes	14	IV	1kw	250w	Majority
Auburn, N.Y.	WMBO	1927	No	13	IV	1kw	250w	Majority
Olean, N.Y.	WHDL	1929	No	14	IV	1kw	250w	Majority
Lumberton, N.C.	WTSB	1946	Yes	14	IV	1kw	250w	Majority
Reidsville, N.C.	WREV	1950	Yes	14	II	1kw	. . .	Majority
Rocky Mount, N.C.	WCEC	1947	Yes	13	II	1kw	. . .	Majority
Ashtabula, Ohio	WREO	1937	Yes	14	II-B	5kw	1kw	Majority
Marietta, Ohio	WBRJ	1964	Yes	14	III	5kw	. . .	Majority
Enid, Okla.	KCRC	1926	No	13	III	1kw	1kw	Majority
Muskogee, Okla.	KBIX	1936	Yes	13	IV	250w	250w	Majority

Bend, Ore.	KGRL	1960	No	14	II	1kw	. . .	Minority
Coos Bay, Ore.	KOOS	1928	No	15	IV	1kw	250w	Majority
Grants Pass, Ore.	KAGI	1939	Yes	14	III	5kw	1kw	Majority
Lancaster, Pa.	WGAL	1922	Yes	12	IV	1kw	250w	Majority
Lewistown, Pa.	WMRF	1941	Yes	14	IV	1kw	250w	Minority
Anderson, S.C.	WAIM	1935	Yes	13	IV	1kw	250w	Majority
Aberdeen, S.D.	KSDN	1948	Yes	14	III	1kw	1kw	Majority
Dyersburg, Tenn.	WDSG	1946	Yes	14	IV	250w	250w	Majority
Johnson City, Tenn.	WETB	1947	Yes	13	III	1kw	. . .	Majority
Fredericksburg, Va.	WFLS	1960	Yes	14	III	1kw	. . .	Majority
Centralia-Chehalis, Wash.	KITI	1954	No	15	III	1kw	. . .	Minority
Port Angeles, Wash.	KONP	1945	No	14	IV	250w	250w	Majority
Bluefield, W.Va.	WHIS	1929	No	14	III	5kw	500w	Majority
Morgantown, W.Va.	WAJR	1940	Yes	14	III	5kw	500w	Majority
EIGHT COMMUNITIES WITHIN METROPOLITAN AREAS								
Gary, Ind.	WLTH	1950	No	01	III	500w	. . .	Majority
Dubuque, Iowa	KDTH	1941	Yes	11	III	5kw	1kw	Majority
Brockton, Mass.	WBET	1946	Yes	09	III	5kw	1kw	Majority
New Bedford, Mass.	WNBH	1921	No	09	IV	1kw	250w	Majority
Easton, Pa.	WEEX	1956	Yes	04	IV	250w	250w	Majority
Woonsocket, R.I.	WWON	1946	No	03	IV	1kw	250w	Majority
Newport News, Va.	WGH	1927	Yes	06	III	5kw	5kw	Majority
Racine, Wis.	WRJN	1926	Yes	09	IV	1kw	250w	Majority

[1] Population Code: 01 = 2 million or more; 02 = 1–2 million; 03 = 500,000–1 million; 04 = 250,000–500,000; 05 = 225,000–250,000; 06 = 200,000–225,000; 07 = 175,000–200,000; 08 = 150,000–175,000; 09 = 125,000–150,000; 10 = 100,000–125,000; 11 = 75,000–100,000; 12 = 50,000–75,000; 13 = 25,000–50,000; 14 = 10,000–25,000; 15 = 5,000–10,000; 16 = 2,500–5,000.

[2] A Class I station operates on a "clear" channel and employs 10,000, 25,000, or 50,000 watts power to serve remote rural areas as well as a large center of population. (1 kilowatt = 1,000 watts.)

A Class II station is a secondary station which operates on a clear channel with a power of 250, 500, 1,000, 5,000, 10,000, 25,000, or 50,000 watts. It serves a population center and an adjacent rural area, and is operated so as to not interfere with the extensive services rendered by major clear-channel stations.

A Class III station, which shares a "regional" channel with several similar stations, uses power of 500, 1,000, or 5,000 watts and serves a center of population and adjacent rural area.

A Class IV station operates on a "local" channel (shared by many similar stations elsewhere) and employs up to 250 watts nighttime and not more than 1 kilowatt daytime.

[3] Majority ownership comprises 50 per cent or more.

Sources: Testimony of Former FCC Chairman E. William Henry before the Antitrust Subcommittee of the Judiciary Committee, House of Representatives, 88th Congress, 1st session, 1963. The transcript of these hearings, held March 13, 1963, was never published. See transcript in files of Representative Emanuel Celler's office, House Office Building.

TABLE XXXI *Ranking by Revenues of Newspaper-Owned AM Radio Stations in Markets Classified by Number of Stations in Each Market, 1961* [1]

Rank in Market	*Total Number of Newspaper-Owned Stations in Market with 2 or More Stations (182 Markets)*	*16 to 31 Stations (13 Markets)*	*10 to 15 Stations (18 Markets)*	*8 or 9 Stations (14 Markets)*	*6 or 7 Stations (24 Markets)*	*4 or 5 Stations (32 Markets)*	*3 Stations (29 Markets)*	*2 Stations (52 Markets)*
1	92	3	10	9	9	17	16	28
2	66	6	6	2	9	9	9	25
3	25	1	4	3	5	7	5	
4	14	2	3	4	1	4		
5	6	0	2	0	2	2		
6	1	0	0	1	0			
7	3	0	1	1	1			
8	1	1	0					
9	2	0	2					
10	2	1	1					
Lower than 10	10	10	—	—	—	—	—	—
Totals	222	24	29	20	27	39	30	53

[1] Based on Annual Financial Report for 1961.

Source: Testimony of E. William Henry, former FCC chairman, before the Antitrust Subcommittee of the Judiciary Committee, House of Representatives, 88th Congress, 1st session, 1963. The transcript of these hearings, held March 13, 1963, was never published. See transcript in files of Representative Emanuel Celler's office, House Office Building.

TABLE XXXII *Twenty-seven Communities with One Commercial Television Station and One Daily Newspaper, with Newspaper Having Ownership Interest in Station*

TV Station in Which Newspaper Has Interest				
City and State	*Call Letter*	*Extent of Newspaper Ownership*	*Station Under Original Licensee*	*Year Station Began Operations*
FOURTEEN COMMUNITIES WITH NO OTHER TV STATION IN MARKET				
Fort Smith, Ark.	KFSA-TV	Majority	No	1956
Dodge City, Kan.	KTVC	Minority	Yes	1957
Topeka, Kan.	WIBW-TV	Majority	Yes	1953
Columbus, Miss.	WCIB-TV	Majority	Yes	1956
Meridan, Miss.	WTOK-TV	Minority	Yes	1953
Watertown, N.Y.	WWNY-TV	Majority	Yes	1954
Akron, Ohio	WAKR-TV	Minority	Yes	1953
* Astabula, Ohio	WICA-TV	Majority	Yes	1965
* Zanesville, Ohio	WHIZ-TV	Majority	No	1953
Anderson, S.C.	WAIM-TV	Majority	Yes	1953
San Angelo, Tex.	KCTV	Majority	No	1953
Bluefield, W.Va.	WHIS-TV	Majority	Yes	1955
LaCrosse, Wis.	WKBT	Minority	Yes	1954
Cheyenne, Wyo.	KFBC-TV	Minority	Yes	1954
FOUR COMMUNITIES WITH ONE OTHER TV STATION IN MARKET				
Albany, Ga.	WALB-TV	Majority	Yes	1954
Quincy, Ill. [1]	WGEM-TV	Majority	Yes	1953
Hannibal, Mo. [1]	KHQA-TV	Majority	Yes	1953
Temple, Tex.	KTEM	Majority	. . .	1953
NINE COMMUNITIES WITH TWO OR MORE OTHER TV STATIONS IN MARKET				
* Rock Island, Ill.	WHBF-TV	Majority	No	1950
Mason City, Iowa	KGLO-TV	Majority	Yes	1954
Paducah, Ky.	WPSD-TV	Majority	Yes	1957
* Hastings, Neb.	KHAS-TV	Majority	. . .	1956
Lancaster, Pa.	WGAL-TV	Majority	Yes	1949
Greensboro, N.C.	WFMY-TV	Majority	Yes	1949
Winston-Salem, N.C.	WSJS-TV	Majority	Yes	1953
Greenville, S.C.	WFBC-TV	Minority	Yes	1953
Texarkana, Tex.	KTAL-TV	Majority	Yes	1953

* Stations added to update list to Jan. 1, 1967

[1] The Hannibal station is located in Quincy, Ill., although the station is licensed to the Lee Enterprises, newspaper-broadcasting chain which owns the Hannibal newspaper.

Source: Testimony of Former FCC Chairman E. William Henry before the Antitrust Subcommittee of the Judiciary Committee, House of Representatives, 88th Congress, 1st session, 1963. The transcript of these hearings, held March 13, 1963, was never published. See transcript in files of Representative Emanuel Celler's office, House Office Building.

TABLE XXXIII *Seventeen Communities with Two Commercial Television Stations and One Daily Newspaper, with Newspaper Having Ownership Interest in One of Two Stations*

TV Station in Which Newspaper Has Interest		*Extent of Newspaper Ownership*	*Station Under Original Licensee*	*Year Station Began Operations*
City and State	*Call Letter*			
SEVEN COMMUNITIES WITH TWO TV STATIONS IN MARKET				
Columbus, Ga.	WRBL-TV	Majority	No	1953
* Idaho Falls, Idaho	KIFI-TV	Majority	. . .	1961
* Terre Haute, Ind.	WTHI-TV	Minority	. . .	1954
* Jackson, Miss.	WJTV	Minority	No	1953
Springfield, Mass.	WHYN-TV	Majority	Yes	1953
Springfield, Mo.	KYTV	Majority	No	1953
Wausau, Wis.	WSAU-TV	Minority	Yes	1954
TEN COMMUNITIES WITH THREE OR MORE TV STATIONS IN MARKET				
Mobile, Ala.	WKRG-TV	Majority	No	1955
* Tampa, Fla.	WFLA-TV	Majority	. . .	1955
* Cedar Rapids, Iowa	KCRG-TV	Majority	No	1953
* Des Moines, Iowa	KRNT-TV	Majority	Yes	1955
Baton Rouge, La.	WBRZ	Majority	Yes	1955
Portland, Maine	WGAN-TV	Majority	Yes	1954
Syracuse, N.Y.	WSYR-TV	Majority	Yes	1950
Fargo, N.D.	WDAY-TV	Majority	Yes	1953
Harrisburg, Pa.	WTPA-TV	Majority	Yes	1953
Johnstown, Pa.	WJAC-TV	Majority	Yes	1949

* Stations added to update list to Jan. 1, 1967.

Source: Testimony of Former FCC Chairman E. William Henry before the Antitrust Subcommittee of the Judiciary Committee, House of Representatives, 88th Congress, 1st session, 1963. The transcript of these hearings, held March 13, 1963, was never published. See transcript in files of Representative Emanuel Celler's office, House Office Building.

TABLE XXXIV *Various Measures of the Revenue Shares of Newspaper-Owned Television Stations, 1961.*[1]

1. Newspaper-owned Television Stations as a Proportion of all Commercial Television Stations (excluding network-owned and operated stations).

Stations	*Revenues*
24 per cent	36 per cent

2. Newspaper-owned Television Stations as a Proportion of all Commercial Television Stations in the Top 25 Television Markets, Excluding New York, Chicago, and Los Angeles.[2]

Stations	*Revenues*
37 per cent	40 per cent

3. Newspaper-Owned Television Stations' Shares of Market Revenues.[3]

NINETEEN TWO-STATION MARKETS		
	50 Per Cent and Over	*9*
	50–60	6
	60–70	1
	70–80	0
	80–90	2
	Less Than 50 Per Cent	*10*
	40–50	6
	30–40	3
	20–30	1
TWENTY-SIX THREE-STATION MARKETS		
	33.3 Per Cent and Over	*13*
	33.3–43	8
	43–53	5
	Less Than 33.3 Per Cent	*13*
	20–33.3	13
SEVEN FOUR-STATION MARKETS		
	25 Per Cent and Over	*6*
	25–30	1
	30–35	3
	35–40	2
	Less Than 25 Per Cent	*1*
	20–25	1

[1] Based on Annual Financial Report for 1961.

[2] The three networks (ABC, CBS, NBC) own and operate the network affiliated stations in New York, Chicago, and Los Angeles. That, apparently, is the reason data for these three markets were excluded from this FCC information.

[3] In each market cited, commercial television stations are either all VHF or all UHF. In each market only one station is affiliated with a newspaper; the others are not. Excluded are three two-station markets, nine three-station markets, and two four-station markets where more than one station is affiliated with a newspaper.

Source: Testimony of E. William Henry, former FCC chairman, before the Anti-trust Subcommittee of the Judiciary Committee, House of Representatives, 88th Congress, 1st session, 1963. The transcript of these hearings, held March 13, 1963, was never published. See transcript in files of Representative Emanuel Celler's office, House Office Building.

TABLE XXXV *International Telephone and Telegraph: Principal Divisions and Subsidiaries*

NORTH AMERICA	MANUFACTURING—SALES—SERVICE
Canada	ITT Canada, Ltd., Montreal; Royal Electric Co. (Quebec), Ltd., Pointe Claire, P.Q.
Jamaica	ITT Standard Electric of Jamaica, Ltd., Kingston.
Mexico	Industria de Telecomunicación S. A. de C. V., Mexico City; Materiales de Telecomunicación S. A. Toluca; McClellan, S. A., Mexico City; Standard Eléctrica de México S. A., Mexico City.
Panama	ITT Standard Electric of Panama S. A., Panama City.
Puerto Rico	ITT Caribbean Manufacturing, Inc., Rio Piedras; ITT Caribbean Sales and Service, Inc., Rio Piedras.
United States	Airmatic Systems Corp., Saddle Brook, N.J.; Avis Rent A Car System, New York; Barton Instrument Corp., Monterey Park, Calif.; Federal Electric Corp., Paramus, N.J.; Hamilton Management Corp., Denver; Industrial Products Div., San Fernando, Calif.; Intelex Systems, Inc., Paramus, N.J.; International Standard Electric Corp., New York; ITT Corp., Sud America, New York; ITT Arkansas Div., Camden, Ark.; ITT Bell & Gossett Hydronics Div., Morton Grove, Ill.; Stover branch, Freeport, Ill.; ITT Cannon Electric Div., Los Angeles; ITT Data and Information Systems Div., Paramus, N.J.; ITT Direct Fired Equipment Div., Columbus, Ohio; Mercer, Pa.; Torrance, Calif.; ITT Electron Tube Div., Easton, Pa. and Roanoke, Va.; ITT Export Corp., New York; ITT Federal Laboratories Div., Nutley, N.J.; ITT Financial Services, Inc., New York; ITT Aetna Finance Co., St. Louis; Kellogg Credit Corp., New York; ITT Credit Corp., New York; Great International Life Insurance Co. (50 per cent interest), Atlanta; ITT General Controls Div., Glendale, Calif.; ITT Gilfillan, Inc., Los Angeles; ITT Hammel-Dahl Div., Warwick, R.I.; ITT Industrial Laboratories Div., Fort Wayne, Ind.; ITT Kellogg Communications Systems Div., Chicago; ITT Kellogg Telecommunication Div., New York; Corinth, Miss.; Milan, Tenn.; Raleigh, N.C.; ITT Mackay Marine Div., Clark, N.J.; ITT Marlow Div., Midland Park, N.J.; ITT Mobile Telephone, Inc., San Fernando, Calif.; ITT Nesbitt Div., Philadelphia; ITT Process Systems Div., Lawrence, Mass.; ITT Semiconductors Div., West Palm Beach, Fla., and Lawrence, Mass.; ITT Telephone Corp., Harrisburg, Pa.; ITT Wire and Cable Div., Pawtucket, R.I.; Woonsocket, R.I.; Clinton, Mass; Jennings Radio Manufacturing Corp., San Jose, Calif.
Telephone Operations	
Puerto Rico	Puerto Rico Telephone Co., San Juan.
Virgin Islands	Virgin Islands Telephone Corp., Charlotte Amalie.

SOUTH AMERICA	MANUFACTURING—SALES—SERVICE
Argentina	Compañía Standard Electric Argentina S. A. I. C., Buenos Aires.
Brazil	Standard Eléctrica S. A., Rio de Janeiro; Electrônica Industrial S. A., Sao Paulo.
Chile	Compañía Standard Electric S. A. C., Santiago.
Colombia	ITT Standard Electric de Colombia S. A., Bogotá.
Venezuela	Standard Telecommunications C. A., Caracas.
Telephone Operations	
Brazil	Companhia Telefônica Nacional, Curitiba.
Chile	Compañía de Teléfonos de Chile, Santiago.
Peru	Compañía Peruana de Teléfonos Limitada, Lima.

EUROPE, MIDDLE EAST, AFRICA MANUFACTURING—SALES—SERVICE

Algeria	Société Algérienne de Constructions Téléphoniques, Algiers.
Austria	Standard Telephon und Telegraphen Aktiengesellschaft, Czeija, Nissl & Co., Vienna.
Belgium	Bell Telephone Manufacturing Co., Antwerp; ITT Europe, Inc. (branch), Brussels; ITT Industries Europe, Inc. (branch), Brussels.
Denmark	Standard Electric Aktieselskab, Copenhagen.
Finland	Standard Electric Puhelinteollisuus Oy, Helsinki.
France	Centre Français de Recherche Opérationelle, Paris; Compagnie Générale de Constructions Téléphoniques, Paris; Les Téléimprimeurs, Paris; Compagnie Générale de Métrologie Annecy; Laboratorie Central de Télécommunications, Paris; Le Matériel Technique Industriel, Paris; Le Matériel Téléphonique, Paris; Société Industrielle de Composants pour l'Electronique, Courbevoie.
Germany (*West*)	Standard Elektrik Lorenz Aktiengesellschaft, Stuttgart, and subsidiaries.
Iran	Standard Electric Iran AG, Tehran.
Italy	Fabbrica Apparecchiature per Comunicazioni Elettriche Standard S.p.A., Milan; Società Impianti Elettrici Telefonici Telegrafici e Costruzioni Edili S.p.A., Florence; ITT Domel Italiana S.p.A., Milan.
Netherlands	Internationale Gas Apparaten N. V., The Hague (joint venture); Nederlandsche Standard Electric Maatschappij N. V., The Hague.
Nigeria	Kollerich (Nigeria), Ltd., Lagos.
Norway	Standard Telefon og Kabelfabrik A / S, Oslo.
Portugal	Standard Eléctrica S.A.R.L., Lisbon.
Republic of South Africa	Standard Telephones and Cables (South Africa) (Proprietary), Ltd., Boksburg East, Transvaal; Supersonic Africa (Proprietary), Ltd., Johannesburg, Transvaal.
Spain	Compañía Internacional de Telecomunicación y Electrónica S. A., Madrid; Compañía Radio Aérea Marítima Española S. A., Madrid; Standard Eléctrica S. A., Madrid.
Sweden	ITT Norden AB, Barkarby; Standard Radio & Telefon AB, Barkarby.
Switzerland	Intel S. A., Basle; ITT Standard S. A., Basle; Standard Téléphone et Radio S. A., Zurich, Steiner S. A., Berne.
Turkey	Standard Elektrik ve Telekomünikasyon, Ltd., Sirketi, Ankara.
United Kingdom	Creed and Co., Ltd., Brighton; ITT Industries, Ltd., London and subsidiaries; Standard Telephones and Cables, Ltd., London; Standard Telecommunication Laboratories, Ltd., London and other subsidiaries.

FAR EAST AND PACIFIC MANUFACTURING—SALES—SERVICE

Australia	Standard Telephones and Cables Pty., Ltd., Sydney.
Hong Kong	ITT Far East and Pacific, Inc. (branch), Hong Kong; ITT Far East, Ltd., Hong Kong.
Japan	ITT Far East and Pacific, Inc. (branch), Tokyo.
New Zealand	Standard Telephones and Cables Pty., Ltd. (branch), Upper Hutt, Wellington.
Philippines	ITT Philippines, Inc., Makati, Rizal.

TABLE XXXV *Continued*

INTERNATIONAL COMMUNICATIONS OPERATIONS

American Cable & Radio Corp., New York; All America Cables and Radio, Inc.; Commercial Cable Co.; ITT Cable and Radio, Inc.—Puerto Rico; ITT Central America Cables & Radio, Inc.; ITT Communications, Inc.—Virgin Islands; ITT World Communications, Inc.; Mackay Radio and Globe Wireless of the Philippines; Companhia Rádio Internacional de Brasil, Rio de Janerio; Compañía Internacional de Radio Boliviana, La Paz; Compañía Internacional de Radio S. A., Buenos Aires; Compañía Internacional de Radio S. A., Santiago; Cuban American Telephone and Telegraph Co. (50 per cent interest), Havana; Radio Corp. of Cuba, Havana.

ASSOCIATE LICENSEES FOR MANUFACTURING (MINORITY INTEREST)

Australia	Austral Standard Cables Pty., Ltd., Melbourne.
France	Lignes Télégraphiques et Téléphoniques, Paris.
Italy	Società Italiana Reti Telefoniche Interurbane, Milan.
Japan	Nippon Electric Co., Ltd., Tokyo; Sumitomo Electric Industries, Ltd., Osaka.
Spain	Marconi Española S. A. Madrid.

Source: *Broadcasting,* Dec. 13, 1965, pp. 35, 38.

Notes

1 The Daily Newspaper: Development and Decline

1. Burns W. Roper, *Emerging Profiles of Television and Other Mass Media: Public Attitudes 1959–1967*, Television Information Office, 1967. See also Richard Carter and Bradley Greenberg, "Newspapers vs. Television: Which Do You Believe?" *Journalism Quarterly*, Spring 1965, pp. 29–34.
2. Frank Luther Mott, *American Journalism* (New York: Macmillan, 1950), p. 22.
3. *Ibid.*, p. 28.
4. The author is deeply indebted to Frank Luther Mott's outstanding journalism history, *American Journalism*, and Morris Ernst's first edition of *The First Freedom* (New York: Macmillan, 1946) for much of the historical data presented in this chapter.
5. Mott, p. 318.
6. *Ibid.*, p. 527. See also Oliver Carlson and Ernest Sutherland Bates, *Hearst: Lord of San Simeon* (New York: Viking, 1936), p. 92; and John K. Winkler, *W. R. Hearst: An American Phenomenon* (New York: Simon and Schuster, 1928), p. 146.
7. There is disagreement as to how many daily newspapers were in existence in 1909. The figure 2,600 is from 1910 Census Bureau data. Royal Ray reported there were 2,200 English-language dailies of general content in 1909. The 2,600 figure undoubtedly includes foreign language and specialized daily newspapers.
8. The number of dailies started and discontinued was determined by comparing *Editor & Publisher Yearbook* listings, two years at a time, during the period 1944–66.
9. College and university-affiliated daily newspapers were not included in these figures. Specifically, daily noncommercial newspapers at the University of Iowa and University of Missouri, both listed in *Editor & Publisher Yearbook*, 1967, as community daily newspapers are not included in these data.
10. The number of newspaper competitive cities declined from 689 in 1910 to 552 in 1920, a percentage decline of 19.9. For other decades the figures are: 1920 to 1930, a decline of 251 equal to a rate of 45.5 per cent; 1930 to 1940, a 120 drop, 39.9 per cent rate; 1940 to 1950, a 64 decline, 35.4 per cent; 1950 to 1960, a 41 decline, 35 per cent. Source: *N. W. Ayer Newspaper Directory*.
11. The seventy-eight-year-old Indianapolis *Times* ceased publication October 11, 1965, after suffering "substantial losses for years." The employee-owned Milwaukee *Journal* bought the *Sentinel*, 1962, and halted the *Sentinel*'s Sunday edition. The Atlanta *Times*, founded to give conservatives a voice in Georgia's

major metropolis, suspended publication August 31, 1965, after incurring deficits in excess of $2.6 million. The *Arizona Journal*, begun as a model offset-daily February 14, 1962, first suspended publication from January to August 1963, and finally quit April 22, 1964.

12. William J. Farson, executive vice-president American Newspaper Guild, statement before the Subcommittee on Antitrust and Monopoly, U.S. Senate Committee on Judiciary, July 14, 1967.

13. Combined circulation of the *Herald Tribune, Journal-American,* and *World-Telegram & Sun* was 1,227,779 daily, and of the *Herald Tribune* and *Journal-American,* 1,161,939 Sunday (*Editor & Publisher Yearbook,* 1966); The *World Journal Tribune* circulation was 691,156 daily and 888,336 Sunday (*N. W. Ayers,* 1967). Four thousand jobs were lost. But most serious, one of America's great newspapers, the *Herald Tribune,* disappeared, thus ending one publication (the *Herald*) begun by James Gordon Bennett in 1835 and another (the *Tribune*) founded by Horace Greeley in 1841.

14. New York, 3, each independently owned; Chicago, 4, owned by two publishers; Philadelphia, 3, owned by two publishers; Detroit, 2; Houston, 2; and Los Angeles, 2. Source: *Editor & Publisher Yearbook,* 1967.

15. *Editor & Publisher Yearbook,* 1951.

16. Houston in the mid-1960's became the sixth American city with a population in excess of one million. That city is served by two independently owned daily newspapers with combined circulations of 540, 908; *Editor & Publisher Yearbook,* 1966.

17. Circulations are from *Editor & Publisher Yearbook,* 1966.

18. John Hay Whitney, whose New York *Herald Tribune* died in the three-newspaper merger in New York City of the *Herald Tribune, World-Telegram & Sun,* and *Journal-American,* September 12, 1966, said in the 1964 Lovejoy Address at Colby College, Waterville, Maine, November 12, 1964, ". . . the profit still lies in monopoly situations where, too often, there is more income than excellence."

19. *United States* v. *Chattanooga News-Free Press Co.,* Cr. 7978 (E.D. Tenn.; filed June 13, 1940). Defendants found guilty on one of two charges on December 11, 1940, and fined one cent each in lieu of costs.

20. *United States* v. *Lorain Journal Company,* Civ. 26823 (N.D. Ohio; filed September 22, 1949).

21. 342 U.S. 143, December 11, 1951.

22. *United States* v. *The Mansfield Journal Company,* Civ. 28235 (N.D. Ohio; filed May 31, 1951).

23. *United States* v. *The Kansas City Star Co.,* Cr. 18444; *United States* v. *The Kansas City Star Co.,* Civ. 7989. Defendants found guilty on February 22, 1955; 240 F. 3d 643 (8th Cir. 1957). And the U.S. Supreme Court refused to review the case; *cert. denied* 354 U.S. 923. The civil case was terminated with the entry of a consent decree which prohibited forced combination sales of newspapers or advertising space, November 15, 1957.

24. *United States* v. *Wichita Eagle Publishing Company, Inc.,* Civ. W-1876 (D. Kan.), complaint filed and consent decree entered on June 20, 1959.

25. The Federal Trade Commission on March 1, 1967, notified Dow Jones & Co., Inc., publishers of the

Wall Street Journal, that it had undertaken an investigation to learn if the *WSJ* had engaged in unfair or discriminatory practices within the meaning of Section 5 of the Federal Trade Commission Act and 2(a) of the Clayton Antitrust Act. See Dow Jones & Co., Inc., *Common Stock and Prospectus*, for secondary offering of Dow Jones stock, dated April 5, 1967, p. 10.

26. *United States* v. *Times Picayune Publishing Company*, Civ. 2797 (E.D. La.; filed June 14, 1950). The Federal District Court for the eastern district of Louisiana on May 28, 1952, entered a verdict against the defendant. However, the U.S. Supreme Court on May 25, 1953, reversed the lower court without passing on the legality of similar advertising arrangements "in other circumstances or in other proceedings," thus leaving the Justice Department free to enter other proceedings. 345 U.S. 594.

27. *United States* v. *Harte-Hanks Newspapers, Inc.*, Cr. 15393 (N.D. Tex.). See 170 F. Supp. 227 (N.D. Tex., 1959).

28. *United States* v. *The Lima News*, Civ. 64–178 (W.D. Ohio). The complaint was filed November 19, 1964, and terminated on November 30, 1965, with the consent judgment.

29. *Editor & Publisher*, June 25, 1966, p. 12.

30. *United States* v. *Lindsay–Schaub Newspapers, Inc.*, Civ. No. 6748D (E.D. Ill.); filed March 27, 1967.

31. Portion of the transcript of the hearing in *United States* v. *Citizen Publishing Company*, Civ. 1969-Tucson (D. Ariz.), January 24, 1966. The complaint was filed January 4, 1965; the motion by the government for a summary judgment was filed April 16, 1965; a hearing on that motion was held on August 4, 1965; and the court issued its order stating the issues for trial October 26, 1965. The trial was conducted in April 1966. No decision on the one issue in trial has been handed down.

32. Joint operations cities as of May, 1967: Birmingham, Ala.; San Francisco; Miami, Fla.; Honolulu; Evansville and Fort Wayne, Ind.; Shreveport, La.; St. Louis; Lincoln, Neb.; Albuquerque; Columbus, Ohio; Tulsa; Franklin-Oil City and Pittsburgh, Pa.; Nashville and Knoxville, Tenn.; El Paso; Salt Lake City; Bristol and Lynchburg, Va.; Spokane; Charleston, W. Va.; and Madison, Wisc.

33. Raymond B. Nixon and Jean Ward, "Trends in Newspaper Ownership and Inter-Media Competition," *Journalism Quarterly*, Winter 1961, p. 7.

34. See, especially, testimony of John J. Flynn, associate professor of Law, University of Utah; Evan Mecham, publisher of Tucson (Ariz.) *American*; Fred J. Martin, publisher of *Park County News*, Livingston, Mont.; and Edgar F. Elfstrom, publisher of Fullerton (Calif.) *Daily News Tribune*, before the Subcommittee on Antitrust and Monopoly, U.S. Senate Committee on Judiciary, July and August 1967.

35. The government contends in the Tucson case that the joint operation entered into in 1940 was intended to create a monopoly. Also pertinent to the Tucson case, stockholders of the Tucson *Daily Citizen*, through agreements contained in the joint operation plan, bought the *Arizona Star* in 1964 after sale of the *Star* had been negotiated with the Brush-Moore chain. *Editor & Publisher*, April 9, 1966, p. 11; April 16, 1966, p. 9.

36. This joint operation began July 30, 1966. Under the agreement costs are allocated to the "tenant" newspaper; profits will be shared based on a formula set forth in the agreement, thus guaranteeing the Cox organization a profit where it previously had sustained losses. This was the price the Knight chain paid to prevent sale of the *News* to a competitor, possibly to another large chain. About 520 employees were dismissed from the *News* staff. *Editor & Publisher,* August 6, 1966, pp. 9–11.

37. Senate 1312, introduced March 16, 1967. Two joint sponsors have been intimately related to newspapering: Thomas H. Kuchel (D-Calif.), whose father owned and published a newspaper in Anaheim, Calif., for forty-eight years, and Jennings Randolph (D-W.Va.), former owner and publisher of weekly newspapers. All of the others except Senator Strom Thurmond (D-S.C.) represent states where joint operations are or recently have been in existence: Senators Paul J. Fannin (R-Ariz.), Daniel K. Inouye (D-Hawaii), Hirman L. Fong (R-Hawaii), Vance Hartke (D-Ind.), Birch Bayh (D-Ind.), A. S. "Mike" Monroeny (D-Okla.), Fred R. Harris (D-Okla.), Hugh Scott (R-Pa.), John G. Tower (R-Tex.), Wallace F. Bennett (R-Utah), and Frank E. Moss (D-Utah). The bill was introduced by Senator Carl Hayden (D-Ariz.).

38. Among the cases wherein the "natural monopoly" was introduced were *United States* v. *Harte-Hanks Newspapers, Inc.*, in which Harte-Hanks was acquitted after forcing another newspaper in Greenville, Tex., to sell via economic pressures. The other and more important case involved cross civil antitrust suits by *Union Leader Corporation* v. *Newspapers of New England, Inc.* and *Haverhill Gazette Company* v. *Union Leader Corporation,* 284 F. 2d 583 (1st 1960). In essence, Haverhill, Mass., businessmen invited William Loeb, publisher of the *Union Leader Corporation,* 284 F. to publish a shopper during a three-day strike of the Haverhill *Gazette.* He converted his free circulation shopper into a daily, paid merchants fifty dollars a week to induce others to advertise in his Haverhill *Journal* and not advertise in the *Gazette.* Both newspapers engaged in unfair advertising practices, the *Gazette* as a defensive move, the court held. Loeb offered to buy the *Gazette,* but his offer was refused. Instead, the *Gazette* was sold to members of a nonprofit trade association of New England publishers, formed as the Newspapers of New England. Loeb brought a civil antitrust suit against NNE, complaining, among other things, that his *Journal* failed and his other newspapers then faced unfair competition in that he was opposing thirty publishers. Although the trial court found the *Gazette* competed unfairly, the U.S. Court of Appeals, First Circuit, Massachusetts, reversed this decision, holding the *Gazette* acted in defense. Further, the appellate court held that Loeb's other newspapers were in no apparent danger of unfair competition from NNE. Both courts cleared NNE on other charges. And, of course, the most important aspect of the decision was that Haverhill was declared incapable of supporting more than one viable newspaper and so was a "natural monopoly."

39. *United States* v. *The Times-Mirror Company,* Civ. 65–366–WF (C.D. Calif.); complaint filed

March 5, 1965; trial began May 2, 1967.

40. *United States* v. *E. W. Scripps Company*, Civ. 5656 (S.D. Ohio); complaint filed May 27, 1964; scheduled for trial beginning February 12, 1968.

41. Mr. Wright, also board chairman of Humble Oil & Refining Co., Houston, made these remarks at a San Francisco Chamber of Commerce meeting. The text of his address appears in *Editor & Publisher*, October 1, 1966, pp. 104, 110, 114.

42. Testimony of Loyal B. Phillips before the Antitrust Subcommittee of the Judiciary Committee of the U.S. House of Representatives, "Concentration of Ownership in News Media," March 14, 1963. See Official Verbatim Transcript in the chairman's office, Representative Emanual Cellers, p. 289.

43. *United States* v. *World Journal Tribune, Inc.*, Civ. 66–2967 (S.D. N.Y.). Major concern in this case was the unfair competition the new afternoon *World Journal Tribune* might pose to the New York *Post*, its only general circulation afternoon competition.

44. Testimony of Loyal B. Phillips before the Antitrust Subcommittee of the U.S. House of Representatives, March 14, 1963.

45. Speech by Gene Wendorf at the Southern Illinois Editorial Assn. annual spring meeting in Carbondale, Ill., April 14, 1967, and interview after his talk.

46. *United States* v. *Associated Press*, Civ. 19–163 (S.D. N.Y.) filed August 28, 1942; judgment entered January 13, 1944. Affirmed by the U.S. Supreme Court, June 18, 1945 (326 U.S. 1).

47. *Broadcasting*, June 5, 1967, p. 52.

48. The plaintiff, Richard W. Nowels, and his newspaper, the Buena Park *News*; defendants, W. J. McGiffin Newspapers, publishers of the Buena Park *Pony Express*. Trial was in Orange County Superior Court, Santa Ana, Calif., judgment entered February 10, 1967. *Editor & Publisher*, February 19, 1967, p. 10.

2 Accelerated Chain Take-over of Newspapers

1. Frank Luther Mott, *The News in America* (Cambridge, Mass., 1952), p. 187.

2. Raymond B. Nixon, "Who Will Own the Press in 1975?" *Journalism Quarterly*, Winter 1955, p. 14.

3. The average sizes of chains by years: 1910, 4.7; 1923, 4.9; 1930, 5.6; 1940, 5.3; 1945, 4.85; 1954, 5.1; 1960, 5.1; 1967, 5.28. Source for years other than 1967: Raymond B. Nixon and Jean Ward, "Trends in Newspaper Ownership and Inter-Media Competition," *Journalism Quarterly*, Winter 1961, p. 5.

4. The number of chains holding interests in 10 or more dailies: 10—2, 11—1, 12—1, 13—1, 14—2, 16—4, 17—1, 18—2, 21—1, 22—1, 27—1, 30—1, 36—1. Note: Interests in some newspapers are held by more than one chain. Source: *Editor & Publisher Yearbook*, 1967, corrected.

5. The other states in which chains own 50 per cent or more of the dailies: Alabama (68.6), Arkansas (54.5), Idaho (60), Louisiana (68.2), Maine (55.5), Minnesota (53.3), Nevada (71.4), New Hampshire (50), North Dakota (54.5), Oregon (60), South Dakota (50), Vermont (75), Washington (54.2), West Virginia (50). Source: *Editor*

& *Publisher Yearbook,* 1966, corrected to April 1967.

6. See article by A. Kent MacDougal, *Wall Street Journal,* December 15, 1965, p. 1.

7. William J. Farson, executive vice-president American Newspaper Guild, testimony before the Senate Subcommittee on Antitrust and Monopoly, July 14, 1967.

8. H. R. Horvitz testimony before the Senate Subcommittee on Antitrust and Monopoly, August 1967. See also Luther A. Huston, "Many Call, Few Are Chosen to Comment on Hayden Bill," *Editor, & Publisher,* August 12, 1967, p. 62.

9. Nixon and Ward, "Trends in Newspaper Ownership and Inter-Media Competition," p. 7.

10. Circulation figures from Jerome H. Walker, "Weekly Circulation Totals Show How the Groups Stand," *Editor & Publisher,* April 9, 1966, pp. 9–10; "Taking Another Look At Group Standings," *Editor & Publisher,* May 21, 1966, pp. 48, 50; *Editor & Publisher,* June 4, 1966, p. 72; corrected to reflect acquisitions since those dates.

11. Roy Thomson throughout the world controls in excess of 100 newspapers and 200 magazines, 25 printing companies, 17 television stations, 12 radio stations, 7 book publishing companies, 2 airlines, and other interests. Russell Braddon, *Roy Thomson of Fleet Street* (New York: Walker, 1965).

12. Two nonchain Sunday papers compete in Little Rock; Bridgeport, Conn.; Washington, D.C.; Columbia, Mo.; and Dallas. One of the two in Columbia is operated by the School of Journalism, University of Missouri, as part of its instructional program.

13. Cities where chain and nonchain Sunday newspapers compete: Champaign-Urbana, Ill.; Baltimore; Boston; Detroit; Las Vegas, Nev.; Newark, N.J.; New York; and Fort Worth.

14. Chain control of Sunday circulation by years: 1923, 44.7 per cent; 1933, 45.9 per cent. Source: Alfred McClung Lee, *The Daily Newspaper in America* (New York: Macmillan, 1937) pp. 215–16. 1935, 52.4 per cent 1945, 53.8 per cent; 1953, 53.9 per cent; 1960, 54.2 per cent; 1962, 53.7 per cent. Source: Raymond B. Nixon, "118 Owner Groups; 4.9 Average Holds," *Editor & Publisher,* April 21, 1962, pp. 86, 92.

15. Data compiled from *Editor & Publisher Yearbook,* 1966 and 1967, corrected to April 1967.

16. Thomson buys mostly small dailies and weeklies in the United States.

17. "Roy Thomson Invades America," *Harper's,* February 1962, p. 70. Also, Braddon, *Roy Thomson of Fleet Street,* where it is noted that his 40,000 one £ shares "within two years became so valuable that they made possible the purchase of Lord Kemsley's entire chain of British newspapers," p. 233. Thomson paid the equivalent of $31.5 million for the Kemsley chain, consisting of 18 important newspapers, including the prestigious *Sunday Times* of London and the *Empire News,* p. 251. It should be noted that the *Sunday Times* was not then associated with the historic and premier British London *Times.* However, Thomson bought the London *Times* in 1966 and merged it with his *Sunday Times.*

18. "Eighty per cent of all newspaper sales since the war (World War II) have been to other newspapers," Ben H. Bagdikian said. "The American

Newspaper Is Neither Record, Mirror, Journal, Ledger, Bulletin, Telegram, Examiner, Register, Chronicle, Gazette, Observer, Monitor, Transcript, Nor Herald of the Day's Events, It's Just Bad News," *Esquire*, March 1967, p. 143.

19. "Instead of paying out huge sums in taxes he (Newhouse) buys additional properties . . . and then plows back earnings to rehabilitate or expand them." Jerry H. Walker, "Newhouse Builds Empire For Family and Charity," *Editor & Publisher*, March 11, 1967, pp. 9–10.

20. John A. Lent, *Newhouse, Newspapers, Nuisances* (New York: Exposition Press, 1966), p. 88.

21. Braddon, p. 321.

3 The Nondaily American Press

1. *N. W. Ayer Newspaper Directory*, 1915.

2. See, especially, John Cameron Sim, "Decline in Weeklies' Numbers Starts from Misleading Peak," *Journalism Quarterly*, Spring 1966, pp. 121–124; and "Statistical Note" to the Appendix, Alfred McClung Lee, *The Daily Newspaper in America* (New York: Macmillan, 1937), pp. 705–9.

3. Morris L. Ernst, *The First Freedom* (New York: Macmillan, 1946), p. 104.

4. Malcolm M. Willey and William Weinfeld "The Country Weekly: Trends in Numbers and Distribution, 1900–1930," *Social Forces*, October 1934, pp. 51–56.

5. Wilbur Peterson, "Loss in Country Weekly Newspapers Heavy in 1950's," *Journalism Quarterly*, Winter 1961, pp. 15–24. Peterson identified 6,548 small town "country" weeklies and 1,440 metropolitan weeklies listed in *N. W. Ayer Newspaper Directory*, 1950. He excluded from his study more than a thousand weeklies listed by *Ayer*; "these included religious, racial, political, foreign language, college, military, trade, labor, legal . . . and free circulation newspapers."

6. Approximately 30 per cent of the dailies which suspended during 1945 to 1965 reverted to less frequent publication. *Editor & Publisher Yearbook*, 1944–66.

7. Department of Labor, "Small Daily Newspapers Under the Fair Labor Standards Act," June 1942.

8. Ernst, p. 105.

9. Willey and Weinfeld, "The Country Weekly and the Emergence of 'One-Newspaper Places,' " *Journalism Quarterly*, September 1934, p. 246.

10. Peterson, p. 23.

11. Kenneth R. Byerly, *Community Journalism* (Philadelphia: Chilton, 1961), p. 14.

12. Thomas J. Scheiber, "The Newspaper Chain of W. B. Harris," *Journalism Quarterly*, Spring 1951, p. 219.

13. Interview with Howard R. Long, chairman, Department of Journalism, Southern Illinois University, who was employed as editor of one of the Woodyard newspapers in the 1930's.

14. Data on chains was compiled from weekly newspapers listed in *N. W. Ayer Newspaper Directory*, 1967, and *Editor & Publisher Yearbook*, 1966, both corrected to reflect weekly newspaper acquisitions, October 1965 to May 1967.

15. Theodore Peterson, "Changes Ahead in the Print Media: Their Im-

plications for Educational Communication," talk at annual convention of American Assn. of Agricultural College Editors, Athens, Ga., July 14, 1966.

16. Morris Janowitz, *The Community Press in an Urban Setting* (Glencoe, Ill.: Free Press, 1952), pp. 35–46.

17. Data from N. W. *Ayer Newspaper Directory*, 1967, and *Editor & Publisher Yearbook*, 1966, corrected for changes since the publication of the two annuals.

18. Janowitz, p. 46. Cities and city limit newspapers with suburban weeklies in parentheses are: New York, 25 (70); Chicago, 82 (99); Los Angeles, 57 (51); Philadelphia, 48 (59); Boston, 22 (29); Detroit, 22 (29); Pittsburgh, 10 (43); San Francisco, 4 (6); Cleveland, 11 (6); Baltimore, 5 (3).

19. N. W. *Ayer Newspaper Directory*, 1967, and *Editor & Publisher Yearbook*, 1966, corrected to May 1967.

20. N. W. *Ayer Newspaper Directory*, 1967, and *Editor & Publisher Yearbook*, 1966, corrected to May 1967.

21. *Ibid.*

22. Rick Friedman, "The Weekly Editor, Suburban Chicago Story," *Editor & Publisher*, September 10, 1966, p. 32.

23. *Editor & Publisher*, October 15, 1966, p. 40.

24. *Editor & Publisher*, May 7, 1966, p. 12; October 30, 1966, p. 90.

25. *Editor & Publisher*, May 27, 1967, p. 55.

26. Floyd Stein, "The Revolution in Suburbia," *Grassroots Editor*, July 1966, p. 5.

27. Associated with Ingersoll are Mark Goodson and William Todman, television show producers. *Editor & Publisher*, December 3, 1966, p. 11; January 7, 1967, p. 45.

28. Gene Wendorf, sales promotion manager and assistant to the publisher of Des Plaines Publishing Co., a suburban weekly chain competitor of the two Field dailies, speaking at the Southern Illinois Editorial Assn. Spring meeting, Carbondale, Ill., April 14, 1967. See *Grassroots Editor*, July 1967, p. 11.

29. Stein, p. 6.

30. Boyd L. Miller, "More Dailies Zoning for Suburban Readers," *Journalism Quarterly*, Summer 1965, p. 460.

31. "Lust for Advertising, Post Threatens Weekly Papers," *Grassroots Editor*, January–February 1967, pp. 18–20, reprinted from *Cervi's Rocky Mountain Journal*. Also, Wendorf, *Grassroots Editor*, July 1967, pp. 11, 29.

32. Carter Publications, publisher of the Fort Worth *Star-Telegram*, bought an interest in its fifth Fort Worth area weekly in January 1967. *Editor & Publisher*, January 7, 1967, p. 44.

33. Stein, pp. 3–7; Wendorf, p. 29.

34. Janowitz, p. 44.

35. James Force, "The Daily Press in Suburbia: Trends in 15 Metropolitan Areas," *Journalism Quarterly*, Autumn 1962, pp. 460–63.

36. Miller, p. 462.

37. Robert Ezra Park, *The Immigrant Press and Its Control* (New York: Harper & Bros., 1922); *Society, Collective Behavior, News and Opinion, Sociology and Modern Society* (Glencoe, Ill.: Free Press, 1955), pp. 152–81; and elsewhere.

38. *News Workshop*, New York University, May, 1967, p. 5.

39. Frank Luther Mott, *American Journalism*, (New York: Macmillan, 1950), p. 29; Carl Wittke, *The German-Language Press in America*

(Lexington, Ky.: University of Kentucky, 1957), pp. 13–14.

40. Wittke, *German Language Press in America*, p. 208.

41. Park, *The Immigrant Press and Its Control*, p. 318.

42. *N. W. Ayer Newspaper Directory*, 1917, 1920.

43. *Ibid.*, 1925, 1935, 1940, 1950, 1960, 1965, 1966, 1967.

44. Park, *Society, Collective Behavior*, pp. 165–75.

45. See, for example, Frederic C. Coonradt, "A New Tone of Voice in the Negro Newspaper," *Grassroots Editor*, July 1966, pp. 17–18. Mr. Coonradt studied the Los Angeles *Sentinel*, circulation more than 40,000, before and after the explosive Watts race riots of August 1965. His conclusion: The *Sentinel* "is less a Negro newspaper than it is a community weekly that circulates in a largely Negro community."

46. Armistead S. Pride, "The Negro Newspaper: Voice of a Minority," *Midwest Journal*, Winter 1950–51, pp. 94–95.

47. Willis D. Weatherford and Charles S. Johnson, *Race Relations* (New York: D. C. Heath, 1934), p. 485.

48. Irvine Garland Penn, *The Afro-American Press and Its Editors* (Springfield, Mass.: Willey, 1891), p. 28.

49. Armistead S. Pride, "Negro Newspapers: Yesterday, Today and Tomorrow," *Journalism Quarterly*, Spring 1951, p. 179.

50. *Ibid.*, p. 179.

51. *Ibid.*, pp. 179–80.

52. Ernst, p. 113.

53. Pride, "The Negro Newspaper: Voice of A Minority," p. 93.

54. Pride, "Negro Newspapers: Yesterday, Today and Tomorrow," p. 181.

55. Letter from Armistead S. Pride, dated June 10, 1967.

56. *Negro Newspapers in the United States*, 1966, Department of Journalism, Lincoln University.

57. *Editor & Publisher*, November 12, 1966, p. 94.

58. *Editor & Publisher*, March 4, 1967, p. 52.

4 Newspaper Problems and Outlook

1. "The Newspaper Collector," *Time*, July 27, 1962, p. 56.

2. *Editor & Publisher*, October 16, 1965, p. 63.

3. Testimony before the Subcommittee on Antitrust and Monopoly of the Committee on the Judiciary, U.S. House of Representatives, March 14, 1963. See p. 289 of the Official Verbatim Transcript in Representative Emanuel Celler's office.

4. Jay Horwitz, "Blood, Sweat, Tears—and Angels Help New York *Post* Toward 166th Birthday," *News Workshop*, Department of Journalism, New York University, May 1967, p. 6.

5. The Associated Press, May 7, 1967.

6. *The Guild Reporter*, September 10, 1965, p. 3.

7. *Editor & Publisher*, October 16, 1965, p. 61.

8. "Annual Newsprint Supplement," 1964, Newsprint Assn. of Canada, Table 19.

9. *Editor & Publisher*, March 4, 1967, p. 12; April 8, 1967, p. 10.

10. Jon G. Udell, *1975 U.S. Newsprint Consumption*, American Newspaper Publishers Assn., (n.d.) pp. 9, 11.

11. "ANPA Newspaper Information Service Newletter," February 20, 1967.
12. Robert U. Brown, "On Larger Newspapers, Revenue Increases Outpace Expenses," *Editor & Publisher*, April 23, 1966, p. 20.
13. *Editor & Publisher*, August 20, 1966, p. 29.
14. *FoI Digest*, January–February 1967, p. 4.
15. Frank Luther Mott, *American Journalism, A History: 1690–1960*, 3rd ed. (New York: Macmillan, 1962), p. 230.
16. *Ibid.*, p. 268.
17. *Ibid.*, p. 279.
18. *Ibid.*, p. 570.
19. Herbert Brucker, "Mass Man and Mass Media," *Saturday Review*, May 29, 1965, p. 44.
20. *Editor & Publisher*, May 13, 1967, p. 69.
21. Kirby Freeman, "The Death of a Daily: Auction in Atlanta," *Editor & Publisher*, March 19, 1966, p. 10.
22. *Editor & Publisher*, March 19, 1966, p. 14.
23. *The Guild Reporter*, September 10, 1965.
24. Frank Murray, "The Birth of a Daily: Everything's 'Go' in Florida," *Editor & Publisher*, March 19, 1966, p. 9.
25. Jerry Walker, Jr., "*Suffolk Sun* Begins to Rise With Cowles Co. Capital," *Editor & Publisher*, August 20, 1966, p. 14.
26. *Editor & Publisher*, September 24, 1966, p. 12.
27. Landon Wills, speech at Southern Illinois University Journalism Week, April 1965.
28. *Editor & Publisher*, November 24, 1962, p. 70.
29. *Editor & Publisher*, March 19, 1966, p. 56.
30. Alan S. Donnahoe, president, Richmond Newspapers, Inc., in talk to the Richmond Society of Financial Analysts. See *Editor & Publisher*, May 13, 1967, p. 38.
31. "Technological Developments in Newspaper Publishing," Appendix B, p. 12, a prepared statement by the American Newspaper Publishers Assn. presented before the Antitrust Subcommittee of the Judiciary Committee, U.S. House of Representatives, March 14, 1963.
32. *Daily Newspapers in 1966*, publication of the American Newspaper Publishers Assn.; see also *Editor & Publisher*, April 29, 1967, p. 58.
33. *Daily Newspapers in 1966*, American Newspaper Publishers Assn.; see also *Editor & Publisher*, April 29, 1967, p. 58.
34. Stephen J. Rogers, president, Syracuse *Herald-Journal*, "Move to Automation Frustrating, Costly," *Editor & Publisher*, November 12, 1966, p. 81.
35. E. B. Weiss, vice-president merchandising services for Doyle Dane Bernbach and columnist for *Advertising Age*, "A Revolution in Communication," Part 4, *Marketing Insights*, December 5, 1966, p. 16.
36. *Editor & Publisher*, September 18, 1965, p. 64.
37. *Editor & Publisher*, March 19, 1966, p. 44.
38. Jerry Walker, Jr., "Offset Trend Faces Cutoff at 70,000," *Editor & Publisher*, June 11, 1966, p. 14.
39. Installation was scheduled to be made in early 1967. *Editor & Publisher*, November 12, 1966, p. 84.
40. Wilbur Peterson and Mark Guldin, "Study Shows Breakdown of Income, Expenses for Nine Weeklies, Seven Dailies in Iowa," *The Iowa Publisher*, August 1965, p. 7.
41. *Statistical Abstract of the United*

States, U.S. Department of Commerce, Bureau of Census, 1956, p. 713; 1961, p. 695.

42. *Member's Service Bulletin*, Inland Daily Press Assn., November 10, 1965, pp. 175–76.

43. *The Guild Reporter*, July 30, 1965, p. 10.

44. Tony Brenna, "Meyer Assails 'Criminal Approach' to New Newspaper," *Editor & Publisher*, May 13, 1967, p. 12.

45. *Editor & Publisher*, April 1, 1967, p. 65.

46. Based on hourly rate increases and fringe benefits for the 250 printers. For rates see *Editor & Publisher*, October 29, 1966, p. 9.

47. Rates quoted in Associated Press dispatch, April 6, 1966. Number of employees from *Editor & Publisher*, April 16, 1966, p. 12.

48. *Editor & Publisher*, October 29, 1966, p. 9; March 25, 1967, p. 13.

49. *Editor & Publisher*, April 1, 1967, pp. 9, 65.

50. The Associated Press, May 6, 1967.

51. The Associated Press, October 28, 1965.

52. *FoI Digest*, November–December 1964, p. 6.

53. *Newsweek*, August 20, 1962, p. 53.

54. The MacManus, John, and Adams advertising firm in a survey of Detroit newspaper readers during the 134-day newspaper strike learned that readers and many retailers had not found suitable substitutes for the closed newspaper, "but the longer the strike continues, the more acceptable the substitutes appear to become. . . . Newspapers are a habit with most Americans; deprive them long enough and they will find a new habit." Quoted in *FoI Digest*, November–December 1964, p. 6.

55. *Editor & Publisher*, August 20, 1966, p. 12.

56. *Newsweek*, August 20, 1962, p. 53.

57. *FoI Digest*, November–December 1964, p. 6.

58. *Detroit Newspaper Strike*, Freedom of Information Center Publication No. 143, June 1965, p. 1.

59. See ANPA list of grievances against the unions, submitted to the Antitrust Subcommittee of the Judiciary Committee, U.S. House of Representatives, March 15, 1963.

60. A. H. Raskin, "Who Needs Newspapers?" *The Reporter* as reprinted in the St. Louis *Post-Dispatch*, October 19, 1965, editorial page.

61. Miles P. Patrone, ANPA labor relations chairman, in a speech at the annual AFL-CIO International Typographical Union convention in Colorado Springs, September 6, 1966, said there were 231 strikes from 1955 to 1965. The figures here cited were adjusted to the period 1957 to 1966.

62. The 67th Annual Report of the ANPA Labor Relations Committee as reported in *Editor & Publisher*, April 29, 1967, p. 70.

63. The Associated Press, April 5, 1965.

64. The Associated Press, April 5, 1965.

65. United Press International, September 12, 1966.

66. William A. Mindak, Andrew Neibergs, and Alfred Anderson, "Economic Effects of the Minneapolis Newspaper Strike," *Journalism Quarterly*, Spring 1963, p. 217.

67. The 1940 and 1950 circulation per adults ratio probably reflects heavy male deaths in World War II rather than newspaper gains. See Census figures for male adults for the two years.

68. Based on *N. W. Ayer* and Bureau of Census data; except for 1966 both were corrected to September 30, 1966.
69. *N. W. Ayer* and Bureau of Census data; except for 1966 both were corrected to September 30, 1966.
70. *Ibid.*
71. Harvey J. Levin, *Broadcast Regulation and Joint Ownership of Media* (New York: New York University, 1960), Table 21, p. 109.
72. Television Bureau of Advertising study as reported in *Broadcasting,* May 29, 1967, pp. 24–25.
73. American Newspaper Representatives, Inc., report, shows 8,478 weekly newspapers in 1956 with 18,529,199 circulation; 8,003 weeklies in 1966 with 26,088,230 circulation. Letter from J. Kay Aldous, administrative assistant, dated December 22, 1966.
74. Jerry Walker, Jr., "For the Record," *Editor & Publisher,* April 15, 1967, p. 16.
75. *Editor & Publisher,* March 25, 1967, p. 6.
76. Automation as herein used is defined as "the use of advanced mechanical equipment, especially in combination with high-speed computers and other self-regulating controls, in manufacturing, accounting, distribution and all other operations." This is the definition used by McGraw-Hill Co. in various of its studies and reports and by the United States Department of Labor, see *Automation, Productivity and Manpower Problems,* undated.
77. *Editor & Publisher,* February 11, 1967, p. 56.
78. Weiss, "A Revolution in Communication," Part 3, *Marketing Insights,* November 28, 1966, p. 17.
79. Weiss issued this warning in "A Revolution in Communication," Part 2, *Marketing Insights,* November 12, 1966, p. 18.

5 News and Feature Services: Boon or Blight?

1. The writer is deeply indebted to the excellent book by Alfred McClung Lee, *The Daily Newspaper In America* (New York, Macmillan, 1937), for much of the detail on the history of the news services.
2. *United States* v. *Associated Press,* Civ. 19–163 (S.D.N.Y.); filed August 28, 1942; judgment entered January 13, 1944.
3. *United States* v. *Associated Press* (326 U.S. 1); affirmed June 18, 1945.
4. *Ibid.*
5. See, among others, Walter Millis, *Road to War: America, 1914–1917* (Boston: Houghton Mifflin, 1935); and Kent Cooper, *Kent Cooper and The Associated Press, An Autobiography* (New York: Random House, 1959).
6. Frank Luther Mott, *American Journalism* (New York: Macmillan, 1950), pp. 710–11.
7. *Associated Press* v. *International News Service* (248 U.S. 215).
8. Edwin Emery, *The Press and America,* 2nd ed., (Englewood Cliffs, N.J.: Prentice-Hall, 1962), p. 662.
9. *Editor & Publisher,* May 31, 1958, p. 14.
10. Dow Jones services its several editions of the *Wall Street Journal* with perforated tape transmitted at a speed of 1,000 words a minute, *Editor & Publisher,* April 8, 1967, p. 11. The Washington *Post* uses an electronic transmission system between London and Washington capable of

transmitting 1,300 words a minute, ANPA *Newspaper Information Service Newsletter*, November 30, 1965.

11. *Editor & Publisher*, March 11, 1967, p. 13; April 22, 1967, pp. 17, 158; *Broadcasting*, March 13, 1967, p. 54; April 24, 1967, p. 44.

12. *Editor & Publisher*, April 22, 1967, p. 17; and letter from Ted Boyle, AP administrative assistant to the General Manager, dated June 2, 1966; Roger Tutarian, vice-president and editor, UPI, in Allen Memorial Lecture, University of Oregon. See, also, "A Million Dollars a Week," *Editor & Publisher*, April 22, 1967, p. 48.

13. *Broadcasting*, March 27, 1967, p. 5.

14. Richard A. Schwarzlose, "Trends in U.S. Newspapers' Wire Service Resources, 1934–66," *Journalism Quarterly*, Winter 1966, p. 629.

15. *Ibid.*, p. 630.

16. *Ibid.*, p. 633.

17. *Editor & Publisher*, April 9, 1966, p. 24.

18. Schwarzlose, p. 636.

19. Robert H. Sollen, "Nationalistic Bias in Reporting Cold War," *Editor & Publisher*, July 8, 1961, p. 64.

20. An unpublished research report by the author conducted during the summer, 1956.

21. Bryce W. Rucker, "News Services' Crowd Reporting in the 1956 Presidential Campaign," *Journalism Quarterly*, Spring 1960, pp. 195–98.

22. Blair Bolles, "The Grass Roots Foreign Correspondent," *Nieman Reports*, July 1956.

23. Edwin Lahey in the Detroit *Free Press*, June 12, 1961. See also *FoI Digest*, May–June 1961.

24. Henry Shapiro, "Interpreting the Soviets," *Nieman Reports*, June 1964. Reprinted by Louis M. Lyons (ed.) *Reporting the News* (Cambridge, Mass.: Belknap Press, 1965), pp. 313–17.

25. "Reporting a Revolution," *Time*, February 12, 1959, pp. 50, 52; "Semper Fidel," *Newsweek*, February 2, 1959; and Howard L. Lewis, "The Cuban Revolt Story: AP, UPI and 3 Papers," *Journalism Quarterly*, Autumn 1960, pp. 573–78, 646.

26. Neal D. Hougton, "The Cuban Invasion of 1961 and the U.S. Press, in Retrospect," *Journalism Quarterly*, Summer 1965, pp. 422–32.

27. Wilbur Schramm, *Responsibility in Mass Communication* (New York: Harper, 1957), pp. 219–20.

28. *Editor & Publisher*, September 2, 1967, p. 11.

29. Evan Mecham testimony before the Subcommittee on Antitrust and Monopoly, Committee on the Judiciary, U.S. Senate, July 13, 1967, p. 203 of unpublished testimony.

30. Richard L. Tobin, "Straws of an Ill Wind," *Saturday Review*, July 13, 1963, p. 41.

31. *Ibid.*

32. Letter from Ted Boyle, June 2, 1966; *Editor & Publisher*, April 22, 1967, p. 48.

33. Mecham, pp. 211–15.

34. Luther A. Huston, "Agency Plan Saves Papers from Graveyard, Hart Told," *Editor & Publisher*, July 29, 1967, p. 52.

35. Luther A. Huston, "Newspaper Problems Are Complex," *Editor & Publisher*, August 5, 1967, p. 47.

36. Luther A. Huston, "New Approach to 'Failing' Papers' Problem Is Hinted," *Editor & Publisher*, August 19, 1967, p. 10.

37. Luther A. Huston, "Antitrust Exemption Bill: 5 Plead for It, 9 Against," *Editor & Publisher*, July 22, 1967.

38. Luther A. Huston, *Editor & Publisher*, August 5, 1967, p. 47.

39. Norman Cherniss testimony before the Senate Subcommittee on Antitrust and Monopoly, July 19, 1967.
40. Elmo Scott Watson, *A History of Newspaper Syndicates in the United States*, 1865–1935 (Chicago: Elmo Scott Watson, 1936), pp. 5–27.
41. Alfred McClung Lee credits these two syndicates with increasing the number of daily newspapers from 574 in 1870 to 971 in 1880 and 1,610 in 1889. See *The Daily Newspaper in America*, pp. 511–12.
42. Watson, pp. 42–44.
43. *Ibid.*, pp. 44–48.
44. Ralph C. Darrow, "Effects of Readyprint Loss on Iowa Weekly Papers," *Journalism Quarterly*, Spring 1953, pp. 230–31.
45. Watson, pp. 54–62.
46. Lee, pp. 542–43.
47. Watson, pp. 67–68.
48. *Ibid.*, p. 69.
49. *FoI Digest*, May–June 1963, p. 4; Emery, *The Press and America*, p. 425.
50. Mott, p. 796.
51. Emery, p. 684; *FoI Digest*, May–June 1963, p. 4.
52. *Time*, August 11, 1958, p. 56.
53. *Editor & Publisher*, December 3, 1966, p. 15.
54. *Editor & Publisher*, August 20, 1966, p. 10.
55. *Editor & Publisher*, January 8, 1966, p. 20, estimated *This Week* in 1965 sold $19,774,500 and *Parade* $17,774,550.
56. *Editor & Publisher 41st Annual Syndicate Directory*, July 30, 1966.
57. Morris Ernst, *The First Freedom* (New York: Macmillan, 1946), p. 92.
58. *Editor & Publisher Syndicate Directory*, pp. 26–27.
59. *Editor & Publisher*, January 7, 1967, p. 11.
60. *Editor & Publisher*, June 24, 1967, p. 46.
61. *Editor & Publisher*, April 1, 1967, p. 58.
62. Luther A. Huston, "Agency Plan Saves Papers from Graveyard, Hart Told," *Editor & Publisher*, July 29, 1967, p. 13.
63. Cook Coen, National Analysis Service, "Cost Study, Daily Must Have 5% More Revenue to Maintain Its 20% Profit Rate," *Editor & Publisher*, April 1, 1967, p. 14.
64. *United States* v. *The Times Mirror Company*, Civil 65–366–WF (C.D. Calif.), pp. 2273–2274.
65. Cherniss, July 19, 1967.
66. *Seminar*, December 1966, p. 15.
67. *United States* v. *The Times Mirror Company*, p. 2275.
68. Loyal B. Phillips testimony before the Subcommittee on Antitrust, Committee of the Judiciary, U.S. House of Representatives, March 14, 1963.
69. Mecham, p. 212.
70. Luther A. Huston, "Many Call, Few Are Chosen to Comment on Hayden Bill," *Editor & Publisher*, August 12, 1967, p. 62.
71. Luther A. Huston, *Editor & Publisher*, August 19, 1967, p. 10.
72. Jack R. Howard, president and general editorial manager, Scripps-Howard Newspapers, testimony before the Senate Subcommittee on Antitrust and Monopoly, July 18, 1967.
73. *Wall Street Journal*, April 7, 1964, p. 2.
74. Statement read by Senator Philip A. Hart (D-Michigan), chairman of the Senate Subcommittee on Antitrust and Monopoly, July 19, 1967.
75. *Editor & Publisher*, July 29, 1967, p. 48.
76. *United States* v. *Newspaper Enterprise Association, Greater Buffalo*

Press, Incorporated, and three subsidiaries: International Color Printing Company, Wilkes Barre, Pa., Dixie Color Printing Corporation, Sylacauga, Ala., and Southwest Color Printing Corporation, Lufkin, Texas. See also *Editor & Publisher,* July 29, 1967, p. 48.

77. *United States* v. *Stamps-Conhaim-Whitehead, Incorporated* (Civ. 1338, n.d. Iowa), cease and desist order filed August 29, 1963; *United States* v. *Metro Associated Services, Incorporated* (Civ. 1337, n.d., Iowa), cease and desist order filed April 3, 1964.

78. The writer observed this event while residing at San Marcos, Tex. For current circulations, see *Editor & Publisher Yearbook,* 1967.

79. *Time,* April 16, 1959, p. 50.

80. Number of Sunday comics appearing in Boston newspapers for five-year periods since 1900–1904 shows a rather consistent increase, excluding data for 1905–9. They reached a peak of 133 in the most recent years of the study, 1955–59. See Francis E. Barcus, "A Content Analysis of Trends in Sunday Comics, 1900–1959," *Journalism Quarterly,* Spring 1961, p. 173.

6 Radio's Serious Problems

1. Herbert Hoover said, "It is inconceivable that we should allow so great a possibility for service, for news, for entertainment, for education and for vital commercial purposes to be drowned in advertising chatter." Hoover's comments were quoted by FCC Chairman E. William Henry. See *Broadcast Advertising,* Government Printing Office, 1963, p. 37.

2. The 1927 level was not equaled until 1940 when 765 stations were authorized.

3. The phrasing is from the Communications Act of 1934.

4. Chairman Fly said in 1959 that there had been only three license revocations for bad programming, and these occurred during the earliest days of broadcasting when Doc Brinkley's stations were denied licenses because of his prescribing "goat gland" operations over the air. *Broadcasting and Government Regulation in a Free Society,* publication of the Fund for the Republic, Inc., 1959, pp. 5, 11.

5. *AM-FM Broadcast Financial Data—1965,* FCC mimeo., October 1965.

6. *Ibid.*; *Broadcasting Yearbook,* 1966, p. 10.

7. *Television,* June 1957, p. 61.

8. Proportions for 1960 were 5.8 and for 1965, 5.9. Source: *Printer's Ink,* February of each year.

9. Total radio income for 1946 was $334,078,914 and for 1965 was $827,782,000. Source: FCC files.

10. *Broadcasting Yearbook,* 1966, p. A-158. The rate of growth was affected by a freeze on applications for new or changed AM facilities imposed May 10, 1962, and lifted July 2, 1964. New AM station assignment rules were adopted to minimize interference of new stations with existing stations in the increasingly crowded AM spectrum. See *29th FCC Annual Report,* 1963, Government Printing Office, 1963, p. 75; *30th Annual Report, 1964,* Government Printing Office, 1964, p. 120; and FCC files, docket 15084.

11. *Broadcasting Yearbook,* 1966, p. B-226.

12. KADS (FM), formerly KGLA (FM) Los Angeles, broadcast all-advertising (classified ads) for nine months beginning November 5, 1966. However, the experiment failed. The FCC on July 1, 1966, granted McLendon Pacific Corp. permission to buy that station and initiate an all-advertising format on a one-year experimental basis. Los Angeles was selected by McLendon for this experiment because the Los Angeles *Times* each year publishes the largest number of classified advertisements of any newspaper in the world. In 1965 the *Times* published 4,057,967 classified ads.
13. *Broadcasting Yearbook*, 1966, pp. D-33–34.
14. FCC dockets 5618, 5640, 8516.
15. FCC docket 8516. See *Report on Editorializing by Broadcast Licensees*, FCC mimeo., 1949, and Section 315 (a) of the Communications Act.
16. *Applicability of the Fairness Doctrine in Handling of Controversial Issues of Public Importance*, FCC mimeo., July 1, 1964.
17. *Broadcasting*, November 7, 1966, p. 54. It should be pointed out that Frank Stanton and CBS were among the strongest advocates of editorial freedom for broadcasting. See various FCC hearings and speeches by Stanton on the subject.
18. *Ibid.*, p. 53. House Speaker John W. McCormack, Representative Emanuel Celler, chairman of the powerful House Judiciary Committee, and Representative Harley O. Staggers, chairman of the Commerce Committee, among others criticized the practice of stations endorsing political candidates. Representative Staggers, who also heads the subcommittee that periodically investigates broadcasting problems, threatened to investigate editorial endorsements by broadcasting stations.
19. *Statement of Policy Concerning Loud Commercials*, FCC mimeo., July 9, 1945.
20. Charles A. Siepmann, *Radio, Television and Society* (New York: Oxford University Press, 1950), p. 13.
21. See FCC publication *Public Service Responsibility of Broadcast Licensees*, Government Printing Office, 1946, p. 44.
22. *E. G. Robinson* v. *Federal Communications Commission*, U.S. Court of Appeals, F.2d, March 19, 1964.
23. Testimony before a Subcommittee of the Committee on Interstate and Foreign Commerce, U.S. House of Representatives, 88th Cong., 1st Sess., November 6–8, 1963. See the subcommittee report, *Broadcast Advertising*, 1963, p. 38.
24. *Ibid.*
25. *TV Guide*, March 31, 1962, p. 14.
26. *Broadcast Advertising*, 1963, pp. 20–97 *passim*.
27. *Broadcasting*, October 17, 1966, pp. 34, 36.
28. *Ibid.*, p. 35.
29. *Ibid.*, p. 39.
30. *Ibid.*, p. 91; *FCC Annual Report to Congress*, 1966, as reported in *Broadcasting*, March 6, 1967, p. 45.
31. Charles A. Siepmann, *Radio's Second Chance* (Boston: Little, Brown 1946) pp. 157–60.
32. See, e.g., writings of Vance Packard, Thorstein Veblen, and John K. Galbraith.
33. A peak for recent years of 43 per cent of approximately 13,000 complaints received in 1964 criticized advertising, *30th FCC Annual Report, 1964*, Government Printing Office, p. 51. In 1965 the percentage dropped to 32 of approximately

21,000 complaints; 34 per cent complained about programming, *31st FCC Annual Report*, 1965, Government Printing Office, p. 105.

34. *Statement of Policy Concerning Loud Commercials*, FCC mimeo. See docket 14904. A summary is provided in *31st FCC Annual Report*, pp. 92–93.

35. See *30th FCC Annual Report*, p. 65, and *31st FCC Annual Report*, p. 94.

36. A I-A station is a dominant station operating at 50,000 watts day and night on a clear channel and designated to render primary and secondary service over an extended geographic area. Its primary (ground) service is free from objectionable interference from other stations on the same or adjacent channels, and its secondary (skyway) service area is free from interference except from stations on adjacent channels.

37. A I-B station may operate with power up to 50,000 watts on a channel occupied by other high power day and night service stations. Each I-B station is required to avoid interfering with the signal of another I-B station on the same channel. Both WABC and KOB use directional antennas to protect signals of the other station.

38. Ownership of the 13 I-A stations already duplicated or to be duplicated: American Broadcasting Company, WLS Chicago; Columbia Broadcasting System, WBBM Chicago, WCBS New York, KMOX St. Louis, WCAU Philadelphia; National Broadcasting Company, WMAQ Chicago, WKYC Cleveland; *Chicago Tribune* newspaper-broadcasting chain, WGN Chicago; Cox newspaper-broadcasting chain, WSB Atlanta; Westinghouse Electric Corp., WBZ Boston, KDKA Pittsburgh; Rust Craft greeting cards and broadcasting chain, WHAM Rochester, N.Y.; Capital Cities broadcasting chain, WJR Detroit.

39. Ownerships of 11 I-A stations not to be duplicated: AVCO manufacturing-broadcasting chain, WLW Cincinnati, WOAI San Antonio; Palmer broadcasting chain, WHO Des Moines; *Dallas Morning News*, WFAA Dallas, and *Fort Worth Star-Telegram*, WBAP Fort Worth, sharing time on channel 820; *Louisville Courier-Journal* and *Times*, WHAS Louisville; *Minneapolis Star and Tribune* and Ridder publications, both newspaper-broadcasting chains, WCCO Minneapolis; Loyola University of the South, a Roman Catholic university, WWL New Orleans; Bonneville International Stations, broadcasting chain arm of the Mormon Church, KSL Salt Lake City; NBC, WNBC New York; National Life and Accident Insurance Co., WSM Nashville; and Earle C. Anthony, Inc., KFI Los Angeles.

40. More than 18 million, in excess of 70 per cent, of those who receive no primary (ground) night radio service live east of the Mississippi River. Source: Testimony of Roy Battles, director, Clear Channel Broadcasting Service, at hearings before a Subcommittee of the Committee on Interstate and Foreign Commerce, U.S. House of Representatives, 87th Cong., 2d Sess., February 1, 1962. See *Clear Channel Broadcast Stations*, Government Printing Office, 1962, p. 57.

41. Responding to numerous complaints from small stations in WLW's coverage area to what they regarded as unfair competition for advertising and listeners, the Senate in 1938 passed a resolution opposing increasing the power of any AM sta-

tions to more than 50,000 watts. See: Senate Resolution 294, 75th Cong., 2d Sess., adopted June 7, 1938.

7 Commercial Television and How It Grew

1. Television ownership figures are from Advertising Research Foundation estimates as reported in *Broadcasting,* December 27, 1965, p. 29. The total number of sets in operation is based on estimates of sales through October 1966.

2. One can understand the vast spectrum requirements of television more clearly and FCC's dilemma at dealing with it through the years when comparing requirements for standard (AM) broadcasting with telecasting. A standard broadcasting station requires only 10 kilocycles. Therefore, the standard spectrum (540 to 1600 kilocycles) can accommodate 105 channels, enough to permit more than 4,000 stations to operate without interference. A television station, however, requires a minimum of 6,000 kilocycles (6 megacycles) to transmit an intelligible picture. Hence, one channel requires only slightly less space than the total spectrum assigned to standard broadcasting. For this reason only 12 channels may be assigned to that portion of the very high frequency spectrum (megacycles 54–216) reserved for television and another 70 to the ultrahigh frequency (megacycles 470–890). Source: Benedict P. Cottone, attorney, former general counsel, FCC, *Broadcasting and Government Regulation in a Free Society,* published by the Center for the Study of Democratic Institutions, The Fund for the Republic, Inc., Santa Barbara, Calif., 1959.

3. As of September 7, 1967, there were 519 commercial VHF and 276 commercial UHF stations authorized, of which all but 18 VHF and 141 UHF were on the air. *Broadcasting,* September 11, 1967, p. 94.

4. The advertising Research Foundation estimated that 53.7 million households had 66.4 million sets as of August 1965. R. H. Buskin Associates, market researchers, said its studies, as of October 1966, showed increases reflected in figures cited here.

5. FCC docket 15858, February 1965.

6. Statistics on stations were taken from *Broadcasting Yearbook,* 1966, pp. A3–A68.

7. Notice of Proposed Rule Making, FCC docket 12782, mimeo. 64453, March 22, 1965, p. 6.

8. FCC Chairman E. William Henry, speaking at NAB convention, Washington, D.C., March 23, 1965.

9. Advertising Research Bureau reported that for the months of March 1963 and 1964, three VHF station market affiliates devoted an average of slightly more than 95 per cent of their prime hour programming to network shows. In a four VHF station market network affiliates devoted an average of more than 97 per cent of their prime time to network programs. *Television Age,* June 8, 1964, p. 31.

10. Hearings before Subcommittee No. 6, Select Committee on Small Business, U.S. House of Representatives, 89th Cong., 2d Sess., May 10, 1966. See *Activities of Regulatory and Enforcement Agencies Relating*

to Small Business, Part 2, Government Printing Office, 1966, p. 554.

11. FCC docket 12859, 1963.

12. Committee under the chairmanship of Senator Charles Potter.

13. The *Barrow Report* was issued by a special FCC network study staff with Roscoe L. Barrow, dean of the University of Cincinnati Law School, director. This study was initiated in September 1955; its report was issued in October 1957.

14. See docket 12859, FCC mimeo, September 14, 1960.

15. *Times-Mirror Broadcasting Co.* v. *United States,* C.A.D.C., No. 16,608. In effect, the Antitrust Division of the Department of Justice joined with Times-Mirror Broadcasting Co. in this suit filed in the U.S. Court of Appeals for the District of Columbia.

16. *29th Annual FCC Report,* 1963, Government Printing Office, 1963, p. 71. The Justice Department took the position that option time violated antitrust laws and was comparable to "block booking" practices forced upon movie theaters by the film industry until the U.S. Supreme Court in 1950 declared that procedure illegal. As with movie exhibitors then, option time, Justice argued, forced TV stations to take some undesirable programs from the networks in order to gain access to desirable ones. The U.S. Court of Appeals remanded the case to the FCC, upon the Commission's request.

17. See docket 12859. The prohibition was adopted May 28, 1963, to become effective September 10, 1963.

18. *Ibid.*

19. *29th Annual FCC Report,* 1963, pp. 71–72.

20. See transcript of testimony, docket 12859, FCC files.

21. *Report on Chain Broadcasting,* FCC, Government Printing Office, 1941. Also, see network contracts printed in *Activities of Regulatory and Enforcement Agencies,* Part 2. ABC, pp. A604–A608; CBS, pp. A584–A586; NBC, pp. A645–A649.

22. "Statement of Criteria Governing Affiliation and Disaffiliation Policy of the CBS Television Network," *Activities of Regulatory and Enforcement Agencies,* Part 2, pp. A572–A573.

23. FCC mimeo. 65461, Rep. No. 5466, March 22, 1965, p. 2.

24. FCC Chairman Henry, speaking before the International Radio and Television Society, September 24, 1965.

25. Chairman Minow in a letter to Representative Oren Harris, chairman, House Committee on Interstate and Foreign Commerce, February 4, 1963. See *Television Network Program Procurement,* H. R. Rep. No. 281, Government Printing Office, 1963, p. 4.

26. *Ibid.,* p. 99.

27. Notice of Proposed Rule-Making, FCC docket 12782, p. 17.

28. In 1964, 74 of 92 programs were licensed to networks. Networks produced another 8½ programs. In all, networks held no proprietary interest in only 9½ programs. Of the 74 programs licensed to networks, networks held syndication interests in 56.

29. *Television Network Program Procurement,* p. 103. In 1964, the *Little Report,* a study financed by the networks, shows the networks earned $23.5 million from their syndication operations, a figure that does not reflect shares of profits received from programs syndicated by other than network entities. Source: *Activities of Regulatory and Enforcement Agencies,* Part 2, p. A378. For com-

plete *Little Report* see pp. A323–A473. CBS Films in 1964 made 2,000 sales to television broadcasters in 76 countries to set a new syndication record. CBS Films' gross on 1964 foreign sales was up 28 per cent and on domestic sales was up 8 per cent. Source: *Broadcasting,* January 25, 1965, p. 68. CBS and Twentieth Century-Fox tied for total number of hours of new prime television service for international syndication, 10 hours each, in 1966, *Broadcasting,* May 16, 1966, p. 29.

30. *Television Network Program Procurement,* pp. 77–78. See also FCC files, docket 12782.

31. *Television,* September 1962, p. 60.

32. NBC testified that the series was dropped because it had lost its audience. NBC cited that program's Nielsen National Average Audience rating for November–December 1956, of 16.6, lower than those for such other dramatic series as "Playhouse 90," 24.0; "Theatre Guild," 21.8; "Studio One," 20.3; "Alcoa / Goodyear Theatre," 19.5; "Kraft Television Playhouse," 19.0; "Armstrong Circle Theatre," 17.0. Source: *Activities of Regulatory and Enforcement Agencies,* p. 597. However, see comments in Chapter 8 relative to the audience-rating services.

33. *Ibid.,* p. 506.

34. *Ibid.,* p. 507.

35. The two pilots in question are "A Man Named McGhee" and "Meet Maggie Mulligan." This suit was filed in the U.S. Dist. Ct., S.D. Calif., Cent. Div. Civ. No. 65–1350–JWC. See *Activities of Regulatory and Enforcement Agencies Relating to Small Business,* Part 1, 1966, pp. A186–A193.

36. Notice of Proposed Rule Making, FCC docket 12782, p. 19.

37. *Ibid.,* p. 21.

38. *Advertising Age,* editorial, November 9, 1959.

39. Notice of Proposed Rule Making, FCC docket 12782, p. 21.

40. Television Bureau of Advertising, *TV Basics,* May 1962, p. 19.

41. *Television Network Program Procurement,* pp. 57–58.

42. Testimony of Stanton, Committee on Interstate and Foreign Commerce, U.S. Senate, 84th Cong., 2d Sess., *The Television Inquiry,* Government Printing Office, 1956, p. 2138.

43. Sarnoff in speech before the Los Angeles Chamber of Commerce. See *Broadcasting,* February 16, 1959, p. 48.

44. "U.S. TV Set Production—1946–1966," *Broadcasting Yearbook,* 1967, p. 14.

45. "TV Broadcast Financial Data—1966," FCC mimeo.

46. The FCC reported that television networks and stations received $1,834.8 million in time sales during 1966, an increase of 9.1 per cent over 1965 figures. Of that amount, of course, they paid commissions to agencies, and program and other operating expenses. Dividing $1,834.8 million by the number of television households, estimated at 53,922,840, shows each household paid an average of $34.03. Sources: television income, *Ibid.;* number of television households, *Broadcasting,* January 17, 1966, p. 83.

47. Harry J. Skornia, *Television and Society* (New York: McGraw-Hill, 1965). See especially pp. 88–119, 205–10.

48. *Ibid.,* p. 96.

49. *Ibid.,* p. 210.

50. "TV Broadcast Financial Data—1966."

51. The number of stations affiliated

with one or more networks was calculated by counting each affiliated station only once even if affiliated with more than one network. The network lists of stations appear in *Activities of Regulatory Enforcement Agencies,* Part 2, CBS, pp. A577–A581, ABC, pp. A600–A603, NBC, pp. A623–A626.

52. "TV Broadcast Financial Data—1966."

53. Testimony of Adam Young, president, Adam Young, Inc., New York. See *Activities of Regulatory and Enforcement Agencies,* Part 2, p. 398.

54. "TV Broadcast Financial Data—1966."

55. "TV Broadcast Financial Data—1966." Investments in tangible broadcast properties: three networks and their owned-and-operated stations, $204,569,000 original cost, $126,051,000 depreciated cost; other VHF stations, $1,013,451,000 original cost, $375,376,000 depreciated cost; UHF stations, $204,569,000 original cost, $48,298,000 depreciated cost.

56. *Ibid.* Expenses: three networks, $825,152,000; 15 network-owned stations, $154,359,000; other VHF stations, $663,500,000; 114 UHF stations, $671,000,000.

57. *Ibid.* Total times sales: networks, $372.5 million; network-owned stations, $306.2 million; other stations, $1,156.1 million.

58. *Ibid.* National spot advertising sales: 15 network-owned stations, $230.9 million; 593 other stations, $640.8 million. It may be of passing interest that the FCC in October 1959, ordered networks to cease selling nonnetwork spots for other than the network's owned stations.

59. All three networks own stations in New York (1), Los Angeles (2), Chicago (3); in addition ABC owns stations in Detroit (6) and San Francisco (7), CBS in Philadelphia (4) and St. Louis (12), and NBC in Cleveland (8) and Washington (10). Further, network rate cards and minimum-buy stipulations pressure advertisers to use stations in large markets, including network-owned stations. See recent rate cards in *Activities of Regulatory and Enforcement Agencies,* Part 2, CBS, pp. A573–A583; ABC, pp. A597–A603; NBC, pp. A619–A638.

60. "TV Broadcast Financial Data—1966."

61. *Activities of Regulatory Enforcement Agencies,* Part 2, pp. A577–A578, A600, A623.

62. *Broadcasting,* September 12, 1966, p. 42.

63. Harlan M. Blake and Jack A. Blum, "Network Television Rate Practices: A Case Study in the Failure of Social Control of Price Discrimination," *Yale Law Journal,* July 1965, pp. 1343–44.

64. Hearings, Committee on Interstate and Foreign Commerce, U.S. House of Representatives, 85th Cong., 2d Sess., Rep. No. 1297, *Network Broadcasting,* Government Printing Office, 1958, p. 207.

65. *Activities of Regulatory and Enforcement Agencies,* Part 2, p. A650.

66. "TV Broadcast Financial Data—1966."

67. *Television Network Program Procurement,* p. 373. See also Transcript 1019–20, Vol. VII, FCC files.

68. *Broadcasting,* November 7, 1966, p. 5.

69. *Television Network Program Procurement,* pp. 370–71. See also Transcript 1060–62, Vol. VII, and Transcript 3622, Vol. XXVI, both FCC files.

70. FCC Chairman E. William Henry speech at the International Radio and Television Society Newsmaker Luncheon, September 24, 1965.

71. Television Bureau of Advertising report, *Broadcasting,* August 22, 1966, p. 38.

72. *Broadcasting,* April 17, 1967, p. 38.

73. *Ibid.*

74. *Ibid.*; March 20, 1967, pp. 40B–40D; April 3, 1967, p. 56.

75. Television Bureau of Advertising estimated there were 1,309 spot television advertisers in 1965, *Broadcasting,* March 28, 1966, p. 54.

76. Although the subject is beyond the scope of this book, it should be noted that small advertisers pay much higher rates for television advertising than do large advertisers. A major reason officers of some large and profitable businesses have given for selling to the largest television advertisers is to gain higher TV advertising discounts. See "Network Television Rate Practices: A Case Study in the Failure of Social Control of Price Discrimination," pp. 1339–1401. See, also, proceedings of the Senate Subcommittee on Antitrust and Monopoly, 1966 and 1967.

77. *Activities of Regulatory and Enforcement Agencies,* Part 2, p. 530.

78. Study conducted by *Broadcast Advertisers Reports,* March 1966. Subcommittee on Antitrust and Monopoly of the U.S. Senate Committee of the Judiciary, see subcommittee's hearing record.

79. Television Bureau of Advertising report, *Broadcasting,* March 21, 1966, p. 42.

80. *Broadcast Advertisers Reports* based on monitoring 243 commercial television stations in 75 major U.S. markets during March 1966. See Senate Subcommittee on Antitrust and Monopoly hearing record.

81. Testimony of Robert W. Morris, Broadcast Advertisers Reports, before Subcommittee No. 6, Select Committee on Small Business, see *Activities of Regulatory and Enforcement Agencies,* Part 2, p. 411.

82. *Ibid.,* pp. 413–14.

83. NBC, whose allocations are assumed to be typical, for December 1965, made available to affiliates 48 thirty-second, 131 forty-second, and 16 one-minute periods during 7:30 to 11 P.M. This would average 1.55 thirty-second, 4.226 forty-second, and .51 one-minute commercial availabilities per night. See testimony of Don Durgin, president, NBC Television Network, House Select Subcommittee on Small Business, *Activities of Regulatory and Enforcement Agencies,* Part 2, p. 610.

84. In 1958, approximately 190 (39 per cent) of the 493 television stations had union contracts covering technicians, and approximately 100 stations (22 per cent) had union contracts for announcers; performing musicians, stagehands, and film department and clerical employees are organized in some of the larger television stations. Source, Charles H. Tower, "Labor Relations in the Broadcasting Industry," *The Duke Law Review,* Winter 1958, pp. 67–68.

85. *Ibid.,* p. 72.

86. The Associated Press, November 16, 1966.

87. Some stations have been struck for long periods. An American Federation of Television and Radio Artists strike against KPOL-AM-FM Los Angeles, for example, was in its 21st month in January 1967.

88. *Broadcasting,* March 15, 1965, p. 147.

89. *Broadcasting,* December 21, 1964, p. 70; January 17, 1966, p. 64; February 7, 1966, p. 9; June 27, 1966, p. 55; November 14, 1966, p. 74.

90. A lesser organization, SESAC, also licenses music performing rights to broadcasters and others.

91. "In 1962 BMI licensed 70% of the current hits listed in the combined polls of *Billboard, Variety* and *Cashbox.* The BMI catalogue contains 84.1% of the top rhythm and blues songs listed in *Billboard*'s R&B Charts for five consecutive years. *Billboard* Music Week's October 1964 polls showed that more than 80% of the selections on the Hot 100 Records chart were BMI songs." *United States of America* v. *Broadcast Music, Inc., and RKO General, Inc.,* U.S. Dist. Ct., S.D.N.Y., No. 64 Civ. 3787, December 10, 1964.

92. See note 91.

93. The Associated Press, November 30, 1966.

94. FCC files. The topic also was discussed in the popular press, see *Newsweek,* October 23, 1950, p. 93.

95. *Newsweek,* February 18, 1952, p. 67.

96. *Time,* April 27, 1953, p. 97.

97. *Time,* December 27, 1953, p. 49.

98. FCC "Broadcast Primer," Information Bulletin No. 2-B, July 1966. Also see FCC files.

99. Letters from Dorothy S. Boyle, manager, Program Records-Information, CBS Television Network, December 7, 1965, and Nancy M. Salkin, director, Corporate Color Information, National Broadcasting Co., Inc., November 22, 1965.

100. *Ibid.* Also, *Broadcasting,* January 3, 1966, pp. 29, 44, 75; May 9, 1966, p. 54.

101. *Broadcasting,* November 7, 1966, p. 44.

102. *Broadcasting Yearbook,* 1966, p. 13. A survey also conducted in November 1965, by the Television Bureau of Advertising reported that of network affiliates responding, 97 per cent could carry network color. The TBA survey, however, was based on fewer replies than was the *Broadcasting* survey.

103. *Broadcasting,* May 16, 1966, p. 56; October 31, 1966, p. 80; May 8, 1967, p. 66.

104. Jack Gould, "Color Television: A Mixed Blessing?" New York Times News Service in the St. Louis *Post-Dispatch,* May 2, 1966.

105. Sources of information about satellites, unless otherwise indicated, are from hearings before the Committee on Commerce and its subcommittee, 88th Cong., 1st Sess., February 18, 19, 27 and March 11, 1963; *FCC Annual Reports* for 1962–66; and the Associated Press and United Press International, 1960–66.

106. Interim control over the Communications Satellite Corporation—until a permanent structure is established, about 1970—is vested in an international board of directors. Founding legislation specified that U.S. interests would hold 61 per cent of the stock and exercise comparable voting power. Up to 50 per cent of the stock can be owned by various U.S. common carriers, limited to those approved by the FCC.

107. The NASA budget as recently as for the 1964–65 fiscal year included a request for $55,771,000 "for research and development and operation incident to the National Aeronautics and Space Administration's communications satellite program," hearings before the Committee on

Commerce, U.S. Senate, 88th Cong., 1st Sess., March 11, 1963. See Serial 6, *Communications Satellite Incorporators,* Government Printing Office, 1963, pp. 84–85.

108. The three Relay satellites were built by RCA on contract for $10 million. NASA estimated launch costs at $2.5 million for each satellite.

109. Comsat manages the communications satellite network for 52 nations. However, 15 European nations have been considering the feasibility of establishing their own satellite system, *Broadcasting,* November 28, 1966, p. 10.

110. Dr. Joseph V. Charyk, president, Communications Satellite Corp., in speech at second annual stockholders meeting in May 1966.

111. Letter from A. Bruce Matthews, financial vice-president, Communications Satellite Corp., July 7, 1966.

112. *Broadcasting,* October 29, 1966, p. 10; November 21, 1966, p. 76.

113. David Sarnoff, "New Dimensions in Mass Communications," an address delivered at the annual dinner of the Advertising Council in New York, December 13, 1965.

114. *Broadcasting,* April 11, 1966, p. 103.

115. General James D. O'Connell, speaking at a meeting of the American Institute of Aeronautics and Astronautics, Washington, D.C., May 1966.

116. *Broadcasting,* December 12, 1966, p. 66.

8 Broadcasting's Embarrassments

1. Although newspaper ownership of broadcasting is criticized elsewhere in this book, fairness demands that the fine record of newspaper retention of broadcasting facilities be mentioned.

2. *FCC Report and Order* relative to "applications for voluntary assignments or transfers of control," docket 13864, mimeo. 17028, March 15, 1962.

3. Designating an action for hearing regardless of outcome of the hearing is a fairly potent FCC weapon. Costs of preparing a case and legal fees place a considerable financial burden on the applicants, opponents may petition for the right to be heard and present evidence detrimental to the applicants, conducting a hearing delays action for several months which often imposes additional financial penalties on both the seller and buyer, and, finally, the outcome of a hearing is always in doubt.

4. The FCC first issues a construction permit. After a station has been built the FCC grants permission for on-the-air-tests. If tests meet specifications set forth in the application and approved by the FCC, a license good for three years and subject to renewal is issued.

5. James Lawrence Fly, former FCC chairman, commenting on the high cost of competing for a broadcasting license said, in part, ". . . it's not extraordinary for a participant to pay $100,000 for the chance to compete unsuccessfully for one of these applications (TV construction permits), and many of them run higher. It's a substantial deterrent." *Broadcasting and Government Regulation in a Free Society,* publication of The Fund for the Republic Inc., 1959, p. 11.

6. Commissioner Lee's concurring statement, *Policy Statement on Comparative Broadcast Hearings,*

FCC mimeo. 71120, July 28, 1965.

7. *Decision in re applications of Ednia Corp., Edina, Minnesota, and Tedesco, Inc., Bloomington, Minnesota, for construction permits,* FCC mimeo. 85913, June 22, 1966, p. 61.

8. *Broadcasting Yearbook,* 1966, p. A-106.

9. *Broadcasting,* December 27, 1965, p. 40.

10. Purchasers, approximate prices, and stations are: Taft Broadcasting, a chain, bought seven stations for $26.9 million (WGR-AM-FM-TV Buffalo, N.Y.; WDAF-AM-FM-TV Kansas City, Mo.; WNEP-TV Scranton, Wilkes-Barre, Pa.). Time-Life, a broadcasting chain-publishing empire, bought KERO-TV Bakersfield, Calif., for $1,565,000. Midwest Television, chain owner of newspapers and broadcasting, bought KFMB-AM-FM-TV San Diego, Calif., for $10,085,000 plus up to $150,000 in tax liabilities. Transcontinental TV Corp. dissolved itself and split the profits among its several stockholders after this transaction. Source: *FCC Order* mimeo. 47207, February 19, 1964.

11. *Ibid.*

12. Transcontinental bought WDOK-AM-FM through its Northeastern Pennsylvania Broadcasting, Inc., subsidiary for approximately $1.4 million (FCC approved in April 1962), *Broadcasting,* April 31, 1962. Northeastern Pennsylvania sold the AM-FM combination to Westchester Corp., licensee of WFAS-AM-FM White Plains, N.Y., for $2.18 million (FCC approved October 6, 1965). One of Westchester's major stockholders is vice-president and director of American Greetings Corp., a greeting card manufacturer. Source: *Broadcasting,* October 18, 1965, p. 110.

13. *Broadcasting,* September 4, 1967, p. 54.

14. Chairman E. William Henry's testimony in hearings before the Subcommittee on Communications, Committee on Commerce, U.S. Senate 89th Cong., 1st Sess., February 26, 1965. See *Progress Report From FCC—1965,* Government Printing Office, 1965, p. 181.

15. Demand for nonbroadcasting spectrum space is tremendous and increasing rapidly. There are more than five million nonbroadcasting transmitters in the United States operated by nearly 1.5 million licensees. The demand for additional spectrum space for the use of the military, other governmental agencies, aviation, industry, land-mobile transportation, public safety, amateurs, and citizens poses tremendous demands on the already overcrowded airways. Many FCC publications discuss these problems. See especially the "Safety and Special Radio Services" section in any recent FCC annual report.

16. FCC Commissioners have expressed concern about the overassignment of AM and FM stations to some large cities, but have done nothing tangible to solve this problem. In *Notice of Proposed Rule-Making* (FCC 63–468, 25 Pike and Fischer, RR. 1615, 1638, May 17, 1963, par. 46) the FCC suggested permitting two or more AM or FM stations "in cities with an abundance of facilities" to merge, with assurance that the deleted frequencies would not be assigned again in that area. Little interest was voiced in the proposal so the FCC decided to consider each such merger application on an *ad hoc* basis. See *Report and*

Order "Amendment of Part 73 of the Commission's Rules, regarding AM station assignment standards and the relationship between the AM and FM broadcast services," docket 15084, FCC mimeo. July 1, 1964, pp. 4, 21. In earlier actions the FCC has acted in a way to encourage maximum entry into each market as long as engineering standards are maintained. The policy was first evolved in *FCC* v. *Sanders Bros. Radio Station* (309 U.S. 470, 474–475; 1940). In at least one instance the FCC called the license of a radio station (WAUB Auburn, N.Y.) up for renewal after the owner of that station opposed granting a construction permit for a second station in that town on the basis that the market could not adequately support two AM stations. The FCC proposed holding a comparative hearing to determine whether, if the market could support only a single AM station, the current licensee or the applicant should operate the station. See *Memorandum Opinion and Order in re appl. by Herbert P. Michels* (*WAUB*) FCC mimeo. 61687 August 5, 1958. Both the current licensee and the applicant were granted AM licenses, but this FCC action has discouraged other licensees from pleading market saturation in attempting to prevent over-assignment of stations.

17. Statistics cited are from *AM-FM Broadcast Financial Data—1965*, FCC mimeo. October 1966. Incidentally, the financial condition of radio is improving. In 1961, 40 per cent were operating at a loss, 34.4 per cent in 1962, 33.5 per cent in 1963, and 28.9 per cent in 1964.

18. Hearings before the Subcommittee on Communications, Committee on Commerce, U.S. Senate, 89th Cong., 1st Sess., February 26, 1965. See *Progress Report From FCC—1965*, Government Printing Office, 1965, p. 181.

19. Statistical information is from *TV Broadcast Financial Data—1966*, FCC mimeo., August 1967.

20. Special subcommittee on Legislative Oversight, Committee on Interstate and Foreign Commerce, U.S. House of Representatives, 86th Cong., 1st Sess. See *Investigation of Television Quiz Shows*, Hearings 1 and 2, Government Printing Office, 1960.

21. Contestants on at least some of these programs signed releases whereby they waived claim to money won and agreed to accept whatever the program producers deemed appropriate.

22. NBC reached a $2.2 million cash settlement with Jack Barry and David Enright, producers of "Twenty-One," "Tic Tac Dough," and other quiz shows on NBC involved in the quiz-show scandal. However, the FCC in July 1964, denied the license renewal application of Barry and Enright for WGMA Hollywood, Fla. A week later the FCC granted renewal applications to NBC for its Philadelphia stations despite the fact that NBC carried the Barry-Enright and other suspect quiz shows. *Broadcasting*, August 3, 1964, and April 12, October 11, and November 22, 1965.

23. For a thorough treatment of the quiz show and related payola and plugola scandals see especially Meyer Weinberg, *TV in America, the Morality of Hard Cash* (New York: Ballantine, 1962).

24. The right of an innocent contestant to sue the network (NBC), "Twenty-One" producers (Jack Barry and David Enright and Barry-

Enright Productions), the sponsor (Pharmaceuticals, Inc.), and the "winning" contestant (Elfrida Von Nardroff) was upheld by the appellate division of the New York State Supreme Court. The plaintiff, Joseph L. Morrison, professor at the University of North Carolina, had brought suit against all of these parties in 1961 for $257,000 in damages. *Broadcasting,* January 3, 1966, p. 125.

25. New York *Times,* May 4, 1960.

26. The Federal Trade Commission issued unfair practices complaints against 103 companies; 57 signed consent agreements to cease payola practices, *Advertising Age,* August 22, 1960.

27. *Variety,* May 4, 1960.

28. Section 317 of the Communications Act of 1934 requires that the sponsor be identified in all broadcast advertising.

29. *Broadcasting,* July 4, 1966, p. 42; July 11, 1966, p. 66.

30. *Broadcasting,* May 23, 1966, p. 58.

31. *Broadcasting,* December 12, 1966, p. 10.

32. Chrysler and Lincoln lease luxury model automobiles to prominent people at around 75 per cent the regular rates. A company spokesman said that approximately one hundred Chryslers were out on lease, about thirty in Washington. St. Louis *Post-Dispatch,* October 26, 1966.

33. New York *Times,* March 18, 1960.

34. Meyer Weinberg in *TV In America, the Morality of Hard Cash* (New York: Ballantine, 1962), argues that the smaller record companies need payola to give them "access to disk jockeys." Otherwise, the giants in the record industry will crush the small operators among the seven hundred record manufacturers. See pp. 202–3.

35. See report of the hearings before a House subcommittee of the Committee on Interstate and Foreign Commerce, 88th Cong., 1st Sess., *Broadcast Ratings,* Part 3, Government Printing Office, 1963, pp. 953–1712, but especially pp. 1561–1609 and 1669–1709. Hereinafter, this four-part report of that subcommittee's hearings will be cited as *Broadcast Ratings.* See also Federal Trade Commission cease-and-desist order (docket C-613), October 23, 1963.

36. *Broadcast Ratings,* Part 3, p. 1709.

37. Information for the remainder of this section, except as otherwise noted, is taken from *Broadcast Ratings,* Part 1, March 5–8 and 18, 1963; Part 2, March 11–15 and 19–20, 1963; Part 3, March 21–April 10, 1963; and Part 4, May 14, 15, 23, June 20, 1963, and January 15 and September 23, 1964.

38. The rating services are discussed here in the same order in which their cases were considered by the subcommittee.

39. *Broadcast Ratings,* Part 2, pp. 419–524.

40. *Ibid.,* pp. 525–96.

41. *Ibid.,* pp. 596–679.

42. *Ibid.,* pp. 679–720.

43. *Ibid.,* pp. 721–86.

44. *Ibid.,* pp. 787–822.

45. *Ibid.,* pp. 823–952.

46. An A. C. Nielsen Co. vice-president testified that Nielsen received 90 per cent of radio and television network audience measurement research revenues.

47. *Broadcast Ratings,* Part 3, pp. 953–1712.

48. Audimeters are attachments placed on radio and television sets to

measure listening and viewing. One audimeter is designed to monitor up to four radio or television sets in a home. Some homes contain more than one audimeter. The audimeter operates 24 hours a day, recording on 16 mm. film, minute by minute, whether a set is on and to what stations or channels sets in operation are tuned. The audimeter was then used primarily to provide data for the national television (Nielsen Television Index) and national radio (Nielsen Radio Index) reports.

49. Nielsen at that time issued national radio (NRI), national television (NTI), metro markets on 220 television markets, metro markets on the top 32 radio markets, both (NSI), and other special broadcast reports. Nielsen began operations as a food and drug marketing service, which it continues; the firm also conducts research for publishing houses.

50. Federal Trade Commission, docket C-290.

51. The Los Angeles *Times*, March 26, 1966.

52. *Broadcasting*, September 5, 1966, p. 9.

53. The recordimeter, used together with the audilog (a diary) in the top 52 television and some radio markets, was attached to a television or radio set to remind viewers or listeners to make entries in the diary. The recordimeter flashed three times each half hour on television and buzzed each half hour on radio. It also recorded the amount of time a radio or television set was on each day, but did not identify channels or time periods. The other approximately 170 television markets were measured by diaries.

54. Federal Trade Commission, docket C-290.

55. Two sigmas refers to two standard deviations, the 95 per cent level of confidence. Since ratings given each of the radio stations did not differ as much as two standard deviations, one could not say that the ratings really differed.

56. *Broadcasting*, January 24, 1966, p. 44.

57. *Broadcasting*, January 2, 1967, p. 5.

58. *Broadcasting*, October 10, 1966, p. 78.

59. *Broadcasting*, March 6, 1967, p. 64.

60. *Broadcasting*, November 28, 1966, pp. 30–31.

61. Gerald T. Arthur was at the time president of Mercury Media and a director of Horizon Broadcasting Corp. These two corporations own television, radio, and weekly newspaper interests. Arthur was, from 1959 to 1963, senior vice-president in charge of all media, including radio and television, for Donahue & Coe, Inc. From 1953 to 1959 he was media manager and later vice-president of Fuller & Smith & Ross, Inc., New York advertising agency. He was in charge of all media at F.S.R. He previously had been assistant media director of the New York office of Campbell-Ewald, a Detroit advertising agency. He also had had broadcasting experience. Source: *Report of Proceedings*, hearing held before the subcommittee on Antitrust and Monopoly of the Senate Committee on the Judiciary, Vol. IV, June 2, 1966, p. 274.

62. Article by D. J. R. Bruckner, the Los Angeles *Times*, April 13, 1966.

63. FCC Chairman Newton N. Minow first publicly referred to television programming as a vast waste-

land at the National Association of Broadcasters 39th annual convention in May 1961. He repeatedly described television in these terms.

9 Broadcasting Networks Dominate Programming

1. Los Angeles *Times,* October 14, 1966.
2. General Electric, Westinghouse, and American Telephone and Telegraph received large shares of Radio Corporation of America stock, which they held for many years.
3. Today, American interests dominate commercial television in Great Britain as well as in many other countries.
4. For a provocative study of those who control ABC, CBS, and NBC, see Harry J. Skornia, *Television and Society* (New York: McGraw-Hill 1965), especially pp. 39–68.
5. Three former MBS officials (Alexander L. Guterma, Hal Roach, Jr., and Garland L. Culpepper, Jr.) were indicted in late summer, 1959, for not registering as agents of a foreign government. They had contracted to broadcast Dominican Republic propaganda of Dictator Rafael L. Trujillo as MBS news. After the matter was publicized, other Mutual officials canceled the contract. Guterma also was convicted of stock manipulation by a New York Federal Court in January 1960.
6. Mutual Broadcasting Co. has been owned at various times by General Tire & Rubber Co., RKO Pictures, Dr. Armand Hammer (oil interests) and associates, Hal Roach Studios (a principal owner, A. L. Guterma, was convicted of stock manipulation), Malcolm Smith (recording interests) and associates, Albert G. McCarthy Jr. (investor), Chester Ferguson (lawyer), Minnesota Mining & Manufacturing Co., and the present owners.
7. *Editor & Publisher,* July 23, 1966, p. 43; *Broadcasting,* May 16, 1966, p. 46; October 17, 1966, p. 9.
8. The FCC was extremely reluctant to approve the transfer of ABC stations, the only role the Commission could play in the matter. But after 21 months, approval was granted, 5–2.
9. Senators Gaylord Nelson (D-Wis.), Wayne Morse (D-Ore.), and Philip A. Hart (D-Mich.), and Representative Silvio O. Conte (R-Mass.).
10. The Associated Press, December 11, 1966.
11. *Broadcasting,* May 9, 1966, pp. 89–92, 98.
12. *Broadcasting-Telecasting,* January 5, 1948, p. 86.
13. *Ibid.*
14. *Ibid.*
15. Philip A. Bennett, *Television as an Advertising Medium,* U.S. Department of Commerce, 1949, p. 6.
16. *Life,* September 17, 1951, p. 63.
17. *Television Yearbook,* 1952, p. 12.
18. Morris Ernst, *The First Freedom* (New York: Macmillan, 1946), especially pp. 135–57.
19. Skornia, pp. 19, 37.
20. Voting for the merger were Chairman Rosel H. Hyde, Robert E. Lee, James J. Wadsworth, and Lee Loevinger; opposed were Nicholas Johnson, Kenneth A. Cox, and Robert T. Bartley. Loevinger, who was in charge of the Justice Department Antitrust Division prior to being appointed to the FCC in 1963, not only voted for the sale, he was

charged by those opposed to the transfer with attempting to discredit an FCC staff member who testified against the transfer. Whether industry jobs await any of those voting "yes," as has occurred previously at the Commission, remains to be seen.

21. Part of the blame lies with a business-oriented Congress which in 1952 amended sec. 310 (b) of the Communications Act to prohibit the Commission from considering whether "the public interest, convenience and necessity might be served by the transfer, assignment or disposal to a person, other than the proposed licensee." As Skornia pointed out (*Television and Society*, p. 83) this action makes it possible for anyone, even those with criminal records, to buy stations. The FCC had established a rule in 1949 whereby competitive bids and proposals would be sought when station transfer requests were before it. The attempt was to stem the tide of newspaper and industrial (AVCO) acquisitions of stations.

22. ABC stockholders received in exchange for each ABC share 0.579 of a share of ITT common stock and 0.579 of a share of ITT preferred stock. *Broadcasting*, May 2, 1966, pp. 50–52.

23. Avis Rent A Car no doubt accounted for most of those 200 facilities. ITT advertisement, *Editor & Publisher*, June 4, 1966, p. 81.

24. The Department of Justice filed a brief in September 1967, asking the United States Court of Appeals, District of Columbia, to reverse the FCC. The merger agreement between ABC and ITT was to expire at the end of 1967 unless consummated. *Broadcasting*, September 11, 1967, p. 64.

25. *Broadcasting*, April 24, 1967, pp. 58–63.

26. New York Times News Service, May 23, 1967; *Broadcasting*, May 29, 1967, pp. 30–34; June 5, 1967, pp. 32–33.

27. *Wall Street Journal*, April 21, 1967, p. 10.

28. ". . . it has taken an average of 20 months to advance an AM application (for new or major changes in facilities) to the point where it may be granted without a hearing or designated for formal hearing." Source: "Administrative Conference of the United States, Committee on Licenses and Authorizations, Licensing of Major Broadcast Facilities by the Federal Communications Commission," report by William K. Jones, Columbia University Law School, Sect. VIII, Ela. See *Activities of Regulatory and Enforcement Agencies*, Part 1, pp. A174–A175.

29. Political forces operating behind the scenes were (1) appointment of John A. McCone, former head of the Atomic Energy Commission and Central Intelligence Agency, as ITT director shortly after the sale was announced. He, incidentally, was the only director of either ITT or ABC to testify at the two-day hearing other than the presidents of the two firms. Source: *Broadcasting*, September 26, 1966, p. 48. (2) ITT was represented at the hearing by Marcus Cohn, partner of Leonard H. Marks, who formerly represented the Johnson family TV interests and at the time was director of USIA. Source: Richard Dudman, Washington correspondent, in the St. Louis *Post-Dispatch*, October 29, 1966, p. 9. (3) An ITT official revealed he had been told by an ITT superior to contribute $1,200 to the "Texas Business and Professional Men's

Committee for Johnson for Vice President" and was promised reimbursement via expense account adjustments. The ITT official who was said to have solicited this contribution denied the story. Further, ITT officials were said to have contributed substantial amounts to President Johnson's President's Club. It is unlawful for corporations to contribute to political campaigns. Source: Information was released by Senator Morse after FCC approved the ABC-ITT merger without asking for the information even though Senator Morse urged the Commission to consider these charges, *Broadcasting*, December 26, 1966, p. 26.

30. *Broadcasting*, December 26, 1966, p. 27.

31. An anonymous FCC official was quoted in *Broadcasting* (December 13, 1966, p. 34) as recounting Commission efforts in the past to strengthen ABC so it might compete more effectively with CBS and NBC. He said that in 1961 the FCC proposed to crowd VHF stations into seven markets at short spacing to give ABC strong affiliates, the plan was abandoned as impractical. In hearings before the FCC, ABC has repeatedly gotten sympathetic consideration for its misdeeds. Elimination of network restrictions on carrying programs of networks other than the affiliate, all-channel television legislation, and many other FCC proposals were designed in part to help ABC.

32. *Broadcasting*, September 26, 1966, p. 48.

33. Total network television income before taxes, including profits of the 15 owned-and-operated stations, was \$111.4 million in 1962, \$136.2 million in 1963, \$156.5 million in 1964, and \$161.6 million in 1965. Since ABC's share was \$13.5 million in 1964 and \$19.9 million in 1965, combined NBC-CBS shares were \$143 million in 1964 and \$141.7 million in 1965, a decline of \$1.3 million versus an ABC increase of \$6.4 million.

34. *Broadcasting*, September 11, 1967, p. 66.

35. *Broadcasting*, October 24, 1966, p. 80.

36. Robert R. Pauley, president of ABC Radio, at annual meeting of ABC radio affiliates, March 27, 1966; quoted in *Broadcasting*, April 4, 1966, p. 69.

37. ABC profits after taxes were \$15,565,000; ITT's profits were \$76 million, equal to \$3.58 a share. *Broadcasting*, March 28, 1966, p. 110.

38. ITT stockholder meeting in Baltimore, April 27, 1966, quoted in *Broadcasting*, May 2, 1966, p. 52.

39. *Broadcasting*, December 26, 1966, p. 29.

40. *Broadcasting*, March 28, 1966, p. 110.

41. *Broadcasting*, September 11, 1967, p. 48.

42. *Broadcasting*, March 6, 1967, p. 40.

43. *Broadcasting*, March 28, 1966, p. 109.

44. Goldenson held 97,061 common shares of stock as announced at the ABC annual stockholders meeting, March 1, 1966. ABC stock closed at 54 on December 1, 1965, and at 86 3/8 on December 22, 1966.

45. ABC owned-and-operated stations: WABC-AM-FM-TV New York, KABC-AM-FM-TV Los Angeles, WLS-AM-FM and WBKB (TV) Chicago, WXYZ-AM-FM-TV Detroit, KGO-AM-FM-TV San Francisco, and KQV-AM-FM Pittsburgh.

46. *Broadcasting,* November 21, 1966, p. 42.
47. *Broadcasting,* December 6, 1965, p. 29.
48. Revenue for 1965: ITT plus ABC, $2.259 billion; RCA, $2.057 billion; CBS, $700 million.
49. *Broadcasting,* December 13, 1965, p. 33.
50. Hearings before Subcommittee No. 6, Select Committee on Small Business, U.S. House of Representatives, 89th Cong., 2d Sess., *Activities of Regulatory and Enforcement Agencies Relating to Small Business,* Part 2, Government Printing Office, 1966, p. A611.
51. *Broadcasting,* July 25, 1966, pp. 55–56.
52. An NBC spokesman said the decision was based on news judgment. *Broadcasting,* September 26, 1966, p. 49.
53. The Associated Press, December 11, 1966.
54. *Broadcasting,* September 26, 1966, p. 51.
55. In the top 50 markets, ABC is affiliated with four NBC primary affiliates and with one CBS primary affiliate. *Broadcasting Yearbook,* 1966, pp. A3–A68.
56. FCC, *Report on Chain Broadcasting,* No. 37, docket 5060, Government Printing Office, 1941.
57. Ernst, p. 135.
58. *Broadcasting,* May 16, 1966, p. 47.
59. AT & T rates: $39.50 / airline mile / 8-hour-a-day / month; $1.15 / airline mile / each hour used. Hence, for 600-mile service, Washington to Chicago, the 8-hour rate is $24,000 a month. For 35 occasional hours between the same cities at the hourly rate, the charge is $24,150. Sports Network, Inc., asked AT & T to provide a 3-hour-a-day service for $14.82 / airline mile. Also, SNI is asking damages of $354,218, five-eighths of the amount paid AT & T for 12 months of service. The FCC also threatened a full-scale study of AT & T's cost, rate, and earnings structure after an FCC-ordered AT & T seven-way cost study showed that where AT & T enjoyed monopoly status, its earning rates were highest and where it competed, as with Western Union, its earning rates were low; earning rates ranged from more than 10 per cent to .3 per cent. The major Western Union complaint was that AT & T was trying to displace WU private wire TELEX and data processing service by using profits earned in monopoly pursuits, primarily private telephone service, to finance its competitive TELEPAK service. Sources: Desmond Smith in *The Nation,* as reprinted in the St. Louis *Post-Dispatch,* January 11, 1966; The Associated Press, November 10, 1966; *Broadcasting,* June 14, 1965, p. 67; December 6, 1965, p. 53; January 3, 1966, p. 118; November 8, 1965, p. 68; and May 9, 1966, p. 46.
60. *Broadcasting,* June 19, 1967, p. 64.
61. Affirmation of the FCC's power to determine "the composition of that (broadcasting) traffic" and denial of abridgment of First Amendment free speech rights under FCC licensing practices as set forth in the Commission's *Chain Broadcasting Regulations* were upheld in the U.S. Supreme Court decision in *National Broadcasting Co.* v. *United States,* 319 U.S. 190 (1943).
62. "Local Blackouts of Network Television," *Columbia Journalism Review,* Spring 1966, pp. 22–28.
63. See Newton N. Minow, *Equal Time,* ed. Lawrence Laurent (New

York: Atheneum, 1964), pp. 75, 94, 103–4, 111, 118, 139.

64. Richard S. Salant, CBS vice president, said that if CBS were to replace its news and public affairs programs with entertainment, CBS would increase its profits by 65 per cent, Yale Roe, *The Television Dilemma* (New York: Hastings House, 1962), p. 163.

65. One reason these programs attract relatively small audiences is that affiliates refuse to carry them. Yale Roe, *The Television Dilemma*, charges that those who advocate better programming, including documentaries, do not support them by watching them, pp. 33–35.

66. Gerald T. Arthur, president, Mercury Media; see unpublished Report of Proceedings, Vol. 4, subcommittee files, "Possible Discrimination in Television Advertising," Subcommittee on Antitrust and Monopoly of the Committee on the Judiciary, U.S. Senate, June 2, 1966.

67. *Broadcasting*, December 19, 1966, pp. 28–32, 34, 36. No more than a dozen network shows were sponsor-supplied in the 1965–66 season; see *Activities of Regulatory and Enforcement Agencies*, Part 2, pp. 538, 571, 620.

68. *Broadcasting*, October 3, 1966, pp. 25–27.

69. *Broadcasting*, March 6, 1967, p. 59.

70. *Broadcasting*, August 8, 1966, p. 38. CBS-TV spent $37.6 million for National Football League television rights for 1966 and 1967 seasons, *Broadcasting*, January 3, 1966, p. 124.

71. Jack Gould, *The New York Times*, November 21, 1966.

72. Robert W. Sarnoff as told to Stanley Frank, "What Do You Want From TV?" *Saturday Evening Post*, July 1, 1961, p. 13.

73. *Broadcasting*, August 8, 1966, p. 10.

74. *Broadcasting*, November 7, 1966, p. 48.

75. *Activities of Regulatory and Enforcement Agencies*, Part 2, pp. A323–A473.

76. *Broadcasting*, April 4, 1966, p. 66.

77. *FCC Annual Report, 1964*, Government Printing Office, 1964, p. 54; *FCC Annual Report, 1965*, Government Printing Office, 1965, p. 109; *Broadcasting*, January 18, 1965, p. 66; February 22, 1965, p. 58.

10 UHF and FM: Broadcasting's Stepchildren

1. In 1948 the FCC reduced the number of VHF channels from 13 to 12 when channel 1 was assigned to nonbroadcast services. At the same time the Commission stopped the sharing of television VHF channels with nonbroadcast services. However, the FCC was experimenting with sharing channel space with land-mobile communications as of this writing.

2. The first UHF commercial station was KPTV, Portland, Ore.; it went on the air September 20, 1952, but expired before a license was issued.

3. All but five of the 40 VHF stations in the top ten markets as of 1966 were in operation by 1949. No new VHF's have gone on the air since 1958 in these markets. Only one station in the top 20 markets has begun telecasting more recently than 1959. VHF station construction in the other top 50 markets cluster around two periods: 1948–50 and 1953–54. Only seven VHF's of the

161 in the top 50 markets began broadcasting during the present decade.

4. Representative Emanuel Celler, testimony March 5, 1962, Committee on Interstate and Foreign Commerce, House of Representatives, 87th Cong., 2nd Sess. See Committee report *All Channel Television Receivers and Deintermixture*, U.S. Government Printing Office, 1962, p. 103.

5. *Ibid.*, p. 102.

6. UHF sets produced by years cited: 1953, 1,459,500; 1957, 779,800; 1961, 370,977. For statistics of other intervening years see *TV Factbook No. 32*, p. 24, for 1953–60. 1961 figures are from *Television Digest*, February 19, 1962, p. 9.

7. *All Channel Television Receivers and Deintermixture*, p. 58. Statistics on station affiliations were summarized from *Broadcasting Yearbook*, 1966, pp. A-3–A-68.

8. The writer checked UHF deleted stations in FCC "station history" files, June 28, 1966, against television stations listed in *Broadcasting Yearbook*, 1966, pp. A-3–A-68.

9. *Broadcasting Yearbook*, 1966, pp. A-3–A-68.

10. "Report on Effects of Deintermixture in Peoria, Springfield and Related Markets in Illinois," prepared by Dallas W. Smythe, Dallas W. Smythe & Associates, for the national Committee for Competitive Television.

11. Although a highly technical discussion on channel coverage is beyond the scope of this book, the reader should be reminded that signals from channels in the lowest portion of the VHF spectrum (channel 2) carry farther than do signals from the next lower channel (channel 3), and so on throughout the VHF spectrum. All VHF channels have greater dispersion radii than do the lowest UHF spectrum channels. Also, lower channels in the UHF spectrum carry farther than do higher-numbered channels in that spectrum.

12. Testimony by former FCC Chairman Newton N. Minow, other commissioners, and Mr. Jacobson, an FCC engineer, before the Committee on Interstate and Foreign Commerce, House of Representatives, March 6, 1966, see *All Channel Television Receivers and Deintermixture*, p. 148 ff.

13. UHF tuners, unlike VHF tuners, do not use a RF (radio frequency) tube. Source of information on tuners: an FCC engineer during an interview with the writer, July 1, 1966. Engineers for the FCC complained in the *31st FCC Annual Report, 1965*, that television set producers, under requirements of the All-Channel set law adopted in 1962, "Unfortunately showed little tendency to greatly exceed the requirements" of the law. Government Printing Office, p. 171.

14. Bakersfield and Fresno are proof of the benefits that can come to television viewers from deintermixture. Only three cities as of November 1, 1965 (New York, Los Angeles, Philadelphia) had television service superior to that of Fresno. The smallest city, other than Fresno, with three network affiliate and two nonnetwork affiliate stations was Washington, D.C. (1960 population 763,956). A smaller market with five stations was Seattle-Tacoma, twentieth in the United States, combined 1960 population, 705,066. Only four cities with smaller populations than Bakersfield had full-time three-network stations (Bangor, Me.; Greenville, N.C.; Fargo, N.D.; and

Las Vegas, Nev. One of the Las Vegas stations was in bankruptcy receivership at the time of this writing.

15. See *All Channel Television Receivers and Deintermixture, passim,* and especially sections wherein FCC members were testifying.

16. E. William Henry, then FCC chairman, estimated that 30 per cent of the television homes had replaced sets with new ones capable of receiving UHF. Source: Testimony before a House Appropriations Subcommittee, The Associated Press, April 30, 1966. Figures released by the U.S. Census Bureau after a study in August 1965, support Henry's figures.

17. *Progress Report From FCC—1965,* p. 114.

18. *Ibid.*, p. 115.

19. *Broadcasting,* January 10, 1966, p. 85; August 8, 1966, p. 90.

20. FCC, in docket 16068, June 15, 1965, adopted an interim policy of designating for hearing the purchase of stations in excess of these guidelines. However, the FCC has failed in at least four recent 1966–67 cases to implement this policy.

21. Kaiser Industries Corporation has invested $30 million in its radio and UHF television subsidiary, Kaiser Broadcasting Corporation. One might question permitting this industrial complex (in 1966 Kaiser Industries and its subsidiaries had a net income of $105,175,126 on revenues of $1,868,871,130) to gain such potentially powerful communications voices. Kaiser is involved in many and diverse enterprises throughout the United States and abroad, including steel and aluminum manufacture and fabrication; chemical production; iron ore, coal, and bauxite mining; manufacture of building materials; development and manufacture of electronic systems and equipment and electronic research and development; manufacture and sales of CATV equipment; automobile, truck, and military vehicle manufacture; engineering; commercial, industrial, agricultural, and residential real estate investment and development; machining of aircraft and missile components; manufacture of wire, cable, and pipes of varying sizes; fertilizer and coke production; natural gas production; and even shipping via its own 52-mile railroad and ocean vessels. Source: *Moody's Industrial Manual,* June 1967, pp. 1684–97.

22. *Broadcasting,* September 25, 1967, pp. 54, 60. It also should be noted that in 1954 the FCC adopted rules limiting broadcasting holdings by a single individual or group to 7 AM, 7 FM, and 7 TV stations of which no more than 5 may be VHF.

23. *Broadcasting,* October 3, 1966, pp. 8, 36.

24. *Broadcasting,* May 16, 1966, p. 5.

25. *Broadcasting,* October 17, 1966, p. 57.

26. David Lachenbruch, "The $200,-000,000 Experiment, UHF," *TV Guide,* December 11, 1965, p. 4. If his estimated additional cost for an all-channel receiver over the cost of a VHF receiver is accurate, the cost to television set owners will exceed half a billion dollars by 1970. Indeed an expensive experiment, as Mr. Lachenbruch points out. It might be noted that VHF station owners opposed deintermixture partially on the basis that the cost to convert would be approximately $250,000 a station. At this rate some two thousand VHF stations, more than four times the number on the air in October 1966, could be converted to UHF at the

same cost the public was forced to pay for tuners, many of which will never be used. Whose interests Congress protected again becomes a matter of conjecture.

27. The financial condition of UHF stations as a group deteriorated in 1965. The one hundred UHF stations as a group reported losing $173,000 during 1965; 92 UHF stations had total profits of $2,700,000 in 1964. In terms of percentages, 34.5 per cent of the UHF stations reported operating at a loss in 1965, an increase from 32 per cent in 1964. In comparison, 396 (87 per cent) of 457 VHF stations reporting had earned profits in 1965. Source: *TV Broadcast Financial Data—1965*, FCC mimeo., August 1966.

28. The FCC is well aware of the grave risks involved in starting a UHF station. In 1965 the Commission adopted standards requiring that applicants for new UHF stations in markets with three or more VHF stations show financial ability to build and operate the stations for two years without advertising income. Incidentally, this further limits entry to UHF broadcasting to persons and groups with financial resources of at least one million dollars. Source: *31st FCC Annual Report*, 1965, p. 102.

29. *Broadcasting*, June 26, 1967, p. 68.

30. Committee on Interstate Commerce, U.S. Senate, 78th Cong., 1st Sess., *Hearings on Wheeler-White Bill (S. 814)*, Government Printing Office, 1943, p. 898.

31. WSM-FM ceased operations in 1951.

32. The opportunities to correct broadcasting's weaknesses when FM replaced AM is the dominant theme in Charles A. Siepmann, *Radio's Second Chance* (Boston: Little, Brown, 1946). See especially pp. 237–76. See also Giraud Chester, Garnet R. Garrison, and Edgar E. Willis, *Television and Radio*, 3rd ed. (New York: Appleton-Century-Crofts, 1963) pp. 38–39.

33. Of the 114 FM-only stations, 111 reported that they lost money during 1949, Chester, *et al., Television and Radio*, p. 39.

34. In 1949 the FCC reported 212 FM commercial deletions. In 1954 only five applications for FM construction permits were pending. See *31st FCC Annual Report, 1965*, p. 124.

35. "Number of Stations: 1922–1965," *Broadcasting Yearbook*, 1966, p. A-158.

36. For fuller quotation see Charles A. Siepmann, *Radio's Second Chance*, (Boston: Little, Brown, 1946), pp. 246–47.

37. *30th FCC Annual Report, 1964*, Government Printing Office, 1964, p. 75.

38. "U.S. Radio Set Production—1922–1965," *Broadcasting Yearbook*, 1966, p. B-226; "U.S. TV Set Production—1946–1965," *Broadcasting Yearbook*, 1966, p. A-157.

39. The FCC on July 1, 1966, granted McLendon Pacific Corp. permission to buy KGLA (FM) Los Angeles and to broadcast advertising exclusively from 6 A.M. to 10 P.M. on a one-year experimental basis. McLendon discontinued his 100 per cent classified advertising format in the Fall, 1967. The FCC since 1955 has permitted FM broadcasters to transmit two different programs simultaneously so that they may offer such auxiliary services as storecasting and background music for business and industry. This was done to provide

supplementary income for the struggling stations.

40. FCC Chairman Henry, in testimony before the Antitrust Subcommittee of the Judiciary Committee, House of Representatives, March 13, 1963. For newspaper ownership of FM stations, 1945 to 1965, see Table 27, Appendix.

41. *AM-FM Broadcast Financial Date—1965*, FCC mimeo., October 1966. For more complete information on the finances of FM stations operated by non-AM licensees, 1954–65, see Table 28, Appendix.

42. These and other financial statistics were calculated from *AM-FM Broadcast Financial Data—1965*.

43. Advertising revenues for 338 independent FM stations were $14.5 million for 1965. Total revenue reported for AM stations was $776.8 million of which $9 million was reported as income earned by FM affiliates. Thus, 3,941 AM stations reported revenues of $767.8 million. AM stations received an average of $197,107.33 and FM stations received an average of $42,899.41.

44. Reported by Lynn Christian, WPIX-FM New York at the National Association of FM Broadcasters convention, March 27, 1966.

45. *31st FCC Annual Report, 1965*, p. 116.

46. Figures for 1957 and 1963 are from "Number of Stations: 1922–1965," *Broadcasting Yearbook*, 1966, p. A-158; and for 1967 from *Broadcasting*, July 3, 1967, p. 63.

47. This FCC rule was adopted July 1, 1964, and affirmed in March 1965. The rule is an outgrowth of repeated hearings. See FCC docket 15084.

48. *Broadcasting Yearbook*, 1966, pp. B-3–B-171.

49. The FCC on July 25, 1963, adopted a table of assignments for FM in which 2,830 channels were assigned to cities throughout continental U.S. (see docket 14185). Most of these channels allocated to large urban areas have been licensed. Therefore, some of these licenses are being sought by speculators at highly inflated prices. The highest price as of this writing was $850,000 paid by Worldwide, Inc., a subsidiary of the Mormon Church's Bonneville International Corp. broadcasting chain, for WRFM (FM) New York City. The FCC approved this sale in May 1966.

11 STV and CATV: Supplementary Services

1. Both NBC and CBS, although admitting concern about the threat of CATV to their financial interests, oppose enlisting governmental intervention to protect themselves. See, for example, NBC Chairman Robert W. Sarnoff's speech to network affiliates, June 3, 1964; and motion by William B. Lodge, CBS-TV vice-president in charge of affiliate relations and engineering, at NAB board meeting June 14, 1964, "that the board pledge itself to refrain from seeking legislation or governmental action to ban or constrain wired pay television." ABC has opposed CATV rather energetically, even to the extent of urging congressional action to bring CATV under FCC regulation. Both NBC and CBS own CATV properties.

2. Chris Welles, "The Tangled Tower of CATV," *Life*, November 18, 1966, p. 56.

3. In the first edition of this book Morris Ernst reported that the networks and broadcasters convinced the FCC to deny an application by Subscription Radio to establish a pay-radio service on three FM channels in New York and Chicago. Subscribers would have paid five cents a day. Morris Ernst, *The First Freedom* (New York: Macmillan, 1946), pp. 177–79.

4. In one week ABC paid $39.5 million for 49 movies (17 Twentieth Century Fox, 32 Paramount); CBS paid $52.8 million for 63 Metro-Goldwyn-Mayer films. The networks bought the right to exhibit each film twice, Jack Gould, New York *Times*, September 29, 1966. CBS paid $37.6 million for rights to telecast the 1966–67 National Football League games, *Broadcasting*, January 3, 1966. Similarly, American Football League, Continental Football League, professional basketball, Olympics, and soccer league rights have been bought.

5. Each of the systems, wired or over the air, except for that used in Bartlesville, Okla., broadcast scrambled pictures and/or sound. An attachment on the receiving set unscrambles these, either when money is deposited or a button is punched to record viewing on a tape or card. Subscribers using the latter system are billed monthly.

6. At the outset the two major financial backers of Subscription Television, Inc., were Lear Siegler, Inc., electronics and aerospace equipment manufacturer, and Rebuen H. Donnelly Corp., a subsidiary of Dunn & Bradstreet, which manages Yellow Pages for several American Telephone and Telegraph Co. affiliates and does direct mail advertising. The Los Angeles Dodgers and San Francisco Giants, professional baseball teams, also held substantial interests in STV.

7. Harry J. Skornia, *Television and Society* (New York: McGraw-Hill, 1965), p. 113.

8. Testimony by Robert W. Sarnoff is contained in a report of the hearings before the Committee on Interstate and Foreign Commerce, U.S. House of Representatives, 85th Cong., 2d Sess., 1958.

9. Files in the FCC, see docket 11279.

10. Resolution adopted by the Interstate and Foreign Commerce Committees of the House (February 6) and Senate (February 19, 1958). The House Interstate and Foreign Commerce Committee asked on July 23, 1958, for a delay into 1959.

11. Connecticut motion picture theater owners on March 28, 1962, filed an appeal in the U.S. Court of Appeals for the District of Columbia, asking the court to set aside the FCC order granting permission for the Hartford test. On March 8, 1962, the court affirmed the FCC's right to authorize the pay-television test. This decision became final when the U.S. Supreme Court, on October 8, 1962, refused to allow a further appeal. *Connecticut Committee Against Pay TV* v. *FCC*, 301 F. 2d 835, 837 (D.C. Cir.), *cert. denied*, 371 U.S. 816 (1962).

12. Press release, Zenith Radio Corp., March 10, 1965.

13. At the conclusion of the third year the system had 4,851 subscribers.

14. *Joint Comments of Zenith Radio Corporation and Teco, Inc., in Support of Petition for Nation-Wide Authorization of Subscription Television*, presented to the FCC on March 10, 1965.

15. See *Further Notice of Proposed*

Rule Making and Notice of Inquiry, docket 11279, FCC mimeo. 80992, March 21, 1966. Examples of favorable comments: ". . . although we have reached no final conclusions thereon, it appears that it may well be in the public interest to authorize such subscription television operations on a permanent nation-wide basis," p. 4. "That subscription television on a nation-wide scale can be effectively integrated into a total TV system, with advantages to the viewing audience, appears to be a reasonably sound conclusion at this point," p. 7, "While it would seem reasonable to suppose that subscription television, as a new competitor for audiences, would exert some competitive impact on the present system, we are unable to conclude on the basis of information available to us that competition would inevitably result in such a serious impairment of the present service as has been so forcefully argued by the opponents," p. 7.

16. Paul O'Niel, "The Box, Will it Revolutionize TV, Reshape the Movies, Retune the American Mind?" *Life*, July 17, 1964, p. 44.

17. Gary A. Steiner, *The People Look at Television, A Study of Audience Attitudes* (New York: Alfred A. Knopf, 1963), pp. 220–23.

18. Franchise agreements with various system promoters had been reached as of mid-1966, with interests in New York, Los Angeles, Chicago, Philadelphia, Washington, San Francisco, Dallas-Fort Worth, Houston, Kansas City, Hartford and New Haven, Conn., Atlanta, Miami, Springfield and Worcester, Mass., Dayton, Ohio, Keene, N.H., and Pittsburgh.

19. Martin Seiden, an economist who conducted a study as a special consultant to the FCC, reported to the Commission on February 12, 1965, that the average CATV installation cost was $27 and the average monthly rate was $4.90. He noted that installation costs have tended to become less in recent years. See *An Economic Analysis of Community Antenna Television Systems and the Television Broadcasting Industry*, FCC, February 1965. Copies of this report have been distributed by the Commission on a limited basis.

20. A survey conducted by Princeton University personnel for an applicant for a New York CATV franchise and presented to the Board of Estimates for the city of New York showed that 50 per cent of the homes in all of the boroughs of New York have substandard television reception. Testimony of former FCC member Frederick W. Ford, the president of NCTA, before the Subcommittee on Communications and Power of the Committee on Interstate and Foreign Commerce, U.S. House of Representatives, 89th Cong., 1st Sess., June 2, 1965. See *Regulation of Community Antenna Television*, Government Printing Office, 1965, pp. 175, 183.

21. Frederick W. Ford, in a talk at a regional NCTA one-day meeting in New York, October 10, 1966, *Editor & Publisher*, October 15, 1966, p. 54; and at NCTA convention, June 28, 1967.

22. Robert H. Beisswenger, president of the Jerrold Corp., CATV equipment manufacturer and operator of 41 CATV systems, said there are 460 CATV systems in the top 100 markets, 119 are under construction, 500 have been awarded franchises, and another 1,200 applications for franchises are pending. See his testimony before the FCC, docket 15971, sec-

ond report and order mimeo. 80218, March 8, 1966.

23. Individual bids were approximately $600,000 for the Santa Monica Mountains area, $235,000 for the Pacific Palisades section, and $10,000 for the Eagle Rock-Highland Park area. Among bidders were NBC; H & B Communications Corp., a giant CATV chain; and two other CATV chains. Sources: *Broadcasting,* August 22, 1966, pp. 52–53; September 26, 1966, p. 54.
24. *Broadcasting,* December 7, 1964.
25. *Regulation of Community Antenna Television,* pp. 158–59.
26. See FCC report and order, docket 12443, April 13, 1959.
27. CATV uses microwave systems to import television signals from stations when signals of those stations cannot be received in sufficient quality by tall CATV antennas. It is possible to relay signals great distances via microwave radio transmission. Indeed, signals from four Los Angeles independent stations have been transmitted to New Mexico CATV systems and from New York stations to Vermont systems via microwave. Licenses to establish microwave systems must be obtained from the FCC. Former Chairman E. William Henry testified that microwave applications seeking to extend signals into communities over 700 miles from the originating stations were on file in mid-1965. See *Regulation of Community Antenna Television,* p. 4.
28. Senator Warren G. Magnuson, recognized generally as a friend of broadcasting, has held minor ownership interests in broadcasting properties for several years.
29. FCC docket 12931; 32 FCC 459, 1963.
30. *Carter Mountain Transmission Corp.* v. *FCC,* 321 F.2d 359, May 23, 1963. Also, see Supreme Court *cert. denied* 375 U.S. 951, January 25, 1965.
31. See docket 14895, December 12, 1962, especially relative to requiring nonduplication for 30 days, later reduced to 15, for private microwave stations in the Business Radio Service relaying programs to CATV systems. See also docket 15233, December 12, 1963, relative to extending the nonduplication to common carriers in the Domestic Point-to-Point Microwave Relay Service serving CATV systems. See also docket 15586, July 29, 1964, and docket 15971, April 22, 1965, in which the FCC instituted an inquiry of rule making concerning regulation of CATV systems in general. At that time nonduplication rules proposed in dockets 14895 and 15233 were adopted.
32. *Broadcasting,* March 14, 1966, p. 53. The FCC might well be wary of allocating scarce microwave space to CATV operators. A single television signal requires capacity equivalent to that capable of carrying 1,860 telephone circuits. See *Nonbroadcast and General Action Report* 1559, FCC mimeo. 55187, July 30, 1964, p. 18.
33. Commissioner Cox vigorously opposed reducing nonduplication requirements from 15 days to 24 hours. See his 12 pages of comments, second report and order, docket 15971, FCC mimeo. 80218, March 8, 1966. Further, the FCC requires carriage of the local station in an effort to reduce the economic impact caused by reduction in audience, especially where the local station is not on the wire. Under such circumstances a weak station might cease operation, with a resultant loss of

service to the public and especially to rural and small-town residents to whom CATV service is not available.

34. The FCC has tended to permit importation of signals into the top 100 markets when (1) broadcasters did not oppose the application and (2) the CATV system apparently posed no threat to UHF development, *Broadcasting,* July 4, 1966, pp. 48–49.

35. FCC second report and order, docket 15971, March 8, 1966. See FCC mimeo. 80218, March 8, 1966. However, although the Commission terminated dockets 14895 and 15233, it specified that docket 15971 proceedings are not terminated and amendments may be made to rules set forth in this second report and order.

36. Many congressmen said they had never received more mail on any single issue. *Life,* November 18, 1966, p. 57, attested to the loyalty of CATV subscribers, saying that "once on the cable, subscribers never want to leave it." *Life* cited "poverty-stricken" Appalachia, Pa., where "less than 2 per cent of the subscribers have been disconnected due to nonpayment of bills."

37. *United Artists Associated* v. *Fortnightly Corp.,* U.S. District Court of New York, May 23, 1966.

38. The House Judiciary Committee reported in October, 1966, that it favored excusing fill-in or master antenna systems from copyright liability. However, it favored full liability for those CATV operators who directly damage the copyright owner and destroy or impair his market, and partial liability for those who indirectly damage the copyright owner by using his work or by discouraging local broadcasters who would be potential copyright licensees. See *Broadcasting,* October 24, 1966, p. 61.

39. A camera scans a teletype printer as it prints the news in such a way that several lines of copy at a time are projected on the television screen over the channel reserved for news. Local news can be fed through the same teleprinter.

40. John W. Gallivan, publisher of the *Salt Lake Tribune* and president of Kearns-Tribune Corp., which owns a TV station and 26 CATV systems, and manufactures CATV news transmission equipment, quoted in *Editor & Publisher,* July 9, 1966, p. 42, and in the Inland Daily Press Assn. *Bulletin,* November 2, 1966, pp. 193–200.

41. NCTA's President Ford estimated that possibly half a dozen were, in 1965, selling advertising. Freedom of Information Center publication No. 152, "CATV: Problems and Promises III," January 1966, p. 8.

42. *Broadcasting,* September 12, 1966, pp. 68, 70.

43. FCC mimeo., docket 15971, March 8, 1966, p. 19.

44. Inland Daily Press Assn. *Bulletin,* November 2, 1966, p. 199. See also *Broadcasting,* May 2, 1966, p. 56; July 4, 1966, pp. 48–49; April 18, 1966, p. 9.

45. These profit percentages exclude deductions for depreciation, amortization, interest, and federal taxes. Only one of the systems studied reported a loss (39 per cent).

46. *Broadcasting,* May 3, 1965, p. 9.

47. See FCC files, hearings before various House and Senate subcommittees and committees, speeches reported in the trade press, literature distributed by those organizations. Here reference is primarily to NAB, Association of Maximum Service Telecasters, Television Accessary Manu-

facturers Institute, and the National Alliance of Television and Electronic Service Association. The industry employed Franklin Fisher, Massachusetts Institute of Technology, to study CATV. See his report issued in 1964 and widely quoted by broadcasters.

48. Of the 548 licensees, 185 are telecasters. This is an increase from the 72 TV licensees, about 22 per cent of the total of all TV licensees, who owned 176 CATV systems at the end of 1964. See *Seiden Report,* February 1965.

49. Report to the NAB board by Roger Clipp, Triangle Stations, a major broadcast and CATV chain, June 21, 1966. See *Broadcasting,* June 27, 1966, p. 65. *Broadcasting,* June 21, 1965, p. 56, reported that 16 of 44 NAB board members have financial interests in CATV, or have applications on file for franchises, or have immediate plans to acquire systems.

50. The Associated Press, July 29, 1965.

51. Testimony of the American Society of Composers, Authors and Publishers before hearings of the Subcommittee on Patents, Trademarks and Copyrights of the Judiciary Committee, U.S. Senate, 89th Cong., 2d Sess., August 1966.

52. Frederick W. Ford, quoted in *Editor & Publisher,* October 15, 1966, p. 54. John W. Gallivan estimated that publishers have interests in 250 CATV systems, *Editor & Publisher,* July 9, 1966, p. 42.

53. *Broadcasting,* August 15, 1966, p. 5.

54. *Regulation of Community Antenna Television,* pp. 5, 28; *Broadcasting,* February 20, 1967, p. 29.

55. *31st FCC Annual Report,* 1965, Government Printing Office, 1965, p. 79.

56. David B. Smith, professor of electrical engineering at the University of Pennsylvania, in a talk at an Institute of Electrical and Electronics Engineers in Philadelphia in June 1966. See *Broadcasting,* June 20, 1966, p. 71.

57. The decree forbade AT & T from engaging in other than common carrier services. It was part of the complaint in which the Department of Justice sought to divorce Western Electric Co. from the Bell System.

58. The NCTA complained to the FCC that the CATV operator under these lease agreements retains ownership only of the equipment at the antenna site, see formal pleadings of NCTA entered October 12, 1966.

12 A Bright Future for ETV?

1. CBS President William S. Paley in comments to the FCC, October 17, 1934. See "Radio as a Cultural Force," CBS pamphlet, 1934.

2. Senator Charles W. Tobey (R-N.H.), chairman of the Senate Commerce Committee, threatened FCC commissioners with repercussions if they converted noncommercial channels to commercial. Since he held the chairmanship of a committee charged with reviewing FCC actions, his influence on commissioners was considerable. For a brief, informative account, see Newton N. Minow, *Equal Time* (New York: Atheneum, 1964), pp. 187–92.

3. *Progress Report of Federal Communications Commission,* hearings before the Subcommittee on Communications, Committee on Commerce, U.S. Senate, 88th Cong., 1st

Sess., Serial 8, Government Printing Office, 1963, p. 149.

4. Many supporters of ETV, led by the National Association of Educational Broadcasters, complained that a disproportionate number of the higher UHF channels, those with less coverage capacities, were assigned to noncommercial television.

5. *Broadcasting,* September 18, 1967, p. 81.

6. *Broadcasting Yearbook,* 1967, pp. A3–A78. Figures are based on number of stations on the air or expected to begin broadcasting by the end of December, 1967.

7. WNDT New York operates on a commercial channel. The station was sold in 1962 to educational interests, after having operated as a commercial station since 1948. Among those who contributed funds were five of the six commercial stations in New York.

8. "Fifth Report and Memorandum Opinion and Order," docket 14229, FCC mimeo. 78383, February 9, 1966, Appendix A.

9. *Broadcasting Yearbook,* 1967, pp. A3–A78.

10. Senator William Benton (D-Conn.) suggested in 1964 that the then 10 per cent excise tax on television receivers be used to finance ETV; "ETV: The Lean Years," Freedom of Information Center, publication No. 139, University of Missouri, March 1965.

11. Lawrence H. Rogers, II, president of Taft Broadcasting Co., radio-TV chain, and *Life* magazine, a publication of Time-Life publishing-broadcasting chain, both recommended that the federal government establish a national educational and cultural authority to support ETV through a tax on commercial TV licenses. Rogers' proposal was discussed by the NAB in 1967. *Life* editorialized in favor of taxing commercial TV to support public TV, February 17, 1967, p. 4.

12. NET as of 1967 provided some 100 affiliates five hours of newly produced programs and two and a half hours of updated children's programs a week plus access to its large library of previously run programs. Source: "Educational Television," FCC mimeo., June 1966, p. 12.

13. The Ford Foundation had contributed $130 million to educational television, mostly to finance NET programming, through 1966. Other foundations, some broadcasters, a few industries and businesses, and agencies of the federal government also have contributed to ETV.

14. The Ford Foundation in December 1966 granted $10 million for a series of educational programs to be carried live over more than 125 noncommercial TV stations, beginning in the Fall 1967. *New York Times,* December 12, 1966. Columbia University contracted with the Foundation to produce these programs. NET provided approximately 75 stations with live coverage of President Johnson's 1967 State of the Union address to Congress. ETV stations in several states, variously estimated at nine to more than a dozen, are linked into networks. The Eastern Educational Network at the beginning of 1966 became the first interconnected regional network. It supplies 80 per cent live evening programs to stations in Maine, New Hampshire, Massachusetts, Connecticut, and New York. EEN plans to expand into a 10-state network.

15. Several aspects of educational television were purposefully excluded from this discussion. Here concern is only with educational broadcasting

which seeks to serve the general public. Consequently, closed-circuit, airborne, fixed service, microwave installation, and other such educational broadcasting were deemed beyond the scope of this book.

13 Broadcasting Control by Chains and Newspapers

1. *Associated Press* v. *United States,* 326 U.S.1, 20 (1945).

2. Doubtless the rate of growth from 1964 to 1967 is exaggerated by figures here presented. The writer and his research assistants exerted considerable effort and time to reflect more accurately than previously has been done, the extent of chain ownership of broadcasting. We identified 115 chains and more than 200 radio stations not so listed in *Broadcasting Yearbook,* 1967. Some sources available to us were not at the disposal of others who have written on this subject.

3. The *Broadcasting Yearbook* definition of a chain, which has wide acceptance in the industry, was adopted for this study: the ownership of three or more radio stations (an AM-FM combination counts as one) and/or two or more television stations.

4. As reported in *Broadcasting,* October 10, 1966—January 9, 1967, inclusive.

5. *Activities of Regulatory and Enforcement Agencies Relating to Small Business,* Part 1, p. 88.

6. Compiled from *Broadcasting Yearbook,* 1966, pp. B3–B171.

7. Order No. 79, FCC mimeo. 48496, March 20, 1941; Order No. 79-A, FCC mimeo. 79-A, July 1, 1941.

8. Daniel W. Toohey, "Newspaper Ownership of Broadcast Facilities," *Federal Communications Bar Journal,* Vol. XX, No. 1, 1966, p. 48.

9. *Broadcasting Magazine,* March 8, 1943, p. 41.

10. H. R. Rep. No. 2326, 82d Cong., 2d Sess. (1952); H. R. Rep. No. 6968, and No. 6977, 84th Cong., 1st Sess. (1955); H. R. Rep. No. 9486, 86th Cong., 2d Sess. (1960).

11. Toohey, p. 52.

12. Official transcript, Antitrust Subcommittee of the Judiciary Committee, House of Representatives, 88th Cong., 1st Sess. (1963). See transcript of testimony in Representative Celler's office. Testimony here cited was given March 13, 1963.

13. Morris Ernst, *The First Freedom,* (New York: Macmillan, 1946), p. 152.

14. Preliminary report filed with the FCC, June 1966, by United Research, Inc., Cambridge, Mass., a firm hired by broadcasters at an estimated cost of $300,000 to study the effects of multiple ownership of television. See *Broadcasting,* June 27, 1966, pp. 68–69.

15. *Broadcasting Yearbook,* 1967, A-166; *Broadcasting,* June 9, 1966, p. 88.

16. Chains owning six television stations were on the air as of January 1, 1967: *A. L. Glassman, *Newhouse, D. H. Overmyer, *Southern Oregon Stations, Springfield TV Broadcasting Co. Stations, Storer Broadcasting Co., Transcontinental Properties, Inc., *Triangle Stations. *Designates newspaper ownerships.

17. In its preliminary report, URI said the average sizes of chains has declined from 3.7 stations in 1956 to 3.3 in 1964. Since the writer does not have access to URI files, this

apparent discrepancy cannot be further examined.

18. *Broadcasting*, April 5, 1965, p. 91, citing FCC files. Mutual funds and broadcasting chains in which they held 1 per cent or more ownership: Drefus Fund—Cowles, RCA, Taft; Fidelity Trend Fund—Metromedia, Taft; Investors Mutual Inc.—AVCO, CBS; Investors Stock Fund, Inc.—AVCO, CBS; Keystone K-2—ABC, Storer; Keystone S-4—AVCO, Capital Cities, Metromedia, Taft; United Accumulative—CBS, General Tire—RKO; United Income—AVCO, CBS; United Service Fund—AVCO, Crowell-Collier, General Tire-RKO.

19. The eight states in which newspapers own half or more of the VHF stations are: Connecticut, 1 of 2; Illinois, 6 of 12; Iowa, 6 of 11; Kentucky, 2 of 4; Maryland, 2 of 3; Nevada, 3 of 5; Pennsylvania, 6 of 10; and Wisconsin, 7 of 12. These and other figures on chain and newspaper ownership of television are based on analyses and comparisons of data reported in *Broadcasting Yearbook*, 1967, *Editor & Publisher Yearbook*, 1966, both revised to reflect changes and corrections, and in FCC data.

20. FCC data prepared for the Antitrust Subcommittee of the House Judiciary Committee, March 13, 1963, and updated by the author using *Broadcasting Yearbook*, 1967, *Editor & Publisher*, 1966, weekly editions of both publications, and reports in the daily press.

21. Chains or newspapers or both own all VHF stations in Arkansas, 6 stations; Idaho, 5; Maryland, 3; Massachusetts, 4; New Hampshire, 1; Ohio, 14; Pennsylvania, 10; Rhode Island, 3; Utah, 3; Washington, 9; and Wyoming 3.

22. Chains or newspapers or both own all but one VHF station in Alabama, 8 of 9; Alaska, 5 of 6; Colorado, 10 of 11; Connecticut, 1 of 2; Hawaii, 7 of 8; Illinois, 11 of 12; Indiana, 6 of 7; Iowa, 10 of 11; Kansas, 10 of 11; Kentucky, 3 of 4; Maine, 6 of 7; Oklahoma, 9 of 10; and West Virginia, 7 of 8.

23. These chain publishing-broadcasting titles were changed from the *Broadcasting Yearbook*, 1966 to *Broadcasting Yearbook*, 1967: Tribune Co. Stations, [owner of the Chicago *Tribune*, Chicago *American*, WGN-AM-TV Chicago, KWGN (TV) Denver, KDAL-AM-TV Duluth, Minn., and interlocking ownership with *New York Daily News*, *Fort Lauderdale* (Fla.) *News*, *Pompano Beach* (Fla.) *Sun-Sentinel*, *Orlando* (Fla.) *Sentinel-Star*, WPIX-FM-TV New York] changed to WGN Continental Broadcasting Co.; Lindsay-Schaub Newspapers Stations, an Illinois-based newspaper and radio-TV chain, to Illinois Broadcasting Co. Stations; Harte-Hanks Newspapers Stations, a Texas newspaper-broadcasting chain, to Harte-Hanks Stations; Gannett Newspapers Stations, a national newspaper-broadcasting chain, to the Gannett Radio-TV Group.

24. Data on the number of stations variously owned as of December 18, 1964, and estimates of percentages of TV homes in top 10 and top 50 markets is taken from "Commission to Designate for Hearing Applications to Acquire Interests in a Second VHF station in Major Markets," FCC Rep. 64–1171, 60894, December 18, 1964. Data on current television ownerships and descriptions thereof in this section, unless otherwise stated are from *Broadcasting Yearbook*, 1966, 1967. Notations in the yearbooks indicate that infor-

mation for various radio and television stations "has been corrected to November 1," p. A-3.

25. Of the 47 newspaper-TV ownerships, 41 are licensed to publishers with other television properties.

26. During the period November 1, 1959—November 1, 1962, daily newspapers acquired 12 VHF stations and sold five. Source: Testimony of former FCC Chairman Newton N. Minow before the Antitrust Subcommittee of the House Judiciary Committee, March 13, 1963.

27. David Berkman, "A Modest Proposal: Abolish the FCC," *Columbia Journalism Review*, Fall 1965, p. 35, and others have criticized the tardiness of this FCC action. Berkman called it, "locking the barn door after the fat calves have escaped."

28. Chains owning more than two VHF stations and/or more than three TV stations in the top 50 markets when the interim policy was adopted: ABC, 5 VHF; CBS, 5 VHF; NBC, 5 VHF; Capital Cities, 5 VHF, 1 UHF; Chris Craft Industries, 3 VHF; *Corinthian Broadcasting Corp., 4 VHF, 1 UHF; *Cox Broadcasting, 5 VHF; AVCO, 5 VHF; *Hearst Corp., 3 VHF; Metromedia Inc., 4 VHF, 2 UHF; *Newhouse Broadcasting Co., 4 VHF, 2 UHF; RKO-General Broadcasting, 5 VHF, 1 UHF; *Scripps-Howard Broadcasting, 4 VHF; Storer Broadcasting, 5 VHF, 1 UHF. *Designates newspaper ownerships.

29. Designating a transfer application for hearing is in itself punishment to applicants. Costs and the length of time before a decision is reached are both greatly increased. Some final decisions are reached only after several years. An indication of the cost is contained in a statement by James Lawrence Fly, former FCC chairman, quoted in *Broadcasting and Government Regulation in a Free Society*, publication of The Fund for the Republic, Inc., 1959, p. 11. Mr. Fly said an unsuccessful applicant for a contested television construction permit may pay $100,000 and "many of them run higher."

30. The proposed rule making, also adopted as an interim policy, was approved, 4–3, June 21, 1965. See FCC mimeo., docket 16068, June 21, 1965.

31. Data from *Broadcasting Yearbook*, 1966, pp. A3–A68.

32. Official transcript, Antitrust Subcommittee of the Judiciary Committee, House of Representatives, 88th Cong., 1st Sess., (1963). See transcript of testimony for March 13, 1963, in Chairman Emanuel Celler's office.

33. Testimony of Roy A. Roberts, managing editor of the Kansas City *Star*, before the FCC. See *Summary of Record*, docket 6051, pp. 27–28.

34. *United States* v. *The Kansas City Star Co.*, Cr. 18444; *United States* v. *The Kansas City Star Co.*, Civ. 7989. Defendants found guilty on February 22, 1955; 240 F. 3d 643 (8th Cir. 1857). The U.S. Supreme Court refused to review the case; *cert. denied* 354 U.S. 923.

35. FCC Public Notice-B, 33087, March 20, 1963, as contained in the record of the Antitrust Subcommittee hearings.

36. *Radio Fort Wayne, Inc.*, 9 Pike and Fischer, R.R. 1221, 1222K.

37. FCC Public Notice-B, 30451, January 31, 1963.

14 Magazines: Will Suicidal Tendencies Abate?

1. Frank Luther Mott, *American Journalism* (New York: Macmillan, 1950), p. 29.
2. *Ibid.*, p. 319.
3. *Ibid.*, p. 320.
4. *Ibid.*, p. 321.
5. *Ibid.*, p. 207.
6. *Ibid.*, p. 395.
7. *Ibid.*, pp. 321, 395.
8. Frank Luther Mott, A *History of American Magazines 1865–1885* (Cambridge, Mass., 1938), p. 5.
9. Earle Brown, president, Industrial Editors Assn. of Chicago, in speech at Southern Illinois University, Department of Journalism, February 21, 1966.
10. Lewis W. Gillenson, "The Struggle for Survival," *Columbia Journalism Review*, Spring 1962, p. 36.
11. Morris J. Gelman, "Magazines, Somber Choice Faces the Ex-Champs of National Media: Adapt or Die," *Television Magazine*, September 1962, p. 36.
12. Theodore Peterson, *Magazines in the Twentieth Century* (Urbana, Ill.: 1956), pp. 10, 11.
13. *Ibid.*, pp. 37–39.
14. Herbert Brucker, *Journalist, Eyewitness to History* (New York: Macmillan, 1962), p. 36.
15. Theodore Peterson, "The Mass Media and Public Enlightenment," talk at meeting of Illinois Library Assn., Rockford, Ill., October 21, 1966.
16. "ABC Circulations of MPA and Non-MPA Member Magazines for Six Months Ending December 31, 1964," Magazine Publishers Assn.
17. Woodrow Wirsig, "Will the Big Magazines Kill Each Other?" *Harper's*, May 1962, p. 8.
18. Barry Gottehrer, "New Look at Curtis," New York *Herald Tribune*, November 13, 1964.
19. *Broadcasting*, March 8, 1965, p. 68.
20. Theodore Peterson, "Magazine Publishing in the U.S., 1960," *Gazette*, No. 6 (1960), p. 34.
21. J. K. Lasser and Co., *Economic Status of the Magazine Industry*, June 1961.
22. A few people claim the general magazines are recouping slightly. See, for example, "Profits in Periodicals, Magazines Have Scored A Comeback With Advertisers And Readers," *Barron's*, February 15, 1964; Robert Root and Christine V. Root, "Magazines in the United States: Dying or Thriving?" *Journalism Quarterly*, Winter 1964; but others disagree, among them "The End of A Beautiful Honeymoon," *Ad Age*, June 20, 1966.
23. Lasser and Co.
24. Advertising data from McCann-Erickson, Inc., reports as published in *Printer's Ink*.
25. Lasser and Co.
26. Peterson, *Magazines in the Twentieth Century*, pp. 90–93.
27. *Ibid.*, p. 93.
28. "Magazine Distributors Cited In Civil Anti-Trust Suit," *FoI Digest*, July–August 1965, p. 3.
29. Simon Norton, at the time he gained control of McCall Corp., controlled Hunt Brothers Packing Co., and Ohio Match Co. Today he also holds large interests in Harbor Plywood Corp., Wesson Oil and Snowdrift Co.; Security Insurance Co.; Northern Pacific Railways; American Broadcasting Co.; and has through McCall bought *Saturday Review*, 1961, and three commercial printers:

National Publishing Co., Washington, D.C., 1962, Foote & Davies, Inc., Atlanta, 1963, and Jersey City Printing and Plimpton Press, Norwood, Mass., 1964.

30. *Printer's Ink*, September 8, 1961, p. 52, reported Simon had placed at least $16 million at *McCall's* disposal.

31. Circulations as of May 27, 1967, *Standard Rate & Data.*

32. *Ibid.*

33. Mott, *American Journalism*, p. 591.

34. Edwin Emery, "William Randoph Hearst: A Tentative Appraisal," *Journalism Quarterly*, Fall 1951, p. 431.

35. *Time*, April 6, 1959, p. 50.

36. *Time*, August 31, 1959, p. 42.

37. *Time*, April 6, 1959, p. 50; August 31, 1959, p. 42.

38. *Editor & Publisher*, April 22, 1967, p. 32.

39. Frank Luther Mott, "Magazines and Books, 1975: A Merging of Two Fields," *Journalism Quarterly*, Winter 1955, pp. 21–26.

40. Sherilyn Cox Bennion, *A Study of Diversification of Operations Among United States Magazine Publishing Companies* (Syracuse, N.Y.: School of Journalism), p. 9.

41. *Ibid.*, p. 4.

42. See, for example, "Turning Curtis Around," *The Gallagher Report*, October 15, 1962, and "Textbook Publishing," *The Gallagher Report*, February 11, 1963.

43. Bennion, p. 10.

44. *New York Times*, February 6, 1966, Sec. III, p. 16.

45. *Time*, June 24, 1966, p. 98.

46. *Quill*, September 1964, p. 8.

47. *The Enduring American Press*, published to commemorate the 200th anniversary of the Hartford (Conn.) *Courant*, October 30, 1964, p. 29.

48. *Time*, March 3, 1967, pp. 76–82.

49. Harlan Logan, "Tomorrow's New Magazines," *Magazine Industry*, Summer 1949, p. 17.

50. Theodore Peterson, "Changes Ahead in the Print Media: Their Implications for Educational Communication," talk at annual convention of American Assn. of Agricultural College Editors, Athens, Ga., July 14, 1966.

51. *Newsweek*, January 10, 1966, p. 42.

52. Peterson, "Changes Ahead in the Print Media."

53. *Newsweek*, January 10, 1966, p. 41.

54. *Publishers' Weekly*, January 9, 1961.

55. Leonard V. Fulton, ed. *Directory of Little Magazines*, El Cerrito, Calif., July 1965. Although this appears to be the most complete directory, others have been compiled by Alan Swallow, *Sage Books*, Denver; James B. May in *Trace*; Lilith Lorraine in *Flame Annual*. Accurate figures are impossible to obtain; many little magazines flower and fade within a half dozen issues. Others move from one locale to another.

56. "E. Oatman on 200–300 'Little' Literary Magazines Being Published in U.S.," *New York Times*, August 28, 1966, Sec. VII, p. 1.

57. *Ibid.*

58. *Ibid.*

15 A Blueprint for Action

1. Thor Severson, "The Copperdust Shadow Over Montana," Denver *Post*, April 6, 1952.

2. William G. Bonelli, *Billion Dollar*

Blackjack (Beverly Hills, Calif.: Civic Research Press, 1954), pp. 113–26. See also Morrow Mayo, *Los Angeles* (New York: Alfred A. Knopf).

3. Michael Pan, "The Influence of Media-Industry Ownership on the Performance of the Press: A Case Study," unpublished Master's thesis, Southern Illinois University, Carbondale, Ill., 1967.

4. John A. Lent, *Newhouse, Newspapers, Nuisances* (New York: Exposition, 1966), p. 116.

5. Frank Luther Mott, *American Journalism* (New York: Macmillan, 1950), pp. 527–33.

6. Gene Fowler, *Timber Line: A Story of Bonfils and Tammen* (New York: Covici-Friede, 1933), p. 408.

7. Excerpts from *Congressional Record*, House debates, June 9, 1934.

8. Per Holting, "Where Does Friction Develop for TV News Directors?" *Journalism Quarterly*, Summer 1957, pp. 355–59.

9. Fred W. Friendly, *Due to Circumstances Beyond Our Control* (New York: Random House, 1967), *passim.*

10. Walter Gieber, "How the 'Gatekeepers' View Local Civil Liberties News," *Journalism Quarterly*, Spring 1960, pp. 199–205.

11. David R. Bowers, "A Report on Activity by Publishers in Directing Newsroom Decisions," *Journalism Quarterly*, Spring 1967, pp. 43–52.

12. Warren Breed, "Social Control in the News Room: A Functional Analysis," *Social Forces*, May 1955, as reprinted in Wilbur Schramm, *Mass Communications*, 2nd ed. (Urbana, Ill., 1960), pp. 178–94.

13. Lewis Donohew, "Newspaper Gatekeepers and Forces in the News Channel," *Public Opinion Quarterly*, Spring 1967, pp. 61–68.

14. Jean S. Kerrick, Thomas E. Anderson, and Luita B. Swales, "Balance and the Writer's Attitude in News Stories and Editorials," *Journalism Quarterly*, Spring 1964, pp. 207–15.

15. Excerpts from address by Walter Lippmann to the International Press Institute, London, May 27, 1965.

16. Cecil H. King, "An English View of American Newspapers," *Editor & Publisher*, April 29, 1967, p. 19.

17. Newton N. Minow, *Equal Time* (New York: Atheneum, 1964), pp. 275–304.

18. David Berkman, "A Modest Proposal: Abolish the FCC," *Columbia Journalism Review*, Fall 1965, p. 34.

19. *Broadcasting*, June 19, 1967, p. 70.

20. UPI, November 23, 1965.

21. King, p. 98.

22. *Ibid.*

23. Howard R. Long, "The Mighty Mice," *Grassroots Editor*, January–February 1967, pp. 2, 34.

24. Morris L. Ernst, "I Have A Concern," *The Villager*, Greenwich Village, N.Y., April 6, 1967.

Index

DATE DUE

GAYLORD			PRINTED IN U.S.A.